The Great
NEW ENGLAND
Food Guide

Kathy Gunst and John Rudolph

■

Photographs by Dan Gair

ARBOR HOUSE
WILLIAM MORROW
New York

For Leonard and Leona Levy

Copyright © 1988 by Kathy Gunst and John Rudolph
Photographs copyright © 1988 by Dan Gair
All rights reserved. No part of this book may be reproduced or utilized in any form or by any means, electronic or mechanical, including photocopying, recording or by any information storage and retrieval system, without permission in writing from the Publisher. Inquiries should be addressed to Permissions Department, Arbor House, William Morrow and Company, Inc., 105 Madison Avenue, New York, N.Y. 10016.

Library of Congress Cataloging in Publication Data

Gunst, Kathy.
The great New England food guide.
Includes index.
1. Marketing (Home economics)—New England—Guide-books. 2. Grocery trade—New England—Guide-books. 3. Farm produce—New England—Guide-books. 4. Stores, Retail—New England—Guide-books. 5. Restaurants, lunch rooms, etc.—New England—Guide-books.
I. Rudolph, John. II. Title
TX356.G86 1988   381'.41'025744   87-24665
ISBN 0-87795-949-8

Manufactured in the United States of America
Published in Canada by Fitzhenry & Whiteside, Ltd.
10 9 8 7 6 5 4 3 2

Symbols © 1988 by Cathy Gair

Contents

Introduction ■ iv

Acknowledgments ■ v

What the Symbols Mean ■ vi

CONNECTICUT ■ 1

MAINE ■ 33

MASSACHUSETTS ■ 85

NEW HAMPSHIRE ■ 149

RHODE ISLAND ■ 179

VERMONT ■ 203

Index ■ 244

Introduction

Traveling with a gastronomic guide tucked in your suitcase is a practice that most of us associate with tours of France or Italy. Many of our fondest memories of European travel have to do with food—the little *pâtisserie* where we discovered an extraordinary fruit tart, the vineyard where we acquired a deeper appreciation for the winemaker's art.

Today these same kinds of experiences are available in New England. Over the past fifteen years the region has gone through a culinary and agricultural renaissance. Small wineries and breweries have been started in almost every New England state. The number of cheesemakers has skyrocketed, and they're making everything from French-style Brie to bold, new, and distinctly American varieties like goat's-milk cheddar. New England has also raised a new crop of organic farmers who sell their high-quality, chemical-free produce at roadside stands, farmers' markets, and specialty food stores. And new smokehouses, bakeries, candy makers, gristmills, and condiment makers are constantly entering the scene with delicious products. Add all this to the region's traditional food providers—dairies, fishermen, sugarhouses, and farmers—and you have a trend worth talking, and writing, about.

The Great New England Food Guide is a combination travel guide, cookbook, and resource guide. With it you will be able to find the best sources for a wide range of foods, including country stores, ethnic markets, farm stands, gourmet food stores, bakeries, health food stores, mail order sources, and farmers' markets. We also tell you where you can watch food being made, from winery tours to tours of experimental farms. In addition we point out scenic and historically significant spots throughout the region that are related to food production—Colonial-era farmsteads that continue as working farms today, old gristmills that are still operating, and beautiful orchards where you can hike and cross-country ski. And, although this is not a restaurant guide, we also highlight a limited number of places where you can enjoy a meal or have one prepared to take out. Finally, *The Great New England Food Guide* is a cookbook, with dozens of recipes that feature native ingredients. Some of the dishes, like clam chowder, are old favorites. Others, such as a lobster and corn terrine, are evidence of more contemporary New England culinary traditions.

We have approached our subject with a firm set of standards and beliefs. First, we believe that locally produced food is better than food that's been shipped in from elsewhere. New England currently imports more than 90 percent of its food. We think that's ridiculous and wasteful. Local food production conserves energy, helps the region's economy, and saves precious agricultural land. Locally raised food is also fresher than food that's traveled thousands of miles in the hold of a ship or in the back of a refrigerated semi-trailer. (In each chapter there is a section on farmers' markets—they are especially good resources for finding out what's being produced in a region and for supporting local agriculture.)

Another thing we feel strongly about is that organically raised food is better than food that's been grown or processed with chemicals or preservatives. Although some of the foods we recommend are not organic, we are happy to say that a growing number of New England farmers are reducing or eliminating the use of chemical fertilizers and pesticides, and other food producers, like bakers and cheesemakers, are avoiding preservatives. These foods are not only healthier, they also taste better.

(We use the term "organic" to describe produce, grains, dairy products, and meat raised without chemical fertilizers, chemical insecticides, hormones, or growth stimulants. Another term we use is "natural." This refers to foods that are made with a minimum of chemicals—for example, bread that's made with nonorganic flour but contains no preservatives.)

To research this book we covered thousands of miles of New England's highways and back roads. And we met literally thousands of people who allowed us a glimpse into their lives and impressed us with their commitment to high-quality, good-tasting locally produced food. Despite our efforts this book is not complete, and it never will be. You can help us with your comments, recommendations, suggestions, and criticisms for future editions. (Please write to us c/o *The Great New England Food Guide,* Arbor House, 105 Madison Avenue, New York, NY 10016.) In the meantime we hope you enjoy the foods and adventures that await you.

Kathy Gunst and John Rudolph
June 1987

Acknowledgments

Dozens of people helped make *The Great New England Food Guide* a reality. They led us to their favorite food stores, cheesemakers, bakeries, farm stands, and fish markets. They lent us their palates for numerous tastings, and they answered our questionnaire. When we were on the road they put us up, and in some cases put up with us. They gave us ideas and inspiration as well as constructive criticism, but most of all they gave us support: Nancy Barr, Bill Bell, Phillip Bragdon, Gene Brown, Kate Coniff and the people at Bread & Circus, Deidre Davis and Chris Cullen, Fran and Barbara Deasy, Karen Frillmann and Judy Wenning, Lee and Nancy Gunst, Andrea, Lee, and Michael Gunst, James Haller, Huson and Polly Jackson, Phyllis Joffee, Johanne Killeen, Dorothee Kocks and Mark Etheridge, Ellen Lesser and Roger Weingarten, Leonard and Leona Levy, Bob, Pixie, and Sarah Lown, Janna McGowan, Kate Meagher, Lisa Mullins, Elisa Newman, Vernice and Shelley Peirce, Jeff Rathaus, Alan and Nancy F. Rudolph, Nancy K. Rudolph, Helen and George Stephenson, Joe and Jane Thomas, and John Voce. We had help from the state Departments of Agriculture and owe special thanks to John Jones (Maine), Commissioner August Schumacher, Jr., and Chris Phillips (Massachusetts), and Commissioner Stephen Taylor and Elizabeth Corell (New Hampshire). Our thanks also to the magazine editors and radio producers and managers who made our lives a little easier so we could finish the book on time, especially our editors at the *Maine Times, The Cook's Magazine,* National Public Radio, and WBUR in Boston.

Thank-you to our agent, Robert Cornfield, for believing in this project from the very beginning, to Lee Simmons of Arbor House for carefully shepherding the book through its various stages, and to Kathie Ness for fine-tuning the manuscript so skillfully.

Special thanks to photographer Dan Gair for his energy, enthusiasm, and unique vision of New England. And to Cathy Lee Gair for designing the graphic symbols and for her willingness to taste any food that was put in front of her.

Finally, we'd like to express our admiration and respect for the many farmers, bakers, fishermen, cheesemakers, brewers, vintners, chefs, and store owners whom we've met on our travels and who make this region so rich and delicious.

What the Symbols Mean

🍎 Apple orchards, "pick-your-own" apple farms, cider mills, and places to get custom-pressed cider.

🍞 Freshly baked breads, biscuits, muffins, pastries, cookies, crackers, and cakes.

🍷 New England's finest vineyards and breweries, with special notes on tours and tastings. Also, places that sell the ingredients and equipment for making your own beer or wine.

🍬 Everything from homemade fudge and chocolate truffles to saltwater taffy, potato chips, and farm-grown popcorn.

🍵 Where to buy freshly roasted coffee and fine teas.

🍯 Maple syrup, honey, herbal vinegars, homemade ketchup, mustards, and jellies and jams made with native fruits and berries.

🐄 Native cheese and yogurt, along with dairies where you can buy unhomogenized cow's milk, fresh cream, and raw goat's milk.

🐟 Fish markets, smoked fish products, and docks and piers where you can buy directly from the fishermen.

🥕 Farm stands and stores that carry exceptional produce, and "pick-your-own" farms.

🌿 Farms, gardens, and shops that sell fresh and dried herbs and herb-related products and crafts. Sources of information about herb gardening and the culinary and medicinal uses of herbs.

🐓 Butcher shops; where to find organically raised meat and poultry; the best game farms, smoked meats, fresh rabbit, sausages, and smoked country ham. Where to order your Thanksgiving turkey.

🍴 Although this is not a restaurant guide, many of the places listed here also serve food and drink. We have made note of the shops and bakeries where you can sit and enjoy a hot mug of homemade soup, a cup of mulled cider, or a full meal.

🏠 The region's finest gourmet food stores, old-fashioned country stores, health food shops, ethnic food shops, pasta shops, and gristmills.

Connecticut

CONNECTICUT

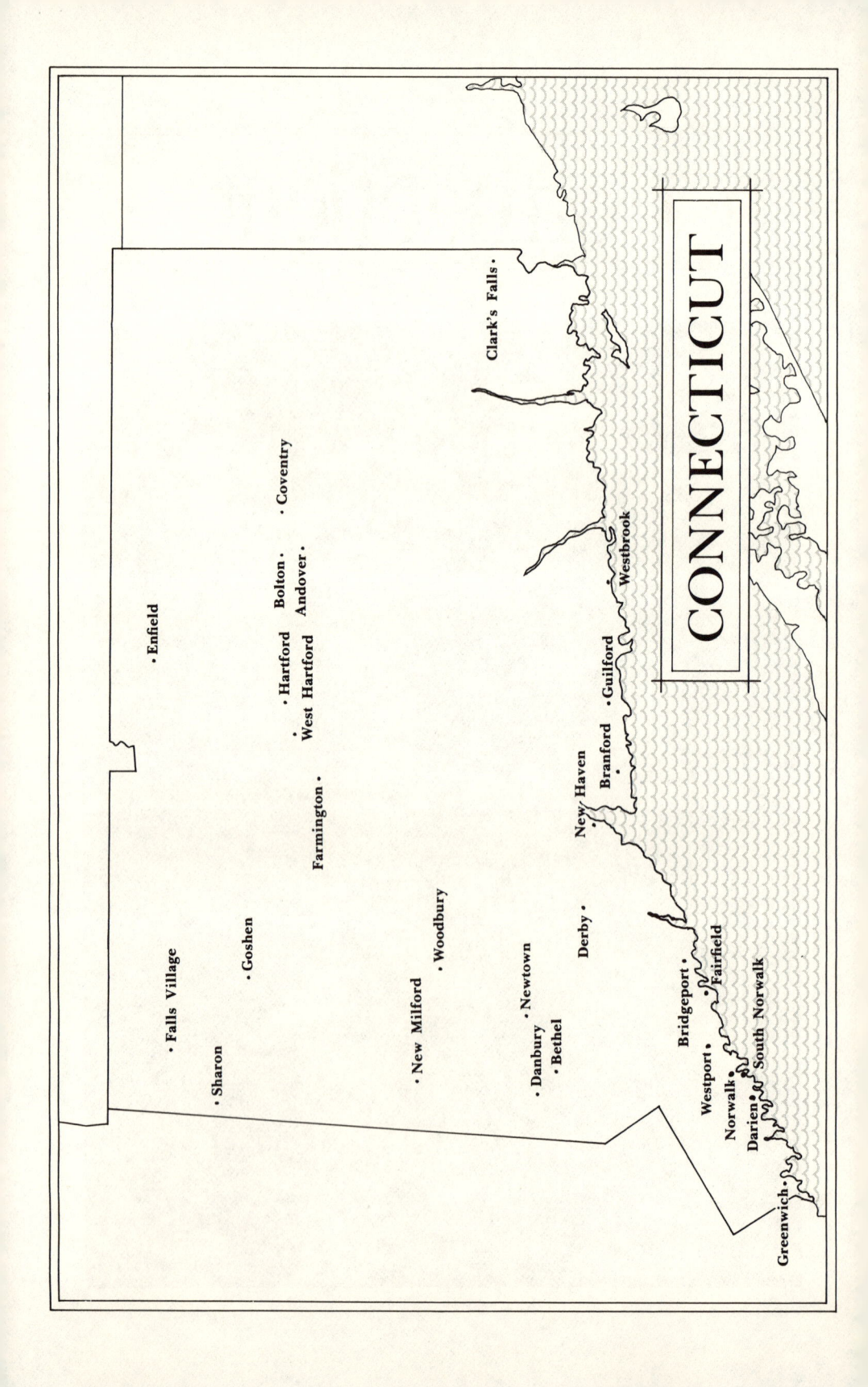

- Enfield
- Hartford
- Bolton
- Coventry
- West Hartford
- Andover
- Farmington
- Clark's Falls
- Westbrook
- Guilford
- Branford
- New Haven
- Derby
- Woodbury
- New Milford
- Danbury
- Newtown
- Bethel
- Bridgeport
- Fairfield
- Westport
- Norwalk
- South Norwalk
- Darien
- Greenwich
- Falls Village
- Sharon
- Goshen

HURST FARM AND GREENHOUSES

46 East Street, Andover, 06232; phone 203-646-6536. Hours: seven days a week 10 A.M. to 5 P.M., later at harvest times. Personal checks accepted. Pick-your-own fruit available; call ahead for conditions.

BLUE JAY ORCHARDS

Plumtrees Road, Bethel, 06801; phone 203-748-0119. Hours: seven days a week 9 A.M. to 5 P.M., later during apple and strawberry seasons. Cash only. Mail order available. Pick-your-own fruit available; call ahead for conditions.

HAUSER CHOCOLATIER

18 Taylor Avenue, Bethel, 06801; phone 203-794-1861. Hours: Monday–Friday 9 A.M. to 5 P.M., Saturday 10 A.M. to 2 P.M.; closed Sunday. Personal checks accepted. Mail order available.

Andover

- "Pick-your-own" is the big attraction here. The Hursts grow strawberries, red raspberries, and the farm's specialties: black raspberries and purple raspberries called "brandywines." Depending on the weather, there are also pumpkins to pick around Halloween.

Other items include fresh vegetables (during the summer months), herb plants (in the spring and summer), their own honey, maple syrup, and preserves, along with dried herbs, local apple cider, and eggs. Over the cash register is a bulletin board full of family recipes. Check them out; some of them look quite good.

Bethel

- When the State of Connecticut decided a few years ago to include this farm in the Connecticut farmlands preservation program, they were not just saving 150 acres of agricultural land in crowded Fairfield County. Blue Jay Orchards is also a great culinary resource and a wonderful place to visit. The farm store, located in a big wooden barn, offers apples grown without alar, along with pears, berries, and vegetables raised with a minimum of chemicals. And for those who are so inclined, many items are available on a pick-your-own basis: strawberries, raspberries, and apples (they grow thirty-eight different varieties).

They also grow their own peaches, nectarines, pears, pumpkins, and sweet corn. You can buy fresh eggs from their flock of laying hens, and organically raised chicken shipped from a farm on Long Island (fresh chickens must be ordered ahead of time). Other products include local honey, Vermont cheeses and maple syrup, their own frozen soups, applesauce, breads, pies, donuts, and excellent preservative-free apple cider.

- Ruedi Hauser's specialty is traditional Swiss-style truffles. Unlike other New England candy makers who are using regional ingredients (like goat cheese and local fruit wines) to create distinctly American truffles, Hauser sticks with recipes and techniques from his native Switzerland. His confections are not wildly innovative, but they are well made and very satisfying.

Hauser, who is a chef as well as a chocolatier, uses imported Swiss and French chocolate to make the truffle shells. They are then filled with creamy chocolate flavored with hazelnuts, raspberry, mocha, and other flavors.

In addition to truffles Hauser makes chocolate pralines, Old Fashioned Almond Bark (a mixture of whole

MUNSON'S CHOCOLATES
Route 6 (P.O. Box 9217), Bolton, 06040; phone 203-649-4332. Hours: Monday–Saturday 9 A.M. to 8 P.M.; Sunday 10 A.M. to 6 P.M. MasterCard and Visa accepted. Mail order available.

BITTERSWEET HERB FARM
777 East Main Street (just off Route 1), Branford, 06405; phone 203-488-1599. Hours: Monday–Saturday 10 A.M. to 5 P.M.; Sunday 11 A.M. to 5 P.M. MasterCard, Visa, American Express, and personal checks accepted. Mail order available.

D AND P OLD FASHIONED CANDY
Dreyden and Palmer Company, 16 Business Park Drive, Branford, 06405; phone 203-481-2276. Factory

almonds in dark, milk, or white chocolate), and Gold Nuggets (a crunchy combination of white chocolate, ground pecans, and hazelnuts). Home candy makers can order unfilled chocolate shells from Hauser, as well as a gingerbread house kit that consists of prebaked pieces ready to be assembled and decorated.

Bolton

■ This is the place to come for really good chocolate-coated strawberry, raspberry, or orange creams. Chocolate-coated crystallized ginger, fudge, chocolate-coated pretzels, and turtles (nut, chocolate, and caramel clusters) are among the many other specialties.

Branford

■ We had heard a lot about Bittersweet Farm—an organic herb farm located near the Connecticut shore that deals in fresh and dried herbs and herbal blends for cooking. So when we drove along Route 1 in Branford and happened upon a mini shopping mall, we wondered what all the fuss was about. But once inside Bittersweet's rambling old farmhouse, inhaling the intoxicating scent of fresh herbs, potpourri blends, and dried spices, we understood.

There are herbs everywhere. The walls are lined with dozens of large glass jars of dried culinary herbs; hanging from the overhead beams are colorful, fragrant bouquets of dried garden herbs and flowers; the fireplace mantels are crammed with jars of herb-flavored vinegars, herb-flavored honeys, herbal tea blends, baskets of exotic-smelling potpourris, and dozens of other herb concoctions.

Bittersweet Farm is best known for their potted herb plants and fresh-cut culinary herbs (available during the spring and summer), as well as their culinary herb blends—salad dressings, curry mixes, salt substitutes, herbal butters and dips, and meat, poultry, and fish seasonings. When we visited around the Christmas holidays, the place was particularly festive, with gorgeous herbal wreaths, pine-scented potpourris, and cinnamon-flavored hot mulled cider.

■ "Originally rock candy had a medical connotation," says Richard Mills Accola, whose family has owned Dreyden and Palmer since 1929. "People used to put it in whiskey to make a cure for sore throats." Now rock candy is sold mainly as a sweet treat. But Accola swears it will soothe your throat when dissolved in bourbon, scotch, or other spirits. For kids he suggests dissolving it in warm milk.

tours available; call ahead.

Sold in candy stores, gift shops, and specialty food stores in the U.S. and Canada.

JUDIE'S EUROPEAN BAKED GOODS
126 Shore Drive, Branford, 06405; phone 203-488-2257. Hours: Tuesday–Saturday 7:30 A.M. to 5:30 P.M.; Sunday 7:30 A.M. to 1:30 P.M.; closed Monday. Cash only.

Dreyden and Palmer claims to be the only manufacturer of rock candy remaining in New England. There just doesn't seem to be much demand for it in this era of sugarless gum and NutraSweet. But rock candy does have a pure sugar taste that artificial sweeteners and most other off-the-shelf candies can't match. And for those old enough to remember the penny-candy store, it has a nostalgic appeal as well.

If you visit the factory in Branford, you'll see strings of rock candy being made, as twine is dipped into hot sugar syrup and then quickly cooled so that jagged sugar crystals form.

■ "I've always baked," says Judie Saleeby. "I remember making mud pies when I was only four years old." In 1976 Judie starting baking bread and cakes for friends, taking on catering jobs as time permitted. No matter how many loaves she made, they always sold out. So in 1979 Judie moved the business from her home kitchen to a small building near the center of Branford, with a view of Long Island Sound. Today Judie's European Baked Goods are sold throughout the New Haven area, and her bread—all seventy-two varieties of it—has become famous. "My accountant says I'm crazy," explains Judie. "Variety, he tells me, is no way to make money. But variety is what keeps me sane. I couldn't stand making the same bread every day."

Judie's breads are flavorful and skillfully made . . . and they have wonderful names. Ode to a Grecian Bean is a hearty wheat bread made with lentils, Bermuda onions, and sunflower nuts. There is also Sargeant Preston's Puffed Corn Bread, Tempestuous Harvest Yam Yam Bread, and Plato's Fig & Lemon Loaf, to name a few. Judie makes more traditional varieties, too, such as Russian Black Bread, Finnish Rye Bread, Challah, and her best-seller French Peasant Bread, an excellent crispy *baguette*-style loaf. Two of her most spectacular breads are what she calls cracker breads. These are flat, crispy loaves, as big around as a large pizza. One of them actu-

Fresh-baked cracker bread at Judie's European Baked Goods.

Judie's Lemon Rice Ricotta Bread

This bread—a wonderful combination of ricotta cheese, rice, and lemon—comes from Judie Saleeby of Judie's European Baked Goods in Branford. "It is much better to wait several hours before eating freshly baked bread," warns Saleeby. "The yeast enzymes are still active and they may give you indigestion. It's best to wait until the next day if you really want to be on the safe side."

2 cups milk
1 cup (2 sticks) unsalted butter
1/3 cup honey
1 teaspoon salt
1 cup cooked rice
About 5 cups unbleached white flour

1 1/2 teaspoons lemon extract
2 envelopes yeast
1/4 cup warm water
1/2 cup ricotta cheese
Grated peel of 1 large lemon

In a medium-size saucepan, boil the milk. Remove it from the heat and add the butter. Stir until the butter has melted. Then pour the milk/butter mixture into a large mixing bowl, and stir in the honey, salt, and cooked rice. After the mixture has cooled, add 4 cups of the flour and the lemon extract. Stir well with a wooden spoon until the mixture is smooth and elastic.

Meanwhile, place the yeast in a small bowl and add the warm water. Let sit for 5 minutes, or until the yeast is thick and foamy.

Add the ricotta cheese, grated lemon peel, and yeast mixture to the dough. Knead the dough on a well-floured surface for 5 minutes, adding extra flour as needed. (The dough should be firm, yet still a bit sticky.) Place the dough in a lightly buttered bowl, cover with a tea towel, and leave in a warm, draft-free spot to rise for 30 minutes. Then punch down the dough and knead another 5 minutes. Cut the dough in half and place in two well-buttered 1-pound bread loaf pans. Cover with a tea towel and leave in a warm spot to rise for another 30 minutes.

Ten minutes before baking, preheat the oven to 375°. Bake the bread for 25 minutes, or until the loaves have a deep, rich golden brown color. Let sit for at least 4 hours before slicing. Makes 2 loaves.

---

ally tastes like a pizza: it's topped with grated cheese, fresh basil, garlic, olive oil, and tomato. The other is loaded with roasted sesame seeds and flavored with extra virgin olive oil.

Judie's breads are not inexpensive, but they are worth the price. The bakery also sells imported jellies and jams, sweet syrups, and mustards. There are a few tables in the front where you can enjoy a morning cup of coffee and some bread or pastries.

CHAVES BAKERY
215 Frank Street,

Bridgeport

■ At fancy bakeries in Greenwich or Westport, these breads might be called *pains de campagne* and *baguettes*. But

Bridgeport, 06604; phone 203-333-6254. Hours: Monday–Saturday 5:30 A.M. to 7 P.M., Sunday 6 A.M. to 3 P.M. Cash only.

CLARK'S FALLS GRIST MILL

Route 216 (a few miles north of the Clark's Falls exit on I-95), Clark's Falls, 06359; phone 203-599-2422. Hours: irregular, call ahead. Cash only.

Also available at Agway stores and general stores in western Rhode Island and eastern Connecticut.

CAPRILANDS HERB FARM

534 Silver Street, Coventry, 06238; phone 203-742-7244. Hours: seven days a week 9 A.M. to 5 P.M. Personal checks accepted. Mail order available.

Herbal luncheons, which include a garden tour, lecture, and five-course meal, are held Monday through Saturday from April 1 through December. On Sundays an herbal high tea is held at 2:00 P.M. Reservations are necessary for both.

Adelma Grenier Simmons stops for a moment during a stroll through her gardens at Caprilands Herb Farm.

this is Bridgeport, so you ask for either the round one or the long skinny one. What's in a name, anyway? This is good, crusty bread. They also make Portuguese sweet bread and Portuguese-style pastries. However, it's the bread that's the real star here.

There's another Chaves Bakery in Bridgeport, at 230 James Street (phone 203-334-0726); same hours.

Clark's Falls

■ This small water-powered gristmill on the Connecticut–Rhode Island border grinds cornmeal for Rhode Island jonnycakes. John Palmer, the miller, also grows much of the corn that is ground at the mill. It's a special variety called Rhode Island white flint corn—and jonnycake aficionados say it has a distinctly sweet flavor.

Palmer, who is also a dairy farmer, eats jonnycakes almost every day. "Jonnycakes and beans, that's good wholesome food," he says. "You can work hard on it."

Coventry

■ The smell of perfume mingles with the scent of fresh rosemary, thyme, and lemon verbena. About a hundred people, mostly middle-aged women, are packed into a warm, steamy greenhouse at the Caprilands Herb Farm, waiting for the lecture to begin. Suddenly there is a stir. Members of the staff seem to come to attention as a tiny person, cloaked in a flowing scarlet cape with a matching red skullcap and long strands of thick beads, enters the room. Someone mutters, half jokingly, "Look, it's the Pope."

Almost. Adelma Grenier Simmons, founder and director of Caprilands, is the dean of American herbalists. Since 1929 Simmons has been studying, growing, writing, and lecturing on herbs with religious zeal. She has penned thirty-two books. "I'm the Agatha Christie of the herb world," she told us proudly.

Lemon Verbena Iced Tea

Lemon verbena is an herb with the scent of fresh lemon. This is a wonderful way to capture its essence.

Chop a few sprigs of fresh lemon verbena and place in ice cube trays. Fill with water, and freeze. Add to a pitcher of iced tea. This also works well with all varieties of fresh mint.

Simmons begins her lecture with arms outstretched. In one hand is a juniper bough. "This is the plant of sanctuary," she explains. "The folded branches protected the Christ Child and the Holy Family." Over the next forty-five minutes Simmons regales her audience with myths, stories, and practical advice about herbs and other plants grown on her 50-acre farm.

Caprilands contains thirty-two different herb gardens. There's a fragrance garden planted with lavender, thyme, heliotrope, and roses; a garden planted with nothing but several varieties of thyme; a culinary herb garden shaped like a butterfly; and a blue garden that contains only flowers and herbs with blue and purple blossoms.

People from around the world have made the pilgrimage to Caprilands to browse through the gardens, hear Mrs. Simmons give her daily lecture, and attend her famous herbal lunches. Visitors dine in Simmons's eighteenth-century farmhouse. The five-course menu, consisting of items like spinach and nutmeg bread, a fresh garden salad with herbal vinaigrette, curried corn soup, and chicken and broccoli casserole, is typical ladies' luncheon fare spiked with fresh herbs. "When we began the [lecture/luncheon] program a few decades ago, nobody knew anything about cooking with herbs," Simmons recalled. "People thought we were trying to poison them when we put chopped parsley in the salad dressing."

Today the people who come to Caprilands are a bit more sophisticated. They can fully appreciate the more than three hundred varieties of herbs displayed in the farm's spectacular gardens. And, as Mrs. Simmons well knows, herbs have become something that people want to own as well as taste and smell.

As lunch winds down, she addresses her visitors once again. This time it's a gentle sales pitch. Herb plants from Caprilands' gardens, along with herb wreaths, herbal teas, vinegars, and garden paraphernalia, are all for sale. "And you'll find my books at the Caprilands bookstore," she says. Then, very discreetly adjusting her skullcap, Simmons adds, "If you do buy a book make sure to have me sign it. It will be worth, oh, so much more."

In the herb gardens at Caprilands Herb Farm.

Spring and summer are the obvious times to visit Caprilands. The gardens are in bloom, an inspiring sight for any gardener. But in mid-December, right around the holidays, this place takes on an especially warm glow. The greenhouse is filled with flowering herb plants and pungent boughs of fresh juniper and other evergreens. The gift shop features tree ornaments from all over the world. In the main house each room contains at least one Christmas tree decorated with fresh and dried herbs. The beehive ovens display Nativity scenes, and everywhere there is the delicious scent of pomander balls and herbal potpourris gently roasting atop wood-burning stoves.

NUTMEG VINEYARD
800 Bunker Hill Road (2 miles north of Route 6), Coventry, 06238 (mailing address: P.O. Box 146, Andover, CT 06232); phone 203-742-8402. Hours: Saturday, Sunday, and holidays 11 A.M. to 5 P.M.; other times by chance or appointment. Personal checks accepted. Call ahead for tastings schedule and driving directions.

■ Vintner Tony Maulucci is a gentle man whose soft-spoken manner and unassuming but pleasant wines belie the rugged landscape where he has carved out vineyards and built a small winery. Before he could even plant grapes (the first vines were planted in 1971), Maulucci and his family had to clear away boulders, a swamp, and untamed woods.

Even today Nutmeg Vineyard has a wild look. The tangled forest underbrush looks as if it still wants to reclaim the neat rows of Seyval, Baco, Foch, and Chancellor grapes that Maulucci has planted on his 38-acre property. The wines, however, are completely civilized, and surprisingly drinkable.

The Antonio red wine is similar to an Italian Chianti, dry with a somewhat fruity flavor and a bouquet reminiscent of cherries. Maulucci calls it his "Sunday red wine." His everyday red is the Baco Noir, also dry but closer to a Bordeaux in character. Similarly, the white Seyval Blanc could be compared to a Bordeaux; it's very dry and astringent. The Seyval Sauterne is slightly sweet and syrupy, and would make a good dessert wine or accompaniment to cheese.

Nutmeg Vineyard also makes fruit wines. We tried the strawberry wine and found it delightfully sweet with a fresh berry flavor. There was also a hint of something that reminded us of pineapple, which cut the sugariness that often overwhelms wines of this type. Another property that was (thankfully) absent was the bitter aftertaste found in many New England fruit wines.

There are a few caveats here: Nutmeg Vineyard wines are good by New England winemaking standards, but they are a bit on the expensive side. Also, these wines are sold only in Connecticut.

Danbury

BALI ORIENTAL FOODS
139 White Street,

■ The smell of grilled meat and fragrant Oriental spices greets you as you enter this tiny shop specializing in Indonesian cuisine. Bali Oriental Foods is both a take-out

Danbury, 06810; phone 203-743-9761. Hours: Tuesday–Saturday 10 A.M. to 7 P.M.; closed Sunday and Monday. Cash only. Catering and take-out available.

CHOCOLATE LACE
8 South Street, Danbury, 06810; phone 203-792-8175. Mail order only.
  Also available at gourmet food stores, gift shops, and candy shops around the country.

restaurant—offering dishes like *sate* (Indonesian-style barbecued meat or chicken) and oversized egg rolls called *lumpia*—and an Oriental grocery that sells items including dried lemon grass, curry paste, tea, and Indonesian condiments.

The owners of the store, Everdina and Bill Koegler, both from Indonesia, make their own condiments and sell them under the brand name Merapi. There is *ketjap manis,* a thick sweetened soy sauce, and several different varieties of *sambals*—thick relish-like condiments that range from moderately hot to get-out-the-fire-hoses hot. These condiments are an excellent adjunct to Western-style roasts and stews as well as Indonesian dishes.

■ Chocolate Lace is a crunchy melt-in-your-mouth caramel candy coated with rich dark chocolate. Like lace, each piece has its own intricate one-of-a-kind pattern.

The story behind Chocolate Lace is almost as unique as the candy itself. At the turn of the century, in Czarist Russia, a young woman named Eugenia Tay made candy whenever there was a snowstorm. The process was simple: She would boil up a pot of sugar and drizzle the hot syrup on the newly fallen snow to form lace-like patterns. The caramelized sugar pieces were then brought indoors and dipped into pans of melted chocolate.

In 1917 the Tay family fled Russia and settled in Manhattan. Eugenia kept the candy-making tradition alive by working in her small urban kitchen with a slab of cold marble. Word got out about her Chocolate Lace, and eventually Eugenia developed a major business. The next step was to invent a machine that would reproduce the same random patterns she first obtained by pouring melted sugar on snow. Eugenia Tay's candy-making machine, affectionately known as Veronica Lace, reminded us of a miniature car wash. To form the lacy patterns, the heated caramel mixture drips through a small hollow pipe perforated with tiny holes. This dispensing wand, as it's called, is constantly moving, so no two pieces of candy look exactly alike. "The candy pieces are like snowflakes," said Stephen Bray, who now owns the company and the machine that Eugenia Tay created.

Once the lacy caramel has been made, it moves along

Getting a Taste of the Portuguese Community

If you are interested in tasting what comes out of Danbury's Portuguese kitchens, you might want to attend one of the Portuguese festivals held in the spring along Liberty Street. The Feast of Saint Anthony usually occurs on the first weekend in June, Portuguese Day is held on or near June 10, and the Feast of Saint John is generally celebrated on the third or fourth weekend in June.

a stainless steel conveyor belt to be sprayed with one of three flavors of hot melted chocolate—dark, mint, or toasted almond milk chocolate. After that the Lace travels through a cooling area where the chocolate hardens; the candy is then trimmed and packaged. Broken bits and pieces are packed separately: Crumbles, as they're called, are delicious sprinkled over ice cream or scattered over pound cake and fruit pies. There is only one problem with this stuff: it's highly addictive.

FERNANDES FOOD STORE
99 Town Hill Avenue, Danbury, 06810; phone 203-748-9181. Hours: Monday–Thursday 8 A.M. to 7 P.M., Friday and Saturday 8 A.M. to 8 P.M., Sunday 8 A.M. to 1 P.M. Cash only.

■ This is an excellent Portuguese market. In addition to a fine selection of fresh meats, fish, and cheeses, they also sell some fresh tropical vegetables. Here you will also find dried cod *(bacalhau)*.

INTERNATIONAL BAKERY
87 East Liberty Street, Danbury, 06810; phone 203-743-1939. Hours: Tuesday–Saturday 6 A.M. to 6 P.M.; Sunday 6 A.M. to 12 N.; closed Monday. Cash only.

■ This small Portuguese bakery specializes in sweet bread *(massa sovada)* and all sorts of Portuguese pastries. We discovered a tiny custard tart with a creamy texture and a rich eggy taste that rivaled any pastry of this kind to come out of a French *pâtisserie*. Also worth trying is something called a Portuguese sausage roll—a small *baguette*-like loaf filled with chunks of spicy *linguica* sausage. On Saturdays and Sundays the specialty is fried dough, and around the holidays you'll find freshly baked Portuguese fruit wreaths.

LISBOA FOOD MARKET
51 Liberty Street, Danbury, 06810; phone 203-748-5938. Hours: Monday–Saturday 8:30 A.M. to 8 P.M., Sunday 8 A.M. to 1 P.M. Cash only.

■ Inside this fairly ordinary-looking shop you will find an extensive selection of Portuguese and Brazilian ingredients and specialty foods. One of the most exciting items is a cheese called Serra da Estrela. This creamy white round cheese, named for a mountain range in Portugal, has a hard crust and comes wrapped in a thin turban-like piece of cheesecloth. Its flavor starts out nutty and almost sweet but leaves a sharp finish in your mouth. The woman behind the counter suggested that we eat it with slices of banana. Despite our skepticism we tried it, and it was delicious.

Other specialties here include freshly made *linguica* sausage, *morcela* (blood sausage), a good variety of fresh whole fish (delivered Tuesday and Thursday), marinated olives, and a big selection of olive oils imported from Portugal. There are some Brazilian ingredients for sale as well, including *dende* (palm) oil, hearts of palm, and *manioca* (yucca flour). Prices are extremely reasonable, particularly for the imported hearts of palm and olive oils.

THE GOOD FOOD STORE
865 Post Road, Darien, 06820; phone

Darien

■ This very attractive food store—with brick walls and lots of beautifully stained wood—offers delicious salads,

203-655-7355. Hours: Monday–Saturday 9:30 A.M. to 6:30 P.M.; closed Sunday. MasterCard, Visa, American Express, and personal checks accepted. Mail order and catering available.

McCONNEY'S FARM CIDER MILL

Roosevelt Drive, Derby, 06418; phone: 203-735-1133. Hours: mid-August to Christmas and late March to late June, seven days a week 9 A.M. to 6 P.M. Personal checks accepted.

VONETES PALACE OF SWEETS

262 Main Street, Derby, 06418; phone 203-734-2061. Hours: Monday–Friday 6:30 A.M. to 5 P.M.; closed Saturday and Sunday. Personal checks accepted.
   Also at 242 Main Street, Ansonia, 06401.

CRAND'S CANDY CASTLE

Route 5 (P.O. Box 3023), Enfield, 06082; phone 203-623-5515. Hours: seven days a week 9 A.M. to 9 P.M. MasterCard, Visa, and personal checks accepted. Mail order available.

breads, muffins, tarts, and pastries. You'll also find a wide array of Oriental, Mexican, Indonesian, British, Italian, French, and American ingredients, along with pâtés, smoked fish, cheeses, and sausages brought in from all over the globe.
   You can put together an incredible picnic at The Good Food Store. They also make gift baskets; we particularly liked the New England Goodies Basket, filled with cheddar cheese, clam chowder, maple syrup, Vermont applesauce and honey mustard, and mulling spices for cider.

Derby

■ You can watch the cider being made in the back room of this small farm stand and then sample its crisp, tart flavor right on the spot. You'll also find apples from local orchards, homemade pies and apple crisp, and super-sweet candy apples. During the spring and summer, vegetable and flowering plants are available in the greenhouse.

■ Vonetes has been a Connecticut institution since 1905. The faded black and white tile floor and the pressed tin ceiling are holdovers from another era. Like much of the Naugatuck Valley, this "Palace of Sweets" seems caught in a time warp.
   There's a long soda fountain manned by an elderly woman and a lanky teenager. Kids come in after school for milk shakes and ice cream sundaes. At the candy counter you find freshly made chocolate bark, orange creams, buttercrunch, chocolate-covered crackers, and popcorn balls. The candy here is not '80s gourmet. The chocolate tastes just a bit waxy, and the nuts in the nut clusters may not be California's finest, but this is real, old-fashioned, homemade candy.
   Vonetes serves breakfast and light lunches, but the real reason to stop by is for a tall frothy milk shake, a bag of candy, and a taste of a life that you seem to find only in the movies these days.

Enfield

■ It is the texture, as well as the flavor, of these candies that tells you that they are of the very highest quality. Crand's chocolates have a kind of "snap" when you bite into them, and not a hint of waxiness. The caramel and nut fillings are crunchy, not tacky. And the taste of all the candies is pure and delicious. We particularly liked the Nut Croquettes, an amalgamation of caramel, chocolate (milk, dark, or white), and nut meats (pecans, almonds, walnuts, or cashews).

Around Christmastime Crand's makes candy canes—big, beautiful pieces of candy that have been shaped by hand. There is no comparison between these and the artificially flavored and colored variety most of us are used to.

Fairfield

DROTOS BROTHERS
849 Kings Highway, Fairfield, 06430; phone 203-333-7530. Hours: Monday–Friday 9 A.M. to 6 P.M., Saturday 9 A.M. to 5 P.M.; closed Sunday. Personal checks accepted.

■ Drotos Brothers carries an extensive line of foods imported from Hungary, including paprika and noodles, but the star attraction is the meat counter, where they sell smoked meats and sausages prepared on the premises.

There are long slabs of smoked spare ribs, smoked ham hocks (primarily used for flavoring stuffed cabbage), and Hungarian farmer's bacon. Almost all the meats have a reddish brown hue that comes from being rubbed with liberal amounts of paprika. The sausage is called *kolbasz*. "It's not kielbasa," the man behind the counter informed us firmly but politely. "Kielbasa is Polish." Drotos Brothers makes three varieties of *kolbasz:* fresh and smoked (both of which must be cooked before eating) and dried, which is ready to eat.

Falls Village

CONNECTICUT FARMHOUSE CHEESE COMPANY
Route 7, Falls Village, 06031; phone 203-824-5878. Hours: Friday 12 N. to 5 P.M., Saturday and Sunday 10 A.M. to 5 P.M.; closed Monday–Thursday. Personal checks accepted.

■ A few years ago Mark Burdick traveled to the Netherlands and returned with a special cheese recipe from a Dutch farmer's wife, along with state-of-the-art cheese-making equipment. Today he and his partner, Katherine Reid, produce several Dutch-style cheeses, using milk from Burdick's herd of Jersey and Holstein cows. Their Gouda is extremely creamy and mild, as is the Herbed Cheese and the Nettle Cheese (nettle, a popular herb throughout Europe, has a slightly salty flavor). The Cheddar (which could stand to be aged longer and have more of a tang) is quite good melted on sandwiches.

All Connecticut Farmhouse Cheeses are made from raw milk, are aged for a minimum of sixty days, and contain no preservatives or colorings. Friday is cheese-making day and visitors are welcome.

Farmington

ANN HOWARD COOKERY
Brick Walk Lane, Farmington, 06032; phone 203-678-9486. Hours: Monday–Friday 7:30 A.M. to 8 P.M., Saturday 7:30 A.M. to 6 P.M., Sunday 8 A.M. to 4 P.M. MasterCard, Visa, and personal checks accepted. Catering and cooking classes available; call for information.

■ There is a lot to be tempted by at this bakery and gourmet take-out store. On the day we visited, the offerings included a chunky chicken and grape salad tossed in a freshly made mayonnaise, a salad of large whole shrimp and pea pods in a ginger vinaigrette, homemade pizza, several pasta salads, and stuffed croissants. When it came time to order our lunch, we opted for a sandwich with dark and white meat sliced fresh from a golden brown roast turkey. The sandwich, on thick slices of homemade sourdough rye, was extremely satisfying.

In addition to sandwiches, soups, entrées, and salads, you'll find a good selection of homemade pies, mousses, and tarts, along with locally made condiments and herbal vinegars, and a dozen varieties of bread.

Ann Howard also owns two restaurants, a catering company, and another gourmet food shop, at 981 Farmington Avenue in West Hartford (203-233-5561).

Goshen

NODINE'S SMOKEHOUSE
Route 63 North, Goshen, 06756; phone 203-491-3511. Hours: Monday–Saturday 9 A.M. to 5 P.M., Sunday 10 A.M. to 4 P.M. MasterCard, Visa, American Express, and personal checks accepted. Mail order available. Tours of the smokehouse available; call ahead.

Also sold at specialty food stores around the country.

■ Nodine's offers more than eighty items, everything from smoked hams to smoked shrimp and smoked venison sausage. But our favorite is their bacon—thick sliced, meaty, and smoked without nitrites.

Nodine's also smokes several other meats without nitrites, including chicken breast, turkey breast, pheasant breast, whole duck, whole goose, hot dogs, and beef tenderloin. And they offer smoked cheeses without nitrites.

We tried some of the smoked fowl products and found them to be flavorful and extremely moist. Other items we recommend are Nodine's *andouille* (a spicy Cajun-style sausage) and smoked venison sausage. Both of these, however, do contain nitrites.

If you have a taste for game but don't have the time or inclination to go out and shoot it yourself, Nodine's may be just your kind of place. They have a big selection of frozen game meat including buffalo, quail, wild boar sausage, pheasant, and several cuts of venison.

Greenwich

BON TON FISH MARKET
343 Greenwich Avenue, Greenwich, 06830; phone 203-869-0462 or 869-0576. Hours: Monday–Saturday 7 A.M. to 6 P.M.; closed Sunday. Personal checks accepted.

■ Fairfield County residents who know about seafood rave about the Bon Ton Fish Market. If it swims and is edible, chances are they carry it. The display case sparkles with such specialties as fresh whole baby salmon and tiny crawfish boiled in a spicy broth and ready to eat. You'll also find more standard fare like sole, swordfish, clams, shrimp, oysters, bluefish, and live lobsters—all at the peak of freshness.

GREENWICH PRODUCE
340 Greenwich Avenue, Greenwich, 06830; phone 203-869-7903. Hours: Monday–Saturday 8 A.M. to 7 P.M.; closed Sunday. Personal checks accepted.

■ This Korean-owned market offers top-quality, strictly fresh produce—common items like lettuce, tomatoes, onions, and potatoes as well as an interesting collection of more exotic fruits and vegetables. We were impressed by the array of brightly colored orange and yellow peppers from Holland, the organic dates from California, fresh kumquats, taro root, celery root, and okra, and the wide variety of mushrooms, including beautiful shiitakes. We also found a good assortment of fresh herbs, ripe fruit from around the world (including Oriental apple pears, which are like a very juicy cross between apples and pears), and Oriental ingredients, including won ton

CONNECTICUT

THE LOBSTER BIN
204 Field Point Road, Greenwich, 06830; phone 203-661-6559. Hours: Monday–Saturday 8 A.M. to 6 P.M., Sunday 9 A.M. to 1 P.M. Personal checks accepted.

MANERO'S MEAT MARKET
559 Steamboat Road, Greenwich, 06830; phone 203-622-9684. Hours: Monday–Friday 10 A.M. to 7 P.M., Saturday 10 A.M. to 9 P.M., Sunday 10 A.M. to 6 P.M. MasterCard, Visa, American Express, Carte Blanche, Diner's Club, and personal checks accepted.

PASTA VERA
88 East Putnam Avenue, Greenwich, 06830; phone 203-661-9705. Hours: Tuesday–Saturday 10 A.M. to 10 P.M.; closed Sunday and Monday. Personal checks accepted. Catering available.

wrappers. Greenwich Produce also specializes in miniature vegetables—those little darlings of nouvelle cuisine chefs. Artfully arranged, with prices to kill, were itsy-bitsy zucchini, pencil-thin French string beans *(haricots verts)*, and carrots the size of a baby's pinky.

- The seafood here just glistens. The swordfish steaks have a pink hue that tells you they are very fresh, and the filet of sole is a beautiful translucent white color. John Tung, the owner, buys fish from all over New England and beyond. There's fresh tuna, smoked and fresh salmon, whole rainbow trout, and of course live lobster. Mr. Tung will also prepare whole poached fish for parties.

- The scene is the meat counter at Manero's, a venerable steak house and butcher shop near downtown Greenwich. A well-dressed couple orders $250 worth of filet mignon. They spend a few minutes chatting amiably with the Italian butchers who run the store and then head for their Mercedes-Benz sports car parked just outside. After the couple leaves, one butcher says to the other, "She's not bad for *beaucoup.*"

"Yeah," says the other. "He's not bad for *beaucoup,* either."

"Yeah, and we're talking *beaucoup de beaucoup,*" says the first butcher.

"I know," replies his co-worker. "And this is old *beaucoup,* too."

Manero's is where the rich and the not-so-rich of Fairfield County come for well-aged prime-quality beef. A sign outside the shop reads "Sssh—Please Let This Sleepy Beef Age Slowly," letting you know that the beef is indeed aged on the premises. Manero's butcher shop also sells lamb, pork, veal, various kinds of poultry, cheeses, steak sauces, and other condiments. They offer sandwiches to go, along with burgers, garlic bread, salads, and Manero's excellent onion rings.

- The spirit of inventiveness pervades this Italian delicatessen, pasta shop, and restaurant. They make ravioli filled with all manner of unusual ingredients: smoked salmon, porcini mushrooms, gorgonzola cheese.

While the emphasis here is on pasta, be sure not to miss their desserts, all baked on the premises. The ricotta cheesecake is remarkably light and flavorful. The cannoli we tried was unusual in that the shell was actually a sweet Italian cookie called a *pizzelle,* rolled up to form a tube and then filled with sweetened ricotta cheese. Delicious!

Virtually everything they make can be packed to go, but not all items are always available, so call ahead if possible.

SAUSAGE EMPORIUM

160 Hamilton Avenue, Greenwich, 06830; phone 203-869-3839. Hours: Tuesday–Saturday 8 A.M. to 7 P.M., Sunday 8 A.M. to 2 P.M.; closed Monday. Personal checks accepted. Catering available.

■ The people of Fairfield and Westchester counties should consider themselves fortunate that Nick Mauro, owner of Sausage Emporium, decided to leave his native Brooklyn and move to Greenwich. Mr. Mauro is a master sausage maker. We have tried several of his Italian-style dried and cured sausages, and they are all superb. The Hot Dry Sausage is similar to pepperoni, but the spices are more subtle and the texture is firm, not dried out like most sausages of this type. The Soppressata is a milder sausage with a pleasing garlic flavor.

Sausage Emporium also offers a full line of fresh uncooked sausages, including veal sausage, pork sausage with cheese and parsley, hot and sweet Italian-style sausages, and Polish-style kielbasa. There is a fine assortment of Italian cheeses, cured olives, marinated peppers, other antipasto ingredients, and fresh Italian bread. Mr. Mauro also makes his own mozzarella cheese, with a wonderful creamy flavor and consistency. It's available plain or marinated in olive oil, parsley, and spicy flecks of red pepper.

TRUFFLES—"FOR FOOD LOVERS ONLY"

1 Grigg Street, Greenwich, 06830; phone 203-629-2993. Hours: Monday 10:30 A.M. to 5:30 P.M., Tuesday–Saturday 9:30 A.M. to 5:30 P.M.; closed Sunday. MasterCard, Visa, American Express, and personal checks accepted. Catering available.

■ It was not one of their better days. When we arrived at Truffles a water pipe had just burst and the employees of this delicatessen and bakery were slogging through the kitchen in rubber boots, wielding mops and pails in an attempt to clean up the mess. The sign outside the door said, "Sorry, temporarily closed." But that didn't deter customers from coming in and practically demanding their sandwiches and salads. Apparently Truffles customers are very dedicated, and for good reason. The food is well prepared, nicely presented, and in many instances it's actually good for you.

The philosophy of the store, explained the woman behind the counter, is to combine the best of two worlds: gourmet food and health food. "But," she went on, "Greenwich is a place that isn't into health food, 'cause health food is kind of . . . well . . . brown." Rest assured, you will not find "brown" food at Truffles, unless it happens to be made of chocolate. One of their most popular desserts is a confection they call Mocha Buttercrunch Pie (it's actually light brown). Basically it's a chewy crust made of ground nuts filled with a generous mound of light mocha mousse and decorated with shavings of rich dark chocolate. Even if they do use unrefined sugar in this concoction, it still doesn't qualify as health food.

The breads, however, are another story. The Millet Bread is a whole wheat loaf studded with crunchy millet grains. They also bake regular whole wheat and white bread. All the grain is ground on the premises.

There are a few tables here for enjoying a light lunch or snack, and of course everything is available to take out. A typical lunch might consist of apple butternut squash soup, veal dijonnaise, a small cup of chocolate mousse, and coffee or Perrier water.

CONNECTICUT

VERSAILLES RESTAURANT

315 Greenwich Avenue, Greenwich, 06830; phone 203-661-6634. Hours: Monday–Friday 7:30 A.M. to 9:30 P.M., Saturday 8 A.M. to 10 P.M., Sunday 8 A.M. to 5 P.M. Personal checks accepted. Catering available.

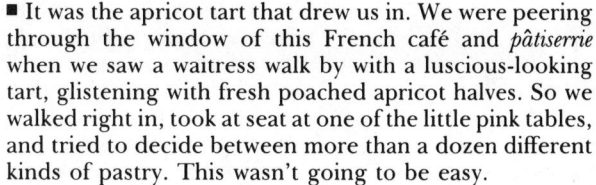

■ It was the apricot tart that drew us in. We were peering through the window of this French café and *pâtiserrie* when we saw a waitress walk by with a luscious-looking tart, glistening with fresh poached apricot halves. So we walked right in, took at seat at one of the little pink tables, and tried to decide between more than a dozen different kinds of pastry. This wasn't going to be easy.

All around us people were enjoying homemade quiches, omelets, crepes, pâtés, and salads. The place had the feeling of a small tea shop you might find in provincial France. We ordered two capuccinos, a slice of the apricot tart, and something called a White Cheese Mousse bedecked with plump fresh raspberries. Each of the pastries fulfilled its visual promise—rich, creamy, and delicately prepared.

The pastry case at Versailles changes daily with an assortment of tarts, cakes, chocolate confections, mousses, and cookies, all available for take-out. The atmosphere here is authentically French, right down to the waitresses who are a bit brusque at times, à la Paris.

Guilford

BISHOP'S ORCHARDS

U.S. Route 1 (I-95 Exit 57), Guilford, 06437; phone 203-453-2338. Hours: Monday–Saturday 8 A.M. to 5:30 P.M., Sunday 8:30 A.M. to 5:30 P.M. Personal checks accepted. Pick-your-own fruits and vegetables available; call ahead for conditions.

■ This is a good farm for fresh apples, pears, blueberries, raspberries, peaches, and vegetables. One of the most unusual items here is their fresh-pressed pear cider. It's similar to a sweet, syrupy apple cider, but has the aroma and flavor of fresh pears. Bishop's apple cider is also good.

Other outstanding products include fresh herbs, Judie's bread (see page 5), local honey, local eggs, and Vermont cheese.

Most of the fruits and berries are available for pick-your-own.

They also run Bishop's Northford Farm Market, Route 17 (3 miles north of Route 22), Northford, 06472 (203-484-9801). Open September and October only; call for hours.

GOZZI'S TURKEY FARM

2443 Boston Post Road (Route 1), Guilford, 06437; phone 203-453-2771. Hours: call ahead. Personal checks accepted.

■ The first, and only, interesting thing you notice when you enter the store at the Gozzi family's turkey farm is a wall full of awards—big silver trophies with turkeys on top, giant blue ribbons decorated with turkeys, plaques with images of turkeys etched into them. It's the Gozzis' shrine to the big bird that has made their business big time, especially during Thanksgiving and Christmas.

The Gozzis raise their own breed of turkey, the Gozzi White. Unlike supermarket poultry, the birds are not given steroids and are raised using a minimum of antibiotics. Fresh turkeys can be ordered for Thanksgiving, Christmas, and Easter. Frozen birds are available the rest of the year. As you would expect, prices are higher than at the supermarket.

PRIME CUT

1300 Boston Post Road (Route 1), Strawberry Hill, Guilford, 06437; phone 203-453-9986. Hours: Tuesday–Saturday, 9 A.M. to 6 P.M.; closed Sunday and Monday. Cash only.

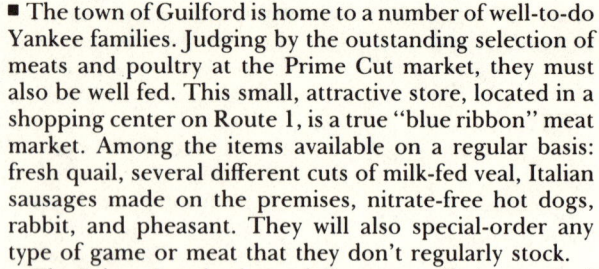

■ The town of Guilford is home to a number of well-to-do Yankee families. Judging by the outstanding selection of meats and poultry at the Prime Cut market, they must also be well fed. This small, attractive store, located in a shopping center on Route 1, is a true "blue ribbon" meat market. Among the items available on a regular basis: fresh quail, several different cuts of milk-fed veal, Italian sausages made on the premises, nitrate-free hot dogs, rabbit, and pheasant. They will also special-order any type of game or meat that they don't regularly stock.

The Prime Cut also has a deli counter offering smoked salmon, pâtés, cheeses, slab bacon, salads, and cold cuts. They sell frozen pasta, some locally made frozen desserts, and fresh breads and bagels.

If we have one reservation about the Prime Cut, it's the lack of locally grown food. Top-quality meat and poultry is being produced in New England, and more of it could be sold here.

Hartford

ADOLF'S MEAT AND SAUSAGE KITCHEN

35 New Britain Avenue, Hartford, 06106; phone 203-522-1588. Hours: Monday–Thursday 8 A.M. to 6 P.M., Friday 8 A.M. to 7 P.M., Saturday 8 A.M. to 5 P.M.; closed Sunday. Cash only.

■ It's a Friday afternoon in June, and Adolf's Meat and Sausage Kitchen is packed with shoppers buying sausages for their weekend barbecues and roasts for Sunday dinner. Housewives and factory workers line up in front of the sparkling glass display case filled with all manner of German sausages and fresh meats. Most speak German as the butchers chop, slice, weigh, and wrap each item to order.

Adolf's makes all their sausage on the premises. There is creamy liverwurst (available both mild and hot), flavorful white sausage, tender bologna, an especially mild veal bologna, fat juicy knockwurst, spicy kielbasa, wieners, a cured ham similar to prosciutto, several kinds of dried sausage, and much more. We tried several of the sausages, and they were all superb. The fresh meats look equally appealing: well-marbled standing rib roasts, steaks, and veal and pork roasts. All the chopped meat is ground to order, and they also custom-grind combinations of veal, pork, and beef.

While sausages and meat are the highlights at Adolf's, they also carry other foods for German- and Polish-style meals. You'll find loaves of heavy, flavorful dark and rye bread, jars of Polish sauerkraut and pickles, cookies and honey imported from Germany, as well as German condiments and spices.

Most of the sausages in the display case are made with nitrites, although some nitrite-free sausages are available on a daily basis. Others may be ordered in advance.

DIFIORE'S PASTA SHOP

■ We were walking through Hartford's South End—past Italian bakeries, pasta shops, butcher shops, and delis—when we came upon DiFiore's. A local chef had recom-

395 Franklin Avenue, Hartford, 06114; phone 203-246-1077. Hours: Tuesday–Saturday 9 A.M. to 6:30 P.M., Sunday 9 A.M. to 1:30 P.M.; closed Monday. Personal checks accepted.

mended their fresh pasta, and we decided to give it a try.

In a small, unassuming-looking display case sat trays of manicotti, jumbo-size stuffed shells, and tiny meat- and cheese-filled tortellini. "In the back we have the fresh ravioli, cannelloni, gnocchi, cavatelli, and egg pasta," said the young woman behind the counter, as if we needed further temptation. "Listen," she confided in a hushed voice. "The broccoli-and-cheese-stuffed shells and the manicotti are the best. You gotta try them."

Several hours later, at home in our own kitchen, we heated up these pasta dishes with some red sauce. After just a few bites it became clear that they were better than what's served in many first-class Italian restaurants. The stuffing in the shells was an unbelievably creamy mixture of ricotta cheese, garlic, spices, and small pieces of fresh broccoli. The manicotti was perfectly tender with a melt-in-your-mouth cheese filling. We only wish we had brought home a dozen more to put in the freezer for a cold, snowy night. For now, we'll just have to settle for the memory.

HARTFORD WEST INDIAN BAKERY

1344 Albany Avenue, Hartford, 06112; phone 203-247-3855. Hours: Monday–Saturday 8 A.M. to 7:30 P.M., Sunday 8 A.M. to 5 P.M. Cash only.

■ Along Albany Avenue in Hartford's North End, numerous restaurants, food stores, and bakeries attest to the culinary contributions made by citizens of Jamaica who have settled in Connecticut. The Hartford West Indian Bakery is a good place to sample some of the traditional foods these immigrants brought with them from their Caribbean island nation.

Displayed on the bakery's counter you'll usually find several different kinds of sweets—banana bread, sweet potato bread, bread pudding, coconut candy, and sweet rolls. The breads and the bread pudding are extremely dense, cake-like desserts that are sweet and spicy at the same time. Each little square is packed with so much sugar, flour, and other ingredients that it can easily serve three people. Despite the heaviness, however, the flavors are light and delicious. There are two varieties of coconut candy: a white and pink candy made with shredded coco-

Choosing a dessert at Bob Cardinale's Marjolaine Pastries and Confections in New Haven.

nut, and a dark candy with large chunks of fresh coconut in a spicy brown sugar base. Both are very sweet and have a pleasant crunchy texture.

The savory offerings at the Hartford West Indian Bakery are just a tad lighter than the sweets. The Jamaican meat patties are similar to beef turnovers or empanadas. They're made with finely ground beef, onions, thyme, and hot red pepper, all wrapped in a flaky pastry crust. It's customary to eat these meat patties tucked into a piece of coco bread, which is like a cross between pita bread and a hot dog roll. We also tried a cornbread fritter filled with spinach and cheese. Similar to an Italian calzone, this fritter had a very creamy filling surrounded by a chewy crust.

Prices at this bakery are extremely reasonable.

RAVIOLI KITCHEN
499 Franklin Avenue, Hartford, 06114; phone 203-247-1330. Hours: Monday–Saturday 8:30 A.M. to 6 P.M., Sunday 9 A.M. to 12 N.; closed Sunday in July and August. Personal checks accepted. Catering available.

Also sold in grocery stores and gourmet food shops throughout central Connecticut and in the Springfield, Massachusetts, area.

■ You'll find just about everything here that you need to cook really fine pasta dishes. There's Italian extra virgin olive oil, freshly made pasta sauces, fresh ricotta, mozzarella, romano, and Parmesan cheese, dozens of varieties of fresh and dried pasta—even pasta-making equipment and oversized pasta bowls imported from Italy.

Ravioli Kitchen's ravioli is tender, and both the meat and the cheese fillings have a fresh, well-seasoned flavor. Other intriguing items include cannelloni with sausage and spinach, meatless lasagna, and artichoke-flavored noodles.

TOP TASTE JAMAICAN BAKERY
551 Albany Avenue, Hartford, 06112; phone 203-548-0185. Hours: Monday–Saturday 9 A.M. to 8 P.M.; closed Sunday. Cash only.

Also at 1113 Albany Avenue, Hartford.

■ The sign outside proclaims that this bakery makes the best Jamaican meat patties in Hartford. Given our limited exposure to this Caribbean specialty we can't say whether that's true, but these meat patties certainly are delicious. A Jamaican meat pattie, as we have noted elsewhere, is a combination of finely ground beef, onions, herbs, and spices in a flaky pastry crust. It's usually eaten inside a roll known as coco bread.

The meat patties at the Top Taste Jamaican Bakery are sold warm. One meat pattie makes a satisfying and filling lunch, especially when accompanied by a bottle of Jamaican-style ginger beer or Ting—a Jamaican soft drink made with grapefruit juice.

New Haven

ATTICUS BOOKSTORE/CAFE
1082 Chapel Street, New Haven, 06510; phone 203-776-4040. Hours: Monday–Friday 8 A.M. to 12 M., Saturday 9 A.M. to 12 M., Sunday 10 A.M. to 5 P.M. MasterCard, Visa,

■ "We've won numerous awards for our cheesecake," reports baker Ken Ayvazian. "People just go nuts for it." Made with a cracker crumb crust and a cream cheese base, it's everything a good cheesecake should be—fluffy, creamy, and slightly tart. There's New York–style cheesecake, cheesecake flavored with chocolate chips, and in the fall, pumpkin cheesecake.

The dark and white Marble Mousse Cake is another

and American Express accepted.
  Also at 160 Main Street, Westport, 06880, 227-4104.

BOB CARDINALE'S MARJOLAINE PASTRIES AND CONFECTIONS

969 State Street, New Haven, 06511; phone 203-789-8589. Hours: Tuesday–Saturday 8 A.M. to 6:00 P.M., Sunday 8 A.M. to 1:00 P.M.; closed Monday. Personal checks accepted.

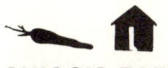

CHICO'S FARM FRESH FRUIT AND PRODUCE

420 Boulevard, New Haven, 06519; phone 203-776-8504. Hours: seven days a week 7 A.M. to 7 P.M. Cash only.

Chico (at right) offering some of the many ethnic specialties at Chico's Farm Fresh Fruit and Produce.

favorite—sweet but not too sweet, with a delicious chocolate crumb crust. Almond Bars combine a frangipane cake base with a sliced almond topping, all dipped in rich chocolate. Also worth trying are the European Fruit Tarts, Carrot Cake, Sweet Potato Pecan Pie, and Cranberry Linzertorte.

■ We have a good friend in New Haven who brings us a cake or torte from Marjolaine every time she visits. One October weekend she arrived with one of their cranberry-walnut tortes—a dense yellow cake laced with whole cranberries, lemon and orange rind, and nut meats, and topped with an indulgent layer of brown sugar and more of the tangy maroon berries. Another time she presented a pear frangipane, sweet with thick slices of fresh pear glazed on top. When we finally came to New Haven to visit our sweet-toothed friend, we all made a trip to Marjolaine together.
  First we tried a croissant. Excellent! Then we moved on to the butter cookies. Ditto! The cheesecake looked incredible, but we didn't dare; we were saving ourselves for the chocolate truffles.
  Marjolaine is an inviting place to spend an hour . . . or two. Sit at one of the cafe tables, sip a cup of coffee, read a magazine or newspaper (supplied by the bakery), and try to resist making a total pig of yourself. It's not easy.

■ Chico's is a little Caribbean oasis set amid the jumble of a typical American suburban highway. Piles of oranges and red peppers and long sticks of fresh sugarcane displayed in front of this roadside stand make a colorful contrast to the seedy used-car dealerships and warehouses that dominate the landscape in this part of New Haven.
  Park your car in front of a sign that says "Stop! Look Out, falling prices," and enter a store stocked with exotic fresh produce including *calabaza* (a kind of tropical

squash), cassava root, and two different types of breadfruit: *pana pan* (large breadfruit) and *pana de pepita* (small breadfruit). Chico (yes, there really is a Chico) also sells fresh coriander, green and yellow plantains, two varieties of fresh coconut, and a wide selection of the root vegetables that are staples of Caribbean cooking. In the summer there are locally grown green beans, collard greens, mustard greens, tomatoes, eggplant, and peppers.

Chico also offers his customers many other ingredients needed to make authentic Puerto Rican and Caribbean dishes: several kinds of dried beans, salted pig tails, smoked ham hocks, and *bacalao* (salted codfish). Chico keeps several grades of *bacalao* on hand, but if you want the good stuff, you have to ask. "I keep it in the back," says Chico with same tone that a jeweler might use in talking about his most valuable gems. For the most part, however, Chico's prices are more in keeping with Filene's basement than with Tiffany's.

CHINA TRADING COMPANY

271 Crown Street, New Haven, 06510; phone 203-865-9465. Hours: Monday–Saturday 9 A.M. to 6 P.M.; closed Sunday. Cash only.

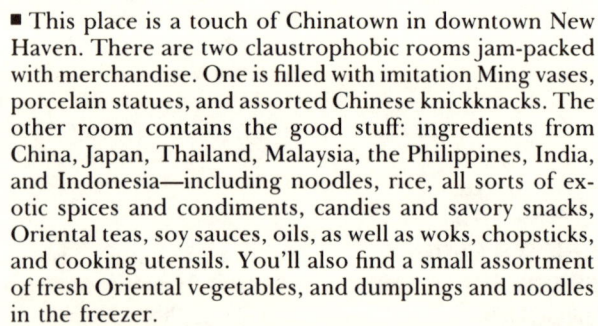

■ This place is a touch of Chinatown in downtown New Haven. There are two claustrophobic rooms jam-packed with merchandise. One is filled with imitation Ming vases, porcelain statues, and assorted Chinese knickknacks. The other room contains the good stuff: ingredients from China, Japan, Thailand, Malaysia, the Philippines, India, and Indonesia—including noodles, rice, all sorts of exotic spices and condiments, candies and savory snacks, Oriental teas, soy sauces, oils, as well as woks, chopsticks, and cooking utensils. You'll also find a small assortment of fresh Oriental vegetables, and dumplings and noodles in the freezer.

Items they don't normally carry can be special-ordered on Tuesday before they make their weekly trip to New York's Chinatown, and picked up on Thursday.

DEROSE'S, INC.

500 Orange Street, New Haven, 06511; phone 203-789-8108. Hours: Tuesday–Friday 8:30 A.M. to 6 P.M., Saturday 8 A.M. to 5 P.M., Sunday 8 A.M. to 12 N.; closed Monday all year and Sunday during June, July, and August. Personal checks accepted.

■ In 1903 the DeRose family ran a fruit and vegetable pushcart in Wooster Square, New Haven's old Italian neighborhood. Years later they expanded the business and opened a small neighborhood grocery store. DeRose's has continued to change with the times: today it is a well-stocked gourmet food shop, bakery, and fruit and produce market.

This is still the place neighborhood residents go to for everyday staples. But now customers also come from all over the New Haven area to buy DeRose's produce, including fresh herbs, Italian lettuce, and locally grown fruit. The variety of domestic and imported cheeses, pâtés, salamis, and smoked meats is one of the best in town. And one entire wall is devoted to nothing but pasta—in every size, shape, and color imaginable.

Each morning customers come in for freshly baked muffins, crusty hard rolls, and scones. There are excel-

EDGE OF THE WOODS

275 Edgewood Avenue, New Haven, 06511; phone 203-787-1055. Hours: Monday–Friday 9 A.M. to 7 P.M., Saturday and Sunday 9 A.M. to 6 P.M. Personal checks accepted.

THOMAS SWEET

1140 Chapel Street, New Haven, 06511; phone 203-562-8179. Hours: Monday–Thursday 10 A.M. to 11:30 P.M., Friday and Saturday 10 A.M. to 12 M., Sunday 10:30 A.M. to 11 P.M. Personal checks accepted. Mail order available.

WILLOUGHBY'S COFFEE AND TEA

1006 Chapel Street, New Haven, 06510; phone 203-789-8400. Hours: Monday–Friday 8 A.M. to 6 P.M., Saturday and Sunday 9:30 A.M. to 6 P.M. MasterCard, Visa, and personal checks accepted. Mail order available.

lent *baguettes,* French pastries, Russian *babkas,* chocolate truffles, and fruit tarts. The deli counter features sophisticated dishes like roasted red and yellow peppers, ginger cream chicken served over curried fettuccine, and egg salad in a lemon-yogurt dressing.

▪ This funky neighborhood grocery store really is on "the edge of the woods" in relation to downtown New Haven. But it is *the* place in town to buy organic vegetables and "health foods." What distinguishes this store from so many other shops is the quality of the produce. The fruit and vegetables are incredibly fresh and tempting, and almost all of them have been raised organically—including the lemons, limes, cranberries, melons, herbs, and Japanese vegetables like daikon and lotus root.

A small take-out counter offers a daily variety of freshly made soups, salads, and sandwiches. There's also a good selection of locally produced honey and maple syrup and a decent choice of imported and domestic cheeses. Of course you'll also find the usual health food store offerings like grains, flours, nuts, oils and vinegars, macrobiotic ingredients, and a wide array of Oriental foods. And considering the quality, prices are surprisingly reasonable.

As of this writing, the store was tentatively planning to move to a new location. Call ahead for information.

▪ This is a pleasant candy store and ice cream parlor in downtown New Haven. They have a good selection of dipped chocolates and chocolate novelties (things like chocolate tennis rackets and edible chocolate "shopping bags" for putting other candies in). The ice cream and most of the candies are made on the premises.

The store has a glass atrium, a perfect place to enjoy an ice cream sundae or a cool drink.

There's another Thomas Sweet in New Haven, at 1456 Whalley Avenue (203-397-4997).

▪ The warm aroma of freshly roasted and brewed coffee fills this small shop in downtown New Haven. This is a place to sit for an hour to enjoy a cup of coffee or tea along with the pastries and cookies they sell. In the summer Willoughby's operates a sidewalk cafe in front of the store.

Willoughby's roasts their own coffee—a process that can be viewed daily in the store's front window. In addition to coffee, they sell a wide selection of automatic and manual coffee makers, espresso machines, and automatic coffee grinders.

New Milford

THE SILO
Upland Road, New Milford, 06776; phone 203-355-0300. Hours: seven days a week 10 A.M. to 5 P.M. MasterCard, Visa, American Express, and personal checks accepted. Mail order available. Cooking classes given; call for information.

■ There is a lot going on inside this old dairy barn, and it ain't cows being milked. The Silo is a fantasyland of fancy food, cookware, and tableware, as well as a highly respected cooking school that offers demonstrations and seminars for home cooks taught by leading chefs and food experts.

But first, let's talk about the merchandise. There are herbal vinegars, fine olive oils, jams, jellies, and candies, all tastefully displayed on rough-hewn wooden shelves or in big wicker baskets. There are also strings of chile peppers and a fine selection of ingredients for making Mexican dishes. There's imported pasta, mustard, olives, and dried herbs, and a good choice of maple syrup, honey, and preserves made in New England. The Silo also sells cookware from around the world.

Like the rest of the store, The Silo's well-equipped demonstration kitchen has been designed to preserve the ambience of an old barn. Exposed beams, wide-paneled floors, and high ceilings make this a comfortable place to watch and learn. Recent classes included a Peking Duck demonstration, chef Jacques Pépin preparing a full French dinner, and a five-day cooking camp for kids.

Newtown

NEWTOWN FRUIT AND FLOUNDER
59 Church Hill Road, Newtown, 06470; phone 203-426-2398. Hours: Monday–Saturday 8:30 A.M. to 6:30 P.M., Sunday 9:30 A.M. to 4:30 P.M. MasterCard, Visa, and personal checks accepted.

■ The name of this roadside market tells you that there's something funny, and slightly off-putting, going on here. But if that's not enough, there's also a sign in the window that gives it away. The sign depicts a hand clutching a bunch of fish by the tail as though they were flowers in a bouquet. Underneath it reads "Say It With Flounders."

The quality of the food at Fruit and Flounder is very good, and compared to most other markets in this part of Connecticut it's excellent. (There just don't seem to be many well-stocked groceries in this area of the state.) But Fruit and Flounder has its problems. Take the cheese section, for example. It's actually a walk-in refrigerator stocked with imported and domestic cheeses. But it's so cold that you need to wear a down parka or you'll freeze before deciding whether to buy the blue cheese or the Brie. Another thing to be careful about is the prices. You may think things are going to be cheap here because it's set up like a food warehouse, but this is definitely a gourmet grocery store.

In the back you'll find wooden crates brimming over with very fresh looking vegetables, most of them locally grown in the summer. There is also a big bulk-foods section where you can scoop out several different kinds of pasta, dried fruits and nuts, coffees and teas. At the seafood counter they sell fresh fish, lobsters, smoked fish, and herring in various sauces. Other items include dried herbs, local apple cider, local honey, and local eggs, and some Chinese and Japanese ingredients.

Norwalk

NORWALK PORK STORE

7 Roger Square (near the East Norwalk train station), Norwalk, 06855; phone 203-866-0025. Hours: Monday–Friday 9 A.M. to 5:30 P.M., Saturday 9 A.M. to 4 P.M.; closed Sunday. Cash only.

■ It is so easy to overlook this German sausage shop—and what a sad mistake. We know from experience. Before we were married John lived a few blocks away from the Norwalk Pork Store for more than a year, passed it on his way to work every day, but never went in. We finally discovered the store when an acquaintance who lives in Fairfield County recommended it for inclusion in this book.

It was a bittersweet discovery, realizing that we could have dined regularly on melt-in-your mouth *weisswurst,* spread our sandwiches with the most heavenly liverwurst you have ever tasted, or made frank-and-bean lunches with some of the best German-style frankfurters this side of the Atlantic. These sausages might have added untold new dimensions to our courtship.

You'll find the Norwalk Pork Store in an old strip-type shopping center, between a Cumberland Farms and a hardware store. Look for the plastic pigs in the window—they will direct you to great sausages. Some of the varieties they make include knockwurst, smoked pork sausage with garlic, skinless franks, coarse liverwurst, smooth liverwurst, liverwurst made with fresh goose liver, Polish-style kielbasa, and Hungarian-style *kolbasz.* They also sell smoked pork chops, fresh pork, and German mustards and condiments. Sandwiches and cold-cut platters are available.

STEW LEONARD'S

100 Westport Avenue, Norwalk, 06851; phone 203-847-7213. Hours: seven days a week 7 A.M. to 11 P.M.; closed Christmas Day. Cash only.

■ Stew Leonard's is as close to Disneyland as a supermarket can be. Employees walk the aisles dressed as cows and chickens, a larger-than-life automated bull wearing a cowboy outfit sings "Thank God I'm a Country Boy" from atop one of the frozen-food cases, a zoo populated with dozens of farmyard animals graces the 500-car parking lot, and everybody here smiles—employees and shoppers alike.

The similarities between "the world's largest dairy store" and the Magic Kingdom are not accidental. Stewart Leonard wants grocery shopping to be fun. And since he opened his store in 1969, Leonard, who started out as a milkman, has demonstrated that running a grocery store like an amusement park can be both fun and profitable. Stew Leonard's is the top-grossing, highest-volume single food store in the world.

But why include Stew Leonard's in this book? Well, there are a few reasons: the quality of many of the products they sell is very high, the prices are reasonable, and, yes, we do admit it's kind of a thrill to shop here.

A sign in the dairy section brags that Stew Leonard's

A New England Afternoon Tea

Most people regard afternoon tea as a silly extravagance, a ritual practiced only by English people and little old ladies in flower-print dresses and silly hats. Well, things have changed and afternoon tea is making a comeback. Many of New England's finer hotels now offer a "tea-time meal," and all sorts of people—young and old alike—can be seen sipping cups of Earl Grey and nibbling away on thinly sliced cucumber sandwiches. As anyone who has experienced afternoon tea knows, it can be the most enjoyable meal of the day.

The trick to a successful afternoon tea, besides inviting the right people, is to make lots of little dishes: small sandwiches made with a variety of ingredients, cheeses, fresh fruit, delicate pastries, and so on. But instead of relying on traditional English favorites, we thought it would be nice to create a New England afternoon tea as a way to sample a wide variety of regional foods. What follows are suggestions for tea sandwiches that use some of New England's best foods. Serve them with New England–made herbal tea or a traditional pot of Chinese or Indian tea.

- Thinly sliced pieces of sharp cheddar cheese over apple cider jelly on whole wheat bread.
- Smoked bluefish topped with horseradish on thin slices of French bread, garnished with a sprig of fresh dill.
- Slices of French bread topped with fresh goat cheese and broiled until the cheese turns golden brown.
- Thin Rhode Island jonnycakes buttered and rolled up with fruit preserves.
- Thick Rhode Island jonnycakes topped with sour cream and caviar.
- A blend of cold baked swordfish, mayonnaise, fresh tarragon, horseradish, and lemon juice, spread on crackers and topped with a thin slice of hard-boiled egg.
- Maine shrimp salad served on Vermont Common Crackers.
- Smoked turkey or chicken on buttered toast, topped with a sprig of fresh watercress.
- Thinly sliced smoked country ham on rye bread with grainy maple mustard.
- Maine crabmeat mixed with a touch of lemon mayonnaise on thinly sliced brown bread.
- Slices of sautéed Connecticut shad roe with lemon slivers, served with buttered black bread and crackers.
- Thin slices of fresh pear topped with fresh chèvre.

sells over 10 million quarts of milk a year. Add that to all the yogurt, butter, ice cream, and cottage cheese they sell and you're talking about a whole lot of dairy products. Because they have such a high turnover, you're just about guaranteed that these will be at the peak of freshness. Further on there is a bountiful display of fresh fruits and vegetables; a meat section featuring pork, beef, and chicken; fresh seafood; a veritable wall of cheeses with everything from Velveeta to Brie; fresh pasta; a giant salad bar; and a counter where they serve up fried chicken, roast duckling, and ribs to go.

Unlike regular supermarkets, Stew Leonard's has only one—very long—aisle. The store is designed so shoppers must walk past every item they sell. Chances are you'll end up buying more than you came for. On your way out you can reward (or console) yourself with a soft ice cream cone.

Also be sure to check out the gallery of snapshots faithful customers have sent in. The photos are all of people holding up Stew Leonard's shopping bags at famous spots around the world. Look, there's one of a lady standing near the Eiffel Tower, and there's another of a man blocking out part of the Taj Mahal with his shopping bag. Isn't this fun!

ELLSWORTH HILL FARM
Route 4, Sharon, 06069
(mailing address: P.O.

Sharon

- Ellsworth Hill Farm began as an apple orchard—30 acres of land planted with five thousand apple trees. The farm was popular for its fresh-pressed cider and fifteen

Cold Spinach Soup with Nutmeg and Cream

This soup must be made several hours ahead of time (or preferably a day ahead), in order to let it chill properly. Nutmeg, the symbol of Connecticut, is a key ingredient; if at all possible, it should be freshly grated.

1 tablespoon lightly salted butter
1 tablespoon safflower oil
2 medium onions, coarsely chopped (about 2 cups)
1 large clove garlic, chopped
1 1/4 pounds fresh garden spinach

7 cups chicken broth, preferably homemade (fat removed)
1/2 teaspoon freshly grated nutmeg
Freshly ground black pepper
About 3/4 cup heavy cream
Freshly grated nutmeg for garnish

In a large stockpot, heat the butter and oil over moderate heat. Add the onions and garlic and sauté about 4 minutes, until tender but not brown. Add the spinach and let it wilt slightly, mixing constantly for 2 to 3 minutes. Add the broth, nutmeg, and a generous grinding of pepper. (If you are using homemade chicken stock, you may want to add a touch of salt; most canned broths are loaded with salt, so there's no need to add any.) Raise the heat to high and bring the soup to a boil. Reduce the heat and let it simmer about 5 to 10 minutes, or until the spinach is soft and tender.

In a blender or food processor, blend the soup in small batches. Place the soup in a large bowl or soup terrine, cover, and refrigerate for several hours (or overnight), until well chilled.

To serve: swirl a tablespoon or two of cream into each bowl of soup, and grind some fresh nutmeg on top. Makes about 10 cups.

Box 76, Cornwall Bridge, CT 06754); phone 203-364-0249 or 364-0546. Hours: April 1 through January 1, seven days a week 9:30 A.M. to 6 P.M. Personal checks accepted. Pick-your-own fruit available; call ahead for conditions.

SO NO SEAFOOD MART

100 Water Street, South Norwalk, 06854; phone 203-866-9083. Hours: seven days a week 9 A.M. to 6 P.M. Personal checks accepted.

NANSHE'S

990 Farmington Avenue, West Hartford, 06107; phone 203-236-1609. Hours: Monday–Friday 10 A.M. to 6 P.M., Saturday 10 A.M. to 5:30 P.M.; closed Sunday. MasterCard, Visa, and personal checks accepted. Mail order and catering available.

varieties of apples, including Mutsu, Empire, and Northern Spy.

Like so many orchards, Ellsworth Hill decided to expand. They planted 5 acres of strawberries and an acre of raspberries, and invited neighbors to come and pick their own. Next, a vegetable garden was planted with tomatoes, summer squash, spinach, lettuce, radishes, sweet sugar peas, snap peas, and onions. Before long the farm was supplying many of the best food shops in the area.

Ellsworth Hill now offers a wide variety of exceptionally fresh produce. In addition to the items mentioned above they also grow grapes and sell grape juice for home vintners. According to manager Jim March, these grapes are not particularly good to eat. But if you are knowledgeable about winemaking, "you can produce some awfully good wine, or very earthy-tasting juice." Over 2 acres of wine grapes are planted, including Chancellor, Foch, and Baco Noir. Grapes should be ordered well in advance.

If you stop by the farm, you can watch them press cider or visit the new greenhouse, offering a good selection of herb, flower, and vegetable plants.

South Norwalk

■ We've never known why, but Norwalk oysters seem to have a fuller flavor than most other oysters. At the So No Seafood Mart you can buy them at their freshest, along with lobsters, clams, swordfish, and other fresh seafood. There's a restaurant and raw bar attached to this fish market, where you can dine on seafood dishes while looking out over Norwalk harbor.

West Hartford

■ Nanshe's is an attractive gourmet food shop with a full take-out menu offering salads, soups, pâtés, cheeses, smoked meats and fish, and sweets. It's a good place to put together a picnic lunch, and if you don't feel like cooking dinner, they'll prepare an entire meal for you.

We tasted their fresh linguine and found it to be tender and flavorful. We also sampled a few of the desserts: both the Lemon Square and the rich, buttery Chocolate Square were excellent. There is just one caveat: like so many other gourmet food shops, prices here are very high.

SHORELINE LOBSTER

5 Boston Post Road (Route 1), Westbrook, 06498; phone 203-669-3477. Hours: Tuesday–Saturday 9 A.M. to 5 P.M., Sunday 10:30 A.M. to 5 P.M.; closed Monday. Cash only.

HAY DAY

1026 Post Road East, Westport, 06880; phone 203-227-9008. Hours: Monday–Saturday 8 A.M. to 7 P.M., Sunday 8 A.M. to 6 P.M. Personal checks accepted. Mail order and catering available.
   Also at 1050 East Putnam Avenue, Riverside, 06878, and 1910 Black Rock Turnpike, Fairfield, 06514. Classes by leading chefs and authors are offered at the Riverside store.

Westbrook

■ There are dozens of places to stop and buy lobsters along the Connecticut shoreline, but there is something particularly appealing about this tiny shack. Here they sell nothing but lobster—locally caught lobster—and the fisherman who runs the place knows his business. The day we stopped by, a couple of nautical characters were inside repairing old lobster traps, grumbling about the weather and the rising cost of seafood. "Better buy this week," they warned us. "Prices are only going one way and that ain't down." Aside from the funky atmosphere and a lot of free conversation, you can buy lobsters here at a reasonable price.

Westport

■ The parking lot was jam-packed. It was Saturday—dinner party day—and it seemed as if everyone in Fairfield County was stopping off at Hay Day to pick up a few last-minute items. A woman in pink tennis sweats ordered a $45 fresh fruit tart for her dinner guests. A preppy young man selected four jars of assorted jams and jellies from New Zealand to bring as a gift to his hostess. And a very distinguished elderly gentleman, bedecked in a tweed jacket, corduroy pants, and suede English walking shoes, asked the woman behind the charcuterie counter for "just a tad of the wild boar pâté."
   Hay Day is the Mercedes-Benz of country farm stores. If money were no object, this is the kind of place we wouldn't mind shopping at every day. There are few stores in Connecticut—or for that matter in New England—that make food, and food shopping, look this appealing.
   A dozen varieties of apples are piled high in wooden crates; cheeses from all over the world are displayed on French straw mats; and seven types of wild mushrooms sit in little baskets, with a card explaining each type and its uses. The wild strawberries from France look ready to be photographed, and the pastry counter is a dieter's nightmare.
   At Hay Day you'll find just about everything that falls into the "gourmet food" category. Looking for fresh guavas, or gooseberries from New Zealand? No problem. Smoked salmon, smoked trout pâté, caviar, Polish sausage, Greek and Italian olives—they have it all.
   The produce here is exceptionally fresh, and the salads, pastries, and pastas are made daily. Hay Day even has its own dairy, supplying fresh milk. You'll also find a small selection of New England–made products, including honey, maple syrup, jams and jellies, herbal jellies and vinegars, and chocolate.

Shopping at Hay Day in Westport.

OLD WORLD DAIRY PURE FARM YOGHURT

Old World Dairy Ltd., 54 Carmel Hill Road, Woodbury, 06798; phone 203-263-5050.

Sold in grocery stores, health food shops, and gourmet food shops throughout Connecticut, as well as some stores in Westchester and Putnam counties (New York) and in the Boston area.

Woodbury

■ This yogurt is rich and tangy. It's unhomogenized, so the first thing you see when you open the container is a layer of yellow cream sitting on top. Old World Dairy Pure Farm Yoghurt has a slightly stronger flavor than most yogurts, so it may take a few bites to get used to it. But you'll probably find, as we did, that it's far more satisfying than most national brands.

Connecticut Farmers' Markets

For more information on any of these markets, contact the Connecticut Department of Agriculture, Marketing Division, State Office Building, Hartford, 06106; phone 203-566-3671 or 566-4845.

* * *

Bethel—Fairfield County Farmers' Market, Fairfield County Extension Office, Stony Hill Road (Route 6), Saturdays from August through October, 9:30 A.M. to 1 P.M.

Bloomfield Farmers' Market, Town Hall, 800 Bloomfield Avenue, Saturdays from mid-July through October, 9 A.M. to 1 P.M.

Cheshire Farmers' Market, Watch Factory parking lot (Routes 68 and 70), Saturdays from July through October, 8 A.M. to 1 P.M.

Danielson Farmers' Market, municipal parking lot, School Street, Saturdays from June through October, 9 A.M. to 12 N.

Granby Farmers' Market, Granby High School parking lot, 315 Salmonbrook Street, Saturdays from mid-July through September, 9 A.M. to 12 N.

Hartford—Albany Avenue Farmers' Market, Fox Middle School, corner of Albany and Blue Hills avenues, Saturdays from mid-July through October, 10 A.M. to 2 P.M.

Hartford—Asylum Hill Farmers' Market, Farmington Avenue (near YWCA), Thursdays from mid-June through October, 10 A.M. to 2 P.M.

Hartford—Downtown Farmers' Market, Market Street (near entrance to G. Fox), Mondays, Wednesdays, and Fridays, mid-July through October, 10 A.M. to 2:30 P.M.

Hartford—Market-on-the-Hill Farmers' Market, corner of Farmington Avenue and Imlay Street, Saturdays from mid-June through October, 10 A.M. to 2 P.M.

Hartford—South End Farmers' Market, 30 New Britain Avenue, Tuesdays from mid-July to mid-October, 3 P.M. to 6 P.M.

Litchfield Farmers' Market, Bankcorp parking lot, Route 202, Saturdays from late July through October, 12 N. to 3 P.M.

Manchester Farmers' Market, St. James Church, 896 Main Street, Saturdays from mid-July through October, 9:30 A.M. to 1 P.M.

Middletown Farmers' Market, South Green, Main Street, Mondays and Thursdays from mid-July through October, 8 A.M. to 1 P.M.

New Haven Farmers' Market, Corner of Chapel and Orange streets, Wednesdays 10 A.M. to 3 P.M., Saturdays 9 A.M. to 1 P.M., from June through October.

New London Farmers' Market, Captains' Walk and Eugene O'Neill Drive, Fridays from mid-July through October, 11 A.M. to 2 P.M.

Norwich—City Landing Farmers' Market, City Landing, Shetucket Street, Saturdays from late June through September, 8:30 A.M. to 12 N. Wednesdays at the Salvation Army, 262 Main Street, 11 A.M. to 2 P.M.

Norwich—Main Street Farmers' Market, 262 Main Street (parking lot), Wednesdays from late June through September, 11 A.M. to 2 P.M.

Plymouth Farmers' Market, Plymouth Congregational Church green, Route 6 and North Street, Thursdays from mid-July through October, 3 P.M. to 6 P.M.

Putnam Farmers' Market, Market Place Restaurant parking lot, Kennedy Drive, Thursdays from July through October, 3 P.M. to 6 P.M.

Rockville—Tri-Town Farmers' Market, East Main Street, Saturdays from mid-July through October, 8:30 A.M. to 12 N.

Sharon Farmers' Market, Low Road and Route 41, Saturdays from July through October, 9 A.M. to 12 N.

Stamford Farmers' Market, Columbus Park, Main Street, Thursdays from August through October, 10 A.M. to 2 P.M.

Torrington Farmers' Market, Haydon Plant parking lot, Route 4, Tuesdays from late July through October, 3 P.M. to 6 P.M.

Willimantic Farmers' Market, corner of Jackson and Union streets, Saturdays 8 A.M. to 12 N., Thursdays 3 P.M. to 7 P.M., from mid-July through October.

Windsor—Aetna/West Green Farmers' Market, Windsor Hill, corner of Addison and Pigeon Hill roads, Tuesdays from mid-July through October, 11:30 A.M. to 1:30 P.M.

Maine

MAINE

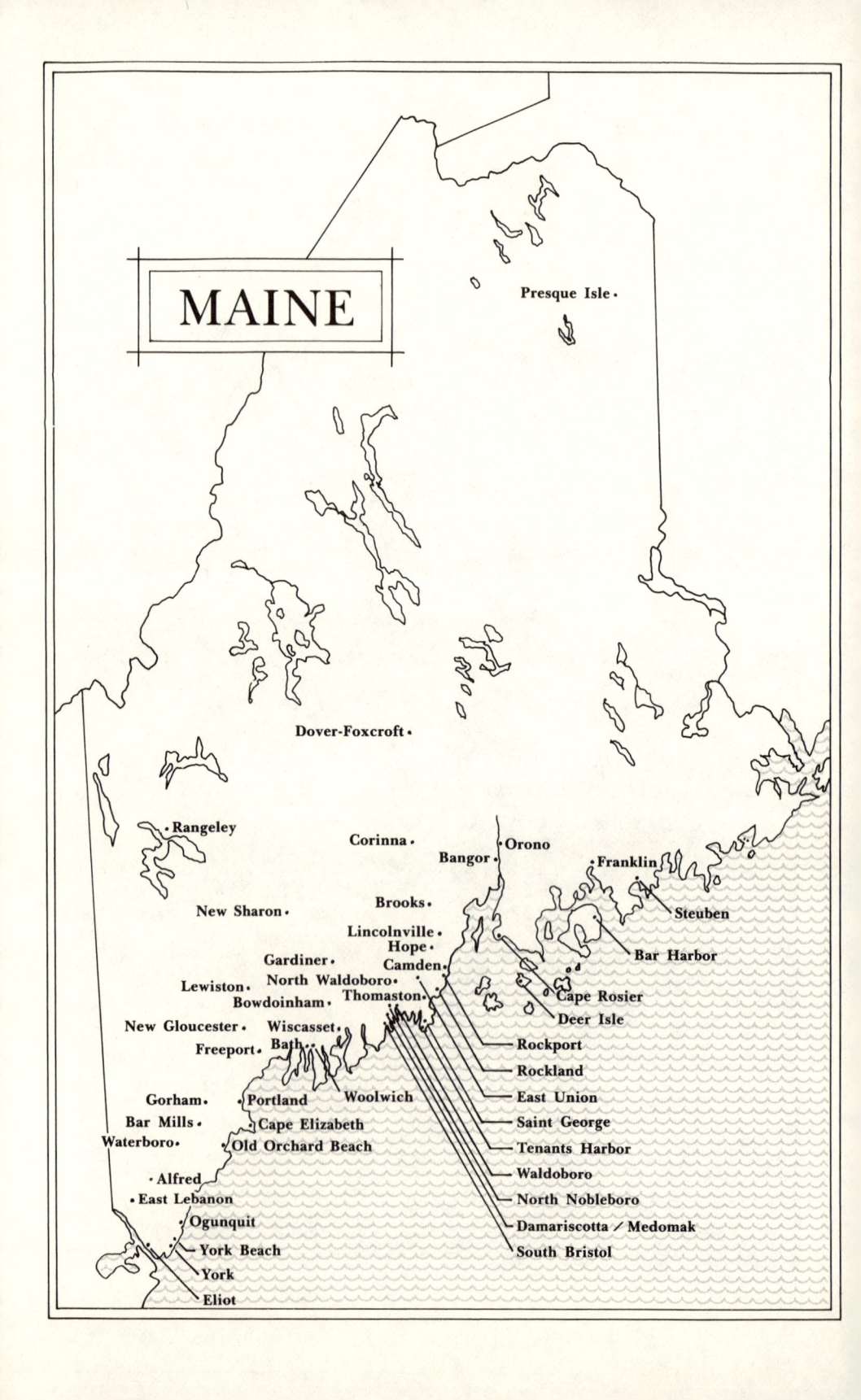

- Presque Isle
- Dover-Foxcroft
- Rangeley
- Corinna
- Orono
- Bangor
- Franklin
- New Sharon
- Brooks
- Steuben
- Lincolnville
- Hope
- Gardiner
- Camden
- Bar Harbor
- Lewiston
- North Waldoboro
- Bowdoinham
- Thomaston
- Cape Rosier
- New Gloucester
- Wiscasset
- Deer Isle
- Freeport
- Bath
- Rockport
- Rockland
- Gorham
- Portland
- Woolwich
- East Union
- Bar Mills
- Cape Elizabeth
- Saint George
- Waterboro
- Old Orchard Beach
- Tenants Harbor
- Waldoboro
- Alfred
- North Nobleboro
- East Lebanon
- Damariscotta / Medomak
- Ogunquit
- South Bristol
- York Beach
- York
- Eliot

Alfred

GILE ORCHARDS
Routes 202 and 4, Alfred, 04002; phone 207-324-2944. Hours: seven days a week 8 A.M. to 5 P.M. Cash only. Pick-your-own apples in the fall; call ahead for information.

■ Cider maker Frank Boucher puts together a well-balanced apple cider. "We try to get it right in the middle, between tart and sweet," he explains. Made from McIntosh, Cortland, Golden Delicious, Spenser, and Macoun apples, the cider has a clean, fresh taste and is produced without preservatives. Visitors are welcome to watch the cider being pressed. They will also custom-press cider for you.

In addition to cider you'll find apples from their orchard, locally produced maple syrup, cheeses, locally grown vegetables, Maine potatoes, a huge selection of penny candy, and jams and jellies.

Bangor

THE BAGEL SHOP
1 Main Street, Bangor, 04401; phone 207-947-1654. Hours: Monday–Friday 6 A.M. to 6 P.M., Sunday 6 A.M. to 2 P.M.; closed Saturday. Cash only.

■ What's a nice Jewish deli doing in a place like Bangor? Who knows? Who cares? The bagels here are fresh and delicious. So are the soft rye bread with caraway seeds and the braided challah.

Other bakery specialties include Russian coffee cake, almond bread, apple strudel, and cheese danish. You can also buy deli items like cream cheese, Nova Scotia salmon, and lox. The only problem is that they seem to run out of many items fairly early in the day.

The Bagel Shop also has a restaurant with a full menu. It's not much on ambience (remember, this is downtown Bangor), but the food is good and plentiful: hot corned beef sandwiches, eggs with kippers and onions, mushroom barley soup, three varieties of knishes. The place does a brisk business at lunchtime. The regular clientele includes personnel from the nearby Bangor Naval Air Station, so while you kvetch over your knish you can converse with a colonel.

BANGOR TAFFY
Pine Tree Confections, Inc., Box 816, Bangor, 04401; phone 207-862-2767. Mail order available.
  Sold in stores throughout Maine, including L. L. Bean (see page 52).

■ It's not much to look at. Open a box of Bangor Taffy and what you see is a plain-looking block of caramel-colored candy, crosshatched into bite-size squares and dusted with powdered sugar. Now take a bite, and be catapulted into ecstasy. This confection has a sweet, buttery flavor with a slight hint of vanilla. The consistency is ultra creamy. You can easily get hooked on this stuff.

"It's dangerous, all right," says Phil Brady, vice-president of sales for Pine Tree Confections. "When I'm on the road I have to keep the samples of Bangor Taffy in the trunk of my car. All day long it calls to me, 'I'm in here.' Every so often I pull over and get out a box to snack on." We sympathize, Mr. Brady. The product is irresistible.

Bangor Taffy is delicious served at the end of a meal

with coffee, or melted down and poured over vanilla ice cream. If you want to be really extravagant, melt down an entire box and make candied apples.

Pine Tree Confections also makes saltwater taffy, several different kinds of fudge, and Bangor Gold, a molasses candy. But Bangor Taffy is the star attraction.

Bar Harbor

NORTHERN LIGHTS GARLIC AND HERBS
P.O. Box 603, Bar Harbor, 04609; phone 207-288-3174. Personal checks accepted. Mail order available.

■ We were walking through the Common Ground Country Fair (see page 72) when we noticed a display of garlic. We've tried to grow garlic in our Maine garden and let's just the say the results have never been very impressive. But there, sitting on a fold-out table, was a collection of garlic that looked as if it had come from the fertile hills of Tuscany. There were garlic bulbs of every size, shape, color, and texture—tiny purple-hued garlic, medium bulbs of rosy pink garlic, and huge sandy-beige garlic bulbs. Being passionate about garlic, we immediately sat down and introduced ourselves to the man who grew these fine-looking plants.

John Navazio told us how he moved to the Maine coast from Oregon in 1984. "In Oregon I had great success with the acre of garlic I grew," he explained. "When I came to Maine everyone told me there was no way I'd grow garlic here. I told them that was ridiculous and planted a small plot, just enough for me and a few friends." After a few successful crops, Navazio realized that he was one of the few people growing garlic in the state. So he increased the size of his crop and now sells several varieties of garlic to customers all over the East Coast. There's a large mild variety that's extremely easy to peel, called German Red—a beautiful bulb with a purple streak running through it. Elephant Garlic (which is not a true garlic at all) is a mammoth, very mild flavored bulb that often reaches 3 or 4 inches in diameter. California Late Garlic is superbly flavored and long-lasting.

Wolfe's Neck Farm, in Freeport.

Navazio's garlic is grown organically. He plants in the fall and harvests his crop each summer. He also grows several varieties of delicately flavored shallots. Write for more details about garlic braids and garlic wreaths. Navazio also plans on planting a good variety of herbs in the near future; write for more details.

Bar Mills

SNELL FAMILY FARM
Route 112, Bar Mills, 04004; phone 207-929-6166. Hours: July to Christmas, seven days a week 9 A.M. to 6 P.M. Personal checks accepted.

Also at the Portland and Saco farmers' markets (see page 84).

■ The Snells make refreshing sweet cider from the apples they grow in their orchard. The cider—made from McIntosh, Delicious, and Cortland apples—is sold without preservatives. They also sell about a dozen varieties of apples along with vegetables grown on the farm, including peas, beans, cauliflower, broccoli, pumpkins, leeks, squash, and brussels sprouts.

Bath

CENTER STREET GRAINERY

36 Center Street, Bath, 04530; phone 207-442-8012. Hours: Monday–Thursday 9 A.M. to 5:30 P.M., Friday 9 A.M. to 7 P.M., Saturday 9 A.M. to 5 P.M.; closed Sunday. Personal checks accepted. Cooking classes held in the winter; call for details.

■ A New Age talk show was playing softly on the radio when we visited the Center Street Grainery one quiet summer morning. We were able to pick up snippets of a conversation about new paths to spiritual enlightenment as we browsed through shelves filled with organic grains, herbal teas, and natural animal crackers. The host of the program began talking about the impact of Eastern philosophy on Western consciousness at about the same time we discovered the store's extensive collection of Japanese ingredients, including just about everything you need to make sushi (except raw fish). It was a cosmic coincidence.

We really shouldn't poke too much fun. This store has a lot to offer anyone who is looking for natural foods or foods made in Maine. They carry a wide variety of salt-free, wheat-free, and dairy-free foods. There are also natural fruit juices at very good prices, and they sell lots of other items in bulk (also at good prices), including peanut butter, tahini, dried fruits, cooking oils, and tamari.

The Center Street Grainery is a good place to pick up a quick lunch or snack. They usually offer a selection of sandwiches, soups, and freshly baked sweets. If you feel like putting together a picnic, they carry whole grain breads from a number of Maine bakeries, along with locally made cheese.

GILMORE'S SEAFOOD MARKET

131 Court Street, Bath, 04530; phone 207-443-5231. Hours: seven days a week 7 A.M. to 6 P.M.. Personal checks accepted.

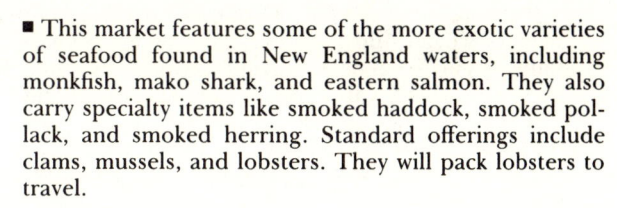

■ This market features some of the more exotic varieties of seafood found in New England waters, including monkfish, mako shark, and eastern salmon. They also carry specialty items like smoked haddock, smoked pollack, and smoked herring. Standard offerings include clams, mussels, and lobsters. They will pack lobsters to travel.

KRISTINA'S BAKERY AND RESTAURANT

160 Center Street, Bath, 04530; phone 207-442-8577. Hours: Tuesday–Saturday 7:30 A.M. to 9 P.M., Monday and Sunday 9 A.M. to 6 P.M. Personal checks accepted. Catering available.

■ This is one of those places where you want to try a little bit of everything. It all looks so delicious, and happily it tastes just as good as it looks. Among the notable items we've sampled: rich and chocolatey cheesecake brownies, sticky buns studded with carmelized pecans and laced with cinnamon, Swedish orange bread flavored with orange peel and anise seeds, and blueberry bran muffins made with wild Maine blueberries.

This is a great place to come for breakfast or brunch. The French toast is, of course, made with their own bread. At lunch or dinner you will also have a chance to try as many of their baked goods as you want. Plan on having two desserts. We did.

Garlic, Leek, and Onion Tart

This tart should be served warm—not straight from the oven. The garlic flavor seems to be at its peak when the tart is allowed to cool for about 10 minutes after baking.

Crust
2 cups flour
Pinch of salt
8 tablespoons (1 stick) lightly salted butter, chilled
3 to 5 tablespoons cold water

The Filling:
3 medium leeks
1 tablespoon olive oil
1 tablespoon lightly salted butter
4 cloves garlic, minced
2 medium onions, thinly sliced
2 cloves elephant garlic or large garlic, thinly sliced
2 teaspoons fresh thyme, or 1 teaspoon dried
1 cup heavy cream
Salt and freshly ground black pepper to taste
1/3 cup plus 2 tablespoons grated Parmesan cheese

Make the pastry crust: Sift the flour and salt into a large bowl. Cut the butter into small pieces, and using 2 kitchen knives (or your hands), work the butter into the flour until it resembles bread crumbs. Make a well in the center of the flour and add 3 tablespoons of the water. Work the water into the pastry, adding more if needed to form a smooth ball of dough. Shape the dough into a ball, wrap in plastic wrap, and chill for at least 1 hour.

Remove the dough from the refrigerator and roll it out to fit into a 9-inch fluted tart (or quiche) pan with a removable bottom. Line the tart pan with the dough, and trim the edges even with the top of the pan. Place it in the refrigerator until ready to bake.

Rinse the leeks well, slice them lengthwise, and cut into 3-inch pieces.

Preheat the oven to 400°. Heat the olive oil and butter in a large skillet over moderate heat. Add the leeks, half the minced garlic, and the onions, and sauté about 5 minutes, stirring occasionally. Add the remaining minced garlic, the sliced garlic, the thyme, and the cream, and raise the heat to medium-high. Let the mixture simmer about 5 minutes, or until the cream is slightly thickened. Remove from the heat, add salt and pepper to taste, and stir in the grated cheese. Spoon the filling into the crust and bake for 10 minutes. Reduce the heat to 325° and bake an additional 50 minutes. Let cool for 10 minutes and serve warm. Serves 4 to 6.

PLANT'S SEAFOOD
203 High Street, Bath, 04350; phone 207-443-2640. Hours: seven days a week 7 A.M. to 6 P.M. (5 P.M. during winter). Cash only.

■ You know that the seafood here is fresh because you can see it and smell it. There's not much room to hide anything in this tiny store. When you walk through the front door, the first thing you're likely to see is Wallace Plant or his sons, Daniel and Chris, standing at the work counter, fileting freshly caught sole or cutting a side of swordfish into thick steaks. A few feet away there's an old ice chest with a glass cover where bright orange salmon, blood-red tuna, and pure white haddock filets are displayed. And the lobster tanks are usually brimming over with frisky crustaceans.

There's nothing fancy here, and they don't sell the widest variety of seafood, but the quality is excellent. They will pack live lobsters to travel.

Bowdoinham

HATTIE'S KITCHEN
The Ledges, Old Post Road, Bowdoinham, 04008; phone 207-666-8827. Hours: May 1 to November 15, Saturday–Thursday 8 A.M. to 8 P.M.; closed Friday. Personal checks accepted. Mail order available for jams, jellies, and pickles. Orchard tours and cider pressing demonstrations by appointment. Pick-your-own apples, plums, and raspberries.

Also at the Brunswick Farmers' Market on Fridays (see page 84).

■ Our first reaction when we tasted Hattie Bouldin's spicy Dilly Beans was "Wow"—not because they were too hot, but because they were so good. These slender green beans are preserved with sprigs of fresh dill, flecks of hot red pepper, and white vinegar. "The rule when making dilly beans," said Hattie's husband, Jim, "is to let your conscience be your guide when it comes to adding the spices." These tasty pickles are conclusive evidence that the Bouldins have very good instincts about this kind of thing.

But dilly beans are only the beginning. Hattie's sauerkraut is crunchy and not too salty (it's great with sausages). Her plum jam is thick and sweet, and is equally good spread on toast or as an accompaniment to roast meat and poultry. The apple butter is also thick and has a pleasing cinnamon flavor. In all, Hattie's Kitchen makes over twenty-five different jams, jellies, and condiments—including a delicious jalapeño pepper jelly that's both hot and sweet at the same time.

All the ingredients that go into these preserves are raised on the Bouldins' 40-acre farm. The vegetables are grown organically, but the fruits are sprayed. "Unfortunately," said Jim, a retired Navy pilot who sounds more like Chuck Yaeger than your typical Maine farmer, "we've screwed up our environment so much that we have to spray the fruit trees."

If you visit the Bouldins' farm, called "The Ledges," you'll find their jams, jellies, and condiments along with fresh fruits in season, vegetables, and their own sweet cider. Jim insists on using at least five different kinds of apples to give the cider balance and flavor. "That's why we don't even start making it until the last week in September," he said. Also look for their dried beans. There are several different types, including the hard-to-find and very tasty variety called Jacob's Cattle, for making such dishes as chile and baked beans.

Brooks

SMITH'S LOG SMOKEHOUSE
Back Brooks Road, Brooks, 04921; phone 207-525-4418. Hours: Monday–Saturday

■ Smith's Log Smokehouse is one of the few places we know that smokes meat without sodium nitrite, a food preservative that has been linked to cancer. One of sodium nitrite's principal benefits is that it gives smoked meat, particularly ham, a "healthy" pink color. Because the Smiths don't use this common additive, their hams, bacon, and sausages generally don't look quite as pretty

Classic New England Clam Chowder

1 dozen quahog or large cherrystone clams
3 strips of bacon or a 2-inch cube of salt pork
2 tablespoons butter
1 medium onion, diced
1 shallot, diced
1/2 teaspoon dried thyme
3 large potatoes, peeled and diced
Freshly ground black pepper to taste
2 cups milk
Paprika to taste

Scrub the clams. Using a clam knife, open the clams over a large bowl, making sure to reserve all the juice. Place the clam meats in a chopping bowl and chop coarsely. Reserve. Strain the clam juice through a fine strainer, and reserve. (It's easier to open the clams if you dunk them in cold water and then quickly in warm, but not hot, water.)

Cut the bacon or salt pork into small pieces, and slowly sauté it in a large soup pot until very crisp. Remove the bacon with a slotted spoon, drain on paper towels, and reserve.

Melt 1 tablespoon of the butter with the bacon fat over moderate heat. Sauté the onions and shallots until they become translucent, about 2 minutes. Add the chopped clams and the thyme, and sauté another 3 minutes. Pour in the strained clam juice, and add the potatoes and the fried bacon. Cover, and simmer until the potatoes are cooked but still firm, about 12 minutes. Add a generous grinding of pepper.

Heat the milk, but make sure it doesn't boil. Stir it into the soup.

(For better flavor, complete all the steps up to, but not including, the addition of the warm milk. Place the chowder in the refrigerator overnight. Heat and add the warmed milk on the following day.)

Cut the remaining tablespoon of butter into small slivers. Serve the chowder in mugs or soup bowls, topped with a sliver of butter and a sprinkling of paprika. Serves 2 to 4.

---

9 A.M. to 5 P.M., Sunday 1 P.M. to 5 P.M. MasterCard, Visa, and personal checks accepted. Mail order available. Custom-smoking available.

as other brands. But don't be swayed by appearances. These products are first-rate.

One Labor Day weekend we took advantage of a special offer from the Smiths and ordered through the mail a ready-made holiday picnic consisting of several different sausages, smoked chicken, and smoked cheese. The summer sausage, made of beef and pork, was slightly grainy and had a very pleasing, somewhat spicy flavor. The pepperoni sausage had a nice bite to it. Because it was a bit soft it tasted fresher than other pepperoni we've had.

Another excellent product was the hot capicola. These thin slices of Italian-style smoked pork tasted like a cross between prosciutto and air-dried beef. For lunch one day we fried up a few slices with garden zucchini and tomatoes, onions, garlic, and olive oil.

In addition to the items we have sampled, Smith's Log Smokehouse produces everything from country ham to slab bacon to smoked kielbasa. They have also started to make some products with sodium nitrite for people who are particularly concerned about the appearance of their food.

Camden

CASPIAN CAVIARS
Highland Mill Mall (P.O. Box 876), Camden 04843; phone 207-236-8313 or 236-4436. Hours: Monday–Friday 9 A.M. to 5 P.M.; closed Saturday and Sunday. MasterCard, Visa, American Express, and personal checks accepted. Mail order available.

Caspian products are also available at The Wine Emporium in Camden and at several other gourmet food shops around New England.

■ Female lobsters are prized for their roe—a cluster of bright red, delicately flavored eggs. Caspian Caviars, a distributor of fancy foods and New England seafood products, sells lobster roe, or coral, under the slightly euphemistic name "lobster caviar." As far as we know, no other company packages lobster roe, and it's easy to see why: it takes 50 pounds of lobster to produce just 1 pound of roe (excuse us, "caviar"). Lobster roe is freshest and most abundant from April through June, so Caspian Caviars collects the roe during these months, cooks it, and flash-freezes it in vacuum-sealed packages. It is also available fresh if ordered ahead.

Now comes the big question. What does one do with lobster caviar? Unlike regular caviar, you wouldn't want to eat these eggs on their own; they tend to have a waxy texture. However, they add a deliciously subtle lobster flavor to fish soups, pâtés, terrines, and sauces. This stuff is not cheap, but when you consider you're buying a flavor that captures the essence of lobster, it's not totally unreasonable.

Caviar from all over the world is the specialty at Caspian Caviars. Caspian claims they "pack everything fresh and import directly." You can order Caspian Beluga, Osetra, and Sevruga, imported from Iran, or domestic sturgeon, salmon, and golden whitefish caviar. Prices are

Boat and gear—ready for the start of lobstering season.

Homarus Americanus—
Cooking the Sweet Maine Lobster

The lobsters caught off the coast of Maine are considered the finest in the world. Crayfish, crawfish, and spiny lobster are all quite tasty, but the sweet, seductive flavor of freshly steamed *Homarus americanus* is the ultimate.

The average Maine lobster weighs in at 1 to 3 pounds, but lobstermen have been known to drag them home as large as 10, 20, even 40 pounds. According to one Maine fisherman we know, despite popular belief these humongous specimens taste every bit as good as their smaller cousins. "Everyone thinks they're tough," he tells us, "but when cooked properly they taste great. The only difference is the texture. The larger the lobster, the coarser the texture."

Each year around 22 million pounds of lobster are caught off the Maine coast. People come from all over the world to taste this great delicacy. But this was not always the case.

In the early 1600s piles of lobsters washed up along the New England coastline. Because they were so plentiful, colonists considered them poor man's food—to serve lobster was an admission of hard times or poverty. Even as late as the 1800s, American cookbooks listed lobster soup (a rich broth made from no fewer than three whole lobsters) in the chapter "Economical Meals."

In the last few years, having consumed an average of one lobster a week, we've come to learn a very basic truth: like all good fresh food, the more simply you prepare lobster the better. Most Down Easters wouldn't think of stuffing a lobster with bread crumbs or setting it aflame with Cognac. The reason being that when you serve lobster plain and simple, subtle flavors emerge that go unnoticed in more elaborate concoctions.

For instance, there's gender to consider. Yes, there is a difference between the taste of male and female lobsters. The males tend to be slightly larger and meatier than their female counterparts. But the females offer meat that is just a bit sweeter, and they often contain roe—a small sac filled with thousands of rich, tiny, coral-colored eggs—which is one of the lobster's great gifts. You can tell the difference between a male and a female lobster by looking between its legs (where else?). Turn the lobster on its back and find the two feelers located at the base of the tail. If they're hard, it's a male; if they're soft and flexible, you've got yourself a lady.

Boiling is the simplest and perhaps most common way to cook lobster, but not necessarily the best. As one local lobsterman explained: "When ya cook chicken in a pot of watah, ya get chicken soup. Same thing with lobstah. It loses all its good flavah." We've found that steaming or broiling produces the juiciest, most tender meat.

To steam a lobster, fill a large pot with about 2 inches of water and sprinkle with salt. (If you have access to fresh seaweed, add a few strips instead of salt.) Bring the water to a rolling boil and add the lobsters to the pot *back first* (so all the juices get caught in the shell and are not lost in the pot). Cover, and let steam about 12 minutes for a 1-pound lobster and about 20 minutes for a 2-pounder. To test for doneness, simply pull off one of the legs; if it pulls off easily, the lobster is ready. Drain, and serve with melted butter, lemon wedges, and plenty of oversized paper napkins.

Broiled lobster is not for the weak at heart. It involves plunging a sharp knife into the abdomen of a squirming, wiggling, lively creature. But the rewards . . . well, just you wait.

Turn the lobster on its back. Place a dish towel over the lobster's head and claws (this will protect your hands and give the poor thing a certain amount of dignity in its final moments). Quickly plunge a very sharp knife down the middle of the lobster, beginning at the head and cutting down through the tail. The lobster may insist on moving around well after you've made the incision, but rest assured it can't feel a thing. Open the body into two halves without separating them completely. The stomach—a round sac located at the head of the lobster—should be removed. Next, lift out the intestinal tract, the thin grayish vein that runs from the head to the tail. Place the lobster in a shallow broiling pan and surround with about ¼ inch of water. Use a nutcracker to slightly crack each of the claws. (This prevents them from exploding under the broiler and makes it easier to get at the meat later.) Scatter about 1 tablespoon of unsalted butter, cut into small pieces, over the entire body of the lobster. Sprinkle lightly with paprika and a touch of finely chopped fresh or dry basil and thyme. Top with a very light sprinkling of fresh bread crumbs and place under a preheated broiler about 2 inches from the flame. Broil about 12 minutes for a 1-pound lobster and up to 16 minutes for a 2-pounder. Serve with melted butter, lemon wedges, a bottle of hot pepper sauce, baked potatoes, cole slaw, plenty of warm biscuits, and a large pitcher of ice-cold beer.

THE WINE EMPORIUM

Highland Mill Mall, Camden, 04843; phone 207-236-2858. Summer hours: Monday–Thursday 9 A.M. to 6 P.M., Friday and Saturday 9 A.M. to 7:30 P.M., Sunday 11 A.M. to 5 P.M. Call for winter hours. MasterCard, Visa, and personal checks accepted. Catering available.

surprisingly reasonable—on a par with any of the big caviar importers in New York.

Also available are live Maine lobsters—from 1¼-pound chicken lobsters to 4-pound monsters—and fresh Maine scallops, shucked or still in the shell. They also sell flash-frozen Maine lobster tails.

Other items you'll find in the Caspian Caviars brochure: smoked fish, truffles and truffle peelings, fresh foie gras, and frozen fresh fruit purées. During the spring, early summer, and fall, wild Maine mushrooms—chanterelles, morels, and cèpes—are sold fresh by the pound and can be ordered through the mail.

■ Ellen Wiland, the owner of The Wine Emporium, says her goal is to have the most comprehensive wine selection in the state of Maine. We can't say for certain whether she has succeeded, although the scope of her wine collection is impressive (there's a 1961 Lafite Rothschild for around $700, along with more modestly priced wines from France, Spain, Italy, Greece, Bulgaria, Hungary, and the United States). What we can say for sure is that the Wine Emporium carries one of the best selections of wine and specialty foods we've found north of Portland.

The Wine Emporium has a cooler filled with treats like fresh caviar, smoked salmon, and a fine assortment of cheeses. There are also cookies and other sweets baked on the premises.

Cape Elizabeth

RAM ISLAND FARM HERBS

Ram Island Farm, Cape Elizabeth, 04107; phone 207-767-5700. Personal checks accepted. Mail order available.

Available at gourmet and specialty food shops. If you have a special interest in visiting the herb farm or would like to pick up your order in person, call ahead to arrange an appointment.

■ Ram Island Farm is a tiny pocket tucked away in a huge family estate on the coast of Maine. If you don't have access to fresh herbs year-round, Ram Island dried herbs are the next best thing. What makes these herbs so incredibly fresh tasting? "Everything is planted by hand, organically grown, harvested by hand, and dried in a humidity- and temperature-controlled environment," answers herbalist Elizabeth Jacques. The group who run this farm are passionate about their work, and they handle their herbs with the kind of care that horse trainers reserve for Thoroughbreds.

Ram Island produces close to fifty types of dried herbs and spices—everything from common herbs like rosemary, tarragon, and thyme to more unusual varieties like raspberry and strawberry leaves, wintergreen, and chive flowers. There are also delicious herbal teas and several blended seasonings—Italian, Poultry, Fish Herbs, and Salad Herbs are our favorites. The herb and spice vinegars are made with garden herbs that are steeped in cider vinegar and infused in the summer sun for about two weeks. Ram Island Farm also produces herbal bath and body scents, herbal lip balms, and spectacular herb wreaths.

Cape Rosier

THE FUNNY FARM

Stanley Joseph and Lynn Karlin, Oar's Cove Road, Cape Rosier, 04642; phone 207-326-4062. Hours: May through October, Monday–Friday 9 A.M. to 12 N., or by appointment; closed Saturday and Sunday. Cash only. Pick-your-own berries available; call ahead for conditions.

■ We always know we're on to a good source of food when it's recommended over and over again. Such was the case with Stanley Joseph of The Funny Farm. "He grows gorgeous organic produce," raved a friend who summers near Cape Rosier. "Oh, definitely," said another. "This guy knows how to work the earth."

Stanley Joseph and his wife, Lynn Karlin, bought their 22-acre farm from Helen and Scott Nearing in 1980. The Nearings—authors, environmentalists, and advocates of a simple, natural country life-style—were responsible for encouraging a number of young New England farmers.

The Funny Farm supplies produce to many of the area's finest restaurants and inns, but they also invite visitors to come to the farm and buy direct. Stanley Joseph plants "all the normal kinds of vegetables for a New England farmer," but what he really enjoys is growing "more exotic things—like fresh fennel, radicchio, and arugula." He also harvests "tons" of fresh basil and other herbs. And throughout the summer there are berries—strawberries, blueberries, and raspberries. The other part of their business is cut flowers, which they use to create beautiful dried flower wreaths.

Joseph has one other claim to fame: scarecrows. He collects driftwood from nearby beaches and constructs elaborate structures to keep away unwanted birds and animals. "There's this one woman who comes here every summer who wants me to start a scarecrow festival or contest," he told us. "She thinks my scarecrows are some sort of artistic creation. I don't know." He laughs. "Maybe one day we'll do that." For now he is content with gardening.

Corinna

COCK PHEASANT FARM POPCORN
Durham Bridge Road (RFD 1, Box 1605), Corinna, 04928; phone 207-278-4553. Call ahead for hours and directions. Personal checks accepted. Mail order available from late fall through winter.

■ You know that Cock Pheasant Farm's popcorn is going to be different the minute you start popping it. Within seconds the whole kitchen fills with the aroma of fresh corn. When it's done you have a huge bowl of pure white hull-less popcorn with a delicious nutty corn flavor. It's so good it doesn't need butter.

John Buckland produces about 5 acres of White Cloud corn every year. "This variety is hard to grow," he told us, "as it requires 110 growing days. So you can see we have to plant early and harvest late and pray for a good year." When you cook this popcorn, Buckland advises, "use very little oil, as oil tends to make the corn tough. An old-fashioned wire basket or a hot air popper works very well."

Damariscotta

MARGO'S MARKET
Off Main Street, Damariscotta, 04543; phone 207-563-5378. Hours: Monday–Saturday 8:30 A.M. to 5:30 P.M.; closed Sunday. Personal checks accepted.

■ You'll find an outstanding variety of Maine foods and culinary offerings from around the world at this specialty food store, which advertises itself as "The best little market in Maine." Among the local products they carry are smoked salmon from Horton's Downeast Foods (page 78), several kinds of Maine goat cheese, and local fruits, vegetables, honey, and maple syrup. On the import side you'll find Italian pasta; cheeses from France, Italy, and Great Britain; olive oil and vinegar; and a good selection of beer and wine.

Although Margo's Market is not a butcher shop, they do carry an extensive selection of frozen meats. Hard-to-find items like quail, squab, and sweetbreads are either in stock or may be special-ordered.

Deer Isle

NERVOUS NELLIE'S JAMS AND JELLIES
Sunshine Road (RFD 474), Deer Isle, 04627; phone toll-free 800-346-4273, or 207-348-6182. Hours: Monday–Friday 8 A.M. to 5 P.M.; closed Saturday

■ There are so many cooks making and marketing homemade jam and jelly these days that it seems you have to have a gimmick to get any attention. So here we have a delightful cartoon character, a squiggly little creature named Nervous Nellie who simmers up fresh Maine berries, fruits, and vegetables to create some memorable conserves.

The Blueberry-Ginger Conserve—a combination of wild Maine berries, crystallized ginger, oranges, and lem-

Fiddleheads, Fiddleheads

We had heard about fiddleheads for years. "They're incredible," a friend raved, "a great delicacy—a cross between asparagus and artichokes." So there we were at a large resort hotel in New Hampshire and the waiter announced that fresh fiddleheads were the "vegetable of the day." At last. What a disappointment when a plate of overcooked greens arrived, looking like a mass of limp, curly spinach. We each took a bite and concluded that fiddlehead ferns were one of the world's most overrated foods.

A few years later, while dining at a Boston restaurant, we decided to give fiddleheads another try. This time we were served a plate of perfectly round, bright green vegetables, sautéed in olive oil with garlic and lots of fresh spring herbs. Finally we understood what the fuss was all about. When properly cooked, fiddlehead ferns, with their unique earthy flavor, are delicious.

According to Robert Chute, a fiddlehead "expert" and biology professor at Bates College in Lewiston, Maine, "There are over 400 species of fern in the U.S. and only one kind worth eating. That's the fiddlehead." Actually the coiled frond of the ostrich fern, fiddleheads resemble the scroll of a violin; hence the name. They grow wild throughout New England—primarily in Maine, New Hampshire, and Vermont—and along the Eastern seaboard of Canada.

Fiddleheads begin to pop up in late April or early May. For many New Englanders they are the first real taste of spring. Peter Cox, the former editor of the *Maine Times*, explained: "Connecticut has shad roe, Maryland has soft-shell crabs, but here in Maine we have fiddlehead ferns." Throughout Maine it is a spring tradition to spend a day rummaging through forests and fields and along streams in search of the wild ferns. Once they discover them, said Cox, "Mainers covet their fiddlehead patches and don't let anyone know about them."

New Englanders have been picking fiddlehead ferns for generations. Lately there's been some controversy about picking wild fiddleheads; many scientists warn that eating fiddleheads can be dangerous. Peter Cox agrees: "They're like wild mushrooms. You learn to be very careful." Before you head for the woods, keep in mind that the ferns are edible only when young and tightly curled, before they unravel and become fully mature. Like hunting for wild mushrooms, be sure to consult a guidebook, or better still, go fiddlehead hunting with someone who knows what to look for.

Years ago there wasn't much demand for fiddleheads. In recent years, however, they've become one of the hot "new" New England foods, featured on spring menus in many of the best restaurants. You can use fiddleheads in several different ways: toss them with a vinaigrette, add them to salads, pickle them, or use them to stuff a roast lamb or pork loin. We like them simply prepared—steamed and tossed with butter, sautéed with garlic and fresh herbs, or puréed into a simple, delicious soup with fresh asparagus. The season is too short and the taste too special to smother fiddleheads with a lot of strong or fancy flavors. (See pages 51 and 61 for recipes.)

and Sunday. Personal checks accepted. Mail order available.

Also available at gourmet food stores and country stores.

PEACEFIELD FARM

Bear Hill Road (RFD 1, Box 268), Dover-Foxcroft, 04426; phone 207-564-3031. Hours: seven days a week, call ahead for an appointment. Mail order available.

Also sold at the Camden Farmers' Market (see page 84).

THE SIROIS FAMILY FARM

Little River Road (Box 68), East Lebanon, 04027; phone 207-457-2046. Hours: late June through Columbus

ons—makes a fantastic topping for ice cream, pound cake, or yogurt. You could also use it to make a sweet, fruity glaze for duck. The Spicy Apple Cider Jelly is thinner than most, with a sharp, sweet flavor that goes well with pork.

We tasted the Red Tomato Marmalade and the Hot Tomato Jelly with a group of friends and the reaction was mixed. Some thought they tasted like tomato juice with pectin; others found the flavors attractive. And a four-year-old friend of ours thinks they would be great on burgers, instead of ketchup.

Other flavors include Wild Maine Blueberry Jam, Sunshine Road Marmalade (made with oranges, pink grapefruit, and lemons), Strawberry Marmalade, and Red Raspberry Jam. Also look for Hot Tomato Chutney, Orange-Mint Jelly, and a spicy jalepeño-spiked jelly.

Dover-Foxcroft

■ "I believe in raw-milk cheese," says Sherri Hamilton adamantly. "More and more state laws are leaning toward pasteurization, but when you pasteurize milk you kill a lot of the good bacteria and the taste that should be developing in a cheese."

Hamilton makes a variety of raw goat's-milk cheeses based on the traditional French chèvre. (In order to get around state pasteurization laws, Hamilton ages all her cheeses for a minimum of sixty days.)

Peacefield Farm Chevri is made from the milk of Saanen goats (a Swiss breed). The animals are fed nothing but natural grain, hay, and organically grown forage. This cheese has a thick, creamy consistency and a slightly sour taste. The Strong Chevri is aged three months and tastes remarkably similar to a French Montrachet—tangy, sharp, and delicious. Best of all is the Herb Chevri, a creamy cheese chock-full of organically grown herbs. Garlic Chevri is outrageously good spread on thick slices of toasted French bread or stirred into thick vegetable soup or chowder. Hamilton also makes a very creamy, mildly flavored feta cheese.

Sherri Hamilton is happy to have visitors come to Peacefield Farm and watch the cheesemaking process.

East Lebanon

■ Sydney Sirois and her husband, Norman, both grew up on farms, and when they started having children of their own they decided it was time to begin farming again. "We wanted our children to know that food doesn't grow in a supermarket," said Sydney. So they bought a 35-acre farm with a 150-year old farmhouse in southern Maine and planted several acres of vegetables. The first summer their garden was so prolific that they opened a small

Day weekend, seven days a week 10 A.M. to 6 P.M. Cash only. Pick-your-own fruit and vegetables available; call ahead for conditions.

MORGAN'S MILLS
Just off Route 17, East Union, 04862; phone 207-785-4900. Hours: Tuesday–Saturday 10 A.M. to 6 P.M., Sunday 12:30 P.M. to 5 P.M.; closed Monday. MasterCard, Visa, and personal checks accepted. Mail order available. Tours available; groups should be arranged in advance.

Morgan's Mills products are also sold at natural foods stores throughout New England.

Richard Morgan of Morgan's Mills.

produce stand, "just to give the kids something to do." Neighbors were impressed by what they saw: the vegetables were beautiful, and they had all been grown organically.

Today the Sirois family has a "real" produce stand, offering a wide variety of organic vegetables. They also sell farm-fresh eggs and their own maple syrup; and when Sydney Sirois has the time, she cooks a variety of fruit jams and jellies, fruit pies, and several types of bread. This is a great place to buy vegetables by the bushel for freezing or canning; prices are extremely reasonable.

Produce is only half the story here. The Sirois also raise several hundred chickens and turkeys; all the birds are grain-fed with a minimum of medication and are sold fresh, never frozen. (Poultry orders are taken by phone in the spring and again in midsummer for fall delivery.) This is also the place to buy piglets if you want to raise your own pork; the Sirois raise close to a hundred piglets every year. Poultry and meat must be ordered in advance.

East Union

■ It's worth going out of your way to find Richard Morgan's gristmill, not just because the freshly ground grains and other regional foods he sells are excellent, or because you can have a lot of fun swimming in the millpond right outside the front door, or because you can watch the mill in action on days when they grind the grain. Morgan's Mills merits a special trip because it combines all the best elements of the New England food revival to which this book is dedicated.

Richard Morgan opened his business in 1982. Like a lot of people who moved to Maine in recent years, he was attracted by the opportunity to live in the country and be an entrepreneur at the same time. But to realize his dream of starting up an old-style gristmill Morgan needed one crucial ingredient: waterpower. The site he choose sits atop a small dam that once drove an earlier

Whole Wheat Almond Pancakes with Maple-Nut Syrup

These pancakes taste best when made with freshly ground whole wheat flour. They should be small—about the size of a large silver dollar. If time allows, mix the batter an hour before serving and let it sit in the refrigerator.

Pancakes
3/4 cup fresh whole wheat flour
1 teaspoon double-acting baking powder
1/2 teaspoon salt
1/3 cup ground or minced almonds
1/2 cup milk
1 egg
2 tablespoons maple syrup
2 tablespoons butter, melted

Syrup
3/4 cup maple syrup
1 tablespoon butter
1/2 cup walnuts and almonds, finely chopped
Drop of vanilla extract

In a medium bowl sift together the flour, baking powder, and salt. Stir in the almonds.

In a separate bowl, gently whisk together the milk, egg, maple syrup, and melted butter. Add the liquids to the flour mixture and stir gently until moistened. Don't be concerned about lumps. Set the mixture in the refrigerator for about 1 hour.

Heat all the syrup ingredients over low heat for about 5 minutes, or until the butter has melted and the nuts are warm. (For a variation, you can also add chopped dried fruit, fresh blueberries, raspberries, or blackberries, or thin slices of fresh apple and pear.) Keep warm.

Remove the batter and stir. If it seems too thick, add an additional tablespoon or two of milk. Heat a griddle or large skillet over high heat. Grease the pan lightly with vegetable oil or butter. (The griddle is hot enough when water dropped on it splatters.) Use a heaping tablespoon of batter to form each pancake. Cook on one side for about 2 to 3 minutes, until bubbles form. Turn the pancakes over and cook an additional 1 to 2 minutes. Serve warm with Maple-Nut Syrup. Makes about 16 small pancakes.

---

gristmill as well. Today in addition to grinding about a dozen different kinds of organic wheat, corn, and rice, Morgan produces 30 kilowatts of electricity. Some of the power is used to drive the mill machinery; the rest is sold to the local electric company.

Although freshly ground grains are his specialty, Richard Morgan also stocks a variety of locally made foods in his store. You can buy organic eggs, organic vegetables, and apple cider in season. Inside the stained-glass-decorated dairy case you'll find cheeses and other dairy products made in New England. From time to time Morgan may also have locally produced smoked meats and fish.

A lot of the flour ground at Morgan's Mills ends up at organic and natural foods bakeries in New England. These flours are also available in bulk to individual consumers at the Morgan's Mills store. If, however, you aren't able to make a trip to East Union, Richard Morgan has a whole line of flours, and muffins and pancake mixes, that can be ordered by mail and are sold in a number of specialty and organic food stores. One of the most popular mixes is Griffles (a combination of griddle cakes and waffles). It's made from a mixture of four different whole grain flours and leavening agents that you mix with eggs, water, butter, and orange or apple juice to make pancakes or waffles. There are also a Buckwheat Griffles, Rice-Corn and Oats Griffles (made without wheat, dairy, or salt), and Blueberry Griffles. Other mixes include Maple Cornbread and Muffin Mix, and Jonny Cakes made from Rhode Island–grown corn.

Because these flours contain no preservatives, Morgan says they should be treated like fresh produce: refrigerated or stored in a cool place.

Eliot

BACK FIELDS FARM
14 Odiorne Lane, Eliot, 03903; phone 207-439-2837. Hours: irregular, call ahead. Personal checks accepted. Tours of the farm can be arranged. Mail order available.
   Also at the Portsmouth, New Hampshire, Farmers' Market (see page 84).

■ We have to confess to a certain lack of objectivity when it comes to Back Fields Farm. The owners of the farm, Connie and Silas Weeks, are our good friends, and they have figured prominently in our education about organic gardening and New England agriculture. Bearing that in mind, we are happy to recommend Back Fields Farm for first-rate vegetables, herbs, and condiments.

The Weekses produce a lot of different items, most in limited quantities. There are gorgeous bouquets of fresh garden herbs, tender green lettuce and spinach, strawberries, colorful sprays of cut flowers, maple syrup, honey, preserves, and pickles. They have their own flock of laying hens for eggs and a small orchard of fruit trees, and they sell freezer lamb. (The lamb is truly superb. It must be ordered well ahead of time for late fall delivery.)

One of our favorite Back Fields Farm products is Connie's pickled watermelon rind. It's sweet and crunchy, with a spicy tang that comes from cloves. It's superb with barbecued meats. Also delicious is her Sunny Strawberry Jam. Tiny, perfectly ripe strawberries are mixed with a minimum of sugar and briefly simmered on the stove. Then they are set out to "bake" in the hot summer sun for several days before being canned.

If you visit Back Fields Farm, allow a little extra time. The Weekses are usually happy to show visitors around their farm, and it's well worth seeing.

KING TUT'S CIDER MILL
307 Goodwin Road (Route 101), Eliot, 03903; phone 207-439-3191. Hours: Labor Day weekend to Christmas, seven days a week,

■ "Made from sound ripe apples with no preservatives," states the label on each jug of King Tut's cider. This cider is both tart and sweet, with a multidimensional apple flavor. King Tut's is our local cider mill, so we're partial to it, but we've tasted ciders from all over the region and few come close.

Charlie Tuttle, who owns the mill, claims King Tut's is

Sautéed Fiddlehead Ferns

This is one of the simplest, most delicious ways to serve fresh fiddleheads. If you like, you can add ½ pound thinly sliced wild mushrooms to the skillet. Serve with roast chicken, lamb, or pork, or toss with buttered fettuccine.

1 pound fresh fiddlehead ferns
2½ tablespoons olive oil
3 cloves garlic, minced
½ pound thinly sliced wild mushrooms (fresh morels or shiitake, oyster, or chanterelle mushrooms), optional
1 tablespoon chopped fresh basil
1 tablespoon chopped fresh chives
Salt and coarsely ground black pepper to taste

Trim the stems of the fiddleheads and wipe off the papery brown covering with a damp paper towel. Blanch the fiddleheads in a pot of boiling water for about 30 seconds. Drain, and refresh under cold running water.

In a large skillet, heat the oil over very high heat. Add the garlic and sauté for a few seconds, until golden brown. Add the fiddleheads (and thinly sliced wild mushrooms, if desired), and sauté for 3 to 5 minutes, or until they begin to get tender but still have a crunchy bite. Stir in the basil and chives, and season with salt and pepper. Serves 2 or 3.

---

8 A.M. to 6 P.M. Custom cider pressing on Saturdays from 8 A.M. to 4 P.M.; call ahead for information. Personal checks accepted.

Also sold at local farm stands and produce markets.

MAINE COAST SEA VEGETABLES

Shore Road, Franklin, 04634; phone 207-565-2907. Personal checks accepted. Mail order available.

Sold in health food stores and specialty food shops throughout New England.

the oldest continuously run cider mill in Maine. "My father put in the mill in 1903," he recalled, "and we've made cider every year since then, except for one year when there was a real scarcity of apples." Today Charlie's son Kenneth presses the cider. "He's got a special touch," Charlie said proudly. "I don't know what it is. I guess we Tuttles just have cider in our blood."

Franklin

■ Kelp, dulse, alaria, and wild nori—four types of seaweed—are available through Maine Coast Sea Vegetables. According to the label, "the kelp is cut from the beds at the head of Frenchman Bay, dried in the sun or wood heated, and packed in clear bags." When we tried it in miso soup, it added a wonderfully fresh, not too salty sea flavor. The wild nori can be used to roll sushi—a Japanese dish of raw fish placed on mounds of vinegared rice and wrapped in seaweed. And the alaria (the Atlantic cousin of Japanese *wakame*) looked so interesting we just ate it raw. "It's like beef jerky for New Agers," says a friend of ours.

Maine Coast Sea Vegetables also makes Sea Seasonings, ground seaweed mixed with spices. It's a low-sodium alternative to table salt.

Baked Buttercup Squash

1 medium-size buttercup squash
1/2 cup apple cider
3 tablespoons maple syrup
2 teaspoons butter

2 teaspoons chopped fresh sage leaves, or 1 teaspoon dried
Freshly ground black pepper to taste

Preheat the oven to 350°. Cut the ends off the squash and cut it in half horizontally. Scoop out and discard all the seeds. Place the squash in a baking dish and fill each cavity with 1 tablespoon cider, 1 1/2 tablespoons maple syrup, 1 teaspoon butter, and 1 teaspoon sage leaves (or 1/2 teaspoon dried). Top with a generous grinding of pepper. Pour the remaining apple cider around the outside of the squash and bake for 1 hour, or until soft. While it is cooking, check the squash to make sure the cider hasn't dried out; if needed, add an additional 1/4 to 1/2 cup. Let the squash sit about 10 minutes before serving. Serves 2.

Freeport

GOOD EARTH FARM AND MARKET
Pleasant Hill Road, Freeport, 04032; phone 207-865-9544. Hours: Strawberry picking mid-June to July 4, seven days a week 10 A.M. to 5 P.M. Fall produce mid-September to November 1, seven days a week 10 A.M. to 5 P.M. Cash only.

■ Strawberries start the season at the Good Earth Farm in mid-June, and visitors are invited to come and pick their own. In the fall the farm reopens with winter crops and over forty varieties of fresh and dried herbs. Almost everything is grown organically—potatoes, several varieties of winter squash, broccoli, and apples. But the big attraction each October is the Good Earth Farm's great pumpkin patch. Come take a hay ride, pick your own pumpkin, have a cold apple and a glass of hot cider, and celebrate the harvest.

L. L. BEAN
Route 1, Freeport, 04033; phone toll-free 800-221-4221, or 207-865-4761. Hours: seven days a week, 24 hours a day. MasterCard, Visa, American Express, and personal checks accepted. Mail order available.

■ In 1912 Mr. Leon Leonwood Bean opened a store in downtown Freeport, catering to sportsmen and outdoor enthusiasts. Today L. L. Bean (or "Bean's," as it is also known) is famous around the globe as *the* place to buy waterproof Maine hunting shoes, sleeping bags, tents, canoes, rain gear, hiking shorts, and anything else that falls under the category of outdoor wear and equipment. But most people don't realize that Bean's also has a large and varied selection of New England–made foods.

L. L. Bean is an enormous store, with four levels of shopping around a central atrium that features a pond stocked with live trout. Up on the fourth level you'll find the home and camp food section. Look for The Gingham Shop's wonderful fruit jams (see page 56), Maine-made honey and maple syrup, applesauce and preserves from the Cherry Hill coop in Vermont (see page 205), saltwater taffy, herb-flavored vinegars, pepper jelly from New Hampshire, and dried spices from the Shaker community

WOLFE'S NECK FARM

Burnett Road (RR 1, Box 71), Freeport, 04032; phone 207-865-4469. Hours: Monday–Saturday 8 A.M. to 5 P.M.; closed Sunday. MasterCard, Visa, and personal checks accepted. Mail order available.

of Sabbathday Lake (see page 59). They also carry a good collection of New England cookbooks, as well as cooking equipment—everything from giant lobster cookers to fish smokers and sausage makers.

■ Does this sound familiar? You love beef, but you don't want all the chemicals they pump into most commercially raised beef. You would like to buy organic beef, but farms that produce it will only sell you half a cow or more, and you don't want all that meat. The solution: beef from Wolfe's Neck Farm.

Since 1959 this farm has maintained a serious commitment to raising organic beef. And they sell it in quantities that make sense for individual consumers as well as large families. You can order as little as 20 pounds of meat through the mail, and if you go to the farm you can buy just one steak if that's all you want. They generally have

---

Bill Bell's New England Boiled Dinner

Serve with a few varieties of mustard and a loaf of dark bread.

6 pounds beef brisket
2 cloves garlic, peeled and left whole
3 whole cloves
5 black peppercorns
2 large bay leaves
2 tablespoons dried rosemary
1/2 cup brown sugar, loosely packed
3 onions, peeled
1/8 cup Dijon mustard
5 carrots, peeled and cut in half
6 large red potatoes
3 medium-size turnips or parsnips, peeled and cut in half
1 large red or white cabbage, cut into quarters

In a large stockpot or casserole, cover the brisket with cold water. Add the garlic, cloves, peppercorns, bay leaves, rosemary, 1/4 cup of the brown sugar, and the onions. Bring the mixture to a boil over high heat. Lower the heat and simmer for 2 to 3 hours, or until the meat is tender.

Preheat the oven to 400°. Remove the meat from the pot and place it in a roasting pan. Reserve the stock. Mix the remaining 1/4 cup brown sugar with the mustard. Spread the mustard glaze over the brisket and set it aside. (The recipe can be made ahead of time up to this point.)

Meanwhile, bring the stock that the meat cooked in to a rolling boil. Add the carrots and potatoes, reduce the heat, and simmer for 10 minutes.

Place the brisket in the oven and bake about 10 minutes, or until the glaze begins to brown. At the same time, add the turnips to the stockpot and cook 5 minutes. Finally add the cabbage and cook an additional 5 minutes, or until tender.

Place the brisket in the center of a large platter. Remove the vegetables from the broth with a slotted spoon, and arrange around the meat. Serves 4 to 6.

an ample supply of steaks, plus beef roasts, brisket, ground beef, beef liver, and other cuts.

The beef itself is outstanding. It's lean, tender, and flavorful. And when they say it's organic they mean it. Everything these cows eat is grown without chemical fertilizers or pesticides. They are fed no growth stimulants or hormones, and unlike western beef cattle that spend their days in crowded feedlots, the cows at Wolfe's Neck Farm have a chance to graze on rolling pastures with spectacular views of Casco Bay. In fact, it's worth a trip to Wolfe's Neck Farm to see this beautiful landscape. Visitors are welcome to walk around the farm.

Wolfe's Neck Farm also sells organically raised lamb from other farms in Maine. Both beef and lamb are sold frozen.

Gardiner

■ "Pure sin" is how a friend of ours likes to describe John Hannon's fudge. The words creamy, buttery, rich, and intense also come to mind. There are hundreds of country stores and candy shops throughout New England that make their own fudge, but very few of them are able to match this stuff. The fudge is made daily, and there are over a dozen flavors to choose from. We've tried the Maple Chocolate Chip, Penuchi, Chocolate Almond, and Nut Fantasy, and let's just say that our friend knows what she's talking about.

The John Hannon Company (named for an Irish immigrant who is said to have been the first chocolate manufacturer in the world) also sells quality chocolates and candies from Europe, Canada, and the U.S. You'll also find Maine-made ice cream here, served in homemade waffle cones.

Gorham

■ Corn and strawberries are the specialties at this attractive farm stand. They also grow tomatoes, beans, peas, peppers, lettuce, and in the fall, pumpkins. We visited in October and found a beautiful selection of winter squash along with some hard-to-find varieties of dried beans. Their Jacob's Cattle beans were superb in our favorite baked bean recipe (see page 174).

Patten's Farm also sells apple cider from the nearby Snell Family Farm (see page 36), cut flowers, and vegetable and flower seedlings for your own garden.

There's another Patten's Farm stand, on North Street in Kennebunkport; same hours.

JOHN HANNON CHOCOLATIER

242 Water Street, Gardiner, 04345; phone 207-582-4990. Hours: Monday–Wednesday 10 A.M. to 5 P.M., Thursday–Saturday 10 A.M. to 6 P.M.; closed Sunday. MasterCard, Visa, American Express and personal checks accepted. Mail order available.

Also at 390 Fore Street, Portland, and at 1 Damariscotta Center, Main Street, Damariscotta.

PATTEN'S FARM

County Road (Box 298, RR 4), Gorham, 04038; phone 207-839-4667. Hours: Mid-May through September, seven days a week 9 A.M. to 7 P.M. October through Christmas, seven days a week 11 A.M. to 5 P.M. MasterCard, Visa, and personal checks accepted. Pick-your-own strawberries and peas.

Terrine of Fresh Corn with Lobster

We first tasted this terrine at Aubergine restaurant in Camden a few years ago. It combines the best flavors of New England—fresh summer corn and sweet Maine lobster—in a classic French terrine. Chef David Grant was kind enough to send us his recipe. There are several steps involved in making this dish, but you can cook the lobster and prepare the sauce a day ahead of time. Serve it as a first course or as a main course lunch or dinner dish along with a cold bottle of Chenin Blanc. (This recipe requires a food processor.)

Lobster Sauce
2 cooked lobsters (1 1/4 pounds each)*
1 1/2 cups dry white wine
1 cup mirepoix (a mixture of carrots, onions, and celery cut into 1/4-inch dice)
2 bay leaves
4 cups heavy cream
1 1/2 tablespoons chopped fresh parsley
1 tablespoon chopped fresh tarragon

Few sprigs fresh tarragon for garnish (optional)

Corn Terrine
8 ears very fresh corn
1 cup heavy cream
2 eggs
8 egg yolks
Salt and pepper to taste

*Be careful not to overcook the lobster or it will be tough. Cook about 1 minute less than usual, remove from boiling water, and let cool. Remove the meat but do not discard the shells. Cut the lobster meat into small chunks and set aside in the refrigerator to cool.

Prepare the sauce: Combine the wine, *mirepoix,* bay leaves, and 4 cups water in a saucepan and bring to a boil. Add the lobster shells (not the meat) to the saucepan. Let the sauce boil until reduced to 1 cup of liquid, 10 to 15 minutes. Add the cream, lower to a moderate heat, and let the sauce simmer until you have about 2 1/2 cups of liquid and the sauce is thick enough to coat a spoon. Strain the sauce through a fine sieve and set aside. (The recipe can be prepared a day ahead of time up to this point.)

Prepare the terrine: Preheat the oven to 275°. Shuck the corn and drop it into a pot of boiling water. Cook for 2 to 3 minutes, remove, and let cool. Using a sharp knife, remove the kernels; you should have about 4 cups. Place the corn kernels in the container of a food processor along with the cream, and process for several seconds. Add the eggs, yolks, and salt and pepper to taste, and process until fully combined. Pour the mixture into a buttered 6-cup terrine or large loaf pan, and cover with aluminum foil. Place the terrine into a shallow baking dish, and surround with enough boiling water to come about halfway up the sides of the terrine. Bake for about 1 1/2 hours. The terrine should not rise or turn brown; reduce the temperature if necessary. To test for doneness, gently insert a skewer or the tip of a knife into the terrine; if it comes out hot and dry without picking up any bits of cream or corn, the terrine is ready. Let it sit for a few minutes, and then gently invert it onto a large serving plate.

Meanwhile, heat the sauce in a small saucepan over moderate heat. Add the lobster chunks, parsley, chopped tarragon, and salt and pepper to taste, and heat until simmering.

To serve: Cut the terrine into fairly thick slices. Spoon the sauce (without the lobster chunks) over or around the slices, and then place the lobster meat around the side. Garnish with a sprig of fresh tarragon. Serves 6 as main course or 8 as an appetizer.

Hope

THE GINGHAM SHOP
Hope Road (Route 105), Hope, 04847 (mailing address: R.R. 1, Box 4379, Camden, ME 04843); phone 207-763-3300. Summer hours: Monday–Saturday 6:30 A.M. to 9 P.M. Winter hours: Monday–Saturday 9 A.M. to 5 P.M. Closed Sunday. Personal checks accepted. Mail order and gift packages available.

Also sold at many New England specialty food shops.

■ We tried all of Carolyn Grey's Maine Berry Jams—blueberry, raspberry, and strawberry—and fought over which one was best. They're thick, not too sweet, with a terrific fresh fruit flavor. Try these jams mixed with yogurt, heated and served as an ice cream topping, as a glaze for poundcake, or as a filling for a layer cake or thin crepes. Grey also makes an outrageously good Cranberry-Almond Conserve in which cranberries, raisins, and currants are mixed with crunchy slivers of almonds. It's delicious with poultry, game, or beef or served inside a steaming-hot baked sweet potato. Other items include apple cider jelly, strawberry-nectarine jam, apricot jam, banana jam, and some twenty other fruit combinations.

In this highly competitive market, Grey has managed to make her products not only taste good but look appealing as well. Each jar is covered with a little square of gingham; gift sets come in handmade wooden crates.

Lewiston

SEAVEY'S NEEDHAMS
Lou-Rod Candy, 1047 Sabattus Street, Lewiston, 04240; phone: 207-784-5822. Hours: Monday–Friday, 7:30 A.M. to 5 P.M.; Saturday 9 A.M. to 5 P.M.; closed Sunday. Personal checks accepted. Mail order available.

Also available at candy stores and supermarkets in Maine.

■ Seavey's Needhams are to Maine what maple sugar candy is to Vermont. Needhams have been the candy of choice since 1872. For those who have never tried one, they're something like a Mounds bar, only round—a creamy, ultra-sweet coconut candy dipped in bittersweet chocolate.

We had always heard about Needhams' association with Maine but were never able to understand the connection. The people at Lou-Rod Candy explain it this way: "In the fall of 1872, the Reverend George S. Needham, a popular evangelist of Needham, Massachusetts, was holding very successful evangelistic meetings in Portland, Maine. Conversions were many and the name of

Carolyn Grey and her jam stand in Hope—"where it all got started."

Needham was on the lips of everyone for miles around. One day Allen Gow, proprietor of a candy store in Portland, Maine, walked into his shop and found his workers dipping coconut squares into chocolate. 'What will you call that candy?' asked Mr. Gow. A young candy maker named A. S. Ellsworth, of Auburn, Maine, said, 'Call them Needhams.' "

Lou-Rod Candy also makes chocolate and peanut butter fudge, and a traditional-style peanut brittle.

Lincolnville

DUCKTRAP FISH FARM

Pitcher Pond Road (RFD 2, Box 378), Lincolnville, 04849; phone 207-763-3960. Hours: Monday–Friday, 8 A.M. to 5 P.M.; closed Saturday and Sunday. MasterCard, Visa, and personal checks accepted. Mail order available.

Also available at fish markets, gourmet food stores, and some supermarkets.

■ There are hundreds, perhaps even thousands, of people who smoke fish in this country, but few of them do it as well as Des Fitzgerald. After graduating from Harvard, Fitzgerald spent several years working in Alaska as a salmon fisherman and then went on to study aquaculture at the University of Washington's College of Fisheries.

In the mid-1970s Fitzgerald settled in the small town of Lincolnville, just 2 miles in from the coast, and set up Ducktrap Fish Farm. We found him one June afternoon working in his "factory" tucked away in the woods. While we waited for Fitzgerald to get off the phone (he was taking an order from a popular Boston restaurant—one of many that serve his seafood), we watched a young woman using tweezers to pluck tiny bones out of a salmon filet. "That's the kind of attention to detail we demand," said Fitzgerald, introducing himself.

We sat outside at a small picnic table dwarfed by a grove of enormous white birches and pine trees. "That's my pride and joy," Fitzgerald said, pointing toward his trout pond, where he raises some 30,000 to 40,000 trout every year. Most of the trout are sold fresh to restaurants, but luckily some of them make their way into the smokehouse.

We had to tell Fitzgerald straight out that we think his smoked salmon rivals any we've tasted. He didn't seem surprised. "We're trying to get Americans over the mystique that Scotch and Irish salmon are the only kind of smoked salmon worth eating," Fitzgerald explained. "Generally speaking, it's fattier and not nearly as fresh as ours."

Ducktrap's Western Smoked Salmon is indeed fresh tasting, with a rich flavor and a tender melt-in-your-mouth texture. We've served it on buttered toast points and in a salad with avocado slices, capers, and lemon juice, and believe us, it really doesn't get better than this. The Eastern (or Scotch Style) Salmon is a touch drier and a bit saltier, but just as flavorful.

Ducktrap smokes a wide variety of fish, and as Fitzgerald explained, "each one is treated with a different brine, and smoked with a different combination of wood chips for varying amounts of time." (No prepared cures or chemicals are ever used.) Small meaty scallops, for

Smoked trout from Ducktrap Fish Farm.

instance, are smoked with a delicate wood like apple, while a strongly flavored oily fish like bluefish is smoked over oak and maple.

We've tasted over a dozen varieties of Ducktrap smoked fish and haven't found one we didn't like. The Whole Rainbow Trout is a masterpiece. Peel the skin off and expose a slightly pink, moist, and unbelievably tender fish. The Smoked Maine Monkfish tastes like sable or smoked sturgeon but sells for half the price. And the tiny Smoked Maine Shrimp and Smoked Mussels make a wonderful fish chowder (see recipe, page 75). Also be sure to look for Ducktrap's Smoked Fish Pâtés (salmon, bluefish, and trout). A mixture of smoked fish, cream cheese, scallions, sour cream, and spices, they are excellent spread on toast or a bagel, melted in a baked potato, spooned into an omelet, or piped on top of a grilled salmon or swordfish steak.

Ducktrap smoked fish makes a wonderful gift. The fish are packed inside a box made of Maine pine, the lid is branded with the Ducktrap fish logo, and each box comes complete with a fresh sprig of green Maine balsam.

Medomak

HOCKOMOCK HOLLOW

'Stache Foods, Route 32, Medomak, 04551; phone 207-529-5879. Hours: by appointment. Mail order available through 'Stache Foods, P.O. Box 705, Damariscotta, ME 04543. Catering available.

■ Hockomock Hollow is the creation of W. Stewart Blackburn, a Bowdoin graduate with a degree in biology and physics who trained as a chef in San Francisco. Blackburn is also the founder of 'Stache Foods, a company he named after his own impressive red handlebar moustache. 'Stache Foods produces an excellent tangy Maple Barbecue Sauce that is sold in some specialty food stores in Maine and can be ordered by mail. It's great on ribs, chicken, even tofu. Blackburn has also developed Maple Seafood Sauce and something called Clipper Ketchup, a condiment sweetened with maple syrup and apple juice concentrate.

What excites Blackburn most these days is his catering business. Blackburn specializes in historical feasts from any period, cooked outdoors over an open fire and served

Stewart Blackburn, creator of 'Stache Foods. holding some of his Maple Barbecue Sauce.

in period costume. For Maine's July Fourth Celebration of the U.S. Constitution's bicentennial, he created a colonial feast, roasting pigs and chickens and serving them with homemade grape and walnut ketchup and thin jonnycakes. All the waiters and waitresses wore eighteenth-century costumes. Blackburn also offers pig roasts, barbecues, medieval and Roman feasts, and clambakes.

New Gloucester

■ Anyone really interested in herbs should make a point of visiting the Shaker community at Sabbathday Lake. Long before cooking with herbs became fashionable in this country, the Shakers were well versed in their culinary and medicinal powers.

The herbs grown, dried, and packaged at the Sabbathday Lake Shaker community are among the freshest and most flavorful we've tasted. Tightly packed in attractive tins, they somehow manage to stay fresh far longer than other dried herbs. In the culinary herb line you'll find a *fines herbes* mixture of thyme, marjoram, basil, tarragon, and parsley as well as standards like summer savory, tarragon, rosemary, chervil, and fennel seed. There are some thirty-five herbal teas such as Pippsissewa, Queen of the Meadow, Lady's Mantle, Vervain, and Colt's Foot. Other teas include Marshmallow Root, a mint blend, Camomile, and Strawberry Leaf.

The Shakers first arrived at Sabbathday Lake in 1783; they became an official Shaker community in 1794. Today there are only eight Sisters and Brothers perpetuating the Shaker life-style and beliefs in this 1700-acre community. You can take a short tour through several of the buildings, where you'll learn about Shaker furniture, farming tools, textiles, and crafts. But if you want to learn about herbs and their importance in Shaker life, leave time for the walking tour, when you'll visit the formal herb gardens and the building where all the herbs are dried and packaged.

THE UNITED SOCIETY OF SHAKERS
Route 26, New Gloucester, 04274 (mail order address: Herb Department, Sabbathday Lake, Poland Spring, ME 04274); phone 207-926-4597. Hours: Memorial Day through Columbus Day, Monday–Saturday 10 A.M. to 4:30 P.M. Personal checks accepted. Mail order available. Tours of the garden and buildings available; call ahead for times.

New Sharon

■ "I began making fresh fruit jams," explained Grace Firth, "because I couldn't find a decent store-bought jam to eat." Using berries, apples, and rhubarb from her 80-acre farm, Grace and her husband, John, began experimenting with low-sugar jam recipes. "I'm a nutrition student," Grace said. "The jams you find in the supermarket are two-thirds sugar and one-third fruit. It's ridiculous. We make our jams with maple syrup and honey. They don't contain any sugar at all. But we still call them 'low sugar' because, let's face it, honey and maple syrup are forms of sugar."

The result of the Firths' experimentation is jam with a

FIRTHS' FRUIT FARM
RFD 1, Box 1460, New Sharon, ME 04955; phone 207-778-3904. Hours: Monday–Saturday 9 A.M. to 5 P.M.; closed Sunday. Call ahead for directions. Personal checks accepted. Mail order and gift packages available. Pick-your-own

YORK HILL FARM CHEESE

York Hill Farm, York Hill Road, New Sharon, 04955; phone 207-778-9741. Hours: seven days a week 9 A.M. to 6 P.M. Personal checks accepted. Mail order available, except during summer months.
 Also available at the Brunswick Farmers' Market (see page 84).

berries available; call ahead for conditions.
 Also sold at local markets.

fresh fruit flavor and no overpowering sweetness. The varieties change from year to year, depending on which fruits are most abundant. Favorites include Rhubarb-Blackberry, Blueberry-Raspberry, Apple Butter, and Strawberry. In addition to jam they also sell fresh raspberries and blueberries during the summer, as well as their own maple syrup and honey.

▪ When Penny and John Duncan started making cheese from the milk produced by their two purebred Nubian goats, they weren't totally committed to the endeavor. But, like many cheesemakers living on small family farms, the Duncans got hooked. They now have over a dozen milkers, have just invested in an on-site pasteurizing plant (so they can legally mail their cheese out of the state), and are making more cheese than they ever expected. Lucky for us, because these cheeses are superb.
 We've tasted a number of cheeses from York Hill Farm. The York Cheddar, an aged and waxed goat's-milk cheddar, is one of the most attractive and unusual cheeses made in Maine. It has a pale yellow color and a sweet, slightly nutty flavor. This cheese combines the texture of cheddar and the flavor of goat's milk. We tried it with apples and pears and used it to make a grilled cheese sandwich, which was excellent.
 But it was York Hill Farm's fresh chèvre that really won us over. The Tarragon Chèvre, made in the classic French style, is a small creamy round of goat's-milk cheese coated with tarragon leaves. The subtle tanginess of the cheese combined with the sweet tarragon creates an almost lemony flavor. It's superb in an omelet or spread on chicken breasts and baked. There is also a fresh garlic and herb chèvre, and a chèvre roll coated with cracked peppercorns.
 Visitors are welcome to the farm, and if you arrive in the morning there's a good chance you can watch Penny Duncan milk the goats and begin the cheesemaking process.

North Nobleboro

RIVENDELL FARM

East Pond Road, North Nobleboro, 04572 (mailing address: RFD1, Box 198, Waldoboro, ME 04572); phone 207-832-4178. Hours: call ahead for appointment and directions. Personal checks accepted.

▪ Tim and Connie Southwick, owners of Rivendell Farm, raise tender, extremely flavorful, naturally grown lamb. The Southwicks sell whole and half lambs for freezing, and they make delicious lamb sausage and lamb salami.
 The sausage—made from fresh lamb, natural casing, and spices—is cold-smoked according to an old German recipe. It contains no nitrates or nitrites. These juicy, delicately flavored sausages are great barbecued on a charcoal grill. They're also excellent added to scrambled eggs or pasta sauce. The salami is well seasoned and has a good, hard texture. The Southwicks are planning to produce lamb bratwurst in the future. Mail order for the salami and sausage will also be available; call for details.

Cream of Fiddlehead and Asparagus Soup

This soup can be served hot or cold.

3 tablespoons butter
1 tablespoon light vegetable oil
3 large onions, peeled and chopped
7 cups chicken stock (preferably homemade), defatted
2 pounds asparagus
1 pound fiddlehead ferns
Salt and freshly ground black pepper to taste
1/2 cup heavy cream

In a large soup pot, heat the butter and oil over moderately low heat. Add the onions and sauté until soft and tender, about 15 to 20 minutes. Do not let them brown. Add the chicken stock, and bring to a boil over high heat.

Meanwhile, trim off the tops (about 1 inch) of the asparagus and set them aside. Trim off the tough bottom part of the asparagus spears (about 1 inch) and discard. Cut the remaining asparagus into 1-inch pieces and throw them into the boiling stock. Trim off the stems of the fiddleheads, and throw them into the stock. Wipe off the papery brown cover with a damp paper towel and throw half of the fiddleheads into the stock. Set the other half aside with the asparagus spears. Cover the pot, reduce the heat, and simmer for about 45 minutes, or until the asparagus and fiddleheads are very soft.

Remove the pot from the heat. Working in small batches, purée the soup in a blender or food processor until smooth and creamy. Strain the mixture into a large bowl. Pour the purée back into the pot and season with salt and pepper to taste. Stir in the cream. (The recipe can be made ahead of time up to this point.)

Add the reserved fiddleheads and asparagus spears to the soup. Place over moderate heat until the soup is hot and the asparagus and fiddleheads are tender, about 10 minutes. Taste for seasoning. If serving cold, let the soup cool down, then place in the refrigerator for several hours. Serves 4 to 6.

North Waldoboro

MORSE'S SAUERKRAUT

Virgil Morse and Son, Route 220 North, North Waldoboro, 04572; phone 207-832-5569. Hours: October 1 through April 1, Monday–Saturday 7:30 A.M. to 4 P.M.; closed Sunday. Personal checks accepted. Mail order available.

■ You don't hear people talking a lot about pickled cabbage these days, but for some reason we just kept meeting folks who couldn't say enough about the quality and flavor of Morse's sauerkraut. "You've got to try it," they advised us. "It's addictive." So we ordered a few jars, and when the sauerkraut arrived by mail we immediately grilled a few sausages and started tasting. One bite of this slightly crunchy, pale white pickled cabbage and we understood what all the excitement was about. As sauerkraut goes, this stuff is damn good. The recipe is a Morse family secret, and all the label tells you is that it's "Made on the Farm, from cabbage, salt and sugar." You really don't need to know much more.

We also tried Aunt Lydia's Beet Relish. If you think the

sauerkraut is good, wait until you try this. It's a deep red sweet-and-sour condiment made from cabbage and beets. It makes hamburgers and chicken or turkey sandwiches taste very special. The addition of horseradish gives the relish its wonderful peppery jolt.

If you visit the Morse farm you'll also find fresh eggs, locally grown popcorn, dried beans, and their own fresh cabbage and potatoes.

Ogunquit

HARBOR CANDY SHOP
26 Main Street (P.O. Box 498), Ogunquit, 03907; phone 207-646-8078. Summer hours: seven days a week 9 A.M. to 11 P.M. Winter hours: Wednesday–Monday 9 A.M. to 5 P.M.; closed Tuesday. Closed January and February. Mail order available. MasterCard, Visa, American Express, and personal checks accepted for mail order only.

- You will have a hard time deciding what to buy at the Harbor Candy Shop—it all looks and smells so delicious. This store specializes in what candy maker Ellen Byrne calls "American traditional chocolates." There are crunchy extra-large turtles made with cashews or pecans and caramel dipped in dark or milk chocolate, as well as several different kinds of fudge including Divinity Fudge (which is whipped with egg whites to make it lighter than regular fudge), glazed fruit dipped in chocolate, peanut butter cups, peanut brittle, pecan brittle, crystallized ginger dipped in chocolate, and many other selections. The Harbor Candy Shop also makes European-style chocolate truffles and Sugar Plums—a combination of ground fruits and nuts dipped in chocolate. All of these items may be ordered through their mail-order catalogue.

If you visit the store you'll find a wide assortment of imported and domestic hard candies, including coffee-

---

Maine Maple Sunday

There is so much good maple syrup made in Maine that we could fill an entire book on syrup alone. One of the best ways to get to know, and taste, Maine syrup is to attend Maine Maple Sunday—generally held the third Sunday in March—when some twenty-three sugarhouses open their doors to the general public. You'll learn how to tap a tree, how to boil sap, and you'll watch it turn from a clear, colorless, tasteless liquid into rich, sweet syrup. Weather permitting, there's sugar on snow (maple syrup is heated up, poured over a patch of clean, cold snow, and then allowed to harden into a sweet candy). Other offerings include a variety of maple-filled baked goods, including maple donuts and homemade maple-flavored ice cream.

The participating sugarhouses are scattered throughout the state; for further information and a free brochure, write or call the Maine Department of Agriculture, Food and Rural Resources, Bureau of Agricultural Marketing, State House Station 28, Augusta, 04333; phone 207-289-3491. Ask for a copy of *Follow the Maine Maple Trail.*

flavored Belgian Hopjes, English sour lemon drops, maple syrup drops, and old-fashioned rock candy. They also sell teas, maple syrup, glazed fruit, saltwater taffy, and jelly beans.

Old Orchard Beach

KATE'S BUTTER
P.O. Box 79, Old Orchard Beach, 04064; phone 207-934-5134.
Available at grocery stores, natural foods stores, gourmet food shops, and country stores throughout New England.

- Kate's Butter is special. It has a fresh, creamy taste that makes you think of homemade butter, and unless you're going to make your own, Kate's is the next best thing. It's made fresh every day, using cream from a local dairy, and it's always packed by hand, which improves the texture considerably. And when things are going according to plan, the butter is never allowed to sit on a supermarket shelf for more than four months. "We have a code on the back of each package indicating when the four months is up," explained Karen Patry, who together with her family makes Kate's Butter. "But we don't really trust some of the big stores, so we go around and check on the butter ourselves. It's got to be fresh or there's no point doing what we do."

Kate's Butter comes salted or unsalted. It's definitely more expensive than other brands you find at the supermarket, but once you've cooked with it you'll see that it's worth the price.

Orono

THE STORE
26 Mill Street, Orono, 04473; phone 207-866-4110. Hours: Monday–Saturday 9 A.M. to 6 P.M., Sunday 9:30 A.M. to 3 P.M. Personal checks accepted. Mail order available.

- Orono is a college town, home of the University of Maine, and this specialty food store/bakery/health food shop caters to the university crowd. In addition to carrying cheeses, spices, teas, imported beer and wine, coffee beans, and fresh-baked breads, cookies, and muffins, The Store makes a real effort to showcase Maine-made foods. You'll find baked beans, State of Maine cheeses (see page 74), Nervous Nellie's Jams and Jellies (see page 45), preserves and chutneys, candy, Geary's Pale Ale (see page 64), and fresh goat's milk. During the summer you can pick up 30-pound flats of wild blueberries grown on a local farm (ideal for freezing or using for jam) and other locally produced fruits, vegetables, and herbs.

Portland

BATTAMBANG ASIAN MARKET
157 Noyes Street, Portland, 04103; phone 207-774-7311. Hours: Tuesday–Sunday 8 A.M. to

- This market sells virtually everything you need to create the spicy and pungent flavors of Thai and Cambodian cuisine, as well as ingredients for Vietnamese, Filipino, and Chinese cooking. As far as we know there is no other store like it anywhere in Maine. But what makes Battambang truly unique is that in addition to the canned and frozen products found in most Asian groceries, they also

8 P.M.; closed Monday. Personal checks accepted.

stock a big selection of fresh Oriental vegetables and herbs. There is fresh lemon grass, used to add an aromatic lemony flavor to soups and sauces; green papaya, which is cut up and added to salads; and fresh tamarind, prized for the sour flavor it adds to dishes.

We are not experts on Southeast Asian cooking, so we won't describe all of the other exotic fresh and dried ingredients sold here. Instead we urge you to visit Battambang and spend a little time with the store's energetic and knowledgeable proprietor, Anchina Bugden. She's happy to take culinary adventurers on a tour of her store, picking up sprigs of various fresh herbs for visitors to smell, giving tips on the use of different condiments and spices, and offering recipe ideas and inspiration.

The Battambang Restaurant, operated by Anchina Bugden's sister, Amara Tev, is located at 1363 Washington Avenue in Portland and serves Cambodian and Thai dishes.

FOODWORKS

205 Commercial Street, Portland, 04101; phone 207-773-9741. Hours: Monday–Friday 10 A.M. to 6 P.M., Saturday 11 A.M. to 5 P.M.; closed Sunday. MasterCard and Visa accepted. Catering available.

■ Housed in what was once a gas station, Foodworks is a gourmet take-out shop and caterer. It's an unassuming little place, with a few cafe tables and a small display case filled with incredible-looking salads, roast meats, pastries, and breads. But what really counts is what goes on in the large open kitchen in the back. Everything here is made from scratch, whether it's the seafood bisque, or the vegetable tart in phyllo pastry, or the lobster salad, or the rich chocolate-coconut balls.

Foodworks is a great place to put together a picnic for the beach or for a ride on the ferry around Casco Bay. The shop is located on Commercial Street, right across from the wharfs, so it couldn't be more convenient.

GEARY'S PALE ALE

D. L. Geary Brewing Company, Inc., 38 Evergreen Drive, Portland, 04103; phone 207-878-2337. Tours of the brewery can be arranged; call or write ahead.

Available in bottles and on tap throughout Maine and in the Boston area.

■ We asked David Geary, president and founder of the D. L. Geary Brewing Company, to describe the ale he brews. "It's a classic British pale ale," he began, "comparable to Bass Ale, Watney's, or Whitbred. It has a bright copper color, is very well hopped, and is quite dry." At this point Geary paused. "Look," he blurted out, "what I really want to say about my ale is that it's made to be drunk in large gulps; empty the glass and refill it."

It's obvious that David Geary is more comfortable in the role of beer drinker than beer connoisseur. And he has designed Geary's Pale Ale to suit his own tastes. "It has more beer flavor than most popular American beers," he told us, "so if you like beer to begin with, it's going to appeal to you."

Geary's Pale Ale is indeed a tasty brew. It's fairly bitter, a characteristic that, Mr. Geary told us, comes from the liberal use of hops in the brewing process. But far from being a turn-off, this bitterness adds depth and dimension to the ale. We also like it because it's not too heavy.

You can drink quite a lot of this ale before you begin to feel full. One other point in its favor: as of this writing, Geary's is the only beer or ale being brewed in Maine.

GOOD DAY MARKET CO-OP

155 Brackett Street, Portland, 04102; phone 207-772-4937. Hours: Monday, Tuesday, Thursday, and Friday 9 A.M. to 8 P.M., Wednesday and Saturday 9 A.M. to 6 P.M.; closed Sunday. Maine personal checks accepted.

■ Don't be put off by appearances. The Good Day Market Co-op does not have the slick look that characterizes much of the "new" Portland. But this store, located on the ground floor of a somewhat shabby brick building, offers one of the best collections we have found of foods made and grown in Maine. There are pancake and cake mixes from several Maine gristmills, locally produced eggs and dairy products, bread from several Maine bakeries, and (in the warmer months) a big selection of organic produce from Maine farms.

The co-op also sells a wide variety of Oriental ingredients, dried herbs, spices, bulk grains, tofu, dried fruits and nuts, organic cereals, and more.

HARBOR FISH MARKETS

9 Custom House Wharf, Portland, 04101; phone 207-775-0251. Hours: Monday–Saturday 8:30 A.M. to 5 P.M., Sunday 9 A.M. to 3 P.M. during summer months. Call collect for mail-order information; ask for shipping department. MasterCard, Visa, and personal checks accepted.

■ "There's been a fish market out on this wharf since the turn of the century," John Alfiero told us. His family has been running Harbor Fish since 1971. "This is what a fish market should look like," he said, gesturing out the back door to a fleet of fishing boats just pulling in to dock. "And this is what a fish market should smell like," he continued, pointing to a fat lone sea gull feasting on a pile of still meaty fish carcasses.

Inside, enormous tanks are filled with lobsters and crabs; another contains live Maine brook trout. The glass display cases overflow with fresh filets of sole and salmon and whole flounder. Enormous piles of clams, mussels, oysters, and shrimp sit on beds of crushed ice in large wooden bins. The majority of the seafood you find here is local—cod, cusk, hake, sole, pollack, haddock, and shellfish. But what sets Harbor Fish apart is the wide variety of fish they offer from all around the country and abroad. Depending on the season, you'll find red snapper and mahi-mahi flown in fresh from Florida, salmon from

Time changes little for lobster fishermen.

MODEL FOOD IMPORTS

115 Middle Street, Portland, 04101; phone 207-774-3671. Hours: Monday–Friday 8:30 A.M. to 6 P.M., Saturday 8:30 A.M. to 5:30 P.M.; closed Sunday. MasterCard and Visa accepted. Mail order available.

PORT BAKEHOUSE

434 Fore Street, Portland, 04101; phone 207-773-2217. Hours: Monday–Friday 7:30 A.M. to 6 P.M., Saturday 8 A.M. to 5:30 P.M., Sunday 8 A.M. to 2 P.M. Personal checks accepted.

Also in South Portland, at 343 Gorham Road, opposite the Maine Mall.

PORTLAND LAGER

Maine Coast Brewing, P.O. Box 1118, Portland, 04104; phone 207-773-7970 or 767-4168.

Available in liquor stores, grocery stores, and specialty food shops throughout the Northeast.

Norway, soft-shell crabs from Maryland, shad roe from Connecticut, swordfish and shark from the South, and much more.

■ "Gourmet Food and Wine From Around The World—39 Countries" says the sign over this popular Portland shop. Model Food Imports has been supplying Maine cooks with hard-to-find and esoteric ingredients since 1928. "We have what you don't find anywhere else," explained the clerk behind the counter. "And if we don't have it, we'll get it for you."

Among the goodies: candied ginger from China, gallon tins of extra virgin olive oil from Italy, pickled herring from Maine, soy sauces from China and Japan, chile peppers from Mexico, cheeses from Scandinavia, kosher hot dogs from New York, chocolates from Belgium, geese from Canada, dried apricot paste from Syria, and maple syrup from Vermont.

■ Port Bakehouse has been a Portland favorite for years. This is one of the best places in town to buy freshly baked bread; there are over a dozen varieties. Be sure to try the Portuguese sweet bread and the Scotch Oatmeal bread—both have a hearty flavor and a wonderfully light texture. The daily specials are also worth checking out. On Monday it's quiche; Wednesday is the day for old-fashioned chicken pies; Saturday it's homemade baked beans and brown bread (the beans are delicious, with a tangy, chile-like flavor); and on Sunday customers line up for coffee cake.

The bakery regularly features fabulous linzertortes, oversized cookies, cheese danish, génoise cakes layered and topped with an intensely rich buttercream, and old favorites like oatmeal raisin cookies, date bars, cream cheese brownies, and coconut macaroons. This bakery gets very busy during the early morning pre-office breakfast hour, again at lunch, and then around 5 for those hoping to get a fresh loaf of bread before heading home. Beware: the bread sells out quickly. There's fresh-brewed coffee and tea to go with the sweets.

■ Words flew around the room like gulls in the harbor: "Rich and malty." "Hoppy." "Mildly effervescent, with no biting aftertaste." "Flowery aroma with a gorgeous amber color." "Thick, hearty, and flavorful."

It was March 1986 and some two hundred people had gathered at a restaurant in downtown Portland to taste, and celebrate the birth of, a new New England beer. They sipped and swallowed, pondered and pontificated, and spewed out adjectives like Frenchmen at a formal wine tasting. As bottle after bottle of the beer was consumed, the consensus was that Portland Lager was a hit.

Maple Sugaring—A Wife's Lament

The clock reads 3 A.M. and my husband is not in bed. This is not a man subject to insomnia, and I am fairly confident that he has not run off with another woman. I head downstairs to find him in his bathrobe, a long wooden spoon in hand, stirring a large bucket of liquid. He carefully pours the clear broth into an immense pot that is simmering on our wood stove. The whole room smells vaguely sweet and I wonder if I'm dreaming. Eventually this scent wakes me up just enough to remember what's going on: it's sugaring season, and my husband is obsessed with making maple syrup.

A few years ago when we moved to southern Maine, we bought an old farmhouse with a few enormous maple trees on the property. We had never tapped a maple before, and if memory serves me well, I remember sitting around talking about how much "fun" it would be. But before I knew it, our entire house was taken over by sap. Every day we brought in buckets of it and boiled it down on the stove. It wasn't until we had been boiling for about a week that someone finally told us it takes 40 gallons of sap to make just 1 gallon of maple syrup.

The wood stove was fired up 24 hours a day, and after about two weeks, when the sap was finally turning into something that remotely resembled syrup, the pots had to be watched constantly. "We can't risk burning this stuff," my husband said as he set the alarm clock for 2:45 A.M.

Hours and hours of work for a few quarts of fresh maple syrup—was it worth it? I wasn't really convinced until the final moment when we looked down into the pot and discovered that all those buckets of clear, odorless, mostly tasteless sap had turned into the most beautiful golden-hued syrup I had ever seen. We dipped our fingers into the pot and took our first taste. It was delicately sweet (not overpoweringly sugary) and rich, as if a few sticks of fresh butter had been stirred into the pot. Maple syrup never tasted so good.

During the weeks that followed, we manage to eat a little syrup almost every day. We poured it over toast, pancakes, ice cream, and vanilla pound cake. We used it to glaze a duck and a smoked country ham. We baked cakes and pies with it and even boiled it up and poured it over a patch of clean snow.

March, which is usually one of the slowest, wettest, most miserable months, suddenly took on a whole new meaning. It was a month with a purpose, a month when we wouldn't get much sleep, but a month that brought great satisfaction. We couldn't wait until next year.

Lager is a German word meaning "to store" or "to age," and Portland Lager is aged about five weeks, versus three weeks for most American beers. No chemicals, additives, starches, or sugars are added. The result is a full-bodied beer with a rich, not heavy, flavor. Portland Lager has a golden-amber color like English ale, with a taste like continental lager and a smooth finish. Unlike most American beers, which are consumed ice-cold, you'll get the maximum flavor from this beer at around 40° to 50°.

The Maine Festival

A diverse cross-section of performers, artists, and craftspeople share the limelight each year at The Maine Festival. A performance by an avant-garde dance troupe may be happening on one stage while across the fairgrounds you can listen to storytellers spin traditional Maine yarns or tap your feet to a jazz band. There are concerts by nationally known rock, folk, and classical artists, lots of events for kids, and an outstanding selection of crafts, art, and furniture on sale.

Good food is an important part of this celebration of Maine culture. Many of the state's most innovative restaurants and organic food producers have booths at the festival. There is sushi, spare ribs grilled with maple barbecue sauce, piping hot eggrolls in whole wheat wrappers, fresh corn roasted in the husk, and cool salads made with fresh Maine fruits and vegetables. Lots of seafood is available; oysters on the half shell, steamed Maine mussels, and of course boiled lobster. You could eat several meals at this festival and have something different each time. Unlike most fairs, the food served at The Maine Festival is generally not greasy and doesn't contain loads of sugar and chemicals. You can enjoy yourself and not worry about how you will feel tomorrow.

The festival is also a good place to find out about new Maine food products. Strolling through the exhibit tents, you're likely to find herbal vinegars, honey and preserves, cheese, and freshly ground grains being sold along side exquisite ceramics, weavings, and furniture.

The Maine Festival is held in Portland on the first weekend in August. For exact dates, location, and a schedule of events, contact The Maine Festival of the Arts, Inc., 29 Forest Avenue, Portland, 04101; phone 207-772-9012.

Entrepreneurs Jon Bove and Hugh Nazor spent months researching old beer recipes in the library. What they came up with is a facsimile of a nineteenth-century French-style lager as it would have been made in Maine in pre-Prohibition days. "It's the kind of beer our great-grandparents drank," says the Portland Lager brochure.

The next step was to find a brewery. "Beer making in Maine pretty much died out after Prohibition went into effect," explained Nazor. "The last commercial brewery in the state, McGlinchey Ale, closed in 1873. We wanted to revive that tradition and brew our beer right here in Portland. Unfortunately no one was willing to give us the funds."

Bove and Nazor spent two years trying to convince Maine banks that they had a good business idea, but according to Bove, "the only thing Portland bankers want to talk about these days is condos, condos, condos." So Portland Lager is currently being made at the F. X. Matt Brewery in Utica, New York. As of this writing, Bove,

PORTLAND WINE AND CHEESE COMPANY

8 Forest Avenue, Portland, 04101; phone 207-772-4647. Hours: Monday–Friday 9 A.M. to 6 P.M., Saturday 10 A.M. to 5 P.M.; closed Sunday. MasterCard, Visa, and American Express accepted. Catering and mail order available.

THE WHIP AND SPOON

161 Commercial Street, Portland, 04101; phone 207-774-4020. Hours: Monday–Wednesday, Friday, and Saturday 9 A.M. to 6 P.M., Thursday 9 A.M. to 8 P.M., Sunday 12 N. to 5 P.M. MasterCard, Visa, American Express, and personal checks accepted. Mail order available.

Also in South Portland, at 198 Maine Mall Road.

Nazor, and their two new partners, Linda Murnik and Lynn Morgan, were still working to find the funds to start a brewery in Maine. According to Bove they should be brewing in southern Maine by mid-1988. Plans for the brewery include tours and tastings, with a European-style pub attached.

■ Portland Wine and Cheese is not the largest gourmet food shop in town, nor is it the most unusual or best priced. But there's a feeling here—a kind of openness and friendliness—that makes us come back time and again. We like the sandwiches they make, and we like the tall wooden tables in the cafe section, where you can sip a really good cup of coffee and linger for hours over lunch. We like exploring the wine shelves, with literally hundreds of vintages from around the world. But most of all we like looking at all that food—everything from vats of marinated olives, cheeses, and pâtés to cookies and chocolates. And finally, what we like about this place is their effort to carry locally produced foods.

At the cheese counter you'll find Maine-made cheddar and goat cheese. There's smoked fish and herring, chutneys, vinegars, herbs, jellies, and jams from local cooks. And in season, much of the fruit and produce comes from Maine farmers.

The bulk of the shop is devoted to wine—one of the best selections in the state. "We specialize in wines for under $5," says owner Michael Hoy. If you buy wine by the case, there are some good bargains to be found.

■ The Whip and Spoon is Portland's most complete gourmet food shop. If you can't find it here, chances are it's not available in the state. The people who run this large, immaculately clean, well-organized store, located on the waterfront in the Old Port, make every effort to educate, tantalize, and fulfill every cook's desire.

The front of the shop is dedicated to cookware and equipment—copper casseroles from France, marble baking slabs, Italian coffee machines, and sushi-making kits. You'll find all the essentials you need to make beer and wine at home (complete with a fairly substantial library of beer- and wine-making books), and you can even attend a free beer-making class held every month or so between September and May. And in the back of the shop a beautiful, fully equipped demonstration kitchen is the scene of some of Maine's most informative cooking classes.

Whip and Spoon makes a point of supporting local food producers. You'll find Maine-made maple syrup; jams, jellies, and preserves; dried herbs, herbal vinegars, and oils; and more. The cheese counter features locally made chèvre and cheddar, as well as cheeses from Italy, France, Scandinavia, and other parts of this country.

Washburn-Norlands Living Center

The Washburn-Norlands Living Center is a 400-acre farm in Livermore Falls (about 20 miles northeast of Augusta), where people come from all over the world to experience nineteenth-century rural New England life. But Norlands is not one of those cute re-created New England villages where visitors stop for a day to watch women in calico dresses make wax candles. Livermore is too isolated for that kind of tourism, and besides, that is not the center's intention. The idea at Norlands is to learn history by living it. And because this is a restored farm community, much of what happens here involves food—growing it, harvesting it, cooking it, and, of course, eating it. Norlands serves some of the best home-cooked meals in the state.

Norlands is made up of five nineteenth-century buildings—a one-room schoolhouse, a Universalist church, a library, and the old Washburn estate (once owned by one of Livermore's most prominent families). There are several ways to experience Norlands. At the three-day Live-In Program, visitors live in the old farmer's cottage and take on the identities of real people who lived in Livermore during the nineteenth century. Days are spent farming, cooking, and researching the history of your "character" by exploring local graveyards, diaries, and town records. But you need not make this kind of commitment to get a sense of life at Norlands. There are several daylong festivals and weekend celebrations open to the public that focus on food in the nineteenth century.

All the recipes used in the Norlands kitchen date from the nineteenth century. Everything is cooked on an old wood-burning cookstove; butter is churned by hand; tea is brewed from garden herbs; and all the ingredients are grown and raised on the farm. You can expect traditional dishes such as baked beans and brown bread, corn chowder, blueberry cake with lemon sauce, and excellent bread pudding with maple syrup. *The Norlands Cook Book*, a collection of nineteenth-century Maine recipes, is available at the Norlands gift shop.

Write (RD 2, Box 3395, Livermore Falls, 04254) or call (207-897-2236) for more information, reservations, and dates of festivals.

Presque Isle

NEW PENNY FARM
Route 2, Box 45, Presque Isle, 04769; phone 207-768-7551. Hours: call ahead. Tours and mail order available.

New Penny Farm potatoes are sold at some specialty food shops in New England.

■ When we first heard about New Penny Farm potatoes, we thought they were the ultimate gourmet food rip-off. Specialty potatoes at specialty prices? Potatoes that are hand picked? Who cares? A potato is a potato, right?

Chris Holmes, owner of New Penny Farm, tried to convince us otherwise. "We are reintroducing several varieties of potatoes that were abandoned by the potato industry when it was mechanized several decades ago. I have a small farm, and rather than get large and keep costs down like many of my neighbors have done, I decided to go the other way. I know the idea of old-fashioned potatoes may sound like a gimmick," he admitted, "but my interest is in taste, not novelty."

Not convinced yet? Neither were we until Holmes sent us a few of his Green Mountain Potatoes. A box of large blemish-free potatoes arrived, along with a card describing them as the ideal baking potato. We heated up the oven, popped a few in, and got out our forks. And were we ever amazed. These potatoes were sweet and rich, with a creamy texture. They didn't need butter. The next morning we fried up the leftovers and had some of the best home fries we've ever tasted.

We called Chris Holmes back and asked him to describe a few of the other potatoes he sells:

Chieftain: a red potato that holds up well when boiled and then baked. The perfect potato for Pommes Anna. Holmes says it "doesn't stick if sliced and prepared au gratin. Also, if you have a recipe that calls for the potato to be peeled, this is the ideal one because it doesn't discolor like so many other varieties."

Bintge: developed in Holland, with unusual yellow flesh. Holmes gets the majority of these from a neighbor. He claims this one tastes so buttery that you'd swear it already had the butter in it.

Potatoes Edwin

Thinly sliced potatoes are layered with onions, butter, a light sprinkling of flour, and then coated with milk and baked until golden brown. They're particularly good served with roast duck or chicken.

4 tablespoons butter
4 medium-size Green Mountain, Irish Cobbler, or other Maine baking potatoes (about 1 1/2 pounds)
1 large onion

About 1/3 cup flour
Salt and freshly ground black pepper to taste
About 1 1/2 cups milk

Preheat the oven to 300°. Grease the bottom of a 9 1/2-inch shallow casserole or gratin dish, preferably earthenware or copper, with 1 tablespoon of the butter. Peel and very thinly slice the potatoes and onion. Arrange a third of the potatoes in the casserole, overlapping the edges slightly. Scatter half the onions on top. Sprinkle on a light coating of flour, and top with 1 tablespoon of the butter, cut into small pieces. Season with pepper, and salt if desired. Repeat with a second layer. Place the third layer of potatoes on top, dot with the remaining tablespoon of butter, and season with salt and pepper. Slowly pour the milk over the potatoes until it reaches about halfway up the side of the casserole.

Place the casserole on a baking sheet (in order to catch any juices), and bake in the lower third of the oven for 1 hour and 10 minutes, checking periodically to make sure the milk hasn't dried up. (If it has, add more.) Raise the heat to 375° and bake an additional 10 to 15 minutes, or until the potatoes are golden brown. Serve immediately. Serves 4 to 6.

Yukon Gold: another yellow variety, with a milder flavor than Bintge.

Irish Cobbler: an early potato, ideal for baking, boiling, or steaming.

Katahdin: developed in the 1940s and a native of Maine, long a favorite. It was the predominant potato in Maine until the 1960s, but it now accounts for less than 7 percent of Maine's potato crop. It has lots of character, says Holmes, and is very versatile. Most of these potatoes are grown by one of Holmes's neighbors.

Kennebec: also grown by a neighbor—a good general-purpose potato.

New Penny Farm potatoes are all picked by hand and stored below ground to keep them fresh. Holmes says he has to spray the potatoes in the summer with a fungicide to combat potato bugs, but he never uses herbicides.

Common Ground Country Fair

The first Common Ground fair, held in 1977, was a modest event. A small group of people got together to celebrate the new values and the revival of old skills that members of the counterculture had brought to rural Maine. Today the fair is still permeated with the spirit of alternative life-styles, organic agriculture, and an appreciation for the old ways of doing things, but its size and scope have expanded dramatically. It includes everything from displays of the latest farm machinery and state-of-the-art solar heating devices to the weaving, pottery, and woodwork of Maine craftspeople.

Because this is essentially an agricultural fair there is lots of food, and it's delicious—grilled lamb sausages made from organically raised Maine lamb, lobster rolls, spinach and feta turnovers, french fries made with Maine potatoes, and whole wheat waffles topped with fresh Maine blueberries and ice cream from Maine dairy cows. The Maine Organic Farmers and Gardeners Association (MOFGA), which runs the fair, has strict rules for all food vendors: whenever possible ingredients must be grown organically in Maine, both white and brown sugar are forbidden, and bleached white flour is frowned upon. That means you get onion rings fried in a whole wheat flour batter and doughnuts sweetened with maple syrup. In other words, junk food without guilt.

Many of Maine's finest organic food producers also come to the fair to sell their wares. You can sample the products put out by smokehouses, cheesemakers, herb farms, gristmills, and aquaculturists.

The fair also has a lot to offer anyone interested in getting new ideas for cooking and growing organic food on their own. Competitions include prizes for the best all-natural lunch box treat and the best all-natural dessert. All during the fair, farmers and gardeners compete for the best organically raised fruits and vegetables, and many of them are happy to share their knowledge of agriculture and gardening techniques.

The Common Ground fair is held around the third week in September at the fairgrounds in Windsor. For exact dates and a schedule of events, contact MOFGA, P.O. Box 2176, Augusta, 04330; phone 207-622-3118.

"And we never spray the skin," he explains. "You don't have to worry about peeling the skins off these potatoes. We encourage people to eat the skin." Prices are high. But from what we've tasted, New Penny Farm potatoes are well worth the extra dollars.

Rangeley

FIRST FARM

Gull Pond Road, Box 392, Rangeley, 04970; phone 207-864-5539. Hours: July through September, Monday, Tuesday, Friday, and Saturday 10 A.M. to 5 P.M. or by appointment; closed Wednesday, Thursday, and Sunday. Personal checks accepted.

■ The conditions could certainly be better. Kit and Linda Caspar's organic vegetable and flower garden, located in the resort community of Rangeley, is at an elevation of 1500 feet. "Cold" and "harsh" are the words most often used to describe this climate. Their growing season is extremely short—only twenty to sixty frost-free growing days a year. Asparagus and peas don't usually come up until well into July. Corn doesn't make it at all. But the Caspars are people who like a good challenge, and despite these conditions, they manage to grow some excellent produce.

The list of fruits and vegetables at First Farm is a long one, and everything is raised organically, without pesticides or sprays of any kind. They grow nine varieties of lettuce (including delicate leaf lettuce, Boston, Bibb, black-seeded Simpson, radicchio, and arugula), three types of beans (purple, yellow, and green), three varieties of peas, five members of the onion family (garlic, shallots, leeks, red and yellow onions), and cold-weather crops like broccoli, cabbage, and winter squash. There's also rhubarb, strawberries, and raspberries, which are sold fresh and also go into their homemade jams and conserves.

Also available at the farm are fresh eggs from the Caspars' flock of laying hens, and maple syrup from their trees.

Rockland

SKANSEN FOOD PACKERS

7 Mirrill Drive, Rockland, 04841; phone 207-596-0044. Hours: Monday–Friday 7 A.M. to 4 P.M.; closed Saturday and Sunday. Personal checks accepted.

Also available at supermarkets, fish stores, and specialty food stores throughout New England.

■ Herring is big business in Maine. However, most of the herring caught by Maine fishermen is used for bait in lobster traps. We've never really understood why this is so. Why not smoke the herring or pickle it, as they do in so many other parts of the world? A few years ago we were thrilled to learn about Skansen Food Packers, a company that prepares several types of Scandinavian-style pickled herring at their Rockland plant.

Using North Atlantic herring (caught primarily off Nova Scotia and Newfoundland), they developed recipes for four types of pickled herring: bite-size herring bits are marinated in Sour Cream Sauce, Wine Sauce, Dill Sauce, and Sweet and Sour Mustard. All four are delicious—not overly salty or vinegary. Even the Sweet and Sour Mustard, which we had doubts about, turned out to be a winner.

STATE OF MAINE CHEESE COMPANY

75 Front Street, Rockland, 04841; phone 207-596-6601. Hours: Monday–Friday 9 A.M. to 4:30 P.M.; closed Saturday and Sunday. MasterCard, Visa, and personal checks accepted. Mail order available.

Also sold in grocery stores and specialty food shops in Maine and New Hampshire.

■ Taylor Mudge, president of State of Maine Cheese Company, was trying to explain why the location of his cheese plant, in full view of the Atlantic surf, affects the taste of the cheese they make. "It's not that the cheese tastes salty or has an ocean flavor of any kind," Mudge explained. "It's just that our environment is unique and the cheese develops a noticeable flavor while it's aging. Let's just say there's an ambience here in Rockland that affects these cheeses in some very subtle, positive ways."

This sounds pretty ephemeral, but the truth is, ocean air or no ocean air, State of Maine Cheese Company makes wonderful cheese. The Penobscot Cheddar has a mild flavor and is excellent melted or served at room temperature. Some of this cheddar gets shipped over to the Ducktrap Fish Farm in Lincolnville (see page 57), where it's smoked over native fruitwood and hardwood coals. Cumberland Smoked, as it's called, is one of the finest smoked cheeses we've tried. Katahdin Cheddar, aged anywhere from nine months to a year, is quite a bit sharper, with a nice peppery bite.

Aroostook Jack is very similar to Monterey Jack—smooth and buttery with a slightly sweet taste. It's delicious served with fruit or melted over French bread or burgers. There are three versions of this cheese: plain; Saco Jalapeño, which is spiked with jalapeño peppers; and Kennebec Dill, which has a mild herb flavor.

Also available (at the Rockland plant only) is fresh cheddar cheese curd. Curd is the final state of cheddar production, before it's pressed into cheese. This curd has a tangy, salty flavor and can be eaten on its own or used in cooking the way you use ricotta cheese.

THE MARKET BASKET

Corner of Routes 1 and 90, Rockport, 04856; phone 207-236-4371. Hours: seven days a week 9 A.M. to 6 P.M. MasterCard, Visa, and personal checks accepted. Mail order available.

Rockport

■ The Market Basket is filled with local specialties, hard-to-find ingredients, and loads of imported products. There's fresh and imported pasta, smoked fish from Ducktrap Fish Farm, jellies and jams, exotic chutneys, and lots of Chinese, Mexican, Indian, and Italian ingredients. The *baguettes* are crisp and brought in fresh every day, and the selection of cheeses, pâtés, wine, and beer is extensive. This is a great place to put together a picnic.

Also, be sure to look for Claudette Boggs's peanut butter balls. You may abandon Reese's after tasting one of these crunchy melt-in-your-mouth candies; see page 78 for more information.

KOHN'S SMOKEHOUSE

Route 131, Saint George, 04857 (mailing address: CR 35 Box 160, Thomaston, ME 04861); phone 207-372-8412.

Saint George

■ If it swims or walks, there's a good chance that Ute and Dietrich Kohn have figured out a way to smoke it. As you might expect, this adventurous approach yields varying results. The smoked mackerel is a real treat. This oily fish

Summer hours: Monday–Saturday 8 A.M. to 6 P.M. Winter hours: Monday–Saturday 9 A.M. to 5 P.M. Closed Sunday. MasterCard, Visa, and personal checks accepted. Mail order available. Custom-smoking available.

JOHN'S BAY SEAFOOD

Maine Mariculture, Inc., Thompson Inn Road, South Bristol, 04568; phone 207-644-8192. Hours: Monday–Friday, 9 A.M. to 4:30 P.M.; closed Saturday and Sunday. MasterCard and Visa accepted. Mail order available.

stands up well to the Kohns' somewhat heavy-handed smoking process, and the result is a tender fish with a robust flavor. The smoked salmon, however, was just too smokey for our taste. Kohn's smoked ham also has a strong smokey flavor and is a bit salty, but the overall taste is excellent and the texture is moist and tender.

Some of the other foods they smoke include eel, herring, trout, bacon, beef, mussels, salami, and lobster.

It's a beautiful drive through rolling farmland and past distant water vistas to the Kohns' tiny store in Saint George (4 1/2 miles south of Route 1). Just up the road you'll find Sylvia's Cakes and Breads (see page 77).

South Bristol

■ This seafood-farming company specializes in growing Belon oysters, a European oyster that was introduced to Maine waters about forty years ago. They are a bit saltier than their American cousins, and they have a tangier flavor which comes from the high amount of iodine they absorb from the ocean. "American oysters are bland by comparison," says Maine Mariculture's Jenny Ruffing.

If you visit the company's plant, you'll have a chance to see the beds where the oysters are raised. You can also stroll around South Bristol harbor, with its picturesque

James Haller's Smoked Mussel Cream Chowder

This recipe comes to us from Jim Haller, one of New England's most innovative chefs. Haller, formerly of the Blue Strawbery restaurant in Portsmouth, New Hampshire, and now the head of his own catering company in South Berwick, Maine, has a reputation for adding unusual ingredients to traditional recipes.

1 cup unpeeled diced potatoes
1/2 cup chopped onions
1/4 pound thick slab bacon
4 cloves garlic, chopped
2 cups smoked mussels

3 cups milk
1 cup heavy cream
2 tablespoons chopped fresh chives
1/4 cup dry sherry (optional)
Freshly grated nutmeg (optional)

Place the potatoes and onions in a large soup or stockpot, and add just enough water to cover them. Place over moderately high heat and cook until the potatoes are soft, about 10 minutes.

In a large skillet, fry the bacon and garlic until the bacon is crisp. Remove the bacon from the skillet, and drain on paper towels. Chop the bacon and add it to the stockpot, along with the smoked mussels. Add the milk, and simmer about 10 minutes. Add the cream, chives, sherry, and nutmeg, and heat until the mixture just comes to a boil. Serves 4.

fishing shacks and lobster boats. Marine Mariculture does not have a formal retail store, but they will sell seafood to customers who come to the plant. You can buy oysters, mussels, clams (both steamers and hard-shell), lobsters, and in the winter, Maine shrimp and sea urchins. Oysters, lobsters, mussels, and hard-shell clams may also be mail-ordered.

Look for Maine Mariculture's booth at The Maine Festival in Portland (see page 68) and at the Damariscotta Oyster Festival.

Maine Mariculture employees sorting fresh mussels.

Steuben

■ Larch Hanson calls himself a "professional harvester." He and his wife, Jan, gather seaweed off the Sally Islands, across from Gouldsboro Bay. They harvest five types of "sea vegetables"—kelp, dulse, alaria, digitata kelp, and nori.

Anyone who has ever walked along a Maine beach is well aware that this part of the world has more than its fair share of seaweed. But did you know that seaweed is loaded with nutrients? It's high in protein, potassium, and iodine, and contrary to popular belief it doesn't taste bad, either. Try roasting dulse or nori in a 200° oven for 10 minutes and you'll get delicious, all-natural seaweed chips. (Some friends of ours in Vermont have their four- and seven-year-old boys hooked on the stuff.) Seaweed can also be used to flavor and thicken soups and stews, vegetables, and rice dishes, or it can be eaten by itself or in salads.

Larch Hanson has written an interesting little book called *Edible Sea Vegetables of the New England Coast* for those who want to know how to harvest their own seaweed, what to do with it when they get it home, how to cook it, and how to use it for medicinal purposes. Both the seaweed and the book can be ordered through the mail.

MAINE SEAWEED COMPANY
Box 57, Steuben, 04680; phone 207-546-2875. Personal checks accepted. Mail order available.

Available at health food stores and gourmet food stores across the country.

Tenants Harbor

THE GREAT EASTERN MUSSEL FARMS

P.O. Box 141, Tenants Harbor, 04860; phone 207-372-6317. Hours: Monday–Friday 8 A.M. to 5 P.M.; closed Saturday and Sunday. Cash only. Tours of the plant can be arranged in advance.

Sold at fish stores throughout the United States.

■ These are big juicy mussels with a fresh, clean taste. Although they are raised under controlled conditions, Great Eastern mussels have all the flavor of mussels grown in the wild, and they have much less grit.

The mussel-growing operation that this company uses is fairly simple. First, tiny seed mussels are placed on ocean-bottom beds. The mussels are spread out so they have plenty of room to grow. (Wild mussels, on the other hand, grow in big clumps. They tend to be smaller than cultured mussels, and have less meat and more shell.)

The cultivated mussels are harvested at about two years of age. They are then put in giant saltwater tanks and purged for twenty-four hours to remove as much grit as possible. Great Eastern mussels are a little more expensive than other mussels, but because they are so clean, they are easier to cook with, and you don't have to worry about whether they come from polluted waters.

Thomaston

SYLVIA'S CAKES AND BREADS

St. George Road (Route 131) (CR 35, Box 82), Thomaston, 04861; phone 207-354-6698. Hours: seven days a week 9 A.M. to 6 P.M. Personal checks accepted. Call ahead for special orders. Mail order available.

■ "When we moved way out here in the country," says Sylvia Hocking, "there wasn't anything for me to do. I was getting bored. Boredom is an awful thing. Why, it's the worst thing in the world. That's why I started baking."

It's hard to imagine Sylvia Hocking sitting around twiddling her thumbs. When we visited her she had two incredible-looking raspberry pies sitting on a cooling rack and was pulling four chocolate pound cakes out of the oven. By the end of the day, she would have baked close to a dozen more pies and cakes. This may not sound like much for most bakeries, but you have to take into account that Sylvia Hocking works alone in her kitchen using two twenty-one-year-old ovens. Modestly, Sylvia refers to her work as nothing more than a "hobby." But the truth is, this woman is one of the best bakers we know.

Sylvia's Apple Spice Buckle with Butter Streusel Topping (see recipe below) is a sweet amalgam of apples, brown sugar, butter, buttermilk, and pecans. She also makes incredible Blueberry Buckle and Raspberry Buckle, using locally picked berries. Her Sour Cream and Butter Coffee Cake is a coffee cake lover's fantasy—a moist, buttery cake with cinnamon and nut streusel layered throughout.

Sylvia will ship her cakes, breads, and brownies, but the fruit pies are too fragile to travel. You can also stop by her home and see what's baking, but your best bet is to call ahead and place an order. Sylvia keeps threatening to retire. We can only hope that her fear of boredom will keep her baking for many years to come.

Sylvia's Apple Spice Buckle

This cake is particularly popular in the autumn, when apples are abundant. The recipe can easily be doubled; serve one buckle now and freeze the other for a cold winter day. "Butter is what really makes this cake," says Sylvia. "You have to use real butter."

Buckle
8 tablespoons (1 stick) butter, softened
1/2 cup plus 1/2 tablespoon granulated sugar
1/2 cup firmly packed brown sugar
2 eggs
1/2 teaspoon salt
1 1/4 teaspoons ground cinnamon
1/4 teaspoon ground nutmeg
1/2 teaspoon lemon extract
2 cups flour
1/2 teaspoon baking soda
3/4 cups buttermilk
2 cups chopped tart (about 3 large) apples

Topping
8 tablespoons (1 stick) butter, softened and cut into small pieces
1/4 cup firmly packed brown sugar
1/3 cup plus 1 tablespoon granulated sugar
1/2 cup flour
1 teaspoon ground cinnamon
1/4 teaspoon ground nutmeg
1 to 1 1/2 cups pecan halves

Preheat the oven to 350°. Grease and flour a 9- or 10-inch tube pan.

Prepare the buckle: In a large bowl, cream the butter, 1/2 cup granulated sugar, the brown sugar, eggs, salt, 3/4 teaspoon of the cinnamon, the nutmeg, and the lemon extract. In a separate bowl, sift the flour with the baking soda. Add the sifted flour to the creamed mixture alternately with the buttermilk. Toss the apples with the remaining sugar and cinnamon, and fold into the batter. Stir well.

In another large bowl, blend all the topping ingredients except the pecans.

Pour the buckle batter into the pan. Sprinkle the topping over the batter, and sprinkle it with the pecan halves, pressing them lightly into the topping. Bake for 50 to 60 minutes, or until a toothpick inserted in the center comes out clean. Remove the pan from the oven and gently loosen the cake from the sides and center. Carefully flip the cake onto a plate. Using another plate, flip it over again so the topping side is up. Let cool. Serves 8 to 10.

CLAUDETTE BOGGS'S PEANUT BUTTER BALLS

Waldoboro, 04572; phone 207-832-5774. Mail order available. Personal checks accepted.

Waldoboro

■ When we called Claudette Boggs to get some information about her homemade peanut butter balls, she seemed genuinely surprised. "Oh," she said, "I've been making peanut butter balls for years. They're an old family recipe. My boys have always loved them."

Well, we thought they were pretty good too. The candy—a dark chocolate shell covering a crunchy, melt-in-your-mouth peanut butter center—is similar in concept to a Reese's Peanut Butter Cup, but worlds apart in flavor. Peanut butter fans will adore them.

Claudette Boggs is not interested in turning her candy-making operation into anything more than a small family business. She does do some mail order from her home, or you can order these sweet nuggets from The Market Basket in Rockport (see page 74). One bit of advice; Don't be skimpy when you order these peanut butter balls. According to Ms. Boggs, if they're refrigerated they'll last quite a while. That is, if you can keep from eating them all the day they arrive.

FOX FERN HERB FARM

Route 32 (1½ miles south of Route 1), Waldoboro, 04572; phone 207-832-4721. Hours: late June through Labor Day, Tuesday–Thursday and Saturday 10 A.M. to 4 P.M. At other times call ahead. Personal checks accepted.

■ A long winding driveway flanked by fields of wild flowers brings you to the Fox Fern Herb Farm. It's a modest place: a small greenhouse, some terraced herb gardens overlooking the Medomak River, and a makeshift store set up in the proprietor's garage. But there are some wonderful things to be found here. Fox Fern Pesto Butter is a delicious combination of butter, fresh basil, Parmesan cheese, olive oil, walnuts, and garlic. We spread it on tomatoes before broiling them and stirred it into white clam sauce. It gave both dishes a fresh basil flavor and added some richness as well.

Other products they make include herbal jellies and vinegars. They also offer an extensive selection of fresh and dried culinary herbs.

Tours of the herb garden and an English-style tea are held on Tuesday afternoons in the summer. Classes in growing and using herbs are given. Reservations required.

Waterboro

HORTON'S DOWNEAST FOODS

Grist Mill Road (P.O. Box 430), Waterboro, 04087; phone 207-247-6900. Hours: call ahead. Personal checks accepted. Mail order available.

Also sold in specialty food stores throughout New England.

■ Don Horton is a trained fisheries biologist. At one time he also ran a company that imported wood stoves. Now it seems Horton has combined his two previous professions; he makes smoked fish. Horton's Downeast Foods has been in business for only a few years, but already they have gained a reputation for producing top-quality smoked seafood including smoked salmon, shrimp, bluefish, mussels, monkfish, and trout.

Like most of their products, the Whole Boneless Rainbow Trout is lightly smoked, moist, and very fresh tasting. Horton seems to understand that trout is a delicate fish. Each fish is boned and left whole. All you have to do is toast some bread and serve the trout with a little horseradish, fresh dill, and lemon wedges.

Wiscasset

CHEVALIER FARMS

The Squire Tarbox Inn, Route 144 (RR 2, Box 620), Wiscasset, 04578;

■ Karen and Bill Mitman, owners of The Squire Tarbox Inn, make a variety of cheeses with the 7 to 8 gallons of milk they get each day from their small herd of purebred Nubian goats. Their most popular cheese is a hard goat

phone 207-882-7693. Hours: seven days a week, 9 A.M. to 5 P.M. MasterCard, Visa, American Express, and personal checks accepted. Mail order available.

TREATS

Main Street (P.O. Box 156), Wiscasset, 04578; phone 207-882-6192. Hours: Columbus Day through July 4, Monday–Saturday 10 A.M. to 5:30 P.M. July 5 through Columbus Day, Monday–Saturday 10 A.M. to 6 P.M., Sunday 12 N. to 4 P.M. Personal checks accepted.

cheese, aged for sixty days, similar to Caerphilly (a Welsh coal miners' cheese). Originally they made only enough of this cheese to serve to their guests at the inn. "People adored it," explained Bill. So they decided to enter the cheese in a national goat cheese competition. "We were amazed to walk off with several awards," Bill recalls. That recognition gave the Mitmans the confidence to expand their cheesemaking venture. They recently added a second cheese room to their house and bought a large Dutch pasteurizer.

Among the other cheeses they make is Herbed Chèvre, which has a slightly sour goaty flavor. The Light Feta was one of the creamiest we've tasted, and not overly salty like so much of the feta you find in supermarkets. It's excellent in salads, baked into a spinach-cheese pie, or spread on a bagel instead of cream cheese. They also make something called Orange Chèvre, a soft cheese flavored with orange that is excellent served at breakfast with nut breads.

■ This wine, cheese, and specialty food store makes a point of carrying Maine-made foods—locally produced goat's- and cow's-milk cheeses, honeys, maple syrup, herring, homemade candies, and more. There's also a good selection of imported and domestic wine and an interesting collection of beers from microbreweries. This is a good place to pick up a gift or put together a simple picnic to enjoy on one of the many beaches near Wiscasset.

Squire Tarbox Inn Chèvre Pound Cake

This goat cheese pound cake is extraordinarily light and fluffy, with an unusual, slightly sour flavor. At the inn the Mitmans serve the cake with whipped cream and brandied blueberries.

1 cup soft goat cheese or cream cheese (1/2 pound)
1 1/2 cups unsalted butter, softened
2 cups sugar

1/8 teaspoon salt
1 1/2 teaspoons lemon or vanilla extract
6 eggs
3 cups flour

Preheat the oven to 325°. Lightly butter and flour a 10-inch tube pan.

Blend the cheese and butter in an electric mixer, or beat vigorously with a whisk. Beat in the sugar, salt, and lemon extract until the mixture is very light. Add the eggs one at a time, and beat until the batter is light and fluffy. Gently fold in the flour, and blend until the ingredients are just incorporated.

Pour the mixture into the prepared pan and bake 1 hour and 15 minutes. Invert on a cooling rack and cool thoroughly before serving. Makes 1 cake, about 10 to 12 servings.

Woolwich

SWANGO FARM
Route 1, Woolwich, 04579; phone 207-442-7627. Hours: mid-June through October, Monday–Saturday 10 A.M. to 5:30 P.M.; closed Sunday. Personal checks accepted.

■ "We grow everything from asparagus to zucchini," said Jim Economou, who along with his wife, Jon, operates Swango Farm. But while their 30-acre farm offers a great variety of fruits and vegetables, asparagus is their specialty. "That's what we're known for," said Jim, "that's our niche."

Other items they sell at their farm stand include raspberries, sweet corn, cut flowers, bedding plants, and herb plants. Some of the produce is raised organically.

The Economous have another farm stand, in Bath, on Old Route 1 near the Bath Shopping Center.

York

FINESTKIND FISH MARKET
Route 1 North, York, 03909; phone 207-363-5000. Hours: seven days a week 10 A.M. to 6 P.M. MasterCard, Visa, American Express, and personal checks accepted. Mail-order lobster and clams available. Clambakes and catering available.

■ Dozens of lobster huts, fish markets, and seafood restaurants line Route 1 between Portsmouth, New Hampshire, and Portland, Maine. Finestkind is one of our favorites. Clams, oysters, mussels, and lobsters are always on hand, as well as shrimp, bluefish, sole, haddock, and squid. In the spring they even manage to find fresh shad roe. Everything is prepared to order, so you can buy your fish whole or have it fileted. You'll also find prepared fish dinners, smoked fish, pickled herring, as well as beer, wine, dairy products, bread, and crackers. One large wall of the shop is devoted to recipes, should you need some new ideas.

Next door to the market is an outdoor clambake that operates during the summer. Stop by for a boiled lobster along with steamed clams, mussels, and corn, and try a cup of creamy clam chowder while you wait. Finestkind will also come to your home and prepare a clambake for 10 to 200 people.

WILD IRIS HERB FARM
Route 91 (RFD, Box 198), York, 03909; phone 207-363-4153. Hours: late April to early fall, Wednesday–Sunday 10 A.M. to 5 P.M., weather permitting; closed Monday and Tuesday. Walking shoes and hat advised. Personal checks accepted.

■ When you gaze at the exquisite colors and shapes that make up the Wild Iris herb and flower gardens, you want to take them home with you. And that's precisely what you can do. There are no potted plants here; the idea behind this herb farm is to stroll through the gardens, pick out what you like, and then let herbalist Lucy Clarke dig it up for you to replant in your own herb garden. While she's digging, and wrapping each plant in newspaper, Clarke will probably offer you some advice—how to plan a perennial herb garden; how to plant it, harvest it, and dry the herbs. She'll even give you some interesting cooking tips along the way. Plan to spend some time here absorbing her expertise.

There are literally hundreds of herbs to choose from—over fourteen varieties of fresh thyme, ten types of mint (ideal for drying and making mint tea), lemon balm, anise hyssop, lavender, French tarragon, horseradish root,

Baked Asparagus with Garlic-Lemon Butter and Parmesan

We usually prefer asparagus prepared simply—steamed and topped with a little lemon butter. But one day we tried cooking fresh spring asparagus this way—baked with a pungent garlic-lemon butter, then sprinkled with grated Parmesan cheese and broiled. And we were hooked.

1 pound asparagus, trimmed
3 tablespoons butter
1 large clove garlic, minced
2 tablespoons fresh lemon juice
Freshly ground black pepper, to taste
1/3 to 1/2 cup grated Parmesan cheese

Place the asparagus in a large skillet and cover with cold water. Bring to a boil, reduce the heat, and simmer for about 5 minutes or until the spears are just tender but still have a "snap." Drain and refresh under cold running water.

Preheat the oven to 350°. Place the asparagus in a shallow casserole or skillet. In a small saucepan, melt the butter over moderately low heat. Add the garlic, lemon juice, and pepper, and simmer until the garlic softens, about 2 minutes. Be careful not to let the butter burn. Pour the garlic-lemon butter over the asparagus, being sure to coat the bottom of the pan thoroughly. Bake for about 5 minutes. Remove from the oven and sprinkle the grated cheese just below the asparagus tips. Turn on the broiler and broil until the cheese is melted and bubbling, about 1 minute. Serves 4 as an appetizer or 2 for a lunch dish—along with a loaf of French bread and bottle of good crisp cold white wine.

THE GOLDENROD
Railroad Avenue (P.O. Box 1140), York Beach, 03910; phone 207-363-2621. Hours: seven days a week 8 A.M. to 9 P.M. (11 P.M. in July and August). Personal checks accepted. Mail order available.

sweet woodruff (used to make May wine), and scented sage and geraniums. There's also a large selection of perennial flowers, including five types of daylilies.

Inside the small herb shed you'll find a selection of herbal wreaths and baskets, herbal teas, and dried flowers and herbs. Wild Iris is an herb lover's fantasy—it's worth a trip if only to experience the overpowering scent of garden herbs mingled with the fresh smell of salt water that drifts up from the nearby York River.

York Beach

■ It's early on a summer evening and you decide to take a drive along Maine's coastal Route 1A. As the sky turns a deep shade of blue, you pull into York Beach and there, shimmering in the twilight, is an immaculately maintained white clapboard building bathed in white light and decorated with blue, yellow, and pink neon signs. The building beckons you. You park the car, join the throng of tourists in this seaside town, and enter The Goldenrod.

This is *the* place in Maine for saltwater taffy. You can

A classic wharf and fisherman's shanty on the scenic coast of Maine.

peer through the plate glass windows that face the street and watch the taffy-pulling machines in action every day. The taffy, called Goldenrod Kisses, is still made according to the recipe E. A. Talbey used when he opened The Goldenrod in 1896. There are a dozen different flavors, ranging from chocolate and maple walnut to molasses and strawberry. Our favorites are peanut butter (chewy on the outside with a soft, creamy peanut-flavored inside) and the very refreshing peppermint. Each year Goldenrod makes over 63 tons of taffy, and once you taste it you'll know why it's so popular.

Once you've picked up some taffy, take a seat at the marble-top ice cream bar or one of the tables in the dining room, decorated in the style of a hunting lodge with a big fieldstone fireplace. You'll be served by one of the "Goldenrod Girls," wearing a neat brown and yellow uniform, white socks, and brown moccasins. The menu is pure 1950s—deviled egg sandwiches, cream cheese and olive sandwiches—but it's the desserts that are really special: ice cream sundaes, frappes, banana splits, ice cream floats, and ice cream sodas. Before you leave, be sure to check out Goldenrod's homemade fudge, peanut brittle, and caramel corn. And pick up an extra box of taffy; you'll probably end up eating it on the way home.

Maine Farmers' Markets

Dates, locations, and times change, so be sure to check with the Department of Agriculture for further details: Maine Department of Agriculture, Food and Rural Resources, Station 28, Augusta, 04333; phone 207-289-3491.

Bath Farmers' Market, Broad and Front Streets, Saturdays from early May through October, 8:30 A.M. to 1 P.M.

Belfast Farmers' Market, Fireman's Museum, Route 3, Tuesdays and Fridays from mid-June to late October, 9 A.M. to 12 N.

Blue Hill Farmers' Market, Blue Hill Fairgrounds, Saturdays in July and August, 9 A.M. to 11:30 A.M.

Brewer Farmers' Market, Brewer Auditorium parking lot, Wilson Street, Fridays and Saturdays from July through October, 7:30 A.M. until sold out.

Brunswick Farmers' Market, Brunswick Mall, Fridays from early May through Thanksgiving, 9 A.M. to 5 P.M. Also at Cook's Corner Shopping Center, Wednesdays and Saturdays, 8:30 A.M. to 5 P.M.

Camden Farmers' Market, corner of Concord and Limerock streets, Tuesdays 3 P.M. to 5 P.M. and Saturdays 9 A.M. to 1 P.M., mid-June through mid-October.

Caribou Farmers' Market, downtown mall, Saturdays from mid-July through September, 7:30 A.M. to 12 N.

Damariscotta Farmers' Market, American Legion parking lot, Business Route 1, Fridays from mid-May to September, 9 A.M. to 1 P.M.

Ellsworth Farmers' Market, High Street, Mondays and Thursdays 2 P.M. to 5:30 P.M., Saturdays 9:30 A.M. to 12 N., July to late September.

Farmington Farmers' Market, The Pizza Shed, junction of Routes 2 and 4, Thursdays from mid-May to October, 9 A.M. to 5 P.M.

Fort Kent—St. John Valley Farmers' Market, corner of Market and Main streets, Saturdays from mid-July to September, 8 A.M. to 1 P.M.

Houlton Farmers' Market, Route 1 south of I-95, Fridays from late May through October, 2 P.M. to dark.

Lewiston—Androscoggin County Farmers' Market, Urban Renewal parking lot, Park Street, Saturdays from mid-May through October, 8 A.M. to 1:30 P.M.

Matinicus Farmers' Market, at the harbor, Matinicus Island, Mondays and Fridays from July to Labor Day, 11:30 A.M. to 1 P.M.

Newport—Palmyra Farmers' Market, Flood's parking lot, junction of Routes 2 and 7, Saturdays from late June to early October, 9 A.M. to 1 P.M.

Portland Farmers' Market, Federal and Pearl streets, Wednesdays from May to Thanksgiving, 7 A.M. to 1 P.M. Also at Deering Oaks Park, Saturdays 7 A.M. to 1 P.M.

Rangeley Farmers' Market, North Main Street, Wednesdays from mid-May to October, 9:30 A.M. to 5 P.M.

Rumford—Androscoggin Farmers' Market, Exchange Street, Thursdays from late May to October, 8 A.M. to 4 P.M.

Saco Farmers' Market, Spring Street at Saco Valley Shopping Center, Saturdays from May through October (and Wednesdays from June through October), 7 A.M. to 12 N.

Skowhegan-Madison Farmers' Market Route 201 North at Racliff Flea Market, Madison, Saturdays from mid-May to October, 9 A.M. to 5 P.M.

South Paris—Oxford County Farmers' Market, Farmers' Union parking lot, Wednesdays 2 P.M. to 5 P.M. and Saturdays 9 A.M. to 12 N. from mid-June to October.

Waldoboro Farmers' Market, Route 1, corner of Depot Street, Tuesdays from mid-June to September, 10 A.M. to 1 P.M.

Westbrook Farmers' Market, municipal parking lot, Wayside Drive, Thursdays and Fridays from April to November, 6 A.M. to 6 P.M.

Massachusetts

MASSACHUSETTS

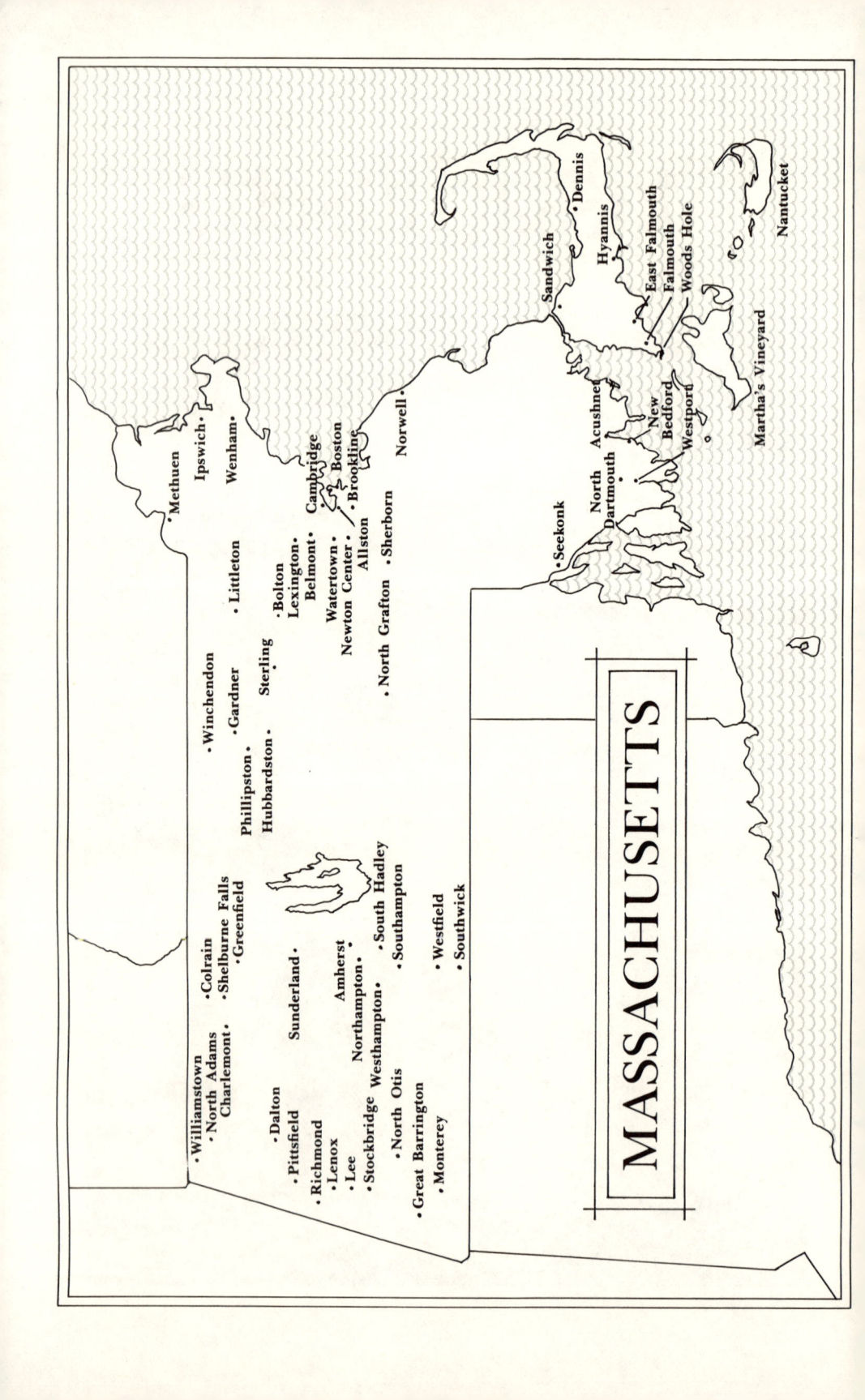

Acushnet

- The Macoun apple is a local favorite here, as it is at orchards throughout the area. Flying Cloud Orchard has one of the older stands of Macoun trees in Acushnet. They also grow a handful of other apple varieties, along with peaches and pears. Other items include home-baked breads, pies, candy apples, preserves, and cider.

FLYING CLOUD ORCHARD
540 Main Street, Acushnet, 02743; phone 617-995-6214. Hours: mid-August to late November, seven days a week 9 A.M. to dusk. Cash only.

- Charlie and May Peters grow about half a dozen varieties of apples along with peaches, pears, and nectarines. Also available are homemade jams, jellies, apple pies, their own sweet cider, and a limited assortment of fresh vegetables. This is a pretty little orchard, a nice place for picnicking and hiking.

PETERS FAMILY ORCHARD AND CIDER MILL
537 North Main Street, Acushnet, 02743; phone 617-995-6533. Hours: irregular, call ahead. Personal checks accepted. Pick-your-own available; call ahead for conditions.

Allston

- A few years ago this Vietnamese fish restaurant was a neighborhood secret. But slowly people from the Boston area have discovered Cao Palace. Now there's almost always a line of customers willing to wait for specialties like Caramel Tuna (a sublime combination of fresh tuna chunks and onion slices in a sweet caramelized sauce), squid stuffed with cellophane noodles and pork, and a very thick and spicy shrimp and rice chowder.

  Cao Palace is also a first-rate fish market. Half the restaurant is taken over by a fish counter displaying some of the best-looking swordfish, tuna, squid, shrimp, and whole whitefish around.

CAO PALACE
137 Brighton Avenue, Allston, 02134; phone 617-783-2340. Store hours: Monday–Saturday 11:30 A.M. to 9:30 P.M.; closed Sunday. Cash only.

- Indian food lovers know that to make a really authentic curry you must have the right ingredients. At House of Spices you'll find all the essentials: two types of store-blended curry powder (hot and mild), a wide variety of Indian spices, sweet and spicy chutneys, killer-hot Indian pickles, ghee (clarified butter), banana chips, lentils, mustard oil, *pappadam* (the crisp Indian bread that is traditionally served with curries), and some excellent Indian teas. There is also a selection of Indian and Middle Eastern cooking equipment, cookbooks, magazines, and music. This small shop is worth a visit if only for the overwhelmingly seductive scent of fresh curry that fills the air.

HOUSE OF SPICES
143 Brighton Avenue, Allston, 02134; phone 617-787-3552. Hours: Tuesday–Saturday 12 N. to 8 P.M.; Saturday and Sunday 11 A.M. to 7 P.M. Personal checks accepted. Mail order available.

Amherst

THE BLACK SHEEP DELI & BAKERY
79 Main Street, Amherst, 01002; phone 413-253-3442. Hours: Monday–Thursday 7:30 A.M. to 6 P.M., Friday 7:30 A.M. to 8 P.M., Saturday 9 A.M. to 6 P.M., Sunday 9 A.M. to 3 P.M. MasterCard and Visa accepted. Catering available.

- The Black Sheep has a cluttered feeling to it, but it's a pleasing kind of clutter. There is a little bit of everything here: ropes of fresh garlic, red chile pepper braids, and wreaths of bay leaves and herbs hanging overhead. Old wooden and glass cases are filled with gorgeous loaves of breads, muffins, and pastries. High-tech metal shelves display coffees, teas, mustards, oils, and jellies from around the world. And at a large island in the middle of the shop you'll find a wide selection of imported and domestic cheeses, fresh pasta, and their own salads and pâtés. Other items include smoked fish, smoked ham, and fresh game, including quail, pheasant, and partridge.

You can sit at one of the tables in the front of the shop and have a cup of coffee and pastry.

SWEETIES FINE CHOCOLATE AND CONFECTIONS
63 North Pleasant Street, Amherst, 01002; phone 413-253-5589. Hours: Monday–Wednesday 10 A.M. to 5:30 P.M., Thursday 10 A.M. to 9 P.M., Friday and Saturday 10 A.M. to 10 P.M., Sunday 12 N. to 5 P.M. Closed Sunday in July and August. Personal checks accepted. Mail order available.

- Chocolate babies, Mary Janes, malted milk balls, red hots, and licorice strings are among the dozens of candies beautifully displayed at this high-tech version of the old penny-candy store. Of course nothing costs a penny any more, and instead of making your selections from a well-worn wood and glass case you can help yourself from huge Lucite bins that reach to the ceiling. In addition to penny candy there are imported and New England–made chocolates, including Champlain Chocolates from Burlington, Vermont (see page 210), and chocolate novelties (things like chocolate telephones and sports cars) from Munson's in Connecticut (see page 4).

There are Sweeties shops in Northampton, at 68 Main Street (413-586-4180), and in Burlington, Vermont, at 101 Church Street (802-863-0309).

Belmont

EASTERN LAMEJUN BAKERS
145 Belmont Street, Belmont, 02178; phone 617-484-5239. Hours: Monday–Friday 8 A.M. to 7 P.M., Saturday 8 A.M. to 6 P.M.; closed Sunday. Cash only.

- There are several excellent Middle Eastern bakeries and food stores in Belmont and Watertown. What sets Eastern Lamejun Bakers apart from the rest is the irresistible smell that greets you when you walk in the door. It's a mixture of spices, herbs, and baking pastry—a smell that makes you hungry.

Take a peek through the doors to the back room and you'll see why it smells so good. There are trays of honey-drenched baklava that have just come out of the oven, Lebanese and Syrian breads, delicate cheese turnovers, and the specialty of the bakery, *lamejun*, which is like a Middle Eastern pizza. *Lamejun* has a thin crust similar to Syrian bread and is topped with finely ground lamb and beef, minced tomatoes, peppers, onions, parsley, and spices. A few *lamejun* warmed in the oven, served with yogurt and a salad, make a delicious and very quick meal.

Eastern Lamejun Bakers is also a well-stocked Middle

Eastern grocery. There are bins filled with red and green lentils, several varieties of wheat flour, and many kinds of rice. The shelves are stocked with jars of Greek honey, jams, and preserves—including bright green pistachio nut preserves and fig marmalade. There are colorful containers of olive oil, olives, dried fruits, feta cheese, and coffee for making the thick brew that is consumed throughout the Middle East. They also sell coffee pots and cookbooks. Prices here are generally reasonable, and there are a few bargains to be found.

Vinegars on display at the Amherst Common Market.

> Here are two other nearby Middle Eastern bakeries that also make *lamejun,* Armenian bread, and pastries such as baklava:
>
> *Massis Bakery,* 569 Mount Auburn Street, Watertown, 02172; phone 617-924-0537. Hours: Monday–Saturday 7:30 A.M. to 7:30 P.M.; closed Sunday. Cash only.
>
> *Sevan Bakery,* 598 Mount Auburn Street, Watertown, 02172; phone 617-924-9843. Hours: Monday–Saturday 8 A.M. to 8 P.M.; closed Sunday. Personal checks accepted.

GREER'S SEA FOODS
353 Trapelo Road, Belmont, 02178; phone 617-484-9000. Hours: Tuesday–Thursday and Saturday 8 A.M. to 7 P.M., Friday 8 A.M. to 8 P.M.; closed Sunday and Monday. Cash only.

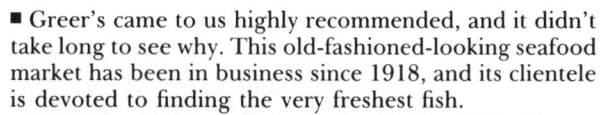

■ Greer's came to us highly recommended, and it didn't take long to see why. This old-fashioned-looking seafood market has been in business since 1918, and its clientele is devoted to finding the very freshest fish.

While we browsed through the display of freshly cut filets of gray sole, thick swordfish steaks, and piles of steamers, clams, crabs, and mussels, we listened to the countermen do business, Greer's-style. "Afternoon, Mrs. Smith. Let me guess. Sole today? No, wait. It's Thursday, and that would make it haddock." The old woman just smiled and replied, "Make it a pound and a half, thank you."

Bolton

BOLTON ORCHARDS
Junction of Routes 110 and 117 (P.O. Box G), Bolton, 01740; phone 617-779-2733. Hours: Monday–Saturday 7 A.M. to 6 P.M., Sunday 8 A.M. to 6 P.M. Personal checks accepted. Mail order available.

■ There is one compelling reason to visit Bolton Orchards. It's their Golden Russet Cider, a blend of Golden Delicious and Russet apples that is like no cider we've ever tasted. It has a light golden color that makes it look more like apple juice than cider, and it's incredibly refreshing—it just goes down so easily. Golden Russet Cider is available Thanksgiving through Christmas only. The rest of the time you'll have to settle for their regular cider, which is also quite good.

Bolton Orchards grows more than thirty varieties of apples, all without alar. They also grow pears, peaches, quinces, plums, and a variety of vegetables. In addition

NASHOBA VALLEY WINERY

100 Wattaquadoc Hill Road, Bolton, 01740; phone 617-779-5521. Hours: seven days a week 11 A.M. to 6 P.M. MasterCard, Visa, and personal checks accepted. Free tours and tastings Friday through Sunday; self-guided tours on weekdays. Pick-your-own strawberries, raspberries, blackberries, peaches, and apples available; call ahead for dates and conditions.

Food and music festivals are held at the winery throughout the summer, and cross-country ski trails are open in the winter.

ANGELO DELUCA MEAT MARKET

119 Salem Street, Boston, 02113; phone 617-227-0430. Hours: Monday–Saturday 6 A.M. to 7 P.M.; closed Sunday. Cash only.

to fresh produce they sell local honey, whole grain breads from New England bakeries, cheese, and regular grocery items.

■ New England fruit wines have a problem that can be summed up in one word: image.

"It's just fermented fruit syrup," sneered a friend of ours. "Sugary, fruit cider," said another. But we have always liked the idea of making wine from native New England fruit. It seems so natural—particularly after tasting so many failed attempts at producing European-style grape wine on New England soil. And besides, in Colonial times wines made from apples, berries, and other native fruits were common. Why not revive an old tradition?

Nashoba Valley is the first modern New England winery devoted solely to the production of fruit wines. Jack Partridge founded the business in 1978. Making wine from fruit was his hobby, and for several years he worked out of his basement in Somerville, Massachusetts. Eventually he became so consumed with the process that he quit his job as a city planner and became a full time winemaker. The winery moved to its present location, a beautiful 55-acre fruit orchard, in 1984. Almost all the apple wine produced at Nashoba is made from apples grown at the orchard, but the majority of the berries and other fruits used are brought in from other New England states, as well as California.

We recently visited the winery, walked among rows of apple trees and berry bushes, and ended up inside the winery building for a tasting. The Dry Blueberry Wine reminded us vaguely of Italian Chianti—dry and warm in the throat, but with a sweet berry scent in the glass. The Pear Wine was the undisputed favorite—full-bodied with a sweet vanilla odor and a dry, astringent taste. It's a wine we would gladly serve with light seafood dishes or as an aperitif with assorted cheeses. There was also a Dry Apple Wine and a slightly sweet Colonial-style wine called Cyser, made from apples and honey. The After Dinner Peach Wine was intensely sweet. We drank it at home with a slice of warm fruit pie, added it to a fruit compote, and poured a few tablespoons over fresh peach slices and a scoop of vanilla ice cream. But we found it to be too syrupy to drink on its own.

Experimenting is what a place like Nashoba is all about. As far as we're concerned, creating new wines from traditional New England fruits has a promising future. Let go of your preconceived notions about fruit wine; it's well worth the effort.

Boston

■ If you love the tang of Italian salami or the buttery texture of prosciutto ham, then head for this butcher

Angelo DeLuca behind a case of his wares.

shop in Boston's North End. Enter, and you're in Italian cold-cut heaven. Hundreds of sausages, hams, and cheeses hang from meat hooks on the ceiling and along the walls. There is *soprasata,* an all-pork salami that has a surprisingly mellow flavor even though it's made with whole black peppercorns. You'll also find sweet and hot pork sausage (dried and cured in olive oil as well as fresh), spicy pork liver sausage, and *cotechini*—a thin dried pork sausage. The butchers at Angelo DeLuca told us that many Italian cooks like to add *cotechini* to their homemade minestrone.

All the sausages and the prosciutto are made and cured on the premises. The owner says the only preservative he uses is salt. No chemicals are added.

Easter is the busiest time of year at Angelo DeLuca, as it is for most of the butcher shops in the North End. Many Italian families order whole baby lambs for their holiday feasts, and so a few weeks before Easter the owner of the market visits sheep farms in Maine and New Hampshire to buy the best of their spring litters.

Angelo DeLuca also sells fresh rabbit raised in Vermont, Maine, and New Hampshire as well as fresh pheasant and baby goat. Whole suckling pigs may be ordered in advance. If you make your own sausage, they will sell you all the ingredients you need, including natural sausage casing.

Many of the items here are seasonal. For example, fresh pork sausage is made only during the winter. If at all possible call ahead to make sure they have the kind of meat you want.

A. PARZIALE AND SONS BAKERY

80 Prince Street, Boston, 02113; phone 617-523-6368. Hours: Monday–Friday 9 A.M. to 6 P.M., Saturday 9 A.M. to 4 P.M.; closed Sunday. Cash only.

▪ When the bread comes out of the oven each morning at A. Parziale and Sons, it seems as if the whole neighborhood around the bakery comes alive. "Boy, it smells good out here," exclaims a woman to her companion as they walk down Prince Street, inhaling the warm yeasty odor that filters out into the open air. A moment later a man pushing a young child in a stroller emerges from the bakery's front door. He hands the baby a piece of still-warm bread and then tears off a chunk for himself.

The smell of fresh bread is like a magnet. People make

their way to the bakery, traveling down the narrow streets of the North End, perhaps stopping to greet a neighbor who already has a loaf tucked under his or her arm, and then entering the warm confines of this shop to secure their own daily ration.

The breads from A. Parziale and Sons Bakery have a satisfying taste and texture. The French-style loaf is crisp on the outside and has a flavorful soft center. The whole wheat Italian bread is light, with a slightly chewy dark brown crust. We heartily recommend a visit both for their fine breads and for the chance to experience this neighborhood bakery.

CHENG-KWONG SEAFOOD MARKET
73–79 Essex Street, Boston, 02111; phone 617-423-3749. Hours: seven days a week 9 A.M. to 8 P.M. Cash only.

■ Although this Chinese grocery sells a little bit of everything, we especially like to shop here for vegetables. For some reason the produce at Cheng-Kwong always looks fresher and healthier than at many of the other nearby markets. Try the Chinese long beans (8-inch-long string beans that are excellent stir-fried; see recipe below), the small purple eggplants, fresh coriander and mint, several types of chile peppers, and very moist, creamy tofu.

CHUNG WAH HONG COMPANY
51–55 Beach Street, Boston, 02111; phone 617-426-3619 or 426-3630. Hours: seven days a week 9 A.M. to 8 P.M. Cash only.

■ A walk through Boston's Chinatown leaves the distinct impression that the residents of this neighborhood are preoccupied with food. Restaurants and food shops occupy most of the storefronts, and on the side streets the sweet smell of freshly baked Chinese pastries fills the air.

There are several excellent stores here where you can buy authentic Chinese ingredients. One of our favorites is Chung Wah Hong, where almost no one speaks English. So unless you speak Chinese, you're pretty much on your own in trying to decide among the ten types of homemade noodles—including lo mein (a narrow noodle that's good in soup and stir-fried with ginger, garlic, and scallions), broad egg noodles, won ton wrappers for mak-

Shopping at Chung Wah Hong.

Stir-Fried Chinese String Beans with Chinese Sausage

½ tablespoon safflower or vegetable oil
1 tablespoon minced garlic
1 tablespoon minced fresh ginger
2 Chinese sausages, or ¾ pound hot Italian sausage, cut into 1-inch pieces
1 pound Chinese string beans, washed and trimmed
2 tablespoons dark Chinese soy sauce
2 tablespoons water
Oyster sauce

Heat a wok or large skillet over high heat. Add the oil by pouring it down the sides of the pan, and heat until almost smoking. Add ½ tablespoon of the garlic and ½ tablespoon of the ginger and cook about 5 seconds, or until they begin to turn a light golden brown. Add the sausage and cook 5 minutes, stirring constantly. Remove the sausage with a slotted spoon and set aside. Add the beans and cook about 2 minutes, stirring constantly until crisp. Add the remaining ½ tablespoon of garlic and ginger and the sausage. Pour in the soy sauce and water and cook 1 minute.

Arrange the beans and sauce on a serving platter, and drizzle lightly with oyster sauce. Serve immediately with a small bowl of oyster sauce on the side. Serves 4.

DAIRY FRESH CANDIES
57 Salem Street, Boston 02113; phone 617-742-2639. Hours: Monday–Thursday 8 A.M. to 5:30 P.M., Friday and Saturday 7 A.M. to 7 P.M.; closed Sunday. MasterCard, Visa, and personal checks accepted.

ing your own Chinese dumplings, and thin rice noodles. In addition you'll find an array of exotic fresh Chinese vegetables (bok choy cabbage, winter melon, fresh water chestnuts, lotus root, and more) and dozens of Chinese sauces: soy, hoisin, oyster, black bean, and spicy chile sauces to name a few.

The fish counter is very popular here; don't be put off if there's a line of women three deep, haggling for the same live carp. The fish is fresh and reasonably priced. Meat here includes everything from pork loin and fresh chicken to pig entrails and piles of chicken feet. Best of all are the lacquered-looking roast ducks, roast pork, barbecued pig, and salted chickens. And before you leave be sure to look past the checkout counter at the array of Chinese medicinal herbs, teas, and potions. There's everything from ginseng root to a very special tonic wine made from dried deer penis.

■ The addictive scent of chocolate and homemade fudge slaps you across the face the minute you walk through the door. And if that isn't enough, you'll find every square inch of this small shop packed with Italian cakes and candies, amaretto biscuits, nut pies, roasted nuts, and large (very reasonably priced) 5-pound bags of pistachio nuts. Dairy Fresh claims to have "the largest variety of fresh candy and nuts in New England." The point is, you can get lost in this place. We'll take a little of each.

Steamed Lettuce with Chinese Oyster Sauce

One of the wonderful things about bottled Chinese sauces is that they add an exotic new taste to fresh native New England vegetables, fish, meat, and poultry. This recipe is a new way to cook lettuce—whether it's in the summer when your garden yields an overabundance of leafy vegetables or during the winter when crispy iceberg and romaine seem to be the only fresh greens at the supermarket that look even halfway appealing. This recipe was inspired by our good friend, chef Ken Hom.

This recipe also works well with Swiss chard, snow peas, broccoli, string beans, or any other green vegetable. Adjust steaming time according to the thickness of the vegetable.

1/4 cup Chinese oyster sauce
1 head iceberg or romaine lettuce
1 teaspoon Oriental sesame oil

Heat the oyster sauce in a small saucepan over low heat until warm.

Core and separate the lettuce leaves, and place them in a vegetable steamer, metal colander, or bamboo steaming tray. Place the steamer in a pot containing about an inch of boiling water (make sure the vegetables don't touch the water), cover, and steam for about 1 minute, or until the leaves are soft.

Arrange the lettuce leaves on a serving plate and pour the warm oyster sauce over them. Drizzle with the sesame oil. Serves 2 to 4.

GIUFFRE FISH MARKET

Corner of Cross and Salem streets, Boston, 02113; phone 617-523-8541. Hours: Tuesday–Thursday 8 A.M. to 5:30 P.M., Friday 7:30 A.M. to 6 P.M., Saturday 7 A.M. to 5 P.M.; closed Sunday and Monday. Personal checks accepted.

HING SHING PASTRY

67 Beach Street, Boston, 02111; phone 617-451-1162. Hours: seven days a week 8 A.M. to 7 P.M. Cash only.

■ This colorful North End fish market carries a wide variety of seafood—a bit more than your ordinary shop. You'll find gorgeous-looking swordfish, lobsters, clams, mussels, crab, sole, haddock, cod, and more unusual items like periwinkles and fresh eel. Giuffre Fish Market is located right near the entrance to the Calahan Tunnel leading to Logan Airport, which makes it an ideal place to pick up a few lobsters before heading out of town. The prices are a lot more reasonable than at the "Lobster to Go" joints at the airport.

■ Chinese cuisine generally doesn't put much emphasis on dessert, so you wouldn't expect much from a Chinese bakery. However, the cookies, cakes, pies, and dumplings made at Hing Shing are very good. Trays of steaming-hot buns, cakes, and cookies are brought from the back room every few hours throughout the day. In the late afternoon, groups of children line up after school for bags of still-warm almond and walnut cookies and light cone-shaped sponge cakes. The black bean donuts are particularly good. We also recommend the sweet rice steamed in bamboo leaves, rich egg tarts, flaky pork buns, and the super-dense honey-drenched Chinese nut pies.

I & A BAKERY

221 Hanover Street,
Boston, 02113; phone
617-227-9618. Hours:
Monday–Saturday
7 A.M. to 7 P.M., Sunday
7 A.M. to 1 P.M. Cash only.

Fresh food and fair prices at Boston's Haymarket.

L'ESPALIERS GREAT FOOD STORE

443A Boylston Street,
Boston, 02116; phone
617-536-6543. Hours:
Monday–Saturday
8 A.M. to 8 P.M.; closed
Sunday. MasterCard, Visa,
and American Express
accepted. Catering and
mail order available.

MODERN PASTRY SHOP

257 Hanover Street,
Boston, 02113; phone
617-523-3783. Hours:
Sunday–Thursday
8 A.M. to 9 P.M., Friday and
Saturday 8 A.M. to
10 P.M. Cash only.

■ Submarine sandwiches on loaves of crisp Italian bread are the big attraction here. Our favorite combination is prosciutto ham and provolone cheese smothered with hot peppers, olive oil, and vinegar. On weekends during the winter they offer a luscious treat called *porchetta*, a whole roasted pig that has been completely boned and then stuffed with its own meat along with garlic and herbs. The meat, which may be eaten cold or warm, is tender and garlicky. The skin is delightfully crispy.

They also carry Italian grocery items including pasta, cheeses, oils, and vinegars.

■ Walk down the stairs into this little shop and be tempted. When we're at L'Espaliers we feel like kids in a candy store. Everything cries out to be tasted: roast leg of lamb stuffed with goat cheese and served with a homemade mango chutney; chunky venison pâté; fried chicken in a crème fraîche, thyme, and sage batter; wild mushroom tartlets . . . Need we go on?

This is one of Boston's most exclusive gourmet food shops, affiliated with L'Espalier restaurant. We can't really afford to make a habit of visiting, but everything we've ever tasted here has been well worth the rather extravagant price. Did we mention the grilled smoked Maine shrimp in a garlic and chile marinade?

■ In Boston's North End, along Hanover Street, there are dozens of little Italian cafes and bakeries serving cannolis, cookies, biscuits, and other sweets. We've visited almost all of them and done our fair share of sampling, and without doubt we've found the cannolis at Modern Pastry to be unsurpassed. They come with a choice of cheese, chocolate, or custard filling. The ricotta cheese filling, our favorite, is soft, creamy, and slightly tangy—the perfect balance to the slightly sweet, very flaky pastry shell. A generous sprinkling of powdered sugar tops the whole thing off. The other specialty here is homemade marzi-

J. PACE AND SON

42 Cross Street, Boston, 02113; phone 617-227-9673. Hours: seven days a week 8 A.M. to 7 P.M. MasterCard and Visa accepted. Mail order available.

POLCARI'S COFFEE

105 Salem Street, Boston, 02113; phone 617-227-0786. Hours: Monday–Saturday 8 A.M. to 6 P.M.; closed Sunday. Cash only. Mail order available.

PURITY CHEESE COMPANY

55–57 Endicott Street, Boston, 02113; phone 617-227-5060. Hours: Tuesday–Saturday 8 A.M. to 5 P.M.; Closed Sunday and Monday. Cash only.

Boston's Haymarket going strong.

pan (almond paste), shaped into very authentic-looking fruits. You may also order very rich Sicilian-style birthday cakes.

■ This supermarket carries all the ingredients you need to cook authentic Italian meals: fennel- and garlic-flavored sausages, dried Italian sausages and prosciutto, thick crusty loaves of Italian bread, imported pasta, and giant vats filled with half a dozen types of Italian and Greek olives. Gallon tins of virgin and extra virgin olive oil go for very reasonable prices. There's also a take-out counter in the back of the shop where you can grab a sub, a bowl of pasta, or a hot calzone.

■ Polcari's has been a North End institution since 1932, selling freshly roasted coffee beans, teas, herbs, and spices. The oversized wooden bins here are filled with dried herbs, nuts, and spices from around the world. Every square inch is packed with merchandise—Italian coffee makers, Turkish dates, California pistachios, ceramic pasta bowls, huge bunches of dried oregano from Greece.

Polcari's doesn't roast their own coffee beans, but the variety and quality of the coffee they sell is consistently good. You'll also find a large assortment of herbal and decaffeinated teas. But perhaps the best thing about Polcari's is the smell—the intense odor of coffee mingled with freshly ground spices like cumin and sage.

■ The difference between fresh mozzarella and the white rubbery brick you find in the supermarket is like the difference between a loaf of homemade bread and air-fluffed Wonder Bread. At Purity Cheese, mozzarella is made by hand. Each kidney-shaped cheese is moist and delicately flavored, with a soft, creamy texture. It's superb sliced and added to salads with fresh basil and olive oil, or melted over pasta, pies, or pizza. The other cheese not to miss here is the ultra-creamy homemade ricotta.

Boston's Haymarket—
The Original New England Market

Every Friday and Saturday throughout most of the year, vendors selling vegetables, fruit, meat, poultry, and fish set up their stands along Boston's Blackstone Street for an open-air market. Haymarket is swirl of bright colors, pungent smells, and raucous sounds. All day long, crowds of shoppers push and squeeze their way through the labyrinth of makeshift wooden stands as vendors call out their singsong sales pitches: "Hey, look at these oranges. Hey, twelve for a dollar. Hey, hey."

There has been a market on or near this site since the 1630s. That makes Haymarket one of the oldest public markets in the country. Originally it was a farmers' market—local farmers would come once a week to sell to both wholesale and retail customers. Over the centuries the market has gone through many changes. Today it is strictly retail and none of the vendors are farmers. Most of the three hundred licensed vendors are Boston residents who depend on the market for all or part of their income. The food they sell comes from all over the country, not just New England.

At Haymarket you can find the best and the worst that Boston has to offer. Because it is so old, the market has a strong sense of tradition. The vending licenses are handed down from father to son in many families. It's also possible to find some real bargains at Haymarket. The produce, in particular, is usually cheap and is always plentiful. But be careful: you can easily end up with a bag of rotten apples if you don't stick up for yourself.

That brings us to the less pleasant side of this market. Haymarket can be an ugly place. Some of the people who operate the stalls are downright hostile. We've often seen vendors, most of whom are Italian, curse their customers and hurl racial slurs at Asian and Hispanic shoppers. As is the case in many of Boston's tightly knit neighborhoods, not everyone is welcome here. But they all come anyway. And the mix of yellow, brown, and white faces along with languages and accents from dozens of nations and neighborhoods makes Haymarket an exciting and vibrant place. It is New England's preeminent urban market.

ROKA'S MARKET

361 Newbury Street, Boston, 02115; phone 617-236-4354. Hours: Monday–Saturday 11 A.M. to 9:30 P.M., Sunday 12 N. to 7 P.M. Cash only.

- This big supermarket and variety store is popular with Boston's Japanese community. The aisles are filled with dozens of types of soy sauce, pickled ginger and vegetables, dried seaweed, Japanese rice, sauces, and teas. You'll find everything here you need to make sushi and sashimi, including a good choice of very fresh fish.

In the front of the shop is a small restaurant counter that serves noodle dishes, sushi, and other traditional Japanese dishes. This place will make you so hungry you'll be tempted to stop for a bite. Don't. Instead head down the street to Genji (327 Newbury Street; phone 617-267-5656). It's one of best (and most skillfully designed) Japanese restaurants in Boston.

SULMONA MEAT MARKET

32A Parmenter Street, Boston, 02113; phone 617-742-2791. Hours: Tuesday–Thursday 8 A.M. to 6 P.M., Friday 8 A.M. to 8 P.M., Saturday 6 A.M. to 6:30 P.M.; closed Sunday and Monday. Cash only.

TRIO'S RAVIOLI COMPANY

222 Hanover Street, Boston, 02113; phone 617-523-9636. Hours: Monday–Saturday 9 A.M. to 6 P.M., Sunday 9 A.M. to 1 P.M. Personal checks accepted.

Also sold in food stores around the country.

KUPEL'S BAKE AND BAGEL

421 Harvard Street, Brookline, 02146; phone 617-566-9528. Hours: seven days a week 6 A.M. to 12 M., Saturdays until 2 A.M. Cash only.

BREAD & CIRCUS WHOLEFOOD SUPERMARKETS

115 Prospect Street, Cambridge, 02139; phone

■ You have to know what you want and ask for it at this tiny, spotlessly clean North End butcher shop. Almost nothing is on display, but the butchers are helpful and the meat is of exceptional quality, whether it's breast of veal, a crown roast of pork, or their superb dried liver sausage.

■ We have to admit that we never were wild about ravioli. Maybe it's because we were served too many of those rubbery little squares as children. Then we tasted Trio's ravioli—large, plump, tender pockets of pasta stuffed with generous portions of ground meat or ricotta cheese and spinach—and our attitude changed. Dining on Trio's spinach-and-cheese ravioli topped with their own thick garlic-laced tomato sauce is ecstasy. It doesn't get this good in most Italian restaurants.

Trio's has been a North End institution for over thirty years. All the pasta is made by hand. In addition to three types of ravioli, there are tortellini (small ring-shaped pasta stuffed with gorgonzola cheese, porcini mushrooms, or a savory pumpkin mixture), manicotti, lasagne, and herb-, vegetable-, and chocolate-flavored fettuccine cut to order (serve chocolate fettuccine for dessert mixed with heavy cream, fresh fruit, and a sprinkling of sugar). You can mix and match the pasta with any of Trio's innovative sauces: Spinach-Walnut, Ginger-Vermouth, Anchovy–Pine Nut, Gorgonzola Cheese, Basic Tomato, and Tomato-Lemon-Scallop.

Brookline

■ There's a lot of debate in Boston about who makes the best bagels. A few years ago, dozens of Kupel's loyal customers signed a petition to protest a newspaper article that claimed the Purity Supreme supermarket down the street made a better bagel. We haven't tasted Purity's bagels, but we can certainly vouch for Kupel's. They're made fresh every few hours and have just the right balance of glazed crust and soft, doughy inside. The poppy seed and Russian raisin are particularly good, but then again so are the egg, sourdough, honey whole wheat, sissle (caraway) rye, black and white, and garlic. You'll also find an assortment of flavored cream cheeses, homemade rye bread, bialys, challah, and other Eastern European pastries.

Cambridge

■ If your local grocery store got rid of all the junk food, processed cheese and bread, chemical-enhanced meat and poultry, and sprayed and waxed fruits and vegetables, chances are there wouldn't be much left on the shelves.

617-492-0070. Hours: Monday–Friday 9 A.M. to 9 P.M., Saturday 8 A.M. to 9 P.M., Sunday 12 N. to 8 P.M. Personal checks accepted. Demonstrations and classes given; call for information.

Also at 392 Harvard Street, Brookline, 02146; 278 Washington Street, Wellesley Hills, 02181; Mountain Farms Mall, Russell Street (Route 9), Hadley, 01035; and Beacon and Walnut streets, Newton Four Corners, 02158.

Now picture a supermarket that sells meat and poultry raised without hormones and steroids, farm-grown fruits and vegetables, fresh pasta and bread made from organic flour, pastries made without white sugar, even dog food produced without additives and fillers, and you'll start to get an idea of what Bread & Circus Wholefood Supermarkets are all about.

Owners Anthony and Susan Harnett started Bread & Circus in 1976 in Brookline, Massachusetts. Both had studied natural foods in Ireland, and when they came to the U.S. they spent time working with Michio Kushi at his Cambridge-based health food store, Erewhon (see page 101). When the Harnetts opened their first shop, it was considered an alternative health food market—a place for people who would eat only tofu, organic vegetables, and dense grain-filled breads. Times have changed. The Harnetts now own five Bread & Circus stores, and their customers are no longer the stereotypical health food fanatics. "There's the yuppie housewife, the Harvard medical student, the lawyer, the caterer, the art student—mainstream people from all over New England," explains Chris Kilham, vice-president of advertising and marketing. "They are people who are willing to pay a bit more for their food because they are committed to eating well."

Aah, yes. A good point. Eat healthy, pay healthy prices. None of this food is cheap. But take a walk around a Bread & Circus store and you'll realize it's worth the extra money.

These supermarkets look a lot friendlier than your typical Shop 'N Save. The music is mellow. The lighting isn t harsh. The sales staff is willing to talk to you about the merchandise; they smile.

The produce section is your first stop. Whatever negative ideas you may have about the look and taste of organic fruit and vegetables will be quickly dispelled. There

The vast display of fresh produce at Bread & Circus.

Fresh bluefish for sale at Boston's Haymarket.

CHAPIN'S FISH AND MEAT MARKET

1728 Massachusetts Avenue, Cambridge, 02138; phone 617-547-3474. Hours: Monday–Friday 9 A.M. to 7:30 P.M., Saturday 9 A.M. to 6:30 P.M., closed Sunday. MasterCard and Visa accepted.

THE COFFEE CONNECTION

36 JFK Street in the Garage, Harvard Square, Cambridge, 02138; phone 617-492-4881. Mail-order address: 342 Western Avenue, Brighton, 02135; phone 617-254-1459.

are piles of oranges and grapefruits from an organic farm in California, a dozen varieties of local and imported melons, eight varieties of apples from a Massachusetts farm, healthy bunches of fresh herbs from Vermont, and an abundant display of lettuce, kale, broccoli, and carrots picked fresh from Massachusetts' lush Pioneer Valley region. Not all the produce is organic, but everything that is, is clearly marked. (Bread & Circus claims to have the largest organic produce section of any supermarket on the East Coast.) During the summer and fall over 50 percent of the fruits and vegetables come from New England farms.

In the dairy case you'll find unhomogenized cow's and goat's milk, along with butter and yogurt from New England dairies and a large selection of New England cheeses. The butcher custom-cuts organically raised beef from Colorado. There are thirteen varieties of tofu, a good selection of fresh seafood, a deli section, a bakery, freshly made pasta, a good selection of wine and beer, and coffee beans and herbal teas from around the world. You can even buy toilet paper and paper towels—made without any dyes or colors, of course.

■ This small market carries a lot of different foods, but their specialties are high-quality meat and fish. The meat counter offers the kind of display that would make anyone contemplating vegetarianism put off their vows for another day. There's filet mignon and thick-cut lamb chops, organically raised chicken and chemical-free sausage. Chapin's will also special-order more exotic meats: quail, partridge, boar. The deli counter offers prosciutto, smoked Vermont ham, several varieties of Italian salami, pâtés, and a wide variety of cheeses.

The fish assortment changes daily, as everything is brought in fresh each morning from the Boston Fish Pier: salmon, swordfish, tuna (great for making sushi or sashimi), shrimp, clams, and squid are standard offerings.

Some people think this place looks too chic and slick to be a neighborhood grocery store, but that's how the owners of Chapin's like to refer to their market. You'll find everything from Cape Cod potato chips, crackers, condiments, and canned soups to imported Italian pasta and rice, herring, and freshly baked cookies and bread. A fragrant assortment of fresh flowers is displayed in the window.

■ There are dozens of cafes and coffee houses around Cambridge and Boston where you can sit and enjoy a really good cup of coffee. After all, this is student-land, where all-nighters and last-minute cram sessions are an integral part of everyday life. Whenever we're in Cambridge and need a little buzz we head over to The Coffee Connection. The coffee here is especially good.

Store hours: Monday–Wednesday 9 A.M. to 7 P.M., Thursday and Friday 9 A.M. to 9 P.M., Saturday 10 A.M. to 9 P.M., Sunday 10 A.M. to 5 P.M. MasterCard, Visa, American Express, and personal checks accepted. Mail order available.

Also at Copley Place, Boston, 02116; Quincy Market, Boston, 02109; 97 Charles Street, Boston, 02114; 61 Union Street, Newton Center, 02159; and 1720 Massachusetts Avenue, Lexington, 02173.

EREWHON NATURAL FOOD GROCERY

1731 Massachusetts Avenue, Cambridge, 02138; phone 617-492-2599. Hours: seven days a week 9 A.M. to 8:30 P.M. Visa and personal checks accepted.

Also at 342 Newbury Street, Boston, 02115, and at 236 Washington Street, Brookline Village, 02146.

LE JARDIN

248 Huron Avenue, Cambridge, 02138; phone 617-492-4534. Hours:

The people at The Coffee Connection are experts at coffee roasting. All the coffee is roasted in small batches and never kept on the shelf for more than three or four days. Each bin of beans is labeled with the "roast date" so you know you are buying really fresh coffee.

If you visit the Cambridge shop, you can sit in the cafe or restaurant and taste up to thirty different coffees from around the world. They also have a good selection of black, green, scented, flavored, and herbal teas from around the world. All the coffees, teas, and coffee-making equipment can be ordered through the mail.

▪ When Michio and Aveline Kushi came to this country from Japan in the early 1960s, they found it hard to find good, wholesome food. The couple began stocking whole grains, seaweed, and other natural foods in the basement of their home in Cambridge. Then in 1966 they opened a small natural-foods grocery store called Erewhon. (The name is "nowhere" spelled backwards—with a few letters transposed.) Michio Kushi is known as the father of the macrobiotic food movement in this country. And since it opened, his store has gained a reputation as one of the best places in the region—if not the country—to buy and become educated about natural foods.

Today there are three abundantly stocked Erewhon stores in the Boston area. Although Kushi no longer owns the chain, Erewhon has maintained his high standards, basic philosophy, and strong sense of "good food."

This is the place to come when you're looking for whole grain breads and cereals, whole wheat pasta, peanut and other nut butters, granola, and organically grown rice. There's unhomogenized milk and nonmedicated eggs from a local farm; Vermont butter, yogurt, and cheese; tofu from Connecticut; and Massachusetts honey, maple syrup, and apple cider. Erewhon makes a point of carrying as much regionally produced food as possible—as long as it's organic. From June through late November a good deal of their produce comes from an organic farmers' collective in western Massachusetts and Vermont. The quality of the produce here is good, but not great. It has that not-quite-prime-time look to it.

In essence, Erewhon is a larger-than-average, better-than-average health food store. You can shop here and feel good about what you eat. You can rest assured that the food has not been pumped up or sprayed with chemicals. How excited you'll be about the experience is up to you.

▪ The sidewalk display of brightly colored geraniums and healthy green herb plants lures you inside. Once you've entered, the overwhelming smell and sight of fresh-cut flowers and a sumptuous array of fresh vegetables make

Monday–Friday
9:30 A.M. to 7 P.M.,
Saturday 9:30 A.M. to
6 P.M.; closed Sunday.
Personal checks
accepted. Fruit and flower
baskets available.

**MAYFLOWER
POULTRY COMPANY**
621 Cambridge Street,
East Cambridge, 02141;
phone 617-547-9191.
Hours: Monday–Thursday,
Saturday, and Sunday
7 A.M. to 4:30 P.M., Friday
7 A.M. to 6 P.M. Cash only.

**NEW DEAL FISH
MARKET**
622 Cambridge Street,
Cambridge, 02141; phone
617-876-8227. Hours:
Tuesday–Saturday
10 A.M. to 7 P.M.; closed
Sunday and Monday.
Cash only.

you want to linger. Le Jardin is a treat for the senses.

In the middle of the store is a display of cut flowers from around the world—a collage of colors and shapes that are both alluring and in some cases a little frightening. (A brown, furry protea from Hawaii looked as though it might bite us if we came too close.) Around this centerpiece are the edibles—bunches of fresh herbs, bright green heads of lettuce, kumquats, passion fruit, guavas, many kinds of fresh mushrooms, asparagus, eggplants, and more. Le Jardin carries an impressive variety of fresh produce.

In addition to fruit, vegetables, herbs, and flowers, Le Jardin sells unhomogenized milk and other dairy products. They also offer fresh game birds, which must be ordered a week in advance. Prices here aren't cheap, but they're not outrageously expensive either.

■ If it's chicken you want, this is the place to get it. They have every conceivable kind of chicken—boilers, capons, stewing fowl, chicken wings, cutlets, backs, necks, breasts, and so on. All the birds are freshly killed on the premises. If you're a real stickler for freshness, you can even pick out the bird you want and have it killed right on the spot (that's a little more expensive). They also sell fresh turkey, rabbit, and Cornish hens. Fresh poussin may be ordered in advance.

■ At the New Deal Fish Market, owner Sal Fantasia does his best to make sure that every customer is satisfied. If someone wants their fish fileted, it's done right on the spot. And if the customer is looking for something a bit unusual, chances are Fantasia not only carries it, but can tell you what it's called in about six different languages. This is one of New England's most unusual fish markets.

"My uncle opened this market during the Depression," Fantasia told us. "He named it in honor of Franklin D. Roosevelt's New Deal." In those days (the early 1930s), the surrounding neighborhood was mostly Italian, and so was the market's clientele. Today the market attracts people of many different ethnic backgrounds who come for the quality and the variety of seafood they offer.

"This is a flying fish," says Fantasia, holding the small fish by one of its "wings." "The Barbadians like it," he says. There is also moray eel, *rouget* (red mullet, a highly prized and very expensive fish from the Mediterranean), octopus, sea urchins, red snapper, squid, and many other varieties. In all the New Deal Fish Market carries about fifty kinds of fish, although generally not all at the same time.

They also sell fine-quality canned sardines and anchovies, imported pasta, Portuguese bread, and other grocery items.

Cranberry-Orange-Ginger Sauce

Serve this with roast turkey, chicken, or goose—or pour it over vanilla ice cream, pound cake, or plain cheesecake.

1 1/2 cups sugar
2 cups water
4 cups fresh cranberries
1/3 cup orange juice, preferably fresh
1 1/2 teaspoons grated orange peel

2 1/2 tablespoons thin julienne strips of fresh ginger
1 teaspoon vanilla extract
2 ounces slivered almonds

Mix the sugar and water in a large saucepan and bring to a boil. Boil for about 5 to 8 minutes, until slightly thickened and syrupy. Add the cranberries and simmer for 5 minutes, or until they begin to pop. Add the orange juice, orange peel, ginger, and vanilla extract, and simmer an additional minute. Remove from the heat and let cool. Add the almonds and refrigerate until cold. The sauce will keep for about 10 days.

ROSIE'S BAKERY

243 Hampshire Street, Inman Square, Cambridge, 02139; phone 617-491-9488. Hours: Monday–Wednesday 7:30 A.M. to 11 P.M., Thursday and Friday 7:30 A.M. to 12 M., Saturday and Sunday 8:30 A.M. to 12 M. Personal checks accepted. Special birthday and wedding cake orders accepted.

Also at 9 Boylston Street, Chestnut Hill Shopping Center, Chestnut Hill, 02167.

■ We were walking around Inman Square in Cambridge when we saw a young woman wearing a rather provocative T-shirt: "I had a chocolate orgasm at Rosie's Bakery." Now, a message like that demands further investigation. So we marched right over to Rosie's and asked about this "chocolate orgasm."

"Oh, that's it right there," said the woman behind the counter, pointing to a plate of dark chocolate brownies topped with glistening chocolate fudge icing. We ordered one (it seemed like the kind of thing you should share), took a bite, and decided that this product had not been falsely advertised. Rosie's Chocolate Orgasm is one of the richest, butteriest, purest chocolate tastes around. The brownie is so rich it should be called fudge. The texture can only be described as sensual; it practically melts in your mouth.

Fortunately we hadn't eaten in a few hours, so we decided to try some ruguluh—a cream-cheese dough filled with raisins, cinnamon, and apricot preserves. Then we sampled a large chocolate chip cookie and decided that this bakery was really good. As luck had it, we were going to a dinner party that evening and had been asked to bring dessert. We surveyed the pastry case and decided on the Snow Queen Cake, a vanilla butter cake layered with raspberry preserves and buttercream and decorated with fresh flowers. It, too, was superb.

Judy Rosenberg, who started Rosie's, trained as an artist. Her pastry work shows an artist's touch: all the cakes and pies are attractively decorated with fresh flowers, fruit, and delicate sugar garnishes. Rosie's has won numerous awards and has a dedicated clientele.

SAVENOR'S MARKET AND SUPPLY COMPANY

92 Kirkland Street, Cambridge, 02138; phone 617-547-1765. Hours: Monday–Saturday 8 A.M. to 8:30 P.M., Sunday 9 A.M. to 6 P.M. MasterCard, Visa, and personal checks accepted.

When we arrived at our dinner party and announced that the cake was from Rosie's, several people starting clapping.

■ Got a hankering for bear stew or llama en brochette? Then hop on over to Savenor's because they've got what you're looking for. The selection of exotic meats here is truly astounding: alligator tails, yak loins, hare fores, elk ribs, venison saddle, turtle, reindeer, and that's just a partial list.

"Our store is unique, and it's because of the environment here in Cambridge," said owner Jack Savenor. "People from all over the world live in this city. If you're from Sweden or Norway, for example, you think nothing of eating elk or reindeer. That's what you eat at home."

Savenor has found a niche making his customers feel at home, even those with more pedestrian tastes. The store offers a wide selection of meats that most of us are more familiar with—everything from well-marbled steaks, to organically raised lamb, to fresh chickens and turkeys.

Savenor, who recently handed the business over to his two sons, Alan and Ron, is probably best known as Julia Child's butcher. He credits Child with helping to transform his store from a typical family-run grocery to a place where cooks come not just to buy good meat but to get advice on how to prepare it as well. "Jack, I'm having a dinner party for four tonight. How big a roast do I need?" asks a customer as she fiddles with a string of pearls around her neck. Savenor, a raconteur as well as a butcher, holds up a boneless roast neatly tied with butcher's twine. "This," he says, "is what we call a honeymoon roast. Two pieces of meat tied together. It should be plenty."

Savenor's Market also sells fresh fish, fresh produce, and other grocery items. But compared to the meat and poultry, these offerings are fairly prosaic. The meat department is where it's happening.

Charlemont

CHARLEMONT APIARIES

Route 2, Mohawk Trail, Charlemont, 01339; phone 413-339-5320. Hours: irregular, call ahead. Personal checks accepted. Mail order available. Beekeeping classes available; call or write for information.

■ Dick and Joan Bonney started Charlemont Apiaries in 1978. But Dick's interest in bees began much earlier; he kept bees as a hobby for many years. His honey ("It's not really mine, it's the bees'," he said with a chuckle) is a light golden color with a sweet, flowery taste that goes down easily. We poured it over cereal and granola, baked with it, and had a spoonful "neat" when we had a sore throat. The Bonneys sell wildflower honey, creamed honey, and crystallized honey, as well as bars of beeswax and beeswax candles. If you're interested in starting your own apiary, Dick Bonney can give you lots of valuable advice; he'll also sell you hives to get you started.

Dick Bonney working with his bees at Charlemont Apiaries.

PINE HILL ORCHARDS

Greenfield Road, Colrain, 01340; phone 413-624-3325. Hours: Monday–Thursday and Saturday 7 A.M. to 5 P.M., Friday and Sunday 7 A.M. to 8 P.M. Personal checks accepted. Mail order available. Pick-your-own available.

Colrain

■ Ever notice that when you have a lot of something, you don't appreciate it nearly as much as you do once it's gone? We first tasted Pine Hill Orchards' Colrain Mountain Cider in late October, which is the peak season for apple cider throughout much of New England. We liked its sweet, fresh flavor and thick, syrupy consistency so much that we brought home a couple of half gallons and stuck them in our freezer. One cold January night we had a craving for a glass of cider. We defrosted one of the Colrain jugs, took a sip, and were immediately transported back to the height of autumn. This crisp liquid tasted like the best cider in the world; we could practically smell the apples being crushed. Did it really taste that good in October?

David Shearer, owner of Pine Hill Orchards, knows apples. He grows some twenty-five varieties on his 150-acre farm. "The altitude and climate in Colrain," explains Shearer, "are ideal for growing apples—particularly McIntosh. You go south into Connecticut, you just won't find the same quality, color, and taste. The range of hills in Colrain is the best in the country."

While some apple farmers might argue with Shearer's assertion, few would be disappointed by his cider. (This is the cider Judith and Terry Maloney use to make their sparkling alcoholic beverage called West County Cider; see page 106). Visitors are invited to pick their own apples and then watch a slide show and video explaining the cider-making process. It's all a bit touristy for our taste, but there is enough quality produce at Pine Hill Orchards to warrant a trip.

An old barn has been turned into a produce stand/gift shop/restaurant featuring homemade fruit pies, apple dumplings, donuts, and cold and hot cider. There's a large selection of New England–made foods, everything

WEST COUNTY CIDER

Catamount Hill Winery (Box 123), Catamount Hill, Colrain, 01340; phone 413-624-3481. Call ahead for hours and directions. Personal checks accepted.

Sold at liquor stores and specialty food stores in western Massachusetts and the Boston area.

from locally grown fruit and vegetables to cheese and smoked meats. Shearer also sells beer- and wine-making equipment. He plans to start making his own fruit wines in the near future. And if Colrain Mountain Wine is anything like Shearer's cider, then we're all in for a nice surprise.

■ This picturesque spot in the foothills of the Berkshires is the home of West County Cider, an ambitious venture by two amateur winemakers from California to produce European-style hard cider using Massachusetts apples. We are happy to report that the efforts of Judith and Terry Maloney are a smashing success. West County Cider is a slightly effervescent, fairly dry alcoholic beverage with a beautiful amber color and a delicious fruity bouquet. It is a straightforward, refreshing drink that is superb by itself or as an accompaniment to food.

The area around Colrain has long been known for producing superior apples. The Maloneys blend juice from four of the most popular local varieties to make their cider—Northern Spy, McIntosh, Delicious, and Baldwin apples. The cider is then aged in steel tanks for about three weeks before being bottled. West County Cider has an alcoholic content of between 5 and 7 percent.

The Maloneys also make Farm Cider, which is available only in Colrain and surrounding towns. But it's worth making the trip to pick up a few bottles of this stuff, because it is out of this world. Farm Cider is a bit more bubbly than the West County Cider, a bit drier, and the flavor of the fruit is a little more recognizable. One of our friends compares it to a good, dry Champagne. We could drink this cider all day long. Unfortunately Farm Cider doesn't keep, so don't buy a case with the idea of saving a few bottles for the future. It's meant to be imbibed right away.

The other notable product from West County Cider is Old Mill Cider Vinegar. This apple cider vinegar, plain or flavored with fresh tarragon or garlic, has an extremely mellow flavor that reminds us of honey. It is superb in salad dressings.

BURGNER FARM

Corner of William Street and Dalton Division Road, Dalton, 01226; phone 413-445-4704. Hours: seven days a week 9 A.M. to 6 P.M. Personal checks accepted.

Dalton

■ Frozen turkey pies and turkey dinners are the specialty here. Fresh turkeys are available during the holidays. The turkeys are sold frozen the rest of the year. Burgner's also sells fresh fruit and vegetables, cider, eggs, and cheese. At their deli counter they feature turkey sandwiches and (guess what) turkey soup.

They also have a store in Lenox, on Lenox Road (413-637-9799).

MASSACHUSETTS 107

Dennis

AQUAGEMS
P.O. Box AC, Dennis, 02638; phone 800-334-1380. MasterCard, Visa, and personal checks accepted. Mail order only.

■ If you love clams on the half shell but worry that they may be tainted by pollution or red tide, Aquagems are the clams for you. These genetically engineered bivalves are raised under carefully controlled conditions designed to ensure their purity. The Aquacultural Research Corporation spent twenty-five years developing the process for growing Aquagems, which includes cultivating them in indoor tanks for several months, feeding them special food, and finally allowing them to mature in Cape Cod waters known for producing high-quality shellfish, including the famous Wellfleet oysters.

Because it takes a lot of time and technology to grow these clams, they are expensive. The cost is more than a dollar per clam, and the minimum order is four dozen. Aquagems are also on the menu at a few seafood restaurants around the country. Call or write the company for a list of restaurants in your area that serve them. You will know that they are Aquagems if you see a V-shaped design on the shell. That's a trait genetically bred into these clams to distinguish them from their undomesticated cousins.

East Falmouth

NEW ALCHEMY INSTITUTE
237 Hatchville Road, East Falmouth, 02536; phone 617-563-2655. Institute hours: seven days a week, 10 A.M. to 4 P.M. Farm stand hours: June 15 to late September, seven days a week, 10 A.M. to 6 P.M. Personal checks accepted. Guided and self-guided tours available.

■ Welcome to the future! At the New Alchemy Institute on Cape Cod they are growing vegetables and herbs, raising chickens, rabbits, and fish, and designing solar structures with the twenty-first century in mind. The institute is a non-profit organization that develops new methods of organic agriculture and solar and wind power for use by families and small communities. It's a very exciting place to visit, whether you're interested in the research they do or just enjoy browsing through the beautiful gardens and greenhouses. They also have a farm stand where you can buy organic produce and herbs from their experimental gardens.

According to head farmer Stan Ingram, the institute's goal is to "build a livable future." To get a glimpse of what that future might look like, Ingram led us into a large, airy greenhouse where concave Plexiglas panels catch and concentrate the sun's rays. The people at the institute call this structure a "bioshelter," which means that it contains several different living systems that help sustain each other with a minimum of outside help. The Cape Cod Ark, as the greenhouse is formally known, is a separate little world, with gardens, fish ponds, even insects, that interact with one another to grow food and conserve heat.

At one end of the Ark vegetables and herbs are planted in neat earthen beds. There's a concrete pond in the middle where bullfrogs perch on lily pads. Toward the front of the structure sit several round fiberglass tanks filled with water, a layer of green algae growing on the surface. The greenhouse, decorated with lush green plants, is heated solely by the rays of the sun.

Basically here's how the system works: The fiberglass water tanks and the concrete frog pond retain heat, which keeps the greenhouse warm when the sun isn't shining. The tanks are also stocked with fish (an African variety called Tilapia). The fish eat the algae, and in turn their waste provides the algae with nutrients. The nutrient-rich water in the tanks is also used to irrigate and fertilize the plants growing in the greenhouse. The vegetables, herbs, and fish are all harvested for human consumption.

If you visit the New Alchemy Institute, plan to spend a few hours exploring the exhibits and gardens. This place is packed with ideas for home gardeners and people who want to make their homes more energy-efficient. There's a beautiful herb garden, where culinary and medicinal herbs are grown. The organic market garden demonstrates ways to increase crop yields without using chemical fertilizers or sprays. They even have a garden that shows you how to cultivate edible weeds. The institute also offers a wide variety of educational programs and workshops, for both adults and children, on cooking, ecology, agriculture, and solar power.

Falmouth

HARBOR VIEW FISH MARKET

227 Clinton Avenue, Falmouth, 02540; phone 617-548-2614. Summer hours: Monday–Saturday 8 A.M. to 6 P.M., Sunday 10 A.M. to 6 P.M. Winter hours: Wednesday–Saturday 9 A.M. to 5 P.M.; closed Sunday–Tuesday. Cash only.

■ This is one of Cape Cod's premium seafood markets. Although the selection is somewhat limited, the fish here is always very fresh. Among the highlights are fresh swordfish and bluefish from Vineyard Sound. They also sell smoked cod and bluefish, pickled herring, and stuffed quahogs.

This is also a very pretty spot to visit. The market is located on Falmouth Inner Harbor, where you'll see fishing boats and pleasure boats tied up at the dock. Beyond the harbor are Vineyard Sound, Martha's Vineyard, and the Elizabeth Islands.

PEACH TREE CIRCLE FARM

881 Old Palmer Avenue, Falmouth, 02540; phone 617-548-4006 (bakery), 548-2354 (stand), 548-2266 (garden). Hours: Monday–Saturday 8 A.M. to 5 P.M. (8 P.M. in July and August), Sunday 10 A.M. to 4 P.M. Personal checks accepted. Catering available.

■ A visit to Peach Tree Circle Farm might go something like this. First, lunch in their restaurant, which includes a pleasant screened-in patio. The meal could include a salad made from greens grown on the farm and a quiche prepared in the farm bakery. Then after lunch, a stroll through the farm's beautifully designed and maintained vegetable and herb gardens and orchards. Finally, a little shopping. You might take home a pie or a loaf of bread, some bright green asparagus, a bunch of cut herbs, fresh ears of corn, or some juicy peaches. They also sell jellies, jams, oils, vinegars, frozen soups, cut flowers, and plants for putting in your own garden.

Elementary-school students tour the future at the New Alchemy Institute in East Falmouth.

PRISCILLA CANDY SHOP

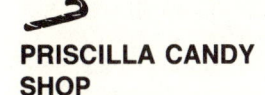

9 Pleasant Street, Gardner, 01440; phone 617-632-7148. Hours: Monday–Friday 9 A.M. to 5:30 P.M., Saturday 9 A.M. to 5 P.M., Sunday 9:30 A.M. to 1 P.M. Personal checks accepted. Mail order available September through June.

Also at 10 Walden Street, Concord.

THE BERKSHIRE COFFEE ROASTING COMPANY

286 Main Street, Great Barrington, 01230; phone 413-528-5505. Hours: Monday–Friday 8 A.M. to 5:30 P.M., Saturday and Sunday 9 A.M. to 5 P.M. Personal checks accepted. Mail order available.

Gardner

■ It was the Coconut Brownie that won us over—a thick square of melt-in-your-mouth milk chocolate, chock-full of grated coconut. We had been skeptical about including Priscilla Candies in this book simply because their list of specialties was almost identical to so many other candy stores around New England. But once we sampled a few morsels—innovative or not—it became clear that this candy was better than most.

Caramel nut chews, peanut butter cups, almond buttercrunch, raisin clusters, and peppermint patties are all made with high-quality chocolate, pure dairy products, and fresh nuts and fruits. Also, around the holidays Priscilla's makes handmade peppermint candy canes. You can visit the store and watch the candy being made; please call ahead.

Great Barrington

■ Coffee beans are freshly roasted in a giant copper and stainless steel roaster nearly every day in the back of this tiny shop. There are about a dozen varieties to choose from, including decaf espresso and decaf cappuccino. You can sit at one of the small cafe tables and enjoy a freshly brewed cup and a light snack, or buy the beans to go. The Berkshire Coffee Roasting Company will also custom-blend your favorite combination of beans; talk to the manager for details.

LOCKE, STOCK & BARREL

Stockbridge Road (P.O. Box 87), Great Barrington, 01230; phone 413-528-0800. Hours: Monday–Saturday 9 A.M. to 6 P.M.; closed Sunday. Personal checks accepted.

TAFT FARMS

21 Division Street, Great Barrington, 01230; phone 413-528-1515. Hours: Monday–Saturday 9 A.M. to 6 P.M., Sunday 10 A.M. to 6 P.M. MasterCard and Visa accepted. Pick-your-own available. Gardening and horticulture classes and workshops offered.

FOSTER'S SUPERMARKET

70 Allen Street, Greenfield, 01301; phone 413-773-9276. Hours: Monday–Saturday 6 A.M. to 9 P.M.; closed Sunday. Cash only.

■ If you love honey, be sure to check out this health food store. Locke, Stock & Barrel has one of the best assortments of honey we've come across anywhere. There is lychee honey from China, chestnut tree blossom honey from Italy, and avocado blossom honey from Mexico, along with several varieties made in New England and New York state.

Locke, Stock & Barrel also sells cheeses, grains, whole grain breads from local bakeries, Oriental ingredients, supplies for Mexican cooking, gourmet food products like sun-dried tomatoes from Italy, and several nonalcoholic sparkling ciders imported from Europe.

■ Dan Tawczynski is a farmer who loves to experiment. He's always trying out some new kind of vegetable or flower, and then gauging how well it grows and whether it's a hit with his customers. When we visited Dan at his 200-acre farm he spoke excitedly about a new variety of potato he had just started cultivating. The Ruby Crescent potato, he explained, is really several little red potatoes that grow together in a half-moon shape. "You've never tasted anything like it," said Dan. "It's so rich, it's like somebody dumped a pound of butter on it."

We can't guarantee that you'll always find these potatoes at Taft Farms, but it's certain that there will be some interesting new vegetable, fruit, or herb to put on your table. "We specialize in varieties that no one else around here carries," Tawczynski explained. That means items like squash blossoms, radicchio, and French *haricots verts*. There is also a big selection of less exotic, but equally attractive, produce: strawberries in late spring; fresh sweet corn, tomatoes, and several varieties of lettuce in the summer; russet potatoes and apple cider throughout most of the year.

Although the vegetables are not grown organically, Taft Farms raises its produce with a minimum of pesticides. The farm has an integrated pest management program: insects are controlled by natural predators instead of chemicals.

Greenfield

■ We would have driven right past this very ordinary-looking supermarket if it hadn't been for August Schumacher, the Massachusetts Commissioner of Agriculture. Schumacher recommended Foster's as a good place to find Pioneer Valley produce. So we parked in the oversized macadam lot, joined dozens of other shoppers, and decided to take a look around. It was a supermarket, all right, with long, rather boring-looking aisles of merchandise. But when we turned the corner into the produce section our eyes lit up. The fruit and vegetables looked terrific, and much of them were from local farms. We also

NEW ENGLAND COUNTRY DAIRY

80 School Street, Greenfield, 01301; phone 413-774-5554.

New England Country Dairy products are sold in supermarkets, health food stores, and gourmet food stores throughout the Northeast.

WESTFIELD FARM

Route 68, Hubbardston, 01452; phone 617-928-5110. Hours: Cheese is available every day from a self-service refrigerator. Mail order available.

Hubbardston cheeses are also sold at gourmet food stores and cheese shops throughout New England.

found a meat counter offering fresh-killed locally raised turkeys, ducks, and geese and a selection of fresh lobster, clams, oysters, and smoked fish that would put many coastal supermarkets to shame.

■ One of the best mass-produced juices we've tasted is Cider Berry from New England Country Dairy. It's made with fresh preservative-free apple cider and berry juice. Both flavors, apple-strawberry and apple-raspberry, have a clean, refreshing taste, and the flavor of the berries really stands out. They also sell plain apple cider under the Cider Berry name, but it's not nearly as good.

If you like yogurt, you might want to try another of their products, East Coast Kefir. This is a cultured milk drink flavored with fruit and sweetened with fruit juice and honey. The taste is similar to buttermilk, and the consistency is thick like a milkshake. A half-pint container of kefir makes a delicious, and very filling, snack. Also try it mixed with granola or other cereal.

Other products made by New England Country Dairy include Lemon Squeeze, premade lemonade sweetened with honey instead of sugar, herbal iced teas, and (around holiday time) eggnog, also made with honey instead of sugar, and containing no coloring or artificial flavoring.

Hubbardston

■ We first tasted Letitia Kilmoyer's Hubbardston Blue at a friend's house. The small, round, surface-ripened cheese with blue mold on the outside was sitting innocuously on a large wooden board, surrounded by several imported cheeses. We took a bite and thought it was a delicious, creamy Roquefort. But it was a complex-tasting cheese; there seemed to be some mystery to it. So we took another bite and discovered the pungent, slightly sour flavor of goat cheese. After a few more bites we realized this was one of the most unusual cheeses we had tasted in a long time. It must be French, we thought. Who else would think of aging pungent goat's-milk cheese in this way? The second pleasant surprise came when we found out it had been made at a small farm near Worcester, Massachusetts.

Letitia and Bob Kilmoyer have been making goat cheese since 1981. When we visited the Kilmoyers on their 20-acre farm, we learned that the key to their success is their willingness to break the rules. "The experts say you can't make cheese the way we do," Letitia explained. "But Bob is a real experimenter. He decided to combine an authentic Roquefort mold with goat's milk, and you can see what happened."

Letitia and Bob are self-taught cheesemakers, which may be one reason why they feel free to try new things. "We had nothing to lose," says Letitia. "Originally

Letitia Kilmoyer of Westfield Farm in Hubbardston, preparing their Hubbardston cheese.

cheesemaking was all about experimenting, but these days everyone is so concerned with consistency that they're scared to try anything new."

The Kilmoyers produce an impressive line of superb cheeses. Capri is a fresh, soft goat cheese that is delicious served on crackers, added to salads (see recipe below), or coated with olive oil and bread crumbs and baked. Herb and Garlic Capri is a variation on the same theme. It's loaded with fresh garlic and dried herbs. Pepper Capri is a creamy goat cheese heavily coated with coarsely cracked black pepper. Westfield Farm's newest creation is Capri Camembert, a very mild, creamy version of the French cheese, aged for at least four weeks.

Fresh goat's and cow's milk is also available, but must be ordered in advance.

Visitors are welcome at Westfield Farm. If they're not too busy, the Kilmoyers will be happy to show you around the farm and the cheesemaking rooms.

Hyannis

CAPE COD POTATO CHIPS

The Cape Cod Company, Breed's Hill Road, Hyannis, 02601; phone 617-775-3358 or 775-3206. Hours: Monday–Friday, 10 A.M. to 5 P.M.; closed Saturday and Sunday.

Sold in supermarkets and food shops throughout New England.

■ We both grew up eating Wise potato chips, and for years they have been the standard by which we compared all other chips. And then along came the 1980s, with designer food and "homemade, all natural" potato chips. It's tough giving up your childhood favorites, but when we tasted Cape Cod Potato Chips we knew things would never be the same.

These chips are thick and they taste . . . well, they taste like potatoes. There's none of that super-greasy, overly salty flavor we've come to expect. They are so good we usually go through an entire bag within a few hours. You can visit the Cape Cod Company factory and see exactly how these chips are made—and of course pick up a few bags, or better yet, a souvenir bucket.

Red Cabbage Salad with Blue Cheese and Bacon

This is a hearty autumn salad that should be made with fresh garden cabbage.

1 pound thick slab bacon, cut into 1-inch pieces
1 large red cabbage (about 2 1/2 pounds)
1/2 pound Hubbardston Blue, Roquefort, blue cheese, or New England goat cheese

Mustard Vinaigrette
1 tablespoon Dijon mustard
1/4 cup plus 1 tablespoon red wine vinegar
3/4 cup olive oil
Salt to taste
Freshly ground black pepper to taste

In a large skillet sauté the bacon until crisp. Drain on paper towels, and set aside. Using a food processor or a sharp knife, thinly slice the cabbage. Place it in a large salad bowl.

Make the vinaigrette: In a small bowl, mix the mustard with the vinegar. Gradually whisk in the oil. Add just a touch of salt (the bacon will be salty) and a very generous grinding of pepper. Pour the vinaigrette over the cabbage, and toss well. Crumble the cheese, and scatter it and the bacon bits over the salad. Toss. Serves 6 to 8.

Ipswich

GOODALE ORCHARDS/THE RUSSELL FAMILY STORE AND CIDER MILL

123 Argilla Road, Ipswich, 01938; phone 617-356-5366. Hours: mid-June through Christmas Eve, seven days a week 9 A.M. to 6 P.M. Personal checks accepted. Pick-your-own fruit and berries available; call ahead for hours and conditions.

■ One of the best things about going to Crane Beach in Ipswich is having a chance to stop at Goodale Orchards. Inside this huge old barn you'll find a great variety of fresh fruit, berries, apples, apple pies, and apple cider. Be sure to try the flaky apple crisp and a few of the Russell family's famous cider doughnuts, hot and fluffy with a fresh cider taste.

Goodale Orchards used to be a small family farm that sold only apples, pears, and preserves. When the Russell family bought the farm in the late 1970s, they planted 8 acres of strawberries, 3 acres of raspberries, and 1 acre of blueberries. (All the berries are available in the store or for pick-your-own.) They also planted three thousand new apple trees, giving the farm some sixteen varieties on 90 acres. The Russells use a minimum of sprays, and they never use alar on the apples.

Fall is definitely the favorite time of year here. On weekends you can watch cider being pressed, take a free hayride through the apple orchards, and pick your own apples. Hot cider, fresh cider doughnuts, frozen cider cups, and apple pies are always on hand.

Lee

HIGH LAWN FARM
Summer Street, Lee, 01238; phone 413-243-0672. Hours: Monday–Saturday 8:30 to 5 P.M.; closed 12 N. to 1 P.M. and Sunday. Cash only.
   High Lawn Farm milk and cream are sold at food stores throughout the Berkshires.

■ There really is a difference between Jersey milk and the milk most of us are used to, which mainly comes from Holstein cows. The milk produced by Jersey cows is richer and creamier. "It adds palatability to any food that it's cooked with," says George Wilde, the owner of High Lawn Farm. And by itself it makes for an incredibly satisfying glass of milk.
   High Lawn Farm produces homogenized and "regular" milk with a layer of thick Jersey cream floating on top. Cream and low-fat milk are also available.

Lenox

NAOMI'S HERBS
11 Housatonic Street, Lenox, 01240; phone 413-637-0616. Hours: seven days a week 10 A.M. to 6 P.M. Closed Sunday in January, February, and March. MasterCard, Visa, American Express, and personal checks accepted. Mail order available. The gardens are on Route 102 in South Lee; open during daylight hours from May through October; phone 413-243-3675.

■ At any time of year Naomi's Herbs is a fragrant refuge from the outside world. In the spring, summer, and fall Naomi Alson and her partner Will (who prefers not to use his last name) invite the public into their herb and flower gardens along the banks of the Housatonic River in South Lee. During the winter their small shop in downtown Lenox is a reminder of the warmer seasons, with bunches of dried herbs and flowers hanging overhead—filling every inch of ceiling space, the sweet smell of herbs perfuming the air.
   Naomi's carries a big selection of organically grown herbs, their own excellent blends of herbal tea, medicinal herbs, and ornamental herbs and flowers. When their gardens are in bloom fresh herbs are available, both cut and potted, along with fresh-cut flowers.

SUCHELE BAKERS
31 Housatonic Street, Lenox, 01240; phone 413-637-0939. Hours: Wednesday–Saturday 8 A.M. to 5 P.M., Sunday 8 A.M. to 1 P.M.; closed Monday and Tuesday. Personal checks accepted.

■ Amy Loveless, owner of Suchèle Bakers, is proud that she's been able to keep her bakery small. People have urged her to expand, but Loveless prefers to operate the bakery on a scale that allows her to personally attend to the details of baking and meeting the needs of her customers.
   Loveless is a stickler for detail. "We bake everything from scratch," she says proudly. "I don't know many bakers that can truthfully make that claim." Whenever possible she uses local ingredients, including fresh fruit in her pies and pastries and rich Jersey milk from a nearby dairy.
   It's a good idea to go to Suchèle Bakers early in the day, before the regular customers have bought up all the croissants (the bakery's specialty), danish pastries, sticky buns, pies, and cakes. And if you want to play it really safe you can order bakery items in advance.

Picnicking at Tanglewood

The chance to listen to a Mozart symphony while the smell of freshly mown grass perfumes the air and a soft breeze caresses your face is what draws most people to the concerts at Tanglewood each summer. These outdoor performances stimulate almost all the senses. Satisfying the taste buds is another important part of this experience. Here are some shops near Tanglewood that prepare picnics.

Crosby's Gourmet Shop, 66 Church Street, Lenox, 01240; phone 413-637-3396. Choose from a menu of soups, their own pâté, cheeses, refreshing cold salads, breads, rolls, and pastries. They will make a picnic box for you, or you can buy the ingredients and put it together yourself.

Loeb's Foodtown, Main Street, Lenox, 01240; phone 413-637-0270. Loeb's offers cold cuts, deli sandwiches, fresh fruits and vegetables, cheeses, beer, and wine. Try some cream from High Lawn Farm (see page 114) and pour it over a bowl of fresh berries.

Nejaime's Stockbridge Wine Cellar and Cheese Shop, 33 Church Street, Lenox, 01240; phone 413-637-2221. Also at Elm Street, Stockbridge, 01262; phone 413-298-3454, and at Guido's Marketplace in Pittsfield (see page 130). Cheeses, pâtés, marinated olives, Middle Eastern specialties, and an extensive selection of wine and beer.

Lexington

WILSON FARMS
10 Pleasant Street, Lexington, 02173; phone 617-862-3900 or 862-3909. Hours: Monday, Wednesday, Thursday, and Saturday 9 A.M. to 6:30 P.M., Friday 9 A.M. to 8 P.M., Sunday 9 A.M. to 5:30 P.M.; closed Tuesday. Personal checks accepted.

There is another Wilson Farms, in Litchfield, New Hampshire (see page 165).

■ If you like quiet, leisurely shopping, then stay away from Wilson Farms. This farm stand and greenhouse is very popular, and is usually bustling with shoppers. But if you're willing to be jostled just a bit as you make your way from the avocados to the hearts of celery, then by all means come on down. Wilson Farms has a great selection of fresh produce, and they grow a lot of it themselves.

A chalkboard at the front of the store lets customers know what's fresh, and what to look for in the coming weeks. When we visited the farm in early spring, they were offering California asparagus. But the board promised that Wilson's own locally grown asparagus would soon be available. We also learned what size eggs their large flock of chickens was laying, and the fortunes of the prize bull they keep at their dairy farm in Falmouth, Maine. Wilson Farms has a lot of resources to draw upon.

The produce at the farm stand is beautifully displayed. There are piles of red, yellow, and green peppers, boxes of plump strawberries, and a truly artful "tower" of celery stalks. They also sell fresh herbs, fresh chicken, both New England and imported cheeses, and hamburger meat from cows they raise themselves. The greenhouse is amply stocked with flowering bedding plants, along with herb and vegetable plants.

Littleton

CHASE FARMS
509 Great Road (Route 119), Littleton, 01460; phone 617-486-3893. Hours: September through June, seven days a week 7 A.M. to 9 P.M. Cash only.
   Chase's cider is also sold at food stores throughout eastern Massachusetts.

■ Chase Farms makes some of the best apple cider around. It's well balanced and refreshing, and made without chemical preservatives. On Sundays during the fall they have an open house, when you can watch the cider being made and sample it right after it's been pressed. They also sell a limited selection of apples in season.

GARY'S FARM STAND
Great Road (Route 119), Littleton, 01460; phone 617-486-8640. Hours: seven days a week 9 A.M. to 7 P.M. Personal checks accepted.

■ There's something special about Gary's corn, but it's hard to define. Sweetness? Maybe. Good texture? Well, yes. Fresh-picked taste? Definitely.
   Gary's also grows a good variety of other fruits and vegetables. There are tomatoes, lettuce, apples, pumpkins, and squash—as well as superb cantaloupe and muskmelon. And then there are the beautiful displays of locally grown peaches, pears, blueberries, raspberries, and grapes. This large farm stand also carries fresh eggs, New England–made cheeses, breads, and fruit pies.

Martha's Vineyard

CHICAMA VINEYARDS
Stoney Hill Road (follow signs off State Road), West Tisbury, 02575; phone 617-693-0309. Hours: April 15 through October, Monday–Saturday 11 A.M. to 5 P.M., Sunday 1 P.M. to 5 P.M. Mid-November to Christmas Eve, Monday–Saturday 1 P.M. to 5 P.M.; closed Sunday. MasterCard, Visa, and personal checks accepted. Mail order available for condiments.
   Chicama Vineyards wines are sold in wine and liquor stores in Massachusetts and New Hampshire. The vinegars are sold throughout the U.S.

■ Catherine and George Mathiesen left New York City and their executive life-style and brought their entire family to Martha's Vineyard. Unlike many people who come to this idyllic island to retire, or fish, or paint, or write books, the Mathiesens had an idea to open a winery. Martha's Vineyard has long been known for its abundance of native Concord grapes. But the Mathiesens wanted to plant European wine grapes in the island's harsh soil. Some people called it risky; others were more straightforward and told them they were nuts.
   Chicama Vineyards opened in 1971, and we have to admit that when we first heard about it we were pretty skeptical too. A few years later, when we tasted our first bottle of Chicama Vineyard's wine, we were unimpressed. But we recently tasted a bottle of their Cabernet Sauvignon and were amazed at the improvement. While we would never call this great wine, it has come a long, long way. Unfortunately many of the other Chicama wines we tasted were not nearly as good.
   The Mathiesens now produce over a dozen varieties of wine, ranging from a dry white Chardonnay to a rich Merlot. You can visit the vineyard and take a free 20-minute tour to see how the grapes are picked by hand, crushed, and aged. At the end of the tour visitors are invited to taste some of the wines. Our overall impression: many of these wines are still very unrefined, but the

Chicama Vineyards' herbal wine vinegars.

reds seem to be far more interesting than the whites.

In addition to selling wine and wine paraphernalia, the gift shop here also offers Chicama's excellent assortment of homemade condiments. This island winery produces over twenty varieties of excellent wine vinegar, made according to the traditional French Orleans method of aging the vinegar in large wooden casks and allowing it to mature slowly and naturally. Our favorite is their Cranberry Vinegar. It has the refreshingly tart flavor of fresh cranberries and is delicious added to vinaigrette, cole slaw, turkey salad, or a hearty vegetable soup.

Also good are Chicama Vineyard's homemade mustards, ice cream sauces, chutneys, salad dressings, and fruit jams.

NIP-N-TUCK FARM

State Road (RFD Box 573), Vineyard Haven, 02568; phone 617-693-1449. Hours: June 1 to October 1, Monday–Saturday 10 A.M. to 5 P.M.; closed Sunday. October to June, Monday, Tuesday, and Thursday–Saturday 1 P.M. to 5 P.M.; closed Wednesday and Sunday. Cash only. Pony and hay rides available by appointment.

Nip-N-Tuck products are occasionally available at the Martha's Vineyard Farmers' Market (see page 147).

■ With some 115 working farms, Martha's Vineyard is one of the most agriculturally vibrant areas in New England. And one of the pillars of Vineyard agriculture is Fred S. Fisher, Jr., owner of Nip-N-Tuck Farm. He's been farming on the island since 1941, providing pure, unhomogenized milk and fresh produce, herbs, and flowers to his customers. Fisher has also helped keep agriculture alive on the island by teaching newcomers some of the tricks of Vineyard farming and by putting 55 acres of his land into the Massachusetts Agricultural Preservation Restriction Fund, a program which guarantees that the land will always be used for farming.

When you visit Nip-N-Tuck Farm, chances are you'll see Fred Fisher working in the pasteurizing room, clad in high rubber boots, an apron, and a railroad engineer's cap. He sells his milk in old-fashioned glass bottles (collected from defunct New England dairies). The milk is rich and delicious, with a thick layer of cream on top—a real treat when poured over fresh island berries or used as a base for clam chowder. You'll also find a nice selection of produce picked fresh daily.

Clams on the Half Shell, Martha's Vineyard Style

Clams on the half shell have the pure flavor of the sea—raw, fresh, and unadorned. And eating clams on the half shell in Menemsha is the ultimate clam experience. Both Poole's Fish Market and nearby Larsen's Fish Market have makeshift clam bars where you can buy freshly shucked bivalves picked from local waters. These clams have a fresh, sweet taste that you just don't find anywhere else.

It's not just the clams that make this a truly special culinary experience. It's the atmosphere. Right outside Poole's and Larsen's back doors is Dutcher Dock, a picturesque wharf where local fishing boats tie up. When it's warm outside you can take your clams, lemon juice, and spicy cocktail sauce and eat them right on the dock. With the smell of salt air filling your head and the taste of fresh clams on your tongue, you may feel, for just a moment, that you are actually eating the ocean in all its richness.

POOLE'S FISH
Dutcher Dock, Menemsha, 02552; phone 617-645-2282. Summer hours: seven days a week 8 A.M. to 6 P.M. Winter hours: Monday–Saturday 8 A.M. to 5 P.M., Sunday 12 N. to 5 P.M. Personal checks accepted. Mail order available.

■ What kind of fish do famous brain surgeons eat to keep their own brains going? Poole's Fish Market is the place to find out. This is where the elite of Harvard, M.I.T., and the literary world come to buy fish while vacationing on Martha's Vineyard.

Owner Everett H. Poole has been in business for over forty years. He offers an impressive array of fresh harpooned swordfish, lobsters (both live and cooked), bluefish, tuna, clams, oysters, sole, and much, much more. It's not unusual to see an enormous just-caught tuna or swordfish being transferred from fishing boats tied up at the adjacent dock directly to Poole's cold-storage building.

But fresh fish is not the only reason why it's worth going out of your way to visit Poole's. Several years ago Everett Poole made a trip to Scotland and brought back a smoker. He now produces some of the most succulent smoked fish you've ever tasted. Our favorite is the smoked bluefish. Poole's method is to add a light smokey taste that doesn't overwhelm the fish's natural flavor. The bluefish is so tender, it's almost like butter. Smoked tuna, eel, haddock, swordfish, scallops, and other varieties are also available.

Poole's also sells its own line of frozen fish dishes and chowder, under the name Menemsha Bites.

One warning: prices at Poole's are high. But so is just about everything else on Martha's Vineyard, and the quality here is exceptional.

THE SCOTTISH BAKEHOUSE
State Road, Tisbury, 02568; phone

■ Every time we go to the Vineyard and drive up-island past the Scottish Bakehouse, we're tempted to stop in. It's the shortbread we're after—thin, super-rich, and loaded with fresh butter. We also like to pick up a loaf of

617-693-1873. Hours: seven days a week 9 A.M. to 6 P.M. (8 P.M. in summer). Personal checks accepted.

bread—either the Oatmeal, Whole Wheat, or Scotch Crusty—and maybe a fresh raspberry or blueberry pie.

Owner Isabel White has lived on Martha's Vineyard since the early 1960s. Originally from Peebles, Scotland, she brought a whole slew of old Scottish recipes along with her and decided to open a bakery. The scones she makes are delicious, as are the meat pies. There are pork and beef pies, a veal and ham loaf with hard-boiled eggs wrapped in pastry, Cornish pasties (potatoes, beef, and onions in puff pastry), and Forfer Bridies, a pork and onion turnover named after Forfer, a small Scottish town. The meat pies make delicious hot hors d'oeuvres and are also good served cold with a tossed salad for lunch or a beach picnic.

SOLVIVA

State Road (Box 582, RFD), Vineyard Haven, 02568; phone 617-693-3341. Hours: Monday–Saturday 1 P.M. to 5 P.M., other times by appointment. Personal checks accepted. Mail order available. Tours available; call ahead for information.

Solviva salads are also sold at food stores on the Vineyard and in Boston and at the Martha's Vineyard Farmers' Market (see page 147).

■ Solviva is the creation of Anna Edey, a strong, outspoken woman who is dedicated to teaching people about the earth and its natural capabilities. "My aim," she explains, "is to produce organic, clean, poison-free food, year-round, without depleting our limited resources."

Edey grows some 150 varieties of lettuce, vegetables, herbs, and edible flowers, using no artificial anything. There's spinach, mache, collard greens, Swiss chard, kale, sweet fennel, mustard greens, bok choy, daikon, watercress, sage blossoms, cilantro, and more. She is able to produce vegetables even during the coldest winter months using a rather extraordinary greenhouse she designed and built herself. The 3300-square-foot building is heated solely by the rays of the sun and the body heat of dozens of chickens and angora rabbits who live in

Anna Edey in the Solviva greenhouse, source of special salad mixtures.

MIDDLE EAST BAKERY

1111 Riverside Drive (Route 110), Methuen, 01844; phone 617-688-2221. Hours: Monday–Friday 8 A.M. to 5 P.M., Saturday and Sunday 8 A.M. to 2 P.M. Cash only.

Joseph's Middle East Style Syrian Breads are sold in supermarkets throughout the East.

ROYAL FEAST POTATO CHIPS

79 Lowell Boulevard, Methuen, 01844; phone 617-683-0961. Hours: Monday–Saturday 9 A.M. to 5 P.M.; closed Sunday. Factory tours available. Also available at grocery stores throughout the Merrimack Valley. Sold in southern New Hampshire and southern Maine under the name Maine Coast Potato Chips.

---

cages inside the greenhouse. The animals also contribute carbon dioxide and manure, which enrich the air and organic soil inside the greenhouse. To complete the cycle, the animals are fed some of the organically grown produce. It is a self-sustaining system.

Solviva's specialty is salad greens. Edey puts together packages of assorted greens, herbs, and edible flowers with a tangy herb salad dressing. No two salads are ever the same; each one contains at least two dozen types of greens and has a wonderful balance of flavors, textures, and colors.

You can visit Solviva year-round and take a self-guided stroll through the greenhouse. Salad packages are pre-made and available all the time. If you want to buy a specific type of green or flower or herb, or want to talk with Edey, be sure to call ahead and make an appointment. During the summer there's also a large outdoor organic garden, open to the public, where you'll find beautiful tomatoes, beans, onions, and other assorted vegetables. If you're interested in learning more about organic gardening, solar greenhouses, as well as designs for various "harmonious living systems," Solviva offers internships, work/study visits, workshops, and tours.

Methuen

■ Syrian pita bread—those soft pockets of dough perfect for making sandwiches and for filling with Middle Eastern salads—is sold in most grocery stores these days. Unfortunately it's difficult to find really fresh pita. (Most of the stuff tends to sit around for a few days, or weeks, before you get your hands on it.) If you visit the wholesale shop attached to Joseph's Middle East Bakery in Methuen, you'll find exceptionally fresh Syrian bread. Whole wheat, white, garlic, onion, and cinnamon raisin pita bread, along with whole wheat bulkie rolls and other breads, are sold at the bakery store for about 20 percent less than you would pay in a supermarket. Of course these breads are not expensive anywhere; the real bonus is freshness. If you're lucky you might even get a bag of still-warm pita.

■ There are a number of New England companies that recently started making "all natural, preservative-free" potato chips. The Royal Feast Potato Chip Company of Methuen claims to have produced natural potato chips since around 1930. These chips are thick, not too oily, and best of all, you can actually taste the potatoes. They're fried in cottonseed oil and packaged without any preservatives or gases.

Royal Feast Potato Chips come in three flavors: plain, unsalted, and sour cream and onion.

Monterey

MONTEREY CHÈVRE

Rawson Brook Farm, New Marlboro Road, Monterey, 01245; phone 413-528-2138. Hours: seven days a week from dawn to dusk. Personal checks accepted. Visitors are encouraged to go on a self-guided tour of the farm.

Also sold in food stores throughout New England and parts of New York.

- Monterey Chèvre is one of the creamiest, most flavorful fresh goat cheeses made in New England. It's a soft, extremely mild cheese that can be used in many different sauces, dips, salads, and egg dishes without overpowering the flavor of the other ingredients. Monterey Chèvre is a fresh cheese that is not intended to be aged. It can be found at its freshest at the farm where it's made.

Cheesemakers Wayne Dunlop and Susan Sellew welcome visitors. You can watch their herd of Alpine goats being milked and get a sense of the cheese manufacturing process.

Monterey Chèvre comes in five flavors: regular, no salt, wild thyme and olive oil, chives and garlic, and black-pepper-coated.

TALL PINE FARM

Wellman Road, Monterey, 01245; phone 413-528-9266. Hours: late June through mid-October, seven days a week 10 A.M. until dark. Cash only.

- "Each summer there's a bit of a struggle over my green beans," says Bob Thieriot, owner of Tall Pine Farm. "They're stringless and they're extremely sweet; maybe that's why they're so popular."

Beans are only one of the vegetables Thieriot grows on his 4 1/2-acre organic farm. The season starts with spinach and moves on to peas, snow peas, lettuce, beets, corn, tomatoes, onions, scallions, and herbs. Thieriot also manages to grow beautiful peaches and apples using a minimum of chemical sprays (during good years he says he uses none at all). Magnificent bouquets of fresh-cut garden flowers are also available during the summer.

Nantucket

BARTLETT'S OCEAN VIEW FARM

Box 899, Bartlett Farm Road, Nantucket, 02554; phone 617-228-9403. Farm hours: mid-June through the first week of December, seven days a week 9 A.M. to 5 P.M. Truck on Main Street: Monday–Saturday 9 A.M. to 1 P.M. Greenhouse: March through December, Monday–Saturday 9 A.M. to 5 P.M.; January through March, call ahead. Personal checks

- The Bartlett family has a reputation for growing some of the best produce on Nantucket. This is the eighth generation of Bartletts to run the farm. It started out as a dairy farm, but they stopped milking cows when pasteurization came into use. After that the family raised sheep. When Phillip Bartlett, the current owner, took over in the early 1950s, he began raising vegetables, herbs, and flowers.

"We plant about 100 acres," explains Dorothy Bartlett, Phillip's wife. "And we grow a little bit of everything. We'd rather not grow half the things we do, but because of the sheer logistics of living on an island, you have to grow everything. Besides, people have come to depend on us."

The farm produces nine varieties of lettuce along with peppers (red, yellow, green, and hot), tomatoes, corn, beets, cucumbers, carrots, all sorts of potatoes and onions, squash, and pumpkins. "We also sell an enormous amount of fresh-cut herbs and bouquets of garden

accepted. Pick-your-own strawberries available; call ahead for information.

flowers," says Dorothy. "But my personal favorites are the melons. We grow gorgeous cantaloupes and watermelons. There's one variety called Yellow Baby Watermelon that has yellow flesh and the most incredible sweet flavor. Once people taste it, they're hooked."

Chile Dilly Beans

In late July and early August, just about every New England garden and produce stand overflows with fresh green beans. By the middle of August you may be hoping never to see another green bean again, but come February you'll crave their fresh, juicy flavor and crisp texture. This recipe combines fresh green (or yellow wax) beans with red chile peppers and fresh dill. The result is a slightly spicy, crisp and refreshing pickle. Serve them with curries, salads, and antipasto platters, or eat them straight from the jar and get back in touch with the flavors of summer.

3 pounds fresh garden beans (green or wax), washed
6 cloves garlic, peeled and cut in half
6 teaspoons yellow mustard seeds
18 small dried red chile peppers

6 large sprigs fresh dill
3 1/2 cups apple cider vinegar or white wine vinegar
3 1/2 cups water
4 1/2 tablespoons kosher or canning salt

Sterilize six pint-size canning jars and lids in boiling water for 15 minutes. Drain and dry.

Trim the beans so that they will fit in the canning jars, making sure to leave 1/2 inch headspace. Distribute the beans evenly among the six jars. Add a clove of garlic, 1 teaspoon mustard seeds, 3 chile peppers, and a generous sprig of fresh dill to each jar.

In a medium stainless steel saucepan, boil the vinegar, water, and salt over high heat. Pour the boiling vinegar solution evenly over the beans, leaving 1/2 inch headspace.

Seal the jars tightly, let them cool, and then let the beans "pickle" in the refrigerator for several days before eating; or process in a boiling water bath for 20 minutes and store in a cool, dark spot for several days before eating. Makes 6 pints.

PASTELARIA COLMEIA
411 Bolton Street, New Bedford, 02740; phone 617-997-9428. Hours: seven days a week 8 A.M. to 6 P.M. Cash only.

New Bedford

■ There must be dozens of Portuguese bakeries in New Bedford, and after a while they all seem to blend together. Pastelaria Colmeia, however, stands out among the many providers of airy Portuguese sweet bread and leaden sweets. The display case here is filled with delicate pastries—creamy chocolate éclairs, soft egg-custard tarts, and light sponge cakes. One particularly good pastry we had was similar to an éclair, only the dough was shaped like a puff pastry shell. It was filled with vanilla pastry cream and topped with chocolate and delicate shavings of candied lemon rind.

The atmosphere here is a bit dingy and reminiscent of a pizza parlor, but don't let it bother you. Take a seat and have a cup of their excellent cappuccino and a pastry. They also bake wedding and birthday cakes to order. Prices are very reasonable.

Newton Center

JOHN DEWAR AND COMPANY
753 Beacon Street, Newton Center, 02159; phone 617-964-3577. Hours: Monday–Saturday 9 A.M. to 6 P.M.; closed Sunday. MasterCard, Visa, and personal checks accepted.

■ This is a small, very classy butcher shop—the kind where they take the time to find you the right cut of meat, tell you how it should be cooked, and suggest what to serve with it. Much of the meat and poultry they sell is organically raised, including organic chicken and natural, grass-fed beef from Wyoming. You'll also find fresh *poussins* (the French name for tiny three-week-old chickens that have a delicate flavor much like a Cornish hen), beautiful lamb chops and racks of lamb, Irish bacon, fresh calves' liver, and all-beef hot dogs. The rotisserie-roasted chickens look so good they just may convince you not to cook your own; they also give the shop an incredible aroma.

There's a very good selection of cheese (both imported and domestic), as well as fresh coffee beans, spices, caviar, fresh butter, and pasta.

North Adams

DELFTREE CORPORATION
234 Union Street, North Adams, 01247; phone 413-664-4907. Hours: Monday–Friday by appointment; closed Saturday and Sunday. Cash only.

■ "I can't really tell you all that much about the mushrooms," said Peter Duble mysteriously. We were sitting in his office in a partially renovated turn-of-the-century textile mill, waiting to hear the story behind Delftree Corporation's shiitake mushrooms. His partner, Bill Greenwald, a mechanical engineer by trade, was walking around in a white lab coat, looking at us suspiciously. "A lot of people want to grow shiitake mushrooms," said Duble. "And we've spent years figuring out a way to grow them from start to finish without using any artificial additives. A lot of this stuff is, um, it's like . . ." Duble stumbled. We weren't sure what he was driving at. "Well," he finally blurted out, "it's a secretive business. Lots of secrets."

Shiitakes have been an important part of the Japanese diet for nearly 1500 years. They are hearty, richly flavored mushrooms that are traditionally grown outdoors on oak logs. At Delftree they've developed a process for growing shiitakes that's faster and more efficient than the old-fashioned method. We managed to pry this much out of Duble: Delftree's shiitakes are cultivated indoors, year-round, on man-made "logs" of packed hardwood sawdust and grain that have been inoculated

Grilled Shiitake Mushrooms Oriental-Style

This recipe was developed by Elizabeth Wheeler for the Delftree Corporation.

1 pound shiitake mushrooms, stems removed
1 teaspoon minced fresh ginger
1 teaspoon minced fresh garlic
1 teaspoon sugar
3 tablespoons Japanese soy sauce
2 tablespoons dry sherry
4 tablespoons peanut oil

Heat a charcoal grill or broiler. In a large bowl, combine the mushrooms with the other ingredients and toss thoroughly. Set aside to marinate for 15 minutes.

Grill the shiitakes for about 1 minute on each side, until lightly browned and tender. Serve immediately or at room temperature. Serves 4.

---

with mushroom mycelium. When grown the traditional way, the mushrooms take 6 to 12 months to mature, but Delftree's take only 6 to 8 weeks. And in the cutthroat mushroom marketplace, time means everything. It was easy to see why Duble wouldn't lay all his cards on the table.

Shiitake (*shii* is a species of oak, and *take* means mushrooms) are larger than regular button mushrooms; they grow up to 6 to 7 inches in diameter. They have a rich, earthy flavor and a texture that can only be described as meaty. Slice a shiitake mushroom and it feels as if you're cutting into a buttery, tender filet of beef. Because they have such a hearty flavor, you use only half the amount you would of regular mushrooms.

According to Duble, these mushrooms are very good for you. "Shiitakes are 99 percent fat free, low in sodium, and contain no cholesterol. And compared with the common button mushroom," he explained, "they have more than twice the amount of protein and fiber, and almost three times the minerals."

Shiitakes are extremely versatile. We broiled them with ginger, soy sauce, and dry sherry (see recipe above) and they took on a distinctly Oriental taste. Another time we sautéed them in butter and garlic, and finished them off with a splash of heavy cream and cognac (see recipe opposite). This gave them an earthy flavor, very much like wild mushrooms.

Of course shiitakes cost a lot more than regular mushrooms—at least eight to ten times more. Delftree's shiitake mushrooms are available in several major U.S. cities, as well as many New England specialty food shops and health food stores. But if you order them directly through Delftree (by picking them up at the factory), you can save a lot of money. Delftree will sell them to you at the wholesale price—about one third the price you find in most stores. You can order a 3- or 7-pound box. If properly refrigerated, shiitakes will keep for close to four weeks, whereas regular button mushrooms keep only seven to ten days.

Shiitake Mushrooms in Cognac-Cream Sauce

Serve on top of buttered toast triangles, or with grilled lamb or veal chops.

2 tablespoons lightly salted butter
2 small shallots, finely chopped
2 cloves garlic, minced
8 large or 16 small shiitake mushrooms, sliced or left whole, stems removed

2 tablespoons cognac
8 tablespoons heavy cream
4 tablespoons chicken broth
Freshly ground black pepper to taste
2 tablespoons coarsely chopped fresh parsley

Heat the butter in a medium skillet set over high heat. Add the shallots and garlic and sauté a few seconds, or until golden brown. Add the mushrooms and sauté 1 minute. Pour in the cognac and let it boil away for a few seconds. Pour in the cream and chicken broth, and simmer until thickened, about 30 seconds to 1 minute. Grind some fresh pepper on top and garnish with the parsley. Serves 4.

North Dartmouth

GASPAR'S SAUSAGE COMPANY

384 Faunce Corner Road (P.O. Box 436), North Dartmouth, 02717; phone toll-free 800-542-2038 or locally 617-998-2012. Hours: Monday–Friday 8 A.M. to 4 P.M., Saturday 8 A.M. to 12 N.; closed Sunday. MasterCard, Visa, and personal checks accepted. Mail order available.

Gaspar's sausages are available in supermarkets and ethnic food shops throughout southern New England.

■ *Linguica* and *chourico* sausages are two staples of Portuguese cookery. In southeastern Massachusetts, with its large Portuguese population, these pork sausages rival hot dogs and hamburgers in popularity and ubiquity. They are served with eggs at breakfast instead of bacon or regular breakfast sausage. They are an essential ingredient in kale soup—a popular Portuguese dish. Barbecued *linguica* and *chourico* are featured at local fairs and festivals. They are even served with baked beans as a substitute for frankfurters.

Gaspar's is the largest and probably best-known Portuguese sausage maker in the area, and for good reason. Although there are lots of people who make *linguica* and *chourico,* few produce sausage that is as tasty as Gaspar's. Both the mild *linguica* and hot and spicy *chourico* are redolent of garlic and paprika. They also make hot and mild Italian sausages, Polish kielbasa, and fresh pork sausage. The Italian and fresh sausages are made without nitrates.

At Gaspar's factory store you can buy the sausages at discount prices.

Portuguese Sausage Stew

Serve this simple, hearty stew with a warm loaf of crusty bread and boiled potatoes.

2 tablespoons olive oil
1 large onion, thinly sliced
4 cloves garlic, minced
1 pound linguica *sausage, cut into 1-inch pieces*
½ pound chourico *sausage, cut into 1-inch pieces*
3 large ripe tomatoes, or 2½ cups canned tomatoes with juice
2 cups cooked white beans (cannelini) or cooked chick-peas
⅔ cup dry white wine
6 tablespoons chopped fresh parsley
1 tablespoon minced fresh thyme, or 1 teaspoon dried
1 tablespoon minced fresh oregano, or 1 teaspoon dried
Freshly grated black pepper to taste
Tabasco or other hot pepper sauce to taste

Heat the oil in a large skillet over moderate heat. Add the onion and half the garlic, and sauté until tender, about 2 minutes. Add the *linguica* and *chourico* and cook for 5 minutes.

If using fresh tomatoes, peel them and slice into small pieces. Add the beans, tomatoes, the remaining garlic, white wine, 4 tablespoons of the parsley, the thyme, oregano, a generous grinding of black pepper, and a splash of hot pepper sauce. Let the stew come to a boil, reduce the heat, cover, and let simmer for about 10 minutes. Sprinkle with the remaining parsley and serve hot. Serves 4.

North Grafton

CREEPER HILL ORCHARD

20 Creeper Hill Road, North Grafton, 01536; phone 617-839-4245. Hours: August 1 to October 1, Tuesday and Wednesday 10 A.M. to 5 P.M., Thursday–Sunday 10 A.M. to 5 P.M.; closed Monday. October 1 to February 28, Saturday and Sunday 10 A.M. to 5 P.M.; closed Monday–Friday. Cash only. Pick-your-own raspberries. Self-guided tours available.

■ At Creeper Hill Orchard you have a chance to get a taste of American history by sampling the antique apple varieties they grow. Bite into the kind of apple that Colonial New Englanders may have eaten, or taste the fruit that sustained the early pioneers as they pushed westward.

Creeper Hill is really a living apple museum. Owners Francis and Margaret Poulin grow about eighty apple varieties, including many that are practically extinct. The oldest is the Roxbury Russet, a small green apple that originated in Roxbury, Massachusetts, around the middle of the seventeenth century. Many of the apples have poetic names suggestive of the places where they were first grown or the characteristics for which they are best known. There is the Washington Strawberry from Washington County, New York; Sops of Wine, an English variety; Duchess of Oldenburg from Russia; and Blue Pearmain, an early American variety with a slightly blue blush on its skin.

The Poulins have been operating Creeper Hill Orchard for about twenty years. They are happy to share their knowledge of apple history and apple culture with visitors. For example, we asked about the Jersey Black Twig apples that were displayed in a big bushel basket and were told that when you cross this exotic variety with a McIntosh you end up with another well-known apple, the Macoun.

In addition to apples, Creeper Hill Orchard grows twenty varieties of peaches, several types of grapes, walnuts, Chinese chestnuts, nectarines, plums, cherries, apricots, and raspberries. They also grow some vegetables and sell cider from nearby cider mills.

North Otis

OTIS POULTRY FARM
Route 8, North Otis, 01253; phone 413-269-4438. Hours: seven days a week 8 A.M. to 6 P.M. (8 P.M. during summer months). Personal checks accepted.

■ Probably the first thing you'll do when you drive up to the Otis Poultry Farm is laugh. There's a series of small red chicken coops with signs spelling out "Egg . . . Eaters . . . Make . . . Better . . . Lovers," a large barn labeled "Chicken Hilton," and at the entrance to the farm store a hand-painted sign advertising: "Otis Poultry Farm. Home of Chicken Gicken Fertilizer—Your Garden's Best Friend." Inside, a small sign tacked up over the cash register explains: "This company has 25,004 employees. The boss, the boss's wife, two sons, and 25,000 chickens."

Otis Poultry Farm is famous throughout the Berkshires for their "Custom Laid Eggs." The man behind the counter told us that "people are willing to drive miles for a crate of our eggs." Why drive out of the way for a dozen eggs? "They're fresh," he told us. "Real fresh."

The farm also sell capons, turkeys, Cornish hens, ducks, and geese. You can find them frozen year-round or special-order them fresh. Other specialties here are chicken and turkey pot pies. Each pie is filled with large chunks of tender meat, smothered in a rich, well-flavored gravy, and blanketed with a thin sheet of flaky pie crust.

The shelves at Otis Poultry Farm are also filled with an eclectic assortment of merchandise—jams and jellies, cheeses, fresh-baked bread and pies, maple syrup, farm-fresh milk, and moccasins, baskets, and sheepskin slippers.

Northampton

**BAKERY—
KONDITOREI
NORMAND**
44 Main Street, Northampton, 01060;

■ An assortment of richly flavored and exquisitely shaped breads is the main reason for visiting this cozy German-style bakery. They bake about twenty different varieties of bread, each so aesthetically pleasing that it looks like the work of a sculptor. There are square loaves decorated with swirl patterns, and oval loaves carefully cross-

phone 413-584-0717.
Hours: Tuesday–Saturday
7:30 A.M. to 5:30 P.M.,
Sunday 8 A.M. to
12:30 P.M.; closed
Monday. Personal checks
accepted.

COFFEE GALLERY
192 Main Street,
Northampton, 01060;
phone 413-584-5116.
Hours: Tuesday-Saturday
10 A.M. to 5:30 P.M.;
closed Sunday and
Monday. MasterCard,
Visa, American Express,
and personal checks
accepted. Mail order
available.

SMOKEHOUSE, INC.
340 Washington Street,
Norwell, 02061; phone
617-659-4824. Hours:
Monday–Saturday
10 A.M. to 6 P.M.; closed
Sunday. Personal checks
accepted. To order by
mail call 617-442-6840 or
write to 15 Coventry
Street, Roxbury, MA
02119.

hatched on top with bits of whole grain peeking through the crust.

The flavors and textures are equally impressive. We tried a loaf of *Bergsteigerbrot*, a dense, earthy bread studded with crunchy wheat berries. It was one of the most satisfying breads we've tasted anywhere.

Also good are the rich butter cookies and tangy cheese crackers. At holiday time German Christmas ornaments hang in the window and the bakery shelves are stocked with tins of imported cookies and cakes.

■ The Amherst area has several shops offering fresh coffee beans, but coffee connoisseurs do their shopping here. Coffee Gallery offers a large collection of freshly roasted beans from Guatemala, Yemen, Armenia, Costa Rica, Peru, Hawaii, and Indonesia. It's a good place to get an introductory coffee education; owners Robert and Mary Lou Heiss have a wealth of information to share.

The Coffee Gallery is also a well-stocked gourmet food shop offering oils, vinegars, mustards, and other condiments; Chinese, Japanese, and Indonesian ingredients; and an excellent variety of imported and domestic chocolates. There's a large array of coffee makers and coffee grinders and a good collection of cookbooks.

Perhaps the most unusual item is a whole wall of imported Dutch licorice in a myriad of shapes, sizes, and textures. These licorice candies, which are common in Holland, range from salty to sweet.

Norwell

■ Dave Nosiglia, who runs the Smokehouse with his father, Victor, is surely one of the best-trained sausage makers in Boston. Dave spent two and a half years as an apprentice in a sausage factory near Bremen, West Germany. After that he went to France to continue his sausage education. Was it worth it? From our perspective, yes. These sausages are exceptional, and besides that, Dave seems to really enjoy his work.

Smokehouse makes over sixty different kinds of sausage from around the world. There are English-style bangers, Lithuanian-style kielbasa, Irish-style black pudding, smoked Polish sausage, Italian fennel-flavored sausage, a Swedish sausage made with barley called *Kor Korv*, peppery Cajun-style andouille, and a dozen varieties of German wurst.

We haven't tried them all, but we can heartily recommend most of the ones we have tasted. The *weisswurst* is a juicy sausage subtly flavored with onions and chives. It has an unusually firm texture. We grilled a few of the *knockwurst* on an outdoor grill, served them with grainy mustard, thick slabs of dark bread, and steins of dark beer, and could have sworn we were in a German beer hall. The Smokehouse slab bacon is extremely lean, very flavorful, and not overly smokey. It's excellent fried and served with a breakfast omelet and gives a subtle smokey flavor to chowders, stews, soups, and sauces. All the products they make are available without nitrates if you order them a week in advance.

There is a Smokehouse store in Wellesley, at 550 Washington Street (617-235-6380); their products are also sold at Bread & Circus Wholefood Supermarkets.

Phillipston

BALDWIN HILL BAKERY

Baldwin Hill Road, Phillipston, 01331; phone 617-249-4691. Hours: Sunday–Thursday around the clock. Personal checks accepted. Tours available; call ahead. Mail order available.

Baldwin Hill bread is sold in health food stores, gourmet stores, and some supermarkets throughout New England and the Mid-Atlantic states.

■ We like a loaf of bread that we can sink our teeth into. Bread that doesn't remind us of air, but of the earth—solid, textured, and substantial. The bread from Baldwin Hill meets this standard.

Owners Hy and Lora Lerner have modeled their bread and bakery after the LIMA Bakery in Belgium, where they first learned to bake and where they "discovered bread more delicious than any we had ever eaten, made only from the simplest and purest ingredients."

At Baldwin Hill organically grown whole wheat flour is stone-ground daily, and rather than adding commercial yeast to the dough they use a slow sourdough fermentation process called *desem*, a Flemish word that means "starter." Each loaf of bread is baked in an extraordinary brick oven that is fired with dry hardwood and can bake up to two hundred loaves at a time. Plan on visiting the bakery on a day when the oven is operating and you'll experience some of the most glorious odors imaginable—fresh sourdough mixed with the smoke from a roaring fire.

Baldwin Hill makes several varieties of bread, but the Natural Sourdough is our favorite—a large round loaf with a beautiful brown glaze, made from organically grown wheat, well water, and sea salt. It's excellent for sandwiches and French toast. Other varieties include Sesame Wheat, Rye, Salt Free Whole Wheat, Cinnamon Raisin, and French bread.

RED APPLE FARM

Highland Avenue, Phillipston, 01331; phone 617-249-6763. Hours: August 1 to April 1, Monday–Saturday 8 A.M. to 6 P.M., Sunday 10 A.M. to 6 P.M. (to 5 P.M. every day, November 1 to April 1).

■ William Rose, the owner of Red Apple Farm, likes to have a little fun with his business, so he has selected one tree out of the two thousand in his orchard and grafted over thirty varieties of apples onto it. You'll find almost as many varieties for sale at Red Apple Farm. In addition to common ones like McIntosh and Red Delicious, there are some less well known apples like Mutsu, Wealthy, and Winter Banana. Unlike many orchards that sell exotic varieties only at the farm, Red Apple Farm will ship apple gift packs that include any mixture of apples you want.

MasterCard and Visa accepted. Mail order available.
 Cross-country skiing and lessons offered during the winter.

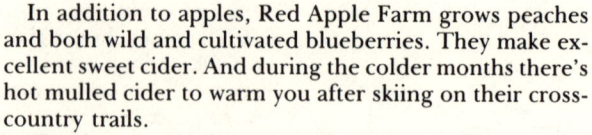

GEORGE'S BREAD
518 Fenn Street, Pittsfield, 01201; phone 413-442-5657. Hours: Monday–Thursday 11 A.M. to 6 P.M.; closed Friday–Sunday. Personal checks accepted. Mail order available.
 Sold at food stores throughout the Berkshires.

GUIDO'S FRESH MARKETPLACE
1020 South Street, Pittsfield, 01201; phone 413-442-9909. Hours: Monday–Saturday 9 A.M. to 6 P.M., Sunday 10 A.M. to 5 P.M. Cash only. Catering available.

In addition to apples, Red Apple Farm grows peaches and both wild and cultivated blueberries. They make excellent sweet cider. And during the colder months there's hot mulled cider to warm you after skiing on their cross-country trails.

The farm uses an integrated pest management program, which means that a minimum of chemical insecticides is sprayed on the fruit.

Pittsfield

■ Like many New England breadmakers, George Boyer was motivated to open his bakery because he couldn't find a decent loaf of bread where he lived. "I wanted bread that had substance to it," says Boyer, "not that mushy stuff." There is plenty of substance in the four varieties of bread Boyer bakes: Coarse Whole Rye Sour Dough, Challah, Whole Grain and Egg, and George's Bread, a whole grain wheat bread that Boyer has justly nicknamed "the toast of the Berkshires."

Although Boyer has succeeded in bringing better bread to the Pittsfield area, he admits that it can be tough getting people to try it. "The loaves are so firm," he says, "that when people squeeze them they sometimes think they are stale." On the contrary, the firmness is a reflection of the whole grains that Boyer uses.

George Boyer works alone. And although his bakery really isn't set up for retail customers, he's happy to have people stop by to buy bread and chat for a moment. A trip to the bakery also offers visitors a chance to see how this bread is made, and to step, for a moment, into the warm, yeasty environment where Boyer spends his working hours.

■ We wish we had known about Guido's sooner. It would have saved us many hours of traveling down winding, sometimes icy country roads searching for unusual foods from the Berkshires. Instead we could have come to Guido's, where many of the region's finest food products have been assembled under one very large roof. Guido's is actually a collection of stores, each with a different specialty.

The Hillsdale Meat Center sells top-quality meats, including some locally raised beef, their own hot and sweet Italian sausages, and chickens and turkeys raised without chemical additives.

At Day's Catch you will find a wide variety of fresh and smoked seafood, along with pickled herring, caviar, and a long menu of prepared seafood dishes, soups, and chowders. They also make clam rolls, shrimp dinners, lobster rolls, fried calamari dinners, and so on, all for take-out.

Nejaime's Bakery and Deli has a big selection of fresh cheeses, including several different varieties of chèvre made on farms in Massachusetts and New York State. They also sell Middle Eastern salads like *tabbouleh, hummus* and *baba ghanoush,* along with pita bread from a local bakery and *zatoons*—imported Greek olives marinated in olive oil, garlic, herbs, and spices.

Another store at Guido's, Pasta Prima, features fresh pasta cut to any size you wish. They will sell uncut sheets of pasta for making lasagne and manicotti.

Rainbow's End Natural Foods has a good selection of organically grown cereals, nuts, and grains. Other items include Mexican and Oriental ingredients, and sauces and condiments made without preservatives.

The Bookloft sells cookbooks and cooking magazines.

Finally, Guido's runs a fantastic produce department. In the summer they carry locally grown fruits and vegetables. And all through the year they maintain a lush display of imported produce, including some hard-to-find items like tomatillos (Mexican husk tomatoes), celery root, fresh shiitake mushrooms, fresh herbs including basil and coriander, bunches of bright green arugula and watercress, ripe melons, berries, plantains, and much more. There also is apple cider from nearby Bartlett's Orchard (see below), local eggs from Otis Poultry Farm (see page 127), and a selection of imported jams, jellies, dried mushrooms, and pickles. A complete dairy section that features local milk and tofu products rounds out the selection of foods at Guido's.

MAZZEO IMPORTING MARKET

251 Fenn Street, Pittsfield, MA 01201; phone 413-448-8323. Hours: Tuesday–Saturday 9 A.M. to 6 P.M., Sunday 9 A.M. to 1 P.M.; closed Monday. Personal checks accepted. Catering available.

BARTLETT'S ORCHARD

Barker Road, Richmond, 01254 (mailing address: Yokun Road, Postal Route 49, Pittsfield, 01201); phone 413-698-2559. Hours: September through May, seven days a week 8:30 A.M. to 5:30 P.M. Personal checks accepted for mail order only. Mail order available until December 1. Tours available.

■ There are certain signs we look for in any Italian market that tell us whether the shopkeeper knows his business. One is fresh sausages, another, crusty bread, a third, good olive oil. Mazzeo's has all of these and more. In addition to making their own hot and sweet sausages, they carry several different types of imported and domestic Italian-style salami and dried sausage, and they have a fine selection of fresh meats. The bread, brought in fresh daily from a bakery across town, has a delightfully crispy crust. And several varieties of olive oil sit side by side with bottles of vinegar, boxes of Italian pasta, and tins of anchovies.

Mazzeo's has an outstanding deli counter with cheeses, olives, and marinated vegetables for antipasto. We tried some red and yellow peppers in a vinaigrette dressing that were out of this world.

Richmond

■ The Bartlett family grows about a dozen varieties of apples, all without alar. They start making sweet cider around the first of October.

Cranberry World

The people at Ocean Spray see the world through cranberry-colored glasses, and at Cranberry World visitors have a chance to share this view. This museum and exhibit hall explores every aspect of the dark red berry, including its history, how it is grown and harvested, and how to cook it. In fact it's just about the only place where you can get a cranberry education. Although southeastern Massachusetts is filled with cranberry bogs, most are not open to the public.

The cranberry is a native American fruit. Wild cranberries were eaten by Indians on both coasts. New England Indians pounded cranberries with venison to make pemmican, a kind of jerky that sustained them through the winter. According to food authority Waverley Root, cranberries may have been the first native American fruit to be shipped to Europe on a commercial basis. The berries were able to withstand the long transatlantic voyage because their high acid content acts as a preservative. (If you've ever bought fresh cranberries you may have discovered that they stay fresh in the refrigerator for months without losing their shape or flavor.)

There are lots of other fascinating facts about cranberries to be discovered at Cranberry World. The atmosphere is a bit touristy, but the exhibits are worthwhile. You'll see antique and modern cranberry picking equipment, a display about the ecology of a cranberry bog, and photographs of people who work on the bogs. The exhibit hints at, but doesn't really explain, the hardships that many cranberry pickers endured in the early part of this century. (Most pickers were immigrants from Finland or the Cape Verde Islands. They were paid minuscule wages, and young children were often forced to work in the bogs alongside their parents.)

At the Cranberry World gift shop, all the employees wear cranberry-colored uniforms. They sell cranberry-flavored honey, cranberry candles, even cranberry-colored yo-yos. They give cooking demonstrations and dispense free ice-cold samples of Ocean Spray juices. There are also some pretty silly exhibits, including a videotape of vintage TV commercials entitled "Remember These Ocean Spray Ads?"

Cranberry World is on Water Street in Plymouth. It is open seven days a week, 9:30 A.M. to 5 P.M., from April 1 to November 30. In October they sponsor all-day tours of nearby cranberry bogs; call for dates and times: 617-747-1000 or 747-2350.

Sandwich

CROW FARM
192 Old Kings Highway (Route 6A), Sandwich, 02563; phone 617-888-0690. Hours: First week in May to Christmas Eve, seven days a week (closed Sunday in July and August); call ahead for

■ Many New England farms have interesting histories, but the story of Crow Farm is unique. According to farmer Howard Crowell, the land he owns has been cultivated for over three hundred years. It used to be the poor farm for the town of Sandwich. "In the old days they didn't put people on welfare, they put them to work," Crowell told us. The old paupers' cemetery is also located on the property. There are no headstones, but according to Crowell, "it's listed as sacred ground on town maps."

DEXTER GRIST MILL

Next to the town hall, Sandwich, 02563 (mailing address: Town Hall, Town of Sandwich); phone 617-888-0157. Hours: Memorial Day to Columbus Day, seven days a week 10 A.M. to 4:45 P.M. Admission charged. Cash only.

Dexter's cornmeal is sold at a few other food stores in the Sandwich area.

hours. Personal checks accepted.

Crow Farm grows a wide variety of fruits and vegetables. In their orchard they have peaches and twenty-five kinds of apples. Autumn is apple cider time at the farm. They also sell local honey and cornmeal from nearby Dexter Grist Mill (see below).

- The Dexter Grist Mill is notable both for the cornmeal that's ground there and for the mill's place in history. It's one of the oldest mills in the United States, dating back to 1654. According to miller Leo Manning, the wooden water wheel and simple gear design represent the earliest type of milling machinery used in this country.

The cornmeal from the Dexter Grist Mill is slightly coarse. It can be used to make traditional New England dishes like jonnycakes and Indian pudding. Manning says many of his customers report that it also makes excellent polenta.

This mill is definitely worth a visit. It's located in a very pretty spot in the center of Sandwich, and tours of the mill allow you to get a close-hand look at the its inner workings.

JOE'S LOBSTER AND FISH MART

Cape Cod Canal, Sandwich, 02563; phone 617-888-2971 or 888-2139. Hours: Sunday–Thursday 8 A.M. to 6 P.M., Friday and Saturday 8 A.M. to 7 P.M. Personal checks accepted.

- There are a few fish markets where the seafood almost jumps up at you, it's so fresh. This is one of them. Located where the Cape Cod Canal spills out into Cape Cod Bay, Joe's Lobster and Fish Mart offers a dazzling array of locally caught seafood, including thick pink swordfish steaks, bluefish, flounder, sole, clams, mussels, and of course lobsters.

QUAIL HOLLOW

Route 130, Sandwich, 02563; phone 617-888-0438. Hours: April 30 to October 1, Monday, Tuesday, and Thursday–Saturday 10 A.M. to 5 P.M., Sunday 10 A.M. to 2 P.M.; closed Wednesday. Personal checks accepted.

- Strictly speaking, this is not an organic farm. But Georgette Pola, who runs Quail Hollow with her father, Peter Cook, makes a point of keeping chemical fertilizers and sprays out of the vegetables they grow and sell. You have to be a little careful here because they also sell fruit and vegetables from other farms that definitely are not organic.

Among the beautifully displayed produce you'll find here: summer squash, zucchini, cucumbers, raspberries, asparagus, sweet white onions, corn, peppers, eggplant, carrots, peas, and scallions. They also sell home-baked breads and nursery stock for landscaping.

Baked Bluefish with Onions, Tomatoes, Basil, and New Potatoes

Bluefish is one of the most flavorful, and least expensive, of all New England fish. It is naturally oily and extremely moist. This is a colorful, simple way to prepare fresh bluefish by layering it with thin slices of onion, tomatoes, and fresh basil and then surrounding the fish with tiny new potatoes. The dish is baked and then splashed with fresh clam juice to create a light sauce. (Begin your meal with fresh clams on the half shell and save the juice for the sauce.) Serve the fish with a tossed green salad, a loaf of warm sourdough bread, and a good bottle of chilled white wine.

8 small new potatoes
Olive oil
1 pound fresh bluefish
1 clove garlic, thinly sliced
1 medium onion, very thinly sliced
3 tablespoons fresh basil leaves, finely chopped, or 1 1/2 teaspoons dried
1 large ripe tomato, or about 10 cherry tomatoes, thinly sliced
Freshly ground black pepper to taste
1/2 cup fresh or bottled clam juice

Place the potatoes in a pot of boiling water and boil for 4 to 5 minutes. Remove and drain. Cut the potatoes in half and set aside.

Preheat the oven to 350°. Lightly oil the bottom of a large ovenproof skillet or baking pan. Place the fish in the skillet, skin side down. Insert the thin slivers of garlic into the flesh of the fish. Place the onions on top, then sprinkle half the basil over the onions. Layer the tomatoes on top, and sprinkle with the remaining basil and freshly ground black pepper.

Place the potatoes around the fish, skin side down. Lightly drizzle the fish and the potatoes with olive oil. Bake for 10 minutes. Remove the fish from the oven and pour the clam juice over it. Bake an additional 5 to 10 minutes, or until the fish is tender and flaky when tested with a fork. Place under the broiler for 1 to 2 minutes, until brown and bubbling, and serve. Serves 2 to 3.

FOUR TOWN FARM

George Street, Seekonk, 02771; phone 617-336-5587. Hours: end of April through October, Monday–Friday 9 A.M. to 6 P.M., Saturday and Sunday 9 A.M. to 5 P.M. Personal checks accepted. Pick-your-own raspberries, strawberries, peas, blueberries, and beans; call ahead for conditions.

Seekonk

■ It's a tax accountant's nightmare. Four Town Farm is literally in four different towns—and two different states. The owners of the farm have to pay property tax in Seekonk and Swansea, Massachusetts, as well as Barrington and East Providence, Rhode Island. The borders are marked by signs near the farm stand. Even so, you can never be sure if it's Massachusetts or Rhode Island produce that you're buying here. But that shouldn't bother you. It's the quality that counts.

Four Town starts out the season with asparagus and rhubarb, and quickly moves on to strawberries and hothouse tomatoes. The tomatoes are ready by the beginning of June, which is a real treat. Other items to look for include sweet corn, cantaloupes, Chinese snow peas, and sugar snap peas.

The greenhouses at this farm are filled with bedding plants and perennials for home gardeners.

Shelburne Falls

■ There are many reasons for visiting Marty's Riverside Restaurant and Bakery. First there's the eclectic menu, combining Mexican, Oriental, and vegetarian-health foods. The ingredients are consistently fresh and the use of fresh herbs and spices abundant. Then there's the atmosphere: a quaint little restaurant with folk-art paintings done by a local artist, gorgeous water glasses and wine goblets made by a local glassblower, and great views of Shelburne Falls and the Bridge of Flowers. Another attraction is the baked goods. The poppy-seed egg bread that came with our meal was moist and buttery with the soft crunch of poppy seeds. For dessert we chose the apple crumb pie, a thin slice of buttery pastry generously topped with tart, slightly undercooked apples, brown sugar, and walnut chunks. The chocolate-rum mousse was extraordinarily rich, with a luscious creamy texture. And because we just couldn't resist, we also got slices of mocha dacquoise and maple syrup cheesecake for the road. It made the ride home so much sweeter.

All of Marty's baked goods and menu items are available for take-out.

MARTY'S RIVERSIDE RESTAURANT AND BAKERY

4 State Street, Shelburne Falls, 01370; phone 413-625-2570. Hours: Tuesday–Sunday 8 A.M. to 10 P.M.; closed Monday. Visa, MasterCard, and personal checks accepted.

McCUSKER'S MARKET & DELI

3 State Street, Shelburne Falls, 01370; phone 413-625-9411. Hours: seven days a week 8 A.M. to 8 P.M. Personal checks accepted. Take-out available.

■ Shelburne Falls is a hip, arty town. Along the main street there's a crafts showroom, a pottery shop, a basket-maker, a weaver, antique shops, and a place that specializes in "Muscle Therapy and Massage." Housed in the historic Odd Fellows Building, McCusker's is just the sort of place you'd expect to find in a town like this. At this combination health food store/country grocery/cafe, you can listen to New Age music while you shop for fresh coffee beans, organically grown vegetables and herbs, locally made cheese, tofu and soy products, baked goods, cider, granola, and so on. There's a lunch counter with a few small tables in the back, serving oversized sandwiches, salads, soups, muffins, bagels with cream cheese, and very large scoops of Bart's ice cream. In the warmer months tables are also set up outside.

Sherborn

ST. JULIEN MACAROONS

White Oaks Farm, 13 Lake Street, Sherborn,

■ Elizabeth Price let out a little sigh before answering our question about how she started making macaroons. "It was the Lord that got me into it," she told us, with just a hint of shyness in her voice. The Price family was going

01770; phone 617-653-5953. Mail order only; write or call for order form. No summer shipment.

through a period of hard times, and Elizabeth says she prayed for work that would solve their financial crisis. Soon after, she met a young man in church who was baking and selling macaroons based on a recipe developed by French nuns in the seventeenth century. Elizabeth worked with the young man, and in 1974 she began her own business selling the macaroons by mail. "The business took off like a bird, and it just soared," Elizabeth said.

Today the entire Price family is involved in making these delicious little cakes. They are very light, with a sweet almond flavor. The outside crust is light brown and has a crunchy texture; the inside is chewy. In a word, they are heavenly.

LUKASIK GAME FARM

Pearl Street, South Hadley, 01075; phone 413-534-5697. Hours: most days 9 A.M. to 5 P.M. Call ahead to check times and to order. Personal checks accepted. Mail order available.

South Hadley

■ Henry Lukasik holds a cleaned and dressed pheasant in the palm of his hand for a visitor to inspect. "We ranch-raise our birds in big outdoor pens covered with nets," he explains. "That means they're a little less gamey than birds grown in the wild, but we gain cookability and good flavor." Then Lukasik strokes the bird as though it still had its glorious plumage. "It's a beautiful product," he says proudly.

Indeed the Lukasik Game Farm raises several kinds of game birds that make for a beautiful, if somewhat expensive, dining experience. In addition to pheasant they grow partridge, wild quail, and wild turkey—all of which can be distinguished from your average chicken or turkey by varying degrees of gaminess, darker meat, or firmer texture. The birds are sold fresh or frozen. Pheasant smoked on the farm is also available.

Tips on Cooking Pheasant

Many cooks shy away from game birds because they are worried about ruining such an expensive and delicate commodity. According to Henry Lukasik, the worst thing you can do is overcook the bird, which will dry it out. To avoid this he suggests the following method: For a 2½-pound pheasant, wash the bird first and pat it dry (if the bird is frozen, wait until it's completely thawed). Douse the cavity with red wine; season the outside of the bird with salt, pepper, and some herbs if you wish. Roast in a 325° oven for approximately 1¼ hours.

If you want to stuff the bird, Lukasik suggests preparing a stuffing that won't overwhelm the subtle flavor of the meat. After all, what's the point of spending all that money if you're not going to taste the difference? Stuffing made of apples, wild rice, or fruits and nuts will work very well.

Game birds are only part of the story here. Lukasik Game Farm distributes high-quality specialty foods from around the world: New Zealand venison, fresh Russian beluga caviar, Norwegian smoked salmon, Black Diamond cheddar from Canada, fresh Long Island duckling, and California squab.

Lukasik raises about ten thousand birds at a time. Unfortunately visitors to the farm are not allowed see them, so the main reason to visit the farm is to avoid the shipping charges that are tacked on to mail orders.

Southampton

PINE HILL FARM
Middle Road,
Southampton, 01073;
phone 413-527-9449.
Hours: by appointment.
Cash only.
 The Touchettes' eggs are also available at the Holyoke Farmers' Market (see page 147).

■ We were sitting in the Touchette family kitchen talking to the youngest son, Martin. The Touchettes, who run Pine Hill Farm, have been in the egg business since 1952; some people in the Pioneer Valley call them the "Egg Family." We too raise chickens and can appreciate the difference between farm-fresh eggs and those found in the supermarket. But we always figured a fresh egg was a fresh egg. However, according to Martin Touchette it's all in the way you raise the birds and what you feed them. Without giving away any family secrets, Touchette let us know that his birds lay some very special eggs.

Although the Touchettes raise mostly chickens, they have also earned a reputation for their goose, quail, and Muscovy duck eggs. Geese, said Martin Touchette, produce the richest and largest eggs of all, with a strong flavor that's ideal for baking. "They're also supposed to be lower in cholesterol than chicken eggs," he told us. Duck eggs, we learned, are slightly larger than chicken eggs, and have a richer flavor. Quail lay tiny eggs that are delicious fried or pickled; they also are popular eaten raw with sushi. (Goose and duck eggs are available only from late winter through midsummer. Quail and chicken eggs are available year-round.)

When you arrive at Pine Hill Farm, the deafening sound of three thousand chickens lets you know you've come to the right place. Ducks, quail, and geese strut around the Touchettes' front yard, their brightly colored feathers fluttering in the breeze. The Touchettes also raise goats and sheep, which are for sale. And plans are underway to sell fresh-killed poultry and game birds. Call for details.

Southwick

THE PUTNAM FARM
Routes 10 and 202,
Southwick, 01077; phone 413-569-5550. Summer hours: seven days a week

■ Suppose that your grandparents live in an old farmhouse. Grandpa grows extraordinary fruits and vegetables and Grandma uses them to make even more extraordinary pies and preserves. Then suppose that these grandparents of yours open their farm to the public

9 A.M. to 6 P.M. Winter hours: Thursday–Monday 9 A.M. to 6 P.M.; closed Tuesday and Wednesday.

Putnam Farm vegetables are also sold at the Holyoke Farmers' Market during the summer and fall (see page 147).

FANEUIL CIDER COMPANY

School Street, Sterling, 01564; phone 617-422-8621. Hours: Monday–Friday 8 A.M. to 5 P.M. Cash only.

Sterling Cider Vinegar is also sold at gourmet and natural food stores in the area.

and sell all this stuff at very reasonable, old-fashioned kinds of prices. Imagine all this, and you'll get a sense of what Jim and Fran Putnam are up to. The Putnam Farm is the kind of New England family farm that was once in abundance. To find it today is like coming upon a great (and sorely missed) treasure.

Step inside the small shop attached to the Putnams' old farmhouse and your senses are all but knocked out by the scent of fruit pies coming out of the oven. Through the large windows you can watch Fran Putnam and her staff making jams and jellies and filling pie crusts with raspberries, apples, blueberries, apricots, and a strawberry-rhubarb combination. During the holiday season there's also pumpkin, pecan, and mincemeat. The majority of Fran Putnam's pies are made with fruit grown on the farm or in the surrounding area. (It's picked in season and flash-frozen.) We tried a raspberry pie in early November and were amazed to find that the berries still had a crunchy texture and a fresh, tart flavor.

The Putnams have been farming this land since 1956—they cultivate around 20 acres. They started out as poultry farmers and in the early 1960s began making old-fashioned chicken pies—meat and gravy on the bottom, homemade biscuits on the top. "I suppose we're most famous for our chicken pies," explained Fran Putnam. But we weren't overly impressed. The pie we brought home contained lots of lean, tender chicken meat, but it was coated in a gelatinous gravy. The biscuits on top, however, were superb—flaky and buttery. (As far as we're concerned, fruit pie is where Fran's real talents lie.)

At Putnam Farm you'll also find delicious fruit preserves and breads. And in the freezer there are containers of excellent homemade baked beans (fresh on weekends), chicken soup (wonderfully soothing), and those very flaky biscuits.

During the summer and into early winter, wooden carts and bins outside are filled with a wide variety of garden vegetables. The Putnams have a reputation for their muskmelons and their broad-leaf spinach ("Don't know what it is but everybody says ours is the best," Jim says proudly). Visiting Putnam Farm gives you a good feeling, like visiting old friends.

Sterling

■ Apple cider vinegar is believed to have been "invented" by the early American colonists. The natural sugars in apple cider were allowed to ferment first into alcohol (or hard cider), and then into vinegar. The tart apple-flavored vinegar was used to pickle vegetables and add flavor to soups, stews, and steamed vegetables. There are those who have long thought that apple cider

Scenic church spires against the backdrop of the Berkshires.

NEJAIME'S OF THE BERKSHIRES

Stockbridge Industrial Park, Stockbridge, 01262; phone 413-298-4246.

Nejaime's Lavasch is sold in grocery, health food, and gourmet stores around the U.S. and in Canada.

RED-WING MEADOW FARM

187 North Main Street, Sunderland, 01375; phone 413-665-3295 or 367-9494. Fishing ponds: 500 Sunderland Road. Pond-hours: weekends 10 A.M. to 3 P.M., weekdays by appointment only. Personal checks accepted. Classes and workshops offered.

vinegar has medicinal properties as well. Many New Englanders have been known to down small doses to aid digestion, fight a cold, or combat arthritis and other ailments.

Most of the apple cider vinegar you find on supermarket shelves these days is made from apple peelings and cores, artificially infused with oxygen and then bottled without being aged. But Sterling Cider Vinegar is different. It is made exclusively from the juice of whole fresh apples and is aged until it develops a mellow, fruity flavor. You can find it in many gourmet food shops throughout the region, or pick up a few bottles (at wholesale prices) at their large warehouse in downtown Sterling.

You'll also find a delicious full-flavored apple cider made here. Just step inside the warehouse and let the person at the front desk know how many gallons you want. Visitors are welcome to watch the cider being pressed.

Stockbridge

- How could bread baked in an industrial park and described by the manufacturer as "user friendly" be any good? It's hard to imagine, but Nejaime's Lavasch is great. Lavasch is actually less of a bread and more of a wafer (perhaps that's where they get the high-tech connection). It's crisp, and it tastes like toast.

The Original Flavor is loaded with sesame seeds. Other flavors include garlic, garlic/dill, onion, and poppy. Nejaime's Lavasch tastes better and fresher than many imported flatbreads, and it's made without preservatives.

Sunderland

- Wouldn't it be great to find a trout pond stocked with so many fish that no matter what the weather or time of day, there would always be plenty of bites at the end of your line? Well, short of building a pond in your own backyard and stocking it full of fish, Red-Wing Meadow Farm is your best bet.

"We raise trout for fun and profit," explained owner Kenneth Bergstrom. Red-Wing has five ponds stocked with thousands of rainbow and brown trout. The hatchery stocks 100,000 fish at any given time, ranging from just a few inches up to several pounds. There are a few ways to get a taste of Red-Wing trout, and the most adventurous is to catch it yourself. On summer weekends you can visit the ponds and fish all day; they'll even rent you the appropriate fishing gear. In winter, weather permitting, there's ice fishing. There's a small entry fee for access to the ponds and then you're charged according to the number of pounds of trout you catch.

Kenneth Bergstrom at Red-Wing Meadow Farm.

If fishing is not your thing, you can simply stop by Red-Wing and buy a live fish or have them gut and clean one for you. The trout range in size from 8 to 14 inches and are as fresh as any fish as you're likely to find anywhere.

Red-Wing is an experimental aquaculture venture. In addition to the trout hatchery, there is an indoor solar-heated greenhouse. Recently Bergstrom got the idea that if he could raise vegetables in the greenhouse, why not raise fish too? So he filled the greenhouse with tanks and began stocking fish called tilapia, a warm-water species from Africa. They have delicate white flesh and a very mild flavor. The fish can be bought whole from the farm. Bergstrom hopes to raise other warm-water species, such as catfish and bass, in the near future.

Kenneth Bergstrom also raises turkeys and beef at his home on the Connecticut River. The turkeys are organically raised and should be ordered early; they are always sold out by holiday time. The beef is also raised without additives; it can be bought by the side or quarter, or you can purchase the entire cow. Custom cutting is also available.

Watertown

KAY'S FRUIT
594 Mount Auburn Street, Watertown, 02172; phone 617-923-0523. Hours: Monday–Saturday 9 A.M. to 7 P.M.; closed Sunday. Cash only.

■ It was a display of small, shiny black Italian-style eggplant that first caught our eye. Actually it was the price—about half what we'd seen them sold for in some of Boston's more upscale neighborhoods. Surrounded by several excellent Armenian bakeries, restaurants, and food stores, Kay's offers a good selection of fresh fruits and vegetables at very reasonable prices. You'll also find open bins of olives, nuts, dried fruits, grains, and seeds.

Wenham

CRAIGSTON CHEESE COMPANY
Box 267, Wenham, 01984; phone 617-468-7497. Personal checks accepted. Mail order available.
Craigston Camembert is sold in gourmet food stores and cheese shops throughout New England.

■ We've all had the experience. You travel to a foreign country, taste a new food, and fall in love. Let's say your trip was to France and you just had your first taste of perfectly ripe Camembert cheese. You come home and find that your local cheese shop carries French camembert, and eager to relive culinary memories, you buy a small wheel. You bring it home, take a bite, and wonder what all the excitement was about. This stuff doesn't taste anything like the cheese you remember.

Susan Hollander had that experience. She claims it's nearly impossible to buy really good imported Camembert in this country. Transporting the cheese, she insists, interrupts the ripening process. So what do you do if you love Camembert and own a farm just 30 miles north of Boston with a small herd of Jersey cows? You beat the French at their own game and start making cheese your-

Trout in Orange Herb Sauce

What could be better than simple pan-fried trout, we asked Ken Bergstrom of Red-Wing Meadow Farm. "Try my trout in orange-herb sauce," he immediately replied. Well, we did, and while nothing can beat the flavor of a freshly caught trout pan-fried over a hot open fire, this sure comes close.

1 trout, 1 1/2 to 3 pounds, cleaned
2 tablespoons minced fresh parsley
2 tablespoons minced fresh tarragon
2 tablespoons minced fresh chives
2 tablespoons minced fresh thyme
8 tablespoons (1 stick) lightly salted butter, melted
1 teaspoon paprika
1 ounce cognac
Juice of 1 large orange

Preheat the oven to 350°. Place the trout in a large well-buttered baking pan. Using a sharp knife, cut three diagonal slices into the side of the trout. In a small bowl mix the parsley, tarragon, chives, and thyme. Stuff the herb mixture into the slashes in the fish. In another small bowl mix the butter, paprika, cognac, and orange juice. Pour this over the fish. Bake for 20 to 30 minutes, or until tender and flaky when tested with a fork. Serves 2 to 4.

---

self. The result: Craigston Camembert, a rich, creamy, mold-ripened cheese that tastes just about as good as anything you'll find in Europe.

We have gone through several wheels of Craigston Camembert and find that we like it more each time. We've served it with a platter of fresh fruit and berries, baked it into a golden cheese tart (see recipe below), and added small wedges of cheese, along with garlic croutons, to a fresh summer green salad. Our only caveat: the cheese generally needs several days to ripen after we buy it at our local cheese shop. Camembert must be slightly soft to very soft in the center, and should always be served at room temperature.

Westfield

FOWLER FARMS
Routes 10 and 202 (College Highway), Westfield, 01085; phone 413-562-7426. Hours: Monday–Saturday 8 A.M. to 7 P.M., Sunday 8 A.M. to 6 P.M. Personal checks accepted.

■ Carrots are the big thing at this roadside market. Fowler Farms claims to be the largest carrot grower in New England. As you might guess, huge piles of carrots are on display here, along with their own parsnips and squash. They also sell peppers, cabbage, potatoes, cauliflower, onions, garlic, and many other fruits and vegetables. The produce is not organic, but it is always fresh.

This is a good place to buy vegetables in bulk for canning. You can make an awful lot of relish and carrot cake with the contents of one of their 50-pound sacks of fresh carrots.

Golden Cheese Tart

This camembert tart comes from friend and food writer Deirdre Davis of Ipswich, Massachusetts. Flavored with fresh ginger, saffron, and orange rind, it's similar to a quiche but much more interesting. She suggests serving it as a first course, or as a luncheon dish accompanied by a salad made of escarole and melon slices with a fresh basil dressing.

The Pastry
1 1/2 cups sifted flour
1/2 teaspoon salt
1/2 teaspoon powdered ginger
8 tablespoons butter
3 to 4 tablespoons cold water

The Filling
1 1/2 cups heavy cream
2 ounces fresh ginger, peeled and sliced into very thin sticks
1 small package or vial of saffron, in threads
2 eggs
2 egg yolks
1 tablespoon flour
Salt and black pepper to taste
8 ounces very ripe Camembert or Brie, rind removed
Grated peel of 1 orange
1 tablespoon butter

Prepare the pastry: In a large bowl, combine the flour, salt, and ginger. Cut the butter into small pieces, and using your fingertips, work the butter into the flour mixture until it resembles bread crumbs. Add the water, 1 tablespoon at a time, adding enough to create a ball of dough. Working on a floured surface, roll out the dough until soft, and then form it into a ball. Wrap in plastic wrap and refrigerate for 1 hour.

Prepare the filling: Put the cream in a saucepan and bring it to a boil. Remove from the heat and add the fresh ginger. Cover, and let it sit for 2 hours. Strain, add the saffron threads, and set aside.

Place the eggs and egg yolks in a blender and mix for a few seconds. Add the flour, salt, pepper, Camembert, and ginger-saffron cream. Blend until smooth. Taste for seasoning, and add the orange peel.

Butter a 10-inch pie plate or quiche dish with the tablespoon of butter. Roll out the pastry and line the pie plate, trimming the edges. Let it rest in the refrigerator for about 30 minutes.

Preheat the oven to 375°. Pour the filling into the prepared pie shell, and bake for 30 to 40 minutes, or until a skewer or toothpick inserted in the center comes out clean. Serves 4 to 6.

Westhampton

OUTLOOK FARM
Route 66, Westhampton, 01027; phone 413-527-0633. Hours: Monday–Friday 6 A.M. to 8 P.M. (7 P.M. in winter),

■ "Your local convenience store and so much more," says the leaflet advertising Outlook Farm's weekly specials. High on a hill a few miles past Smith College, Outlook Farm sells fresh locally grown fruits and vegetables (including close to a dozen varieties of apples in the fall), fresh cider, baked goods, eggs from Pine Hill Farm (see page 137), and all the basics—everything from Campbell's soup to dog, cat, and rabbit food. The meat counter

Saturday and Sunday 6 A.M. to 7 P.M. (6 P.M. in winter). Cash only.

THE VILLAGE STORE/ROOT AND VINE

999 Main Road (Box C-51), Westport, 02790; phone 617-636-2572. (Root and Vine: P.O. Box 3051, Westport, 02790; phone 617-636-5155 or toll-free 800-334-8033.) Summer hours: seven days a week 9 A.M. to 5 P.M. Winter hours: Monday–Saturday 10 A.M. to 5 P.M.; closed Sunday. MasterCard, Visa, and personal checks accepted. Mail order available for beer- and wine-making supplies. Catering available.

here specializes in native naturally raised pork: thick chops, meaty spareribs, Italian sausage, and a deliciously spicy breakfast sausage. You can also pick up homemade soup, sandwiches, and stews at the lunch counter.

Westport

■ The people who run The Village Store have struck a nice balance in the products they sell. While they obviously go out of their way to carry foods made in New England, they also acknowledge that good food comes from many different sources. Their refrigerated display case, for example, is stocked with an extensive selection of New England cheeses. But they also carry imported cheese, including many varieties like blues and triple crèmes that simply aren't made in New England. Other regional specialties to look for include jams and jellies, Vermont maple products, local honey, and New England wines and beers.

The Village Store also bakes bread, pies, cakes, and cookies. In their kitchen they produce salads, soups, sandwiches, hors d'oeuvres, and take-home entrées.

The other part of the business, called Root and Vine, specializes in supplying home beer- and winemakers. They carry virtually everything a home brewer or vintner needs, including starter kits for beginners, exotic flavorings for those who want to experiment, a vast library of how-to books, even corks and bottle caps. Root and Vine also sells liqueur extracts imported from France for making cordials at home. And if you're not interested in making alcoholic beverages but want to have some fun with home brewing, they also carry soft drink extracts with flavors including birch beer, ginger beer, ginger ale, and cream soda. Call or write for a copy of their extensive mail-order catalogue and information about classes in beer- and winemaking.

Do-it-your-selfers can also order cheesemaking supplies, vinegar-making supplies, and sourdough starter from Root and Vine.

CARETAKER FARM

1210 Hancock Road, Williamstown, 01276; phone 413-458-4309. Hours: July 1 to mid-October, seven days a week 9 A.M. to 6 P.M. Personal checks accepted. Self-guided tours available.

Williamstown

■ Elizabeth and Sam Smith like it when people visit their organic vegetable and herb farm. It's not just because they want to show off their beautiful lettuce, carrots, beets, corn, squash, potatoes, and herbs. They also want to communicate their principles and ideas on farming. "We view what we do as educational," said Elizabeth. "Understanding organic farming seems to help people get their head screwed on right." The Smiths chose the name Caretaker Farm because, explained Elizabeth, "we believe we are caretakers of the land and that the land must be kept free, not exploited, for future generations."

Caretaker Farm produce is also sold at local health food stores and gourmet food shops.

THE SLIPPERY BANANA

43 Spring Street, Williamstown, 01267; phone 413-458-4788. Hours: Monday–Saturday 9 A.M. to 8 P.M., Sunday and holidays 9 A.M. to 5:30 P.M. MasterCard, Visa, and personal checks accepted.

WILD OATS FOOD COOP

Colonial Shopping Center, Route 2, Williamstown, 01267; phone 413-458-8060. Hours: Monday–Wednesday, Friday, and Saturday 9 A.M. to 6 P.M., Thursday 9 A.M. to 8 P.M.; closed Sunday. Personal checks accepted.

SMITH'S COUNTRY CHEESE

20 Otter River Road, Winchendon, 01475; phone 617-939-5738. Hours: Monday–Saturday 10 A.M. to 5 P.M., Sunday 1 P.M. to 6 P.M.

The farm's 7 cultivated acres produce some of the finest vegetables in the Berkshires. Mention the name Caretaker Farm and the Smiths' customers start to rave. "You've never seen lettuce like this," one woman exclaimed. "People use chemicals and they still don't get a head of lettuce like this. It's so beautiful you feel guilty eating it." Although the selection is constantly changing, one can usually find romaine, buttercrunch, Winter Density, Green Ice, and red and green leaf lettuce. In late fall the Smiths harvest a large crop of squash, carrots, and potatoes (including a hard-to-find variety called Red Norlands).

Elizabeth Smith also bakes whole grain organic breads, cookies, and fruit pies, and prepares fresh fruit jams and jellies, pickled vegetables, and granola. They also sell honey, maple syrup, and eggs from other local farms. This is a good place to buy naturally raised grass-fed lamb for your freezer.

■ This grocery store and cafe surely must have been designed with the students and faculty of nearby Williams College in mind. Located just a few steps off campus, the Slippery Banana offers everything from overstuffed deli sandwiches for a quick lunch between classes to a fine selection of produce and specialty foods that members of this academic community might desire to challenge their tastebuds.

■ You don't have to be a member of the Wild Oats Food Coop to shop here and take advantage of some of the area's best prices on organic vegetables, health foods, locally made cheese, and bread. The produce section is small but impressive—everything from organic cranberries and grapes to lemons and fresh melons. Shiitake mushrooms from nearby Delftree Corporation (see page 123) are also available. There's a good selection of honeys, nuts, grains, and pasta. You'll often find a line of customers waiting for the morning delivery of breads and cookies from local Clarksburg Bread Company.

Winchendon

■ It was a fluke—one of life's strange coincidences. The day we brought home Smith's Dutch-style Gouda cheese to sample, a friend from Holland arrived for a short visit. We immediately sat him down at the kitchen table and told him we had something for him to taste.

We unwrapped the pale yellow cheese, cut it into small chunks, and passed the plate around. Our Dutch friend brought the cheese up to his nose, like a winemaker savoring a complex bouquet. Then he tasted a small piece

MasterCard, Visa, and personal checks accepted. Mail order available.

Smith's gouda is also available at gourmet food stores, cheese shops, and several New England wineries.

without comment. He tasted several more chunks, again without saying a word. Finally he asked for a glass of water. He cleared his throat. And finally, he spoke. "This," he declared, "is not gouda. However . . . it's good. It's a very good cheese."

And that just about sums up how we feel about Smith's gouda—it's not what they call it, but it's a nice cheese nonetheless. Manufactured on the Smith family's dairy farm in north central Massachusetts, the cheese is made from raw milk and aged over sixty days, and has a mild flavor and creamy texture.

You can visit the Smiths' farm, where they sell "gouda" as well other New England cheeses, smoked foods, preserves, local maple and honey products, and crafts.

Taking care at Caretaker Farm in Williamstown.

PIE IN THE SKY
10 Water Street, Woods Hole, 02543; phone 617-540-5475. Hours: Monday–Friday 7 A.M. to 5 P.M., Saturday 7 A.M. to 3 P.M.; closed Sunday. Personal checks accepted.

Woods Hole

■ The Portuguese sweet bread they bake here has more flavor and substance than most we have tasted. It has a firm texture that makes it perfect for sandwiches.

In addition to selling breads, pastries, and quiches, Pie In The Sky runs a comfortable small cafe where they serve espresso, cappuccino, and light breakfasts and lunches.

Massachusetts Farmers' Markets

For further information, contact the Massachusetts Department of Food & Agriculture, 100 Cambridge Street, Boston, 02202; phone 617-727-3018.

Amesbury Farmers' Market, Amesbury Center, Saturdays from mid-June through October, 8 A.M. to 12 N.

Amherst—The Common Market, Town Common, Spring Street parking lot, Saturdays from early May to mid-November, 7 A.M. to 1:30 P.M.

Attleboro Farmers' & Gardeners' Market, MBTA commuter parking lot, South Main Street, Saturdays from mid-July through September, 8 A.M. to 12 N.

Auburn Farmers' Market, Heritage Mall, Route 12, Saturdays from mid-July through October, 9:30 A.M. to 2 P.M.

Barre Farmers' Market, Barre Common, Saturdays from mid-May through October, 9:30 A.M. to 12:30 P.M.

Belchertown Farmers' Market, Belchertown Center parking lot, Fridays from mid-June through October, 12 N. to 6 P.M.

Beverly Farmers' Market, Ellis Square, Briscoe Street, Thursdays from 12 N. to 4 P.M.

Boston—Brighams Circle/Mission Hill Farmers' Market, Brighams Circle, Osco Drug parking lot, Tremont Street, Thursdays from mid-July through October, 12 N. to 6 P.M.

Boston—Brighton Center Farmers' Market, Bank of Boston, Market Street, Saturdays, 9:30 A.M. to 2 P.M.

Boston—Fields Corner Farmers' Market, Park Street between Dorchester and Geneva avenues, Saturdays from mid-July through October, 9 A.M. to 2 P.M.

Boston—Jamaica Plain Farmers' Market, Curtis Hill (JP Municipal Building) parking lot, Centre and South streets, Tuesdays from June through October, 1 P.M. to 6 P.M.

Boston—Roslindale Farmers' Market, Taft Court, Roslindale Village, Saturdays from mid-July through October, 9 A.M. to 1 P.M.

Boston—South End Farmers' Market, corner of Columbus Avenue and Holyoke Street, Fridays from mid-July through October, 3 P.M. to 7 P.M.

Brockton Farmers' Market, Brockton Fairgrounds, Wednesdays and Saturdays from mid-July through October, 10 A.M. to 3 P.M.

Brockton City Hall Plaza Farmers' Market, City Hall. Fridays beginning mid-July, 11 A.M. to 4 P.M.

Brookline Farmers' Market, Webster Street parking lot, Coolidge Corner, Thursdays from mid-June through October, 1:30 P.M. to dusk.

Cambridge Farmers' Market/Central Square, corner of Bishop Allen Drive and Norfolk Street, Mondays from mid-July through October, 1 P.M. to 6 P.M.

Easthampton Farmers' Market, Union Plaza, Union Street, Tuesdays from May through November, 2:30 P.M. to 6:30 P.M.

Fall River Farmers' Markets, Kennedy Park, Saturdays from mid-May through November, 8:30 A.M. to 1 P.M. Also at Ruggles Park, Wednesdays from mid-May through November, 11 A.M. to 4 P.M.

Fitchburg—Valley West Plaza Farmers' Market, Valley West Plaza, River Street, Tuesdays beginning in July, 9 A.M. to 1 P.M.

Fitchburg—In-Town Garage Farmers' Market, In-Town Garage, Wednesdays beginning in July, 3 P.M. to 6 P.M.

Framingham Farmers' Market, next to St. Tarasis Church, Waverly Street, Saturdays from late June to mid-October.

Greenfield Farmers' Market, Franklin County Courthouse parking lot, Hope and Newton Streets, Saturdays from May through October, 8 A.M. to 12:30 P.M.

Haverhill Farmers' Market, corner of Bailey Blvd. and Main Street, Saturdays from July through October, 8 A.M. to 1 P.M.

Hingham Farmers' Market, Station Street parking lot, Hingham Harbor, Wednesdays and Saturdays from mid-May through October, 11 A.M. to 3 P.M.

Holden Farmers' Market, Chaffins Men's Club grounds, S. Main Street, Thursdays from mid-June to frost, 1:30 P.M. to 5:30 P.M.

Holyoke Farmers' Market, Hampden Park, Chestnut Street, Thursdays from May through October, 3 P.M. to 6:30 P.M.

Huntington Farmers' Market, Huntington Town Common, Saturdays from Memorial Day weekend through October, 9 A.M. to 12 N.

Lawrence Farmers' Market, next to Lawrence City Hall on Pemberton Way, Wednesdays from mid-June to mid-October, 9:30 A.M. to 4 P.M.

Lowell Farmers' Market, Lucy Larcom Park, Merrimack Street, Fridays from mid-May through October, 10 A.M. to 5 P.M.

Martha's Vineyard—West Tisbury Farmers' Market, West Tisbury Agricultural Hall, Saturdays from mid-June through September, 9 A.M. to 12 N.

Nantucket Farmers' Market, Main Street, Monday–Saturday from mid-June through September, 9 A.M. to 1 P.M.

Newton Farmers' Market, Newton City Hall, 1000 Commonwealth Avenue, Tuesdays from July through October, 2 P.M. to 6 P.M.

North Adams Farmers' Market, Berkshire Plaza, facing Route 2 artery and Holden Street, Saturdays from mid-July through September, 8:30 A.M. to 12 N.

Northampton Farmers' Market, Gothic Street next to Main Street, Saturdays from May through October, 7 A.M. to 12 N.

Pittsfield Farmers' Market, Allendale Shopping Center, Route 8, Wednesdays 9 A.M. to 2 P.M. and Saturdays 8 A.M. to 1 P.M. from May through October.

Quincy Farmers' Market, Hancock Street parking lot, Quincy Center, Fridays from June through October, 11:30 A.M. to 5 P.M.

Somerville Farmers' Market, Union Square, Wednesdays from end of June through October, 2 P.M. to 6 P.M.

Southbridge Farmers' Market, Main Street at the Methodist Church, Wednesdays and Saturdays from July through October, 9 A.M. to 1:30 P.M.

Springfield—Avocado Street, 158 Avocado Street, off Route 20, Saturdays from May through November, 8 A.M. to 12 N.

Springfield—Downtown, Springfield Civic Center, corner of East Court and Main Street, Wednesdays from May through November, 11 A.M. to 3 P.M.

Taunton Farmers' Market, Taunton Green, Fridays from late June through October, 10 A.M. to 4 P.M.

Topsfield Farmers' Market, Topsfield Fairground, Route 1, Saturdays from mid-July through September, 8 A.M. to 1 P.M.

Wenham Farmers' Market (Wenham Conservation Commission), Grapevine Road at intersection of Route 22 on Iron Rail Property, Saturdays from mid-July through October, 9 A.M. to 12 N.

West Newbury Farmers' Market, Laurel Grange Hall, Garden Street, Saturdays from August through October, 10 A.M. to 12 N.

Westfield Farmers' Market, Park Square, Saturdays from late May through October, 8 A.M. to 12 N.

Worcester Center Courtyard Farmers' Market, Worcester Center Courtyard, near Filene's. Mondays and Wednesdays from mid-June through October, 9:30 A.M. to 2 P.M.

Worcester S. Main Street Farmers' Market, St. Peter's Church parking lot, 900 block of S. Main Street, Fridays 9:30 A.M. to 2 P.M.

New Hampshire

NEW HAMPSHIRE

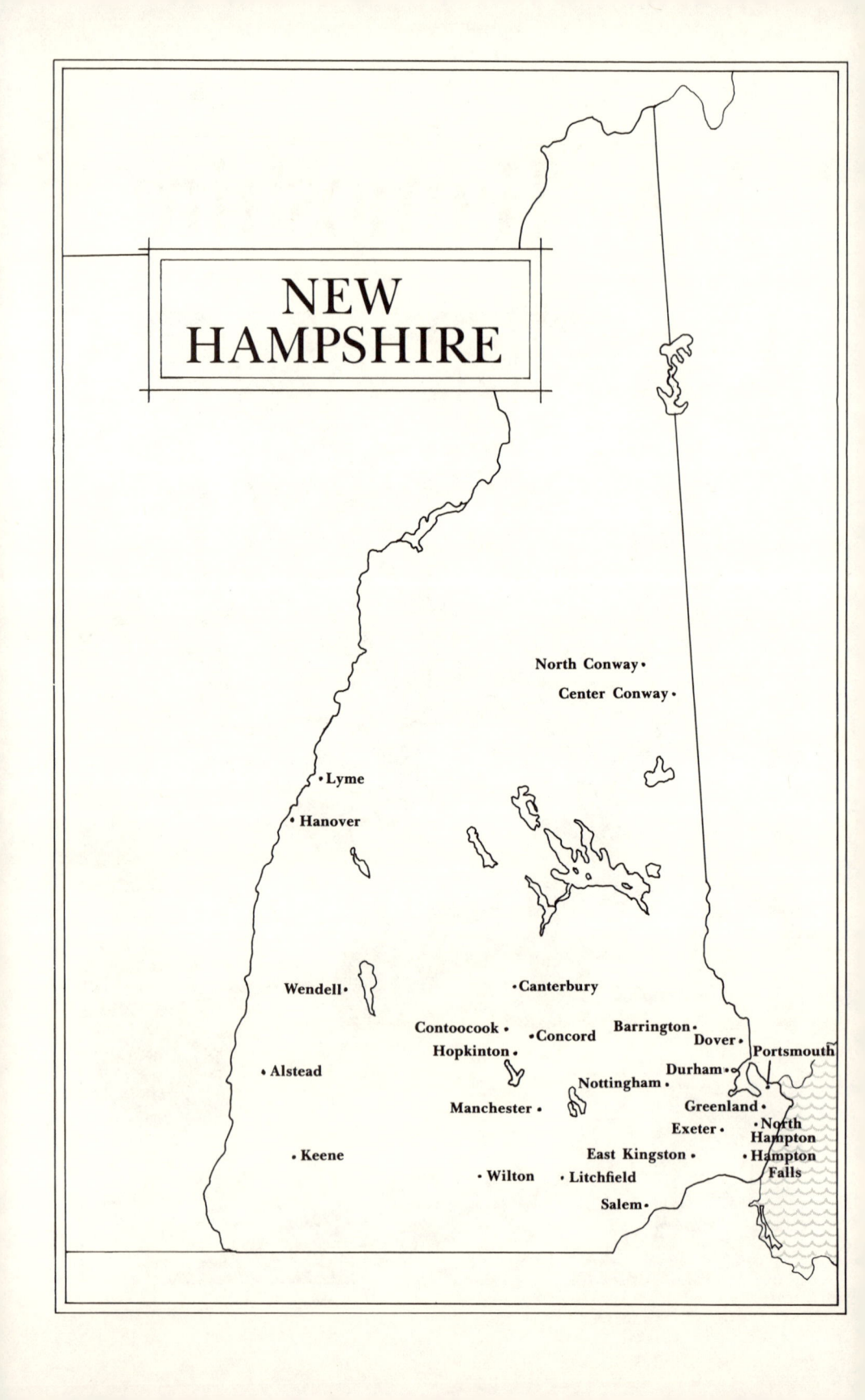

Alstead

BASCOM'S SUGAR HOUSE

RR 1, Box 138, Alstead, 03602 (call for directions); phone 603-835-2230 or 835-6361. Hours: Monday–Friday 7:30 A.M. to 5 P.M. Sugaring season: Saturday and Sunday 11 A.M. to 5 P.M. Visa, MasterCard, and personal checks accepted. Mail order available.

Bascom's maple syrup is sold throughout New Hampshire.

- This is the largest maple sugaring operation in New England. It's a great place to see syrup being made and to taste this natural sweetener in several different forms. During maple sugaring season—March 1 to April 10, approximately—you can watch sap being boiled in huge evaporator pans in the sugarhouse and breathe in the sweet steamy aroma. Bascom's also offers the chance to see how maple trees are tapped these days. Instead of metal buckets, they use miles of plastic tubing to carry the sap from the trees to a central collection point.

During the sugaring season they operate a snack bar that serves maple milk shakes, English muffins spread with maple cream, maple pecan pie, and dough boys—fritters dipped into maple syrup. They also make sugar on snow (a toffee-like candy made by pouring warm maple syrup on snow).

In addition to maple syrup and other maple products, Bascom's sells equipment for both commercial and home sugaring.

Barrington

CALEF'S COUNTRY STORE

Route 9 (P.O. Box 57), Barrington, 03825; phone 603-664-2231. Hours: seven days a week 8 A.M. to 6 P.M. MasterCard, Visa, and personal checks accepted. Mail order available.

- Calef's Country Store has been going strong since 1869, with its wooden barrels of half-sour and dill pickles, tables piled high with penny candy and homemade donuts, and the overwhelmingly seductive scent of smoked hams and bacon. Six generations of the Calef family have kept the store alive.

Local residents shop here for basics like milk, juice, paper towels, and newspapers. Others come from miles around to buy the Calef family's Snappy Cheddar Cheese, Vermont or New York cheddar that is aged for at least 6 months in wooden cheese boxes "down cellar." It comes mild, sharp, very sharp, and smoked. Free samples are always offered and rarely refused.

At the butcher counter you'll find some of the best smoked hams in New England. Around Easter and Christmas, devoted ham lovers line up to the front door, willing to wait for close to an hour for the succulent, moist, tender hickory-smoked meat. The ham contains no preservatives and has a subtle, not overwhelmingly smokey taste. Calef's also smokes thick slab bacon (which doesn't shrink when you cook it), and corns their own beef brisket.

Calef's also stocks a wide assortment of locally made jams and jellies, honeys, and maple syrup. There's extra-fancy molasses from Barbados and freshly made gingersnaps. On Sundays local bakers bring in still-warm loaves of bread and sugar donuts.

During the summer the front porch is filled with bushels of tomatoes, nectarines, and cucumbers grown by local farmers, displayed alongside baseball bats and garden seeds. In the fall it's a classic scene with pumpkins, apples, Indian corn, and fresh cider.

Three Glazes for New England Smoked Ham

Smoking helps preserve ham and brings out the flavor of the meat. Purists like to bake ham without any adornments, but we've found that a few simple seasonings, like whole cloves and fresh apple cider, only make it better. With that thought in mind, here are a few easy glazes for smoked ham, each one full of fresh flavors that will enhance, and not overwhelm, the meat's natural taste. All recipes are for an average 12-pound smoked ham, with the bone in.

Clove, Apple Cider, and Sherry Glaze: Using a small sharp knife, make about 20 "x" marks in the top of the ham. Insert a whole clove into each "x." Pour 2½ cups fresh apple cider and 1½ cups dry sherry over the ham. Let it marinate 2 to 48 hours, covered and refrigerated, before baking. Cook according to butcher's instructions, basting the meat every 30 minutes.

Grainy Mustard and Marmalade Glaze: Mix ½ cup grainy or Dijon-style mustard with 1½ cups orange or mixed-fruit marmalade. Brush on top of the ham during the last 30 minutes of baking, or until the glaze begins to turn brown.

Cassis and Orange Glaze: Pour 1½ cups cassis (black-currant liqueur) and 1½ cups orange juice (preferably fresh) over the ham. Bake according to instructions, basting the ham every 30 minutes.

Canterbury

CANTERBURY HERBS
Hackleboro Road (RR 1, Box 245), Canterbury, 03224; phone 603-783-4578. Hours: by appointment. Personal checks accepted. Mail order available.
  Also available in specialty and gourmet food stores in New Hampshire.

■ When Mary Kerwin went to Europe in 1976 to study farm technology and herb cultivation, she had no idea how much the trip would change her life. Kerwin arrived home and began growing herbs at her 200-year-old farm in Canterbury. She now grows dozens of varieties, as well as several types of garlic, using the "tips, hints, and folklore" she picked up from European herbalists.

"One of the most important things I learned from the older herb farmers," Kerwin recalls, "is that you should never sell pulverized herbs. Always sell the whole herb leaf so that all the volatile oils are retained. The other important lesson is that herbs should be grown organically. You are eating the leaf. If the leaf has chemicals in it, there's no chance to get rid of them before eating."

At Kerwin's farm, herbs are gathered by hand and picked fresh each morning, just after the dew has dried.

All the dried herbs are marked with the date of harvest so you will know exactly how old they are.

Kerwin produces five types of pesto—using dried Italian basil, rosemary, French tarragon, marjoram, and several types of thyme. Mix these herbs with garlic, olive oil, pine nuts or walnuts, and grated cheese and you have a very fresh-tasting sauce for pasta, steamed vegetables, salads, seafood, or grilled meats. You'll find it hard to believe you didn't start with fresh herbs. Also look for Canterbury Herbs' Great Italian Tomato Sauce Kit—a small package of dried basil, oregano, thyme, parsley, marjoram, and celery together with two heads of Kerwin's organic garlic. The recipe inside the package tells you how to put together a delicious sauce for pasta or pizza.

Kerwin grows exceptional garlic. Her crop includes a large-bulb Italian variety and a French variety with small bulbs and a very heady flavor. She makes beautiful garlic braids and wreaths.

Mary Kerwin also sells fresh herbs in season.

Center Conway

EARLE FAMILY FARM

Baird Hill Road, Center Conway, 03813; phone 603-447-6641. Hours: Memorial Day through Columbus Day, seven days a week 9 A.M. to 5 P.M. (self-serve). Personal checks accepted. Pick-your-own fruit available; call ahead for conditions.

The Earles' produce is also available at the Conway Farmers' Market (see page 178).

■ "We grow vegetables, fruit, and herbs naturally," explains Elizabeth Earle, who together with her husband, Thomas, runs the Earle Family Farm. "The flavor of the produce isn't altered in the slightest. Everything tastes good because it's pure."

The Earles cultivate about 3 1/2 acres of land and grow a wide variety of vegetables—everything from rhubarb, asparagus, and bok choy in the spring to corn, tomatoes, beans, squash, and leeks in the summer. They also grow herbs (lovage, Chinese leeks, borage, basil, savory, thymes, and various mints), flowers, and bedding plants. Everything is grown without the use of chemical fertilizers or pesticides. "We don't use anything we can't eat right away," says Elizabeth.

At the height of the season there are strawberries, raspberries, and blueberries. Depending on the weather, you can pick your own raspberries and blueberries, but be sure to call ahead to check on conditions.

ANTHRON'S

9 Depot Street, Concord, 03301; phone 603-224-5677. Hours: Monday–Thursday and Saturday 7:30 A.M. to 6 P.M., Fridays 7:30 A.M. to 8 P.M. MasterCard, Visa, and personal checks accepted. Catering available.

Concord

■ You'll find a bit of everything at this gourmet food shop—pâtés, fresh-baked breads, pasta, salads, sandwiches, cheeses, and frozen entrées. You can put together a picnic here or have Anthron's cater any sort of party, from an afternoon tea to a working luncheon. They'll even bring you breakfast in bed.

BLAKE'S TURKEY FARM

Silk Farm Road, Concord, 03301; phone 603-225-3532. Hours: Monday–Friday 8 A.M. to 5 P.M.; closed Saturday and Sunday except around holidays. Local checks accepted.

Blake's turkey pies are also available at supermarkets and gourmet food stores in central New Hampshire.

LA BOULANGERIE CAFE AND BAKERY

10 Depot Street, Concord, 03301; phone 603-224-6500. Hours: Monday–Saturday 8 A.M. to 6 P.M.; closed Sunday. Personal checks accepted.

GOULD HILL ORCHARDS

Gould Hill Road, Contoocook, 03229; phone 603-746-3811. Hours: August to Labor Day, seven days a week 10 A.M. to 5 P.M. Labor Day to Christmas, seven days a week 9 A.M. to 6 P.M. Christmas through May, Tuesday–Sunday 9:30 A.M. to 5 P.M.; closed Monday, and June and July. MasterCard, Visa, and personal checks accepted. Mail order and pick-your-own available.

■ Blake's turkey pies are made with nothing but meat, a well-seasoned gravy, and a delicate crust. You can buy an all-white-meat turkey pie or a white and dark meat mixture.

Around the holidays Blake's is the favorite place in the Concord area to pick up a fresh-killed bird. You must, however, order your turkey a good month ahead of time, as they always sell out.

■ We were walking around downtown Concord, grumbling about the lack of good food in this city, when we noticed a small bakery in the basement of an old brick building. Inside, the brick walls were painted bright white, the cafe tables were decorated with fresh flowers, and on the walls hung an exhibition of watercolors by a local artist. But most important was what we saw inside the glass pastry case: beautiful-looking tarts, cakes, croissants, cookies, and danish.

As soon as we arrived, a tall basket of just-baked *baguettes* arrived from the kitchen, followed by a plate of strange-shaped pizzas. The *baguette* was superb—a long, thin loaf with a crisp, flaky crust and firm, doughy inside. The pizza, also long and thin, was made of croissant dough rolled out and topped with tomatoes, cheese, and fresh herbs and vegetables. The crust was crisp, buttery, and delicate, a perfect balance to the heady flavors of the topping.

La Boulangerie also offers pies, tarts, cookies, and cakes. But the sweet pastries are not nearly as good as the savory items.

Contoocook

■ This is one of the most beautiful apple orchards in New England. Fields planted with large apple trees slope away beneath you, revealing a spectacular view of Mt. Kearsarge and the White Mountains. The setting is particularly captivating in mid-May, when the apple trees are in bloom. Thousands of tiny white blossoms seem like reminders of the snow that has melted just weeks earlier. In the fall Gould Hill Orchards is the perfect place to pick your own apples. Whenever you get tired of picking, take a moment to look at the view and you're sure to be reinvigorated.

Close to forty different kinds of apples are grown here, including hard-to-find antique varieties and two new types developed by the owners of the orchard. One of these is so new that when we visited it didn't even have a name. They just called it "Brand X."

The quality of the apples is exceptional, and it's noticeable well after apple season has passed. They have a controlled-atmosphere storage system that keeps the ap-

Picking apples—time for cider.

ples "alive" for up to ten months. The result: apples that are crisp, juicy, and exceptionally flavorful even in the spring.

Gould Hill Orchards also presses their own apple cider. Their sugarhouse is open to visitors during maple syrup season. In addition to apples they grow peaches, pumpkins, and winter squash. The orchard is open to hikers, picnickers, and cross-country skiers.

Dover

BROOKFORD FARM
RFD 1, Dover, 03820; phone 603-742-8688. Hours: by appointment. Personal checks accepted.

■ A lot of people we know have stopped eating veal. They've seen the documentaries and television commercials showing baby calves confined to tiny pens where they don't even have enough room to scratch their rear quarters. The message is clear: conditions are barbaric and anyone with a conscience should not be supporting the veal industry. So we, too, stopped eating veal. That is, until we met Robin Aikman at Brookford Farm.

Aikman raises veal organically—on milk, grass, and hay. These are "free-ranging" animals, which according to Aikman means "they are allowed to go out in the open and play." Aikman also raises organically fed lamb on her farm, a gorgeous, hilly piece of land bordering the Salmon Falls River. Both the veal and the lamb are raised to order. You must place your order (for either the whole animal or half) before April 1. Take it from us: you can't buy meat this tender and flavorful in any store.

TUTTLE'S RED BARN

Dover Point Road (Route 16), Dover, 03820; phone 603-742-4313. Hours: seven days a week 8:30 A.M. to 7 P.M. Local checks accepted.

■ "America's oldest family farm" has gone through many changes since John Tuttle first arrived here from England in 1630. Lucy Tuttle, who is the eleventh generation of the Tuttle family to run the farm, has watched it develop from a small one-room farm stand to its current incarnation, a series of huge red barns and greenhouses filled with produce, plants, and specialty foods—sun-dried tomatoes and black olive purée from Italy, bagels and croissants from Boston, raspberry almond tortes and blueberry butter from New Hampshire, pâtés, olive oils, and cheeses from France.

The new, much expanded Tuttle's opened in April 1987 and was met with some skepticism. "A lot of our old-time customers walked in and said, 'Oh gosh, I miss the old atmosphere,' " said Lucy Tuttle. "They thought the place was too big. They missed the little woven baskets everyone used to gather groceries in. They didn't like the new grocery carts." But after a while, Tuttle said, people came back and realized how much the new store has to offer. "People have trouble with change, but change is inevitable," she told us.

Most people in the New Hampshire Seacoast area are just thankful that Tuttle's is still around. As land prices in southern New Hampshire skyrocket and farmland is turned into condos and housing developments, Tuttle's 240-acre farm becomes more and more of a rarity. But the Tuttles are committed to farming, and they use their land to grow a wide variety of vegetables, fruit, and herbs—everything from rhubarb, mustard greens, peas, and strawberries in the spring to lettuce, tomatoes, basil, green beans, corn, and eggplant in the summer. We know one Dover resident who refuses to have her own summer garden. "Why bother," she asks, "when there's such good stuff at Tuttle's?"

We visited Tuttle's recently to get a little perspective on the farm's history.

"No one is exactly sure why John Tuttle came to Dover," Lucy Tuttle began. "We only know that he had received a land grant from the King of England, and being a staunch Quaker, he was probably escaping religious persecution." John Tuttle began homesteading. He cleared the land, which was full of rocks and boulders, and raised enough animals and crops to help his family survive. The Tuttle farm remained a family farm until the early 1900s, when William Penn Tuttle acquired additional land from his neighbors and began growing more fruit and vegetables than his family could eat. William Tuttle took his excess produce, loaded it onto a horse-drawn wagon, and trotted off to town to see if any of his neighbors wanted to buy some vegetables. Word got around. Tuttle's corn was good. His potatoes were even better. With time the business expanded. Years later, driving a Model T truck, Tuttle delivered fruits and vegetables to many of the area's grocery stores.

In the mid-1950s Lucy's father, Hugh Tuttle, sensed changes coming in the food business. All the small family-run stores that Tuttle's supplied were being wiped out by large supermarket chains. "These supermarkets were not particularly interested in buying high-quality locally grown produce," explained Lucy Tuttle. "They did what was easiest and bought from California and Florida, where farmers could guarantee them fruits and vegetables year-round. Father knew he had to either start his own store or go out of business." Hugh Tuttle made the decision not to quit farming, and he turned a few stalls in the farm's early-nineteenth-century barn into a retail store.

"Father sold only what we grew here on the farm," recalled Lucy. "We'd open in the spring with asparagus and put a little tin can out and people would leave their money. Over time people started saying, 'Boy, it's too bad you don't have this and it's too bad you don't have that.' They bought their vegetables here, but they had to go elsewhere for everything else. That was the beginning of the expansion."

In 1956 the barn was turned into a full-fledged store. "Things stayed pretty quiet here until the early '70s when

Baked Green Bean Bundles Wrapped in Prosciutto

Serve these bean "bundles" as an hors d'oeuvre, first course, or as a side dish with grilled lamb chops.

3/4 pound young, tender green beans, washed and trimmed	1 tablespoon olive oil
	1 tablespoon minced garlic
3/4 pound prosciutto, sliced paper-thin	Freshly ground black pepper to taste
3 tablespoons unsalted butter	1/3 cup grated Parmesan cheese

Blanch the beans in a large pot of boiling water for 1 minute. Drain, and refresh under cold running water. Drain again.

Gather about 8 to 10 beans to form a small bundle. Trim the ends so they are all the same length. Fold a slice of prosciutto in half lengthwise and roll it around the bean bundle. Repeat with the remaining beans and prosciutto, and place the bundles in a large shallow baking pan. (The recipe can be prepared ahead of time and refrigerated, covered, up to this point.)

Preheat the oven to 350°. In a small saucepan combine the butter, olive oil, garlic, and pepper, and place over low heat. Simmer 2 to 3 minutes, being careful not to let the butter burn. Pour the garlic butter over the beans, and bake 10 minutes. Remove the dish from the oven and spoon the grated cheese evenly over the beans. Place the dish under a broiler and broil for 1 minute, or until the cheese is bubbling and golden brown. Serve hot. Serves 4 to 6.

my brother and I got involved and started buying local produce from other farms and buying imported items from wholesalers." And then Lucy Tuttle hesitates, but decides to say what's on her mind anyway. "What we did was begin to market this farm and make its future viable."

The members of the eleventh generation of Tuttles now have their own children. Will the twelfth generation continue the tradition? "I'd hate to tell my kids they *have* to work at the farm," says Lucy Tuttle. "But it sure would be sad to see this place go after so many centuries."

Durham

EMERY FARM
Route 4, Durham, 03824; phone 603-742-8495. Hours: Easter through mid-October, seven days a week 8 A.M. to 7 P.M. Mid-October through Christmas Eve, seven days a week 9 A.M. to 6 P.M. Closed Christmas to Easter. MasterCard, Visa, and local checks accepted. Pick-your-own available; call ahead for conditions.

■ In 1655 Joseph Smith began farming this land, and today, eleven generations later, the farm is still maintained by the same family. Fresh berries are the main draw here. On a sloping hill you'll find a strawberry patch (including five different species), five varieties of blueberries, three types of raspberries, and four types of peaches, including a large, particularly juicy variety known as Red Haven. In the spring there's a whole field of tall, thin asparagus and around the holidays, fresh-cut Christmas trees. Pick-your-own is available for strawberries, blueberries, and raspberries.

Emery Farm sells only locally grown fruit and vegetables. In addition to what they grow themselves, their small farm stand is stocked with native apples and summer produce, maple syrup and honey, breads, cookies, and muffins made at nearby bakeries, and crafts and pottery from New Hampshire and Maine artists. A newly designed greenhouse offers annual and perennial flower, vegetable, and herb plants during the spring and early summer.

A curious stare from some New Hampshire beef cattle.

East Kingston

MAPLEVALE FARM
Route 107, East Kingston, 03827; phone 603-642-3381. Hours: Monday–Saturday 9 A.M. to 5 P.M., Sunday 1 P.M. to 4 P.M. Personal checks accepted. Pick-your-own fruit available; call ahead for conditions.

Maplevale Farm products are also sold at the Portsmouth and Dover Farmers' Markets (see page 178).

■ "Around our house," says Judy Levis, who along with her husband, Bruce, runs Maplevale Farm, "chicken is a dirty word." The Levises raise turkeys—lots of them. And in addition to selling whole birds, both fresh and frozen, they produce an astounding array of frozen turkey products. Their all-meat turkey pies are especially good. They come in three sizes and three varieties: all white meat, all dark meat, and mixed. These pies have lots of chunky, tender pieces of turkey mixed with a smooth, light gravy and encased in a light pastry crust.

Maplevale Farm also sells frozen turkey à la king, frozen turkey stuffing, individual roast turkey dinners, turkey soup, and turkey and dumplings. They will even stuff and roast a turkey for you if you give them 48 hours' notice.

And if it's a holiday meal you're planning, they can take care of that too. The farm sells fresh-killed turkeys in the fall, from the end of September through December. They also sell fresh cranberries in November and December, and ready-to-bake apple, mince, and blueberry pies and apple crisp.

While turkey is the star at Maplevale Farm, they also have their own orchards, offering pick-your-own fruit throughout the summer and fall. Raspberries are ready for picking around the first of July; the blueberry season goes from mid-July through September. Peaches and nectarines ripen somewhere around August through September, and fresh, super-juicy pears ripen around the middle of August. The Levis family also raises eight varieties of apples—Jersey Macs begin the season in late August and Ida Reds wind things up in late October. Also available in the fall: pumpkins, gourds, and winter squash.

Exeter

THE CHOCOLATIER
27 Water Street, Exeter, 03833; phone 603-772-5253. Hours: Monday–Saturday 9:30 A.M. to 5:30 P.M.; closed Sunday. Personal checks accepted. MasterCard and Visa accepted for orders over $20. Mail order available, except during summer months.

■ The handmade candies at The Chocolatier range from classics like nut clusters, maple and raspberry creams, peppermint patties, and chocolate-dipped pretzels to more sophisticated items like Tier Mints (mint cream sandwiched between thin layers of dark chocolate), hazelnut truffles, and chocolate-dipped candied ginger. The assortment we sampled was delicious—made with high-quality chocolate and very fresh-tasting fillings. During the spring and summer look for their plump, juicy strawberries hand-dipped in dark chocolate.

Easter is a colorful time at most chocolate shops, but the scene at The Chocolatier is particularly enchanting. Even the most diehard cynic would be hard-pressed to ignore the wonders of this small shop filled from floor to

THE COOK'S CHOICE

33 Water Street Park, Exeter, 03833; phone 603-778-7585. Hours: Monday–Friday 9:30 A.M. to 5:30 P.M., Saturday 9:30 A.M. to 5 P.M.; closed Sunday. MasterCard and Visa accepted for purchases over $20. Personal checks accepted. Mail order available.

HODGDON'S TURKEY FARM

Park Avenue (adjacent to Post Road), Greenland, 03840; phone 603-436-6723. Hours: November through mid-January, seven days a week 8 A.M. to 5 P.M. Personal checks accepted.

YE OLDE ALLEN FARM

Corner of Route 101 and Great Bay Road, Greenland, 03840; phone 603-436-2861. Hours: mid-June through October, seven days a week 8 A.M. to 5 P.M.; closed November to mid-June. Cash only. Pick-your own available; call ahead for conditions.
   Ye Olde Allen Farm

ceiling with enormous chocolate bunnies, chocolate boxes stuffed with jelly beans, and chocolate-dipped fruit.

■ This is the place to come to if you're looking for Spanish sherry vinegar or extra virgin olive oil from Italy, terracotta cookware from Spain, Kona coffee beans from Hawaii, or black-currant tea from England. The Cook's Choice is an attractive, well-stocked shop filled with gourmet foods and cookware from around the world. There's also a freezer full of their own hors d'oeuvres, casseroles, and pastries and a good collection of cheeses and deli meats. At lunchtime you'll find soup and sandwiches to go. Beware: prices here are high.

Greenland

■ Hodgdon's Turkey Farm raises several thousand turkeys every year. The place is wild the day before Thanksgiving, as customers stream in and out. You walk in, announce your name and the weight of the bird you want, and within seconds a person peeks out of a refrigerated closet with your freshly killed turkey. All turkeys should be ordered in advance (although we once saw someone arrive unannounced late on Christmas Eve and walk away with a beautiful 30-pound bird). The turkeys here are raised without chemical feed and are allowed to roam around in outdoor pens. The conditions make for an incredibly tender, juicy bird. Remember: really fresh turkeys take a lot less time to cook than frozen ones.
   In addition to turkey, you'll also find homemade bread and pies, locally pressed apple cider, turkey pies and gravy. A beautiful assortment of dried flowers and holiday wreaths are also available. In the late spring the farm is open for strawberry picking; call ahead to check on conditions.

■ When we heard that Jim Kroitzsh of Ye Olde Allen Farm was selling off more than half his land to real estate developers, we figured the farm would die. But Kroitzsh said "no way," and he is continuing to plant all sorts of fruits and vegetables on his remaining 12 acres and the 20 he rents nearby. The season starts with pick-your-own strawberries, followed by very plump, juicy raspberries. Ye Olde Allen Farm also grows a wide variety of summer vegetables, including some of the best sweet corn around.
   But fall is our favorite time of year at this farm, because that's when they begin making their excellent apple cider. Visitors are welcome to watch the cider being made on the old wooden press, and free samples are always availa-

APPLECREST FARM

Route 88, Hampton Falls, 03844; phone 603-926-3721. Summer hours: seven days a week, 8 A.M. to 7 P.M. Winter hours: seven days a week, 8 A.M. to 5 P.M. Visa, MasterCard, and personal checks accepted. Pick-your-own fruit available; call ahead for conditions.

Apples, cider, and produce are also sold at the Big Apple on Route 1 Hampton Falls and at the Apple Cart in Amesbury, Massachusetts.

cider is also sold at country stores and gourmet food shops in the New Hampshire Seacoast area.

ble. The orchard also offers close to a dozen varieties of apples (all available for pick-your-own), as well as pumpkins, squash, dried flowers, jams, and jellies.

Hampton Falls

■ Peter Wagner admits that it won't be easy holding on to his 500-acre apple farm. The New Hampshire Seacoast continues to experience a real estate boom, and according to Wagner the farm can't survive at its current size for much longer—the land is just too valuable to be used for agriculture. He did tell us, however, that the farm's spectacular orchards will probably stay intact for another ten years. In the meantime maybe we can all buy enough apples to convince Wagner not to sell his land for condos or tract housing.

Over forty varieties of apple grow in this orchard—everything from standards like Mac's and Golden Delicious to lesser-known varieties like Mutsu, Paula Red, Winter Banana, Ida Red, and Russet. The apples are sold by the bushel or by the piece, and several varieties are blended to make sweet cider. Wagner is particularly proud of his Christmas Holiday Blend Cider, which uses the sweet, aromatic (and difficult to grow) Russet apple and is available only around the holidays.

A little more than half the apple trees here are sprayed with alar; if you prefer alar-free apples, just ask and someone will direct you to the ones that have not been sprayed. The same goes for preservative-free apple cider: you have to ask for it.

An orchard lies dormant in the New Hampshire winter.

Be sure to visit Applecrest Farm in the summer, when you can pick your own fruit and berries. There are strawberries, peaches, pears, blueberries, and raspberries. In the fall you can pick your own pumpkin from the farm's large patch. In the summer they sell a good variety of vegetables grown on the farm and on other local farms. And year-round there are freshly baked fruit pies, apple tarts, cookies, and other sweets.

And if you want to work up an appetite, hay rides are given at harvest time, and cross-country ski trails are open in the winter at Applecrest Farm.

Hanover

HANOVER CONSUMER COOPERATIVE SOCIETY

45 South Park Street, Hanover, 03755; phone 603-643-2667. Hours: Monday–Thursday and Saturday 9 A.M. to 6 P.M.; Friday 9 A.M. to 8 P.M.; closed Sunday. Personal checks accepted.

■ We were totally blown away when we visited this sleek, modern supermarket. The Hanover food co-op has one of the finest selections of New England–made, organic, and ethnic foods under one roof available in northern New England. Walking down brightly lit aisles stocked with creamy Vermont goat cheese, plump fresh figs, smoked Maine trout, and organically raised pork and

Is chèvre so popular because the goats are so charming?

Fresh pasta—one of the specialities at Angelina's in Portsmouth.

THE FRAGRANCE SHOP

College Hill Road, Hopkinton (mailing address: 49 Old Concord Road, Henniker, 03242); phone 603-746-4431. Shop hours: mid-April through Christmas Eve, Tuesday–Saturday 10 A.M. to 5 P.M.; closed Sunday and Monday. Garden: May through September, same hours. MasterCard, Visa, American Express, Discover, and personal checks accepted. Mail order available.

lamb, we found it hard to make a connection between this store and the hole-in-the-wall co-ops supported by most communities.

But the Hanover food co-op was once just some sacks of grain and crates of vegetables in somebody's garage. That was in 1936, the year the co-op was founded by seventeen people from Hanover and nearby Norwich, Vermont. Today there are some six thousand co-op members, and manager Arthur Gerstenberger says it's the most successful store of its kind in the country.

The key to the co-op's success seems to be that it has something for just about everyone—from exotics like imported sugarcane and star fruit to New Hampshire apples and everyday household items including laundry detergent and aluminum foil. The co-op's membership is equally diverse, encompassing Ivy Leaguers from nearby Dartmouth College and back-to-the-landers who moved to this part of New England in the '60s.

There is an abundance of regional food on sale here, and it is clearly marked, so for visitors to the area the co-op offers a chance to survey the broad expanse of New England's culinary landscape. Shoppers are also assured that, because it is a consumer's cooperative, the prices will be fair, although not always the rock-bottom cheapest.

Hopkinton

■ Fragrance is the key word here. As soon as we got out of our car we were overwhelmed by the scent of fresh herbs and flowers. We followed the little pathway through the exhibition herb garden, inhaling all the way.

The Fragrance Shop is housed in a large eighteenth-century barn. Dried herbs and flowers hang from the rough-hewn wooden beams overhead, and the barn is filled with culinary herbs, herbal wreaths, herb books, herbal tea mixtures, herbal cooking mixtures, and potpourris. There are dry herbs from all over the world, but a good deal of the fresh herbs you find here come from the shop's own gardens, located directly behind the barn.

The Fragrance Shop offers over a hundred varieties of field-grown herbs and flowering perennials. There are the usual types of culinary herbs, and some unusual varieties as well. You'll find eight kinds of thyme, including lemon thyme, coconut thyme, and nutmeg thyme. There's French sorrel, lovage, and sweet cicely, an old-fashioned herb with a mild licorice flavor and delicate white blossoms. The Fragrance Shop also grows herbs known for their medicinal qualities, such as feverfew, said to have the same properties as aspirin.

All the herbs are grown with composted manure and a minimum of chemical sprays. You can stop by for a tour of the gardens any time and choose whatever herbs or flowers you'd like right out of the ground. The freshly dug herbs are wrapped in newspaper, and some pertinent growing information is included.

The herbal and flower wreaths, potpourris, dried flower arrangements, and herbal cooking blends are all available by mail.

Keene

DRAKE'S DUCK
RD 2, Box 810, Keene, 03431; phone 603-357-5858. Mail order available during winter months only.

Drake's Duck products are available at gourmet food stores in New

- There's nothing like good homemade butter, and it doesn't get much better than the stuff made by Drake's Duck. Using fresh cream from several northern New England dairies, Chris and Marie Drake make a light, fluffy, unsalted sweet cream butter. But they don't stop there. The butter is also used as a base for butters flavored with fresh herbs, fruit, and berries.

We use their herb butter on steamed vegetables, grilled fish, and as a topping for baked potatoes. The Red Raspberry butter is outrageously good. Whether you

---

Herb Baguette

You can make this simple French-style bread using dried herbs, but fresh herbs are preferable. If possible, use a French bread pan to bake the bread. Serve it warm with salads, roasts, or a thick soup or stew.

1 1/2 cups warm water
1 1/2 tablespoons yeast
1 tablespoon honey
4 cups unbleached white flour
1 teaspoon salt
6 tablespoons mixed fresh herbs (thyme, rosemary, sage, lemon verbena, oregano, and basil), or 3 1/2 teaspoons dried
2 tablespoons lightly salted butter, melted
Olive oil

In a large bowl, combine the warm water, yeast, and honey. Let it sit in a warm spot for about 10 to 15 minutes, or until the yeast has dissolved and is starting to bubble. Sift the flour and salt over the yeast mixture, 1 cup at a time, incorporating the flour until the dough forms a large ball.

Lightly flour a working surface and a rolling pin. Cut the dough in half, and roll each half out to form a rectangle about 15 inches long and 8 inches wide. Scatter half the herbs over the surface of one rectangle, and press them into the dough. Drizzle half the melted butter over the surface. Gently roll the dough up, into the shape of a baguette. Repeat with the other half of the dough. Place in a well-greased French bread pan or on a cookie sheet, drape a clean tea towel over the dough, and set in a warm spot for 20 minutes to rise.

Preheat the oven to 450°. Lightly brush the dough with olive oil, and bake for 20 minutes on the middle shelf. Remove, and let cool slightly before serving. The bread can be frozen. Makes 2 loaves.

Hampshire, Massachusetts, and Vermont.

spread it on toast or corn bread, or use it to glaze a duck or roast chicken, the fresh berry flavor comes shining through. The Cranberry Orange butter is also quite good, as is the blueberry. They are like having butter and jam combined in one product.

Drake's Ducks makes excellent pesto (although it's dearly overpriced) and wonderful raspberry linzertortes. They also prepare a line of frozen vegetarian "gourmet entrées" (including Shrimp à l'Orange, Vegetable Fettuccine Alfredo, and Spanakopita)—kind of like yuppie T.V. dinners. We like the idea, especially since these entrées are made with fresh eggs, garden vegetables, and homemade butter, but these frozen foods just don't measure up to the other Drake's Ducks products we've tasted.

Litchfield

WILSON FARM OF NEW HAMPSHIRE

Route 3-A, Litchfield, 03051; phone 603-882-5551. Hours: April 1 through Christmas, Monday–Saturday 9 A.M. to 6:30 P.M., Sunday 9 A.M. to 5:30 P.M.; closed Tuesday. Personal checks accepted. Pick-your-own available; call ahead for conditions.

There is a Wilson Farm store in Lexington, Massachusetts, also (see page 115).

■ Wilson Farm has a reputation for growing top-quality produce. It's been run by the Wilson family since 1884, and many people just won't buy their summer fruits and vegetables anywhere else. This is not an organic farm, but according to owner Debbie Wilson, "sprays are used only when plants are seriously infected."

In addition to the farm-raised produce, they sell fresh eggs from their own flock of hens, local dairy products, and some imported fruits and vegetables. Throughout the growing season Wilson Farm runs a pick-your-own operation. Beginning in mid-June there are strawberries, followed by raspberries, blueberries, tomatoes, and sweet peppers. On weekends, a team of Belgian draft horses takes visitors in and out of the picking fields. (You can also rent the horses for a private hay ride, or in the winter a sleigh ride, around the farm and the surrounding woods.)

Lyme

FOX MORE THAN A MUSTARD

Fox Hollow Farm, RFD 85, Lyme, 03768; phone 603-643-6002. Personal checks accepted. Mail order only.

Also available at gourmet food stores, country stores, and health food stores throughout the Northeast.

■ It doesn't look much like a mustard, and to tell you the truth it doesn't really taste like mustard, either. Fox More Than A Mustard (hereafter referred to as F.M.T.A.M.) is a super-thick, dark colored condiment made with mustard powder, fresh garlic, brown sugar, spices, and vinegar. It is the vinegar, and not the mustard, that makes this product so unique. This is not your ordinary add-a-little-zip type of vinegar; it's balsamic vinegar, or *aceto balsamico*—an intensely sweet dark vinegar made in Modena, Italy, that is aged in wooden casks for several years. It gives F.M.T.A.M. a sweet, pungent, and refined flavor.

When you try this stuff, try not to think of it as mustard or your taste buds might get confused. At first we didn't like it, but once we let go of the idea of "mustard," it started to grow on us. Try it on burgers and sausages, added to salad dressings, or as a glaze for meat, pork, or poultry. Phyllis Fox, the inventor of F.M.T.A.M., suggests mixing 1 tablespoon with ½ cup mayonnaise and serving the sauce with cold shrimp, crab, or lobster salad.

Manchester

ANGELA'S PASTA AND CHEESE SHOP
414 Union Street, Manchester, 03103; phone 603-625-9544. Hours: Monday–Friday 9 A.M. to 6 P.M., Saturday 9 A.M. to 4 P.M.; closed Sunday. During July and August, closed on Saturdays at 1 P.M. Personal checks accepted.

■ The sign in the window urges passersby to "discover the pleasures of fresh pasta." We happily accepted the invitation, and were not disappointed. Angela's makes fresh pasta in several different flavors including spinach, egg, whole wheat, and vegetable. Unlike many fresh pastas where the extra ingredients seem to add nothing more than a bit of color, these have real flavor. The vegetable pasta, for example, has subtle overtones of garlic, tomatoes, and carrots. It marries perfectly with Angela's Alfredo Sauce, a thick, creamy combination of cheese and cream flavored with nutmeg.

Fresh pasta is only part of the story at Angela's. A cold rigatoni salad with artichoke hearts in a herbal tomato sauce was light and flavorful. Another salad, made with orzo, dill, parsley, cherry tomatoes, olive oil, and lemon juice, tasted incredibly fresh and had a wonderful *al dente* texture. We also sampled one of Angela's cannoli. The creamy filling had just the right sweetness, and the shell was crisp and light.

Angela's also makes prepared pasta dishes, including manicotti and lasagna (but the pasta in these dishes is not their own). They have a big selection of imported and domestic cheeses, Italian-style sausages, pâtés, imported oils and vinegars, imported cookies and crackers, and a small wine department.

BAKOLAS MARKET
110 Spruce Street, Manchester, 03103; phone 603-669-2941. Hours: Monday–Saturday 7 A.M. to 9 P.M., Sunday 9 A.M. to 2 P.M. Local checks accepted.

■ This small Greek grocery store doesn't look like much from the outside, and to tell you the truth it doesn't look like much on the inside, either. But take a little time to check it out, and you'll discover some hard-to-find Greek specialties and a family of shopkeepers who are warm, friendly, and eager to educate customers about Greek culinary customs.

What first attracted us to Bakolas Market was the big sign outside advertising spring lamb. We happened to visit the week before Easter, and when we inquired about buying some lamb the man behind the counter looked panicked. "Oh no," stuttered Jim Bakolas. "I'm so sorry, but we sold out. We completely sold out. We got the best lamb around and everyone ordered it all up for the holiday. I'm so sorry. Really, really sorry. Maybe I could find you a leg?"

"It's O.K., it's O.K.," we quickly answered. "We were just asking."

"Oooh," said Mr. Bakolas, breathing a huge sigh of relief. At Bakolas, they like to please.

What they did have on hand was an excellent assortment of Greek olives, both the jumbo black Calamatas and some wonderfully spicy green olives. There was a small assortment of Greek cheeses, as well as bottled *tamara*, the tiny fish roe used to make the Greek appetizer *taramasalata*. Fresh phyllo pastry is always available, ideal for making a spinach and cheese pie. There's Greek orzo and other pasta, coffees, jams and jellies, and Greek olive oil. They also sell some cookware, including those small copper pots used to make that thick, strong Greek coffee.

Orzo Salad with Greek Olives, Tomatoes and Feta Cheese

Serve this refreshing Greek-style salad with warm pita bread. Made with orzo, a rice-shaped pasta, it goes particularly well with roast or barbecued lamb.

1 1/2 cups orzo
1/4 cup olive oil
Juice of 1 large lemon
1 tablespoon red wine vinegar
1/3 cup minced fresh parsley

1/4 cup minced fresh dill
1 1/2 cups cherry tomatoes, halved
3/4 cup Greek olives (pitted if you like)
3/4 cup feta cheese, crumbled or cubed
Salt and freshly ground black pepper to taste

Bring a large pot of lightly salted water to a boil. Add the orzo and boil for about 12 to 15 minutes, or until the pasta is just tender. Drain, and place in a serving bowl. Stir in 1 tablespoon of the olive oil and let cool to room temperature.

When the orzo is cool, gently mix in the remaining ingredients and season to taste. Serves 4 to 6.

THE GREAT NORTHEASTERN PASTRY WORKS

"The Alley" off Main Street, North Conway, 03860; phone 603-356-3925. Hours: seven days a week 7:30 A.M. to 5 P.M. Cash only.

North Conway

■ "This is a small country bakery," explained Neil Hesketh, who together with his wife, Kathy Olsen, runs The Great Northeastern Pastry Works. "We're not real New York-ish. We tend to stand around a lot talking to the locals."

Don't be misled by this laid-back philosophy. Hesketh and Olsen also spend a lot of time baking. Their repertoire includes rich, moist cakes, muffins, breads, croissants, tarts, cookies, and fruit bars. Kathy Olsen trained at the Culinary Institute of America and went on to work as a pastry chef at some of Manhattan's most prestigious restaurants, including Windows on the World and Le Cirque. She later taught her husband, and their collective expertise is what makes The Great Northeastern Pastry Works so special. Their hazelnut cheesecake literally melts in your mouth, and their brownies, topped with a thin layer of chocolate frosting, are what dreams are made of. We also liked the Bourbon Walnut Tart, a not-too-sweet nut-filled pastry in a thin, buttery crust, and the Chunky Chocolate Bar, chock-full of dates, raisins, walnuts, and large chunks of dark chocolate.

You can sit at one of the cafe tables here, enjoy a cup of cappuccino, and sample some of the Great Northeastern Pastry Work's many treats. And you'll be glad that Kathy Olsen and Neil Hesketh didn't stay in New York, but decided instead to share their talents with a small town in New England.

North Hampton

LITTLE MARVEL FARM
2 Exeter Road (Route 101-D), North Hampton, 03862; phone 603-964-9748. Hours: seven days a week 9:30 A.M. to 8:00 P.M. Personal checks accepted.

Products also available at the Portsmouth, Hampton, Dover, and Exeter Farmers' Markets (see page 178).

■ We first discovered Little Marvel Farm at the Portsmouth Farmers' Market. We brought home a loaf of their homemade Anadama bread, toasted a couple of slices, and the bread's grainy texture and fresh-baked flavor won us over.

You'll find other homemade breads here, as well as jellies, jams, pickles, cookies, and pies. They make a delicious apple butter, with the consistency of thick applesauce and a spicy cinnamon flavor. In season, there's also fresh fruit and vegetables.

Nottingham

VAL'S RABBITRY
Route 152, Box 38, Nottingham, 03290; phone 603-679-5451. Hours: irregular. Call ahead to place an order. Personal checks accepted.

■ "I never really meant to start a business," explained Val Adams when asked how she got into raising rabbits. "One day we just said, 'Let's have a pet in the backyard.' My sister raised rabbits, so I figured why not. We got three females and one male and put them together. Nothing happened. So we put them together again. Nothing happened. I told my husband, 'This is ridiculous.' So he borrowed a male rabbit from our neighbor, and before we knew it we had two litters of baby rabbits. Then I said to my husband, 'O.K., now you've done that. What are we supposed to do with them all?' So we cooked one up and had it for dinner and that started the whole thing."

Today Val Adams raises somewhere between two and three hundred rabbits a year. Customers come from all over New England, and some of the most prestigious New England chefs buy her rabbits.

"Everyone wants to know what rabbit tastes like," Adams says. "The standard line is that they're like chicken, but they're not. It's much more like peasant. Only problem is, no one knows what pheasant tastes like." Rabbit is lean, low in cholesterol, and according to Adams, has the highest protein level and lowest number of calories of any meat or poultry. And it's not oily or greasy.

Adams sells rabbit by the pound and will cut it to order.

Rabbits to go—Val's Rabbitry.

All rabbits are sold fresh, never frozen. You can also put in a special order for rabbit livers—a rich, very flavorful treat (see recipe below). All orders must be made in advance and picked up in person. Adams also sells live rabbits for anyone interested in breeding their own. "Just look for the four-foot pink rabbit sign in front of the house," says Adams. "Everyone knows the pink rabbit."

Portsmouth

ANGELINA'S
60 Granite Street, Portsmouth, 03801; phone 603-431-6606. Hours: Monday–Saturday 8 A.M. to 6 P.M.; closed Sunday. Personal checks accepted.

■ Fresh pasta in more than two dozen flavors and shapes and a fine selection of Italian deli foods are just some of the reasons why this shop is worth a visit. Co-owners Angelina Panarese and Fay Zoffoli-Ham can supply you with everything you need to put together an Italian meal, including salads, main courses, bread, desserts, and wine. Many items are made on the premises and all are sold fresh, without preservatives or additives.

One thing we particularly admire about Angelina's is that they are not bashful about the ingredients they use. You can really taste the garlic in their rich, chunky marinara sauce. The same goes for the garlic and basil fettuccine; both of those flavors come shining through.

A magnificent antipasto can be created with items from Angelina's deli case. There are marinated mushrooms, artichoke hearts, sweet roasted peppers, and several different kinds of olives in brine.

Spirited Rabbit Liver Pâté

This recipe comes from chef J. Philip McGuire of the Blue Strawbery restaurant in Portsmouth. It must be made at least eight hours before serving, or preferably the day before. It can also be made using chicken or goose liver. The pâté is made in a food processor.

5 slices bacon, finely chopped
3/4 pound veal stew pieces, minced
Salt and freshly ground black pepper to taste
2 cloves crushed garlic
3 pounds rabbit livers
1 tablespoon lightly salted butter
3 ounces cream cheese

2 teaspoons fresh thyme, or 1 teaspoon dried
2 shots Chartreuse, sweet sherry, or Sambuca
1/4 cup small capers, drained
Bed of greens (optional)
Thinly sliced cucumber (optional)
Nasturtium flowers (optional)

Fry the bacon in a large skillet until crisp. Add the minced veal, and season with salt, pepper, and garlic. When the veal starts to turn brown, add the livers and butter and cook over moderate heat until the livers are just past pink on the inside, about 3 minutes. Add the cream cheese and thyme, and stir together until the cream cheese has melted. Remove from the heat. Using a slotted spoon, remove the meat from the skillet and place it in the container of a food processor equipped with a steel blade.

Add the Chartreuse to the liquid remaining in the skillet, and cook over medium-high heat until reduced by half. Add the liquid from the skillet to the liver mixture in the processor, and blend until coarsely chopped (not puréed). Add the capers, and pulse to mix. Scrape the mixture down with a spatula and pulse again. Check the seasoning, and add salt and pepper to taste.

Line a 3 x 3 x 12-inch terrine or loaf pan with tin foil. Add the liver mixture, cover with tin foil, and chill for at least 8 hours. When ready to serve, turn the terrine upside down, gently peel off the foil, and serve on a bed of greens, garnished with sliced cucumbers and nasturtium flowers. Serves 6 to 12.

THE BAVARIAN PANTRY

41 Pleasant Street, Portsmouth, 03801; phone 603-436-4254. Hours: Tuesday–Saturday 10 A.M. to 5 P.M.; closed Sunday and Monday. American Express and personal checks accepted. Party platters available.

■ The Bavarian Pantry offers a wide assortment of hams, salamis, and sausages, all cured and smoked according to traditional German methods. There's *bratwurst, knockwurst, weisswurst, bockwurst,* and very flavorful German frankfurters. One of our favorites is the *bauernschinken,* a delicious, heavily smoked ham that can be used like prosciutto. Also good are the Black Forest ham and Westphalian ham. You can buy the meats by the pound and have them sliced onto a sandwich on thick brown German-style bread, or ask for one of the sausages to be grilled and served on a hot dog roll with lots of sweet German mustard.

The rest of the shop is filled with imported foods and gifts. There are German baking supplies, German cookies and biscuits, jellies, jams, and teas, and beautiful Austrian tortes (which, unfortunately, are frozen). The cheeses are brought in from all over Europe, including a wonderfully tangy and creamy German variety known as Black Forest Blue. Around Christmas the shop is decorated with German gingerbread houses and Christmas tree ornaments from Germany and Austria.

Starting up a Bean-in-the-Hole supper (left).

Flander's Bean-in-the-Hole beans (right).

CAFE BRIOCHE
14 Market Square, Portsmouth, 03801; phone 603-430-9225. Hours: Monday–Friday 8 A.M. to 6 P.M., Saturday and Sunday 8 A.M. to 5 P.M. Personal checks accepted.

■ This is the only place we know in the New Hampshire Seacoast region that makes real European-style bread. The *pain de campagne* is truly a work of art. It's a dramatic-looking round loaf with a slightly chewy, light brown crust and a delicious white center. We have a loaf of this bread in the house almost all the time.

Also good are the *baguettes, batards,* rye bread, challah, and black bread. Around the holidays they bake extra-large peasant-style loaves that are decorated with swirl or crosshatch patterns; these make elegant centerpieces.

Cafe Brioche also makes a full line of pastries, but they generally don't measure up to the breads, being a bit too sweet for our tastes. There are, however, a couple of exceptions. The Florentine cookies (a lacy confection of chocolate, caramelized sugar, and almond slivers) are among the best we've ever had. Also excellent are the madeleines, a spongy vanilla cookie with a slight hint of lemon.

One other thing you can sample here is the flavor of Portsmouth. Because the cafe is centrally located at the top of fashionable Market Square, it has become a place where many different segments of the community come together. Gray-flannel-suited businessmen and -women sit side by side with camera-toting tourists and young people sporting mohawk hairdos and black leather jackets . . . all sipping cappuccino and eating brioche. The scene is particularly colorful in the summer, when the cafe sets up tables outdoors and you can watch the life of the city roll by at its customary leisurely pace.

Sipping cappucino at Café Brioche.

CERES BAKERY

51 Penhallow Street, Portsmouth, 03801; phone 603-436-6518. Hours: Monday–Friday 5:30 A.M. to 5:30 P.M., Saturday 5:30 A.M. to 3 P.M.; closed Sunday. Personal checks accepted.

■ Every New England town should have a bakery like this one. Each morning at least half a dozen kinds of bread come out of the ovens here, along with dozens of pastries, cookies, and tarts. The oversized chocolate chip cookies are just the way we like them, crisp on the outside and soft and slightly chewy on the inside. Another favorite is the Raspberry Crumble—a soft square of raspberry preserves topped with a brown sugar coating.

The whole wheat French bread, a long, thin loaf with a chewy crust and a soft doughy middle, is also excellent. But then again so are the oatmeal molasses bread, onion-dill bread, cinnamon-raisin bread, and sourdough rye bread. And then there are the brioches, 4-inch-high buttery swirls of dough that literally melt in your mouth. They come plain, with tiny Maine blueberries, or full of sweet pecans.

The bakery has a few cafe tables where you can sip coffee, read the paper, watch the bakers at work, and take in the incredible smells coming out of the kitchen. In addition to coffee, tea, and pastries, they offer their own soups and stews; during the winter months hot cider and hot cocoa are also available.

Beans-in-the-Hole

Beans-in-the-hole are literally beans cooked underground, the landlubbers' version of a clambake. It takes several days of preparation, a good deal of folk wisdom, and a lot of raw muscle power to make this traditional New England festival dish. Each year a number of towns put on public bean-in-the-hole suppers, and many have Flanders' Bean-Hole-Bean Company do the cooking.

George Flanders, company president and master chef, has been baking beans underground for some twenty years. He and his wife, Marlin, are the guardians of a secret bean sauce recipe that gives their beans a sweet, delicate flavor.

Making beans-in-the-hole is not easy. First you have to dig a pit, line it with rocks, and light a hardwood fire at the bottom. In Pembroke, where they serve about five hundred people at the yearly bean-in-the-hole supper, an entire cord of wood is consumed to make a 2-foot-deep bed of hot coals. Only certain types of wood can be used. "It has to be ash or maple," says George Flanders, "or else the beans will smell."

When the fire has burned down to a glowing bed of red-hot embers, giant cast iron pots filled with beans, sauce, onions, and large chunks of salt pork are lowered into the pit. It takes six to eight men to carry each pot.

With the pots in place, the pit is covered, first by some metal pipes and old pieces of corrugated tin that form a makeshift roof, then with a foot of dirt. "When it's all covered up you would never know anything was down there," says George, who recalled that one year in Pembroke someone mistakenly drove over the bean pit in the middle of the night. Fortunately the beans survived. So did the driver.

Almost a full day later the dirt is shoveled off, the cover is removed, and the cauldrons of simmering beans are carefully lifted out of the still-warm coals. If you're downwind when the bean pots are opened, you're sure to get a sweet blast of steaming hot beans, molasses, and brown sugar. The taste is equally tantalizing, but it's hard to describe. These beans are sweet, not at all smokey, and unlike most baked beans, fairly easy to digest. Until you've eaten bean-in-the-hole beans you won't believe that a baked bean could have a flavor this complex, or this delicious.

The traditional accompaniments to bean-hole-beans are sliced ham, hot dogs, or roast beef, along with cole slaw, fresh corn on the cob, rolls, and "tonic" (soda) or iced tea. Bean-in-the-hole suppers are held annually in Northwood, Epsom, and Pembroke. Call or write to Flanders' Bean-Hole-Bean Company for dates (P.O. Box 313, Epsom, 03234; 603-736-9235) and also for information about catering private parties.

EMILIO'S FOODS

87 Daniel Street, Portsmouth, 03801; no phone. Hours:

■ It's lunchtime at Emilio's. The blackboard is set out, listing the daily specials: Italian submarine sandwiches, homemade pizza, Italian tuna sandwich, hummus platter, rice and beans, and burritos.

"Aeey, how you doing?" says Emilio, greeting a young office worker. Wearing a paper deli hat and a slightly rumpled white apron, sporting a small mustache, Emilio

Tuesday–Saturday 9:15 A.M. to 5:30 P.M.; closed Sunday and Monday. Cash only.

looks like the quintessential Italian deli man. But Emilio is more than he appears to be. He's equally comfortable discussing Italian cooking, Washington politics, and New Hampshire real estate. There's a copy of *The New York Times* on the counter and National Public Radio hums quietly in the background. "Feeling better than yesterday?" Emilio asks the young woman. "Let me make you something nice. Prosciutto and provolone on Italian bread with the works. Nice, huh?"

Baked Beans

Short of digging a hole to cook your beans in, this simplified recipe is your best bet. It takes two to three days, but don't be intimidated. There's very little work involved. Serve the beans with ham, cole slaw, biscuits, and lots of cold beer.

2 pounds Jacob's Cattle beans or white pea beans
3 bay leaves
6 peppercorns
2 large onions, peeled and quartered
1/3 pound salt pork, cut in half

3 cups brown sugar
1 cup molasses
4 teaspoons mustard powder
1 1/2 teaspoons Tabasco or other hot pepper sauce
1 1/2 teaspoons ground ginger

Place the beans in a large pot and cover with lots of cold water. Let them soak overnight, or for at least 8 hours. Drain. Place the beans back in the pot and cover with 2 quarts of water. Add the bay leaves, peppercorns, and 1 of the onions. Bring to a boil over moderately high heat. Cover, and simmer—do not boil—over low heat until the skins almost burst when you put the beans on the tip of a serving spoon and blow on them. Be careful not to overcook the beans, as they will get mushy. Total cooking time should be 30 to 60 minutes, depending on the type and size of the bean you use.

Drain the beans over a large bowl, reserving the cooking liquid.

Score the pieces of salt pork by cutting them down the middle without cutting all the way through. Place 1 piece of salt pork and 2 onion quarters in the bottom of a large earthenware, cast iron, or stainless steel casserole or bean pot. Add the beans. Place the remaining piece of salt pork and the remaining onions on top, pushing them into the beans slightly.

Meanwhile, in a medium saucepan, mix 2 cups of the brown sugar along with 1 1/2 cups of the reserved bean liquid. Mix in the remaining ingredients, and heat over low heat until warm and smooth. Pour this over the beans. Scatter the last cup of brown sugar on top of the beans. Cover with tin foil, and place the lid of the bean pot securely over the foil. Place in a cold oven and turn the heat to 250°. Bake for 10 to 12 hours, checking the beans every few hours to make sure the liquid hasn't dried out. If the beans appear dry, add an additional 1/4 to 1/2 cup of the reserved bean liquid as needed. If you're leaving the beans in the oven overnight, lower the temperature to 200°.

Remove the lid for the last 20 minutes of cooking time to crisp up the salt pork. Serve hot or warm. Serves 10 to 12.

"Yo, Emilio," chants a group of three local fishermen. "Well, well, well, it's the three musketeers," Emilio says with a chuckle. The fishermen help themselves to a couple of *pizza rusticas* sitting on the marble counter—small nuggets of pastry rolled around ham, cheese, and spices. "How's my man the D.J.?" says a fisherman. "Hanging in there, holding on," says Emilio dryly. D.J.? someone asks. Deli Jock.

The store continues to fill up. Emilio greets everyone. Most of the customers are regulars, but tourists who walk in off the street get the same treatment. ("Aeey, how you doing? Where you from? What brings you to Portsmouth? Taste this—nice, huh?") They hover around the marble counter where Emilio puts together sandwiches and salads and slices Italian cheeses, or they walk over to his new "Yuppie Bar"—a Formica counter with no stools for "my young people on the go." Before long everyone in the shop is talking or listening to Emilio tell a story, a joke, a fable, a recipe.

"You think I come here to eat?" says one woman. "I come here because I need this guy. My life would be incomplete without Emilio." There's no denying that Portsmouth would be a far less interesting place if it weren't for Emilio Vito Maddaloni. We visit his small, cluttered deli to shop for imported Italian pasta, olive oil and vinegar, marinated olives, cheeses, salami and cured meats—but mostly we come to see Emilio. The man is a born conversationalist, a Johnny Carson of the deli world. And his food's not bad, too.

SANDERS LOBSTER COMPANY

54 Pray Street, Portsmouth, 03801 (off Marcy Street, Route 1B, on the way to Newcastle); phone 603-436-3716. Hours: Monday–Saturday 8 A.M. to 6 P.M., Sunday 10 A.M. to 5 P.M. MasterCard, Visa, and local checks accepted. Mail order available.
Also at 23 Harbor Road, Hampton Beach.

■ There must be a dozen places in the Portsmouth area to buy live lobster, but there's something about Sanders that makes us come back again and again. Perched out on a dock overlooking the harbor, there isn't much to this place except lobster tanks, lobster traps, and other assorted nautical paraphernalia. But Sanders has character.

One of the first things you'll notice here is a large tank right next to the door. This is the "show-off tank," where lobsters up to 32 pounds can often be seen swimming around next to smaller 4-, 5- and 10-pounders. The people at Sanders claim that these larger lobsters are just as tasty as the smaller ones (in fact, you usually get more meat per pound from these monsters). Of course you'll also find regular-sized lobsters here, including chicken lobsters and culls (lobsters with only one claw). They also carry fresh cherrystone and steamer clams, mussels, shrimp, and crabmeat.

Sanders sells lobsters live, or they will cook your lobster for you. They will also ship lobsters anywhere in the country and mail order something called a New England Clambake: four 1½-pound lobsters, 2 pounds of steamer clams, and lots of fresh seaweed all ready to go into your pot at home.

Salem

ANOOSH YOGURT SPREAD

Specialty Cheese, Inc., 47 Cross Street, Salem, 03079; phone 603-898-1260. Hours: Monday–Friday 6 A.M. to 6 P.M.; closed Saturday

■ Anoosh Yogurt Spread is a cross between yogurt and farmer's cheese. It's thicker than regular yogurt, and the taste is on the mild side. It's excellent spread on crackers, toast, or *lamejun,* a Middle Eastern "pizza" topped with ground lamb, ground beef, tomatoes, onions, and spices (see page 88).

Anoosh Yogurt Spread can also be used as a substitute for sour cream in dips, or you can serve it with fresh fruit

---

Crabmeat Salad with Almonds

This is a great lunch or supper dish for a hot summer day. Start with a cold soup and serve the salad with a loaf of crusty bread, herb butter, and an ice-cold bottle of dry rosé or crisp white wine. The salad can be made several hours ahead and kept chilled.

Salad
About 3/4 cup mayonnaise, preferably homemade
Juice of 1 large lime
1 1/2 pounds fresh crabmeat
1 tablespoon butter
3/4 cup chopped or slivered almonds
1 teaspoon olive oil
8 large shrimp, shelled, with tails intact
1 1/2 tablespoons finely chopped mixed fresh herbs (tarragon, chives, and thyme), or 1/2 tablespoon dried

Vinaigrette and Greens
1 teaspoon mustard
Salt and freshly ground pepper, to taste
1 tablespoon chopped fresh chives
4 tablespoons red wine vinegar
9 tablespoons olive oil
1 large head red-leaf lettuce, or 2 to 3 cups mixed greens
Fresh chive flowers (optional)

In a medium bowl, mix together the mayonnaise and lime juice. Gently mix in the crabmeat, and set aside.

In a medium skillet, heat the butter over moderate heat. Add the almonds and sauté for several minutes, stirring constantly until they have turned a light golden brown. (Be careful not to let the almonds burn.) Remove from the heat and drain on paper towels. Set aside.

In another medium skillet, heat the olive oil over moderately high heat. Add the shrimp and sauté about 1 minute. Turn the shrimp over, add the herbs, and sauté another 30 seconds to 1 minute, or until the shrimp turn pink and are firm to the touch. Remove from the heat and set aside.

Prepare the vinaigrette: In a small bowl, mix the mustard with the salt, pepper, and chives. Add the vinegar, and whisk in the olive oil. Set aside.

Place the greens along the bottom of a large serving platter or bowl. Arrange the crabmeat in the center. Spoon the almonds in a line down the middle of the crabmeat. Place the sautéed shrimp alongside the crabmeat, and serve the vinaigrette separately. Garnish with chive flowers. Serves 4 as a main course or 6 as an appetizer.

and Sunday. Personal checks accepted.

Specialty Cheese dairy products are also sold in supermarkets and ethnic and health food stores in Massachusetts, southern New Hampshire, New York City, and Washington, D.C.

GLEN ECHO FARMS

P.O. Box 2, Wendell, 03782; phone 603-863-6780. Personal checks accepted. Mail order available.

STONYFIELD FARM YOGURT

Stonyfield Farm, Barrett Hill Road, Wilton, 03386; phone 603-654-2366.

Stonyfield Yogurt is sold in supermarkets, health food shops, and specialty food stores throughout New England and New York.

salad instead of whipped cream. According to Gary Azarian, president of Specialty Cheese, many Middle Eastern cooks like to mix the yogurt spread with olive oil, chopped garlic, and herbs and serve it with grilled meats, vegetables, and poultry.

In addition to yogurt spread, Specialty Cheese makes regular yogurt and Middle Eastern string cheese. They sell all of these products at their factory store, as well as spices, dried fruit, grains and *lamejun* from a Middle Eastern bakery in Watertown, Massachusetts.

Wendell

■ "This is a very specialized product," said Bill Tuttle in all seriousness. "I don't want to sound like a snob or anything, but this just isn't your ordinary lamb."

Glen Echo Farms raises baby lamb—6- to 8-week-old animals weighing an average of 20 to 24 pounds dressed. These lambs are fed exclusively on mother's milk and are allowed to roam freely around the pasture. The result is meat that is exceptionally light and delicate—so light, claims Tuttle, that many people who don't ordinarily like lamb love this meat. He likes to describe its taste as being more like veal than lamb.

"But," warns Tuttle, "you have to have a very refined sense of taste. This lamb has an incredibly subtle flavor that not everyone would appreciate." Not everyone would appreciate the price, either (it averages about $5 a pound). The majority of Tuttle's customers are fancy restaurants "where the chefs know the difference and know it's worth paying for."

Glen Echo lamb can be ordered by mail or phone, year-round, although according to Tuttle, the summer is not the best time to buy lamb. You must buy the entire lamb; it will be sent whole, or Tuttle can arrange to have it custom-cut at a federally inspected slaughterhouse.

Wilton

■ When you buy a container of Stonyfield Farm Yogurt, you get more than an intensely creamy, rich, and satisfying product. You also get an education. "Did you know," asks the legend on the container, "that the Northeast imports over 90% of the food we eat? Our food travels an average of 1200 miles from field to kitchen? More than 75% of the food we eat is processed?"

Stonyfield Farm Yogurt was started a few years ago by Samuel Kaymen and Gary Hirshberg. "We want to make the supermarket into a classroom," explains Kaymen. "Our mission is to preserve New England's agricultural land and to enhance and encourage organically grown foods in the region. Our yogurt is fresh, local, and wholesome. It's a symbol for what we'd like to see happen all over New England. We don't expect to change the world overnight, but we would like to encourage consumers to support the revival of New England agriculture."

These are not the words of a typical businessman, and Stonyfield Yogurt is not your typical yogurt. It's made from nonhomogenized Jersey milk and comes with a thick layer of custard-like cream on top. Kaymen admits that Holstein and Guernsey cows produce more milk than Jerseys, but he insists that Jersey milk has more protein and butterfat and makes a superior yogurt.

Stonyfield Yogurt comes plain (and low-fat plain, without the layer of cream on top), or flavored with pure maple syrup, strawberries, raspberries, organic wild Maine blueberries, black cherries, or peaches. Other flavors include apricot-mango, French vanilla, cappuccino, lemon, and coffee. All the yogurt is sweetened naturally with fruit juice, rather than honey or sugar. Eat some Stonyfield Yogurt and help support New England agriculture. It's an easy and delicious way to make a statement.

New Hampshire Farmers' Markets

Andover Farmers' Market, next to Andover town offices, Saturdays from mid-July through mid-September, 9 A.M. to 12 N.

Concord Farmers' Market, New Hampshire Savings Bank, Saturdays from July through October, 9 A.M. to 1 P.M.

Conway Farmers' Market, Steamer's Restaurant, Route 16, Saturdays from mid-May through October, 9 A.M. to 12 N.

Dover Farmers' Market, Welby Super Drug Store parking lot, Wednesdays from July through October, 3 P.M. to 6 P.M.

Exeter Farmers' Market, Swazey Parkway, Thursdays from July through October, 3 P.M. to 6 P.M.

Hampton Farmers' Market, Sacred Heart Church parking lot, Lafayette Road (Route 1), Tuesdays from July through October, 3 P.M. to 6 P.M.

Laconia Farmers' Market, Belknap Mill, Beacon Street East, Saturdays from mid-July through October, 9 A.M. to 12 N.

Manchester Farmers' Market (New Hampshire Farmers' Open Air Market), Agway parking lot, Beech and Valley streets, Wednesdays and Saturdays from mid-June through November, 6 A.M. to 12 N.

Milford—Souhegan Valley Farmers' Market, American Stage Festival grounds, Mount Vernon Street, Saturdays from late June through October, 9 A.M. to 1 P.M.

Portsmouth Farmers' Market, Parrott Avenue parking lot, Saturdays from mid-June through October, 9 A.M. to 1 P.M.

Warner Area Farmers' Market, Warner Town Hall lawn, Saturdays from June through October, 9 A.M. to 12 N.

Woodsville Farmers' Market, Central Street, Saturdays from mid-July through October, 10 A.M. to 1 P.M.

Rhode Island

RHODE ISLAND

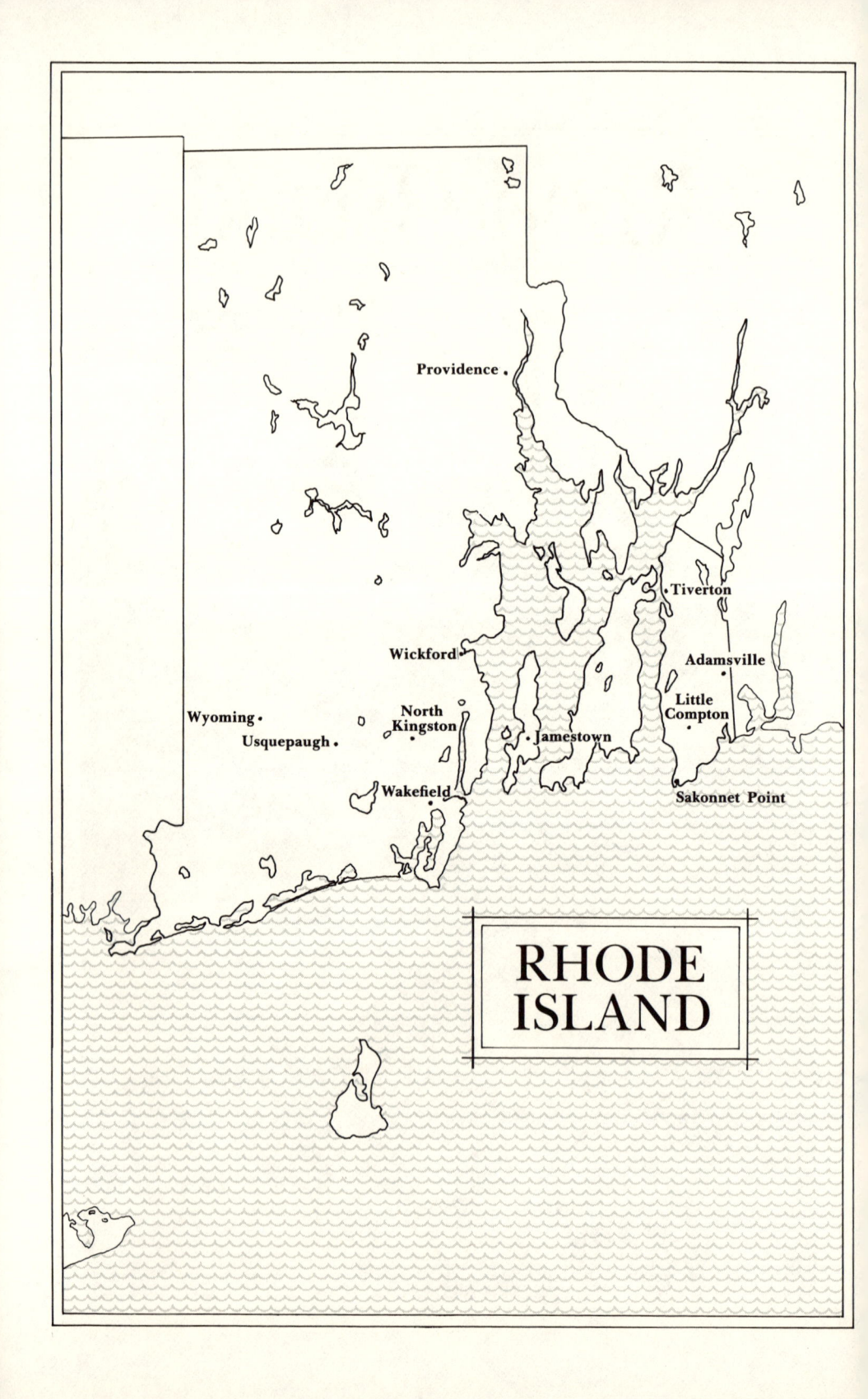

Adamsville

GRAY'S GRIST MILL
P.O. Box 422, Adamsville, 02801; phone 617-636-6075 or 401-849-8844. Hours: irregular, call ahead. Personal checks accepted. Mail order available. Tours can be arranged ahead of time.

Gray's products are sold in specialty food stores in eastern Rhode Island and southeastern Massachusetts, and in a few select stores around the country.

■ When Tim McTague took over the job of miller at Gray's Grist Mill about six years ago, he and the mill's new owner, Ralph Guild, faced a difficult decision. They wanted to preserve and restore the beautiful old mill building, but they also realized that the mill's main product, cornmeal for Rhode Island jonnycakes, is hard to make and has a limited market. "We considered just turning it into a museum," recalls McTague. "That's happened to a lot of old mills." But gristmills have been operating on this site since 1675, and in the end McTague and Guild opted to keep their mill going, grinding Rhode Island white flint corn the way it's been done for hundreds of years. Says McTague: "We're trying to maintain the tradition in as pure a form as possible."

Thirty-year-old McTague had been a carpenter specializing in restoring old homes. He left carpentry to learn the miller's trade from John Hart, the former miller and owner of Gray's Grist Mill, who spent almost his

Gray's Grist Mill.

entire life at the mill. Hart, now in his mid-eighties, was brought up on jonnycakes and still eats them almost every day. He was taught milling by his father, who ran the mill before him.

Gray's is one of the few mills in the country that still make jonnycake meal the traditional way, using Rhode Island flint corn. Native Americans introduced the Pilgrims to flint corn. Gray's uses it almost exclusively, even though it is much harder to grow than modern hybrid corn (you get less corn per acre, and you have to harvest it by hand). McTague says the taste and texture are exceptional: "It's richer and sweeter. The flavor is more fully rounded." It also has a distinctive aroma. "If I go into a mill room and they are grinding flint corn, I can smell the difference," says McTague.

The mill room at Gray's Grist Mill is clean and spare, a study in white and muted grays. There are the round granite millstones, a few wooden tools, and some bins of grain. An old bicycle sits in the corner. The simplicity of the room and the machine it houses speaks eloquently of an earlier era in the history of machines and agriculture.

When the millstone isn't turning, you can hear the rush of water beneath the floorboards. The mill used to be water driven, but in the late 1940s John Hart switched to a more reliable form of power. Today the mill is driven by the same Dodge truck engine that Hart installed. However, he never bothered to take the engine out of the truck. If you go out back you can see the whole rig humming away, with the dashboard and stick shift still in place. Everyone who sees it says the same thing; "Talk about Yankee ingenuity!"

Tim McTague hopes to rebuild the waterwheel eventually, so he can use waterpower when the millpond is high. The rest of the time he'll rely on the old Dodge.

As for Gray's cornmeal, it's as authentic as the mill, and it is truly delicious. McTague works hard to maintain the meal's proper texture, an important part of making good jonnycakes.

In addition to cornmeal, Gray's Grist Mill produces Brown Bread and Muffin Mix, an excellent Pancake and Waffle Mix made from corn, wheat, and rye flours, as well as plain whole wheat flour and rye flour. The corn for the jonnycake meal is grown without pesticides or herbicides, and none of the flours or mixes contain any preservatives.

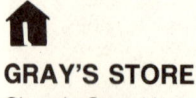

GRAY'S STORE
Church Gray House, Adamsville, 02801; phone 401-635-4566. Hours: Monday–Friday 9:30 A.M. to 6 P.M., Saturday 9:30 A.M. to 5 P.M., Sunday 9 A.M. to 2 P.M. (closed Sunday in winter). Personal checks accepted. Mail order available.

■ They do sell food at Gray's Store, but the main reason to come here is for a taste of history. Gray's claims to be the oldest continuously operating store in the United States. This year (1988) marks the store's two-hundredth anniversary, and manager Grayton Waite is planning a celebration. He has been digging up old newspaper clippings and other memorabilia that document the store's past. And he's doing some modest restoration.

The Great Rhode Island Jonnycake Debate

No New England food stirs greater debate or gives rise to more patriotic sentiments than the Rhode Island jonnycake. Virtually every aspect of this cornmeal flapjack sparks controversy that can be as hot as a griddle on the Fourth of July. There is disagreement over how to make jonnycakes (should they be thick or thin?), how to spell the name (jonny or johnny with an "h"), the derivation of the name (some say it's a corruption of "journey cake," a term used to describe food that was carried by travelers; others suggest the name comes from "Shawnee cake," named after the Shawnee Indians), and the history of the cake itself (did the Pilgrims bring the recipe with them or did they learn it from the native Americans they encountered?).

For those of us who do not live in Rhode Island, all this may sound kind of silly. But for years these issues have engaged, and in some instances enraged, Rhode Islanders, from average citizens up to the state's newspaper editors and members of the state legislature.

The most obvious dividing line in the jonnycake dispute is Narragansett Bay. People who live west of the bay, in the area known as South County, make jonnycakes by scalding the finely ground cornmeal with boiling water before frying the batter. The hot water activates the starch in the meal, resulting in slightly raised cakes. On the other hand, residents of Newport and the eastern part of the state would never think of subjecting their cornmeal to a hot bath. They use cold water or milk, which makes extremely thin jonnycakes with a crisp, lacy fringe. Several years ago the *Providence Journal* described the controversy this way: "When oil and water mix, or cows take unto themselves wings and fly, it may be that South County and Newport will agree on a common recipe for the jonnycake."

While the two sides in the thick-versus-thin debate remain intractable, there have been attempts to foster détente on other fronts. In 1940 the Rhode Island legislature passed a law that defines what constitutes genuine jonnycake meal. The law says that the words "Rhode Island" may not appear on any package of corn unless it's Rhode Island white cap corn grown in Rhode Island. Even so some people claim that it doesn't matter what kind of cornmeal you use, and they continue to grind and sell jonnycake meal made from other varieties of corn. Others, notably the Society for the Propagation of the Jonnycake Tradition in Rhode Island, bristle at this point. The SPJTRI, a group of amateur and professional historians and jonnycake lovers, maintains that Rhode Island white cap corn, or flint corn as it's also called, is the essential ingredient in any jonnycake recipe, thick or thin. They also say the meal must be ground slowly between stones of Westerly (R.I.) granite. But in reality, who's to know? "I don't imagine the state has a jonnycake squad checking up on people," says miller Tim McTague.

Enforcement of the jonnycake law has undoubtedly been lax over the years, and so the SPJTRI and others have become self-appointed defenders of the true jonnycake. It's a time-honored tradition in Rhode Island. In the late nineteenth century Thomas Robinson Hazard, writing under the pen name "Shepherd Tom," gained notoriety through a series of newspaper articles known collectively as *The Jonny-Cake Papers*. It appears that vitriol as well as a love of fried cornmeal motivated Mr. Hazard. In a letter to the Newport *Mercury* (reprinted in the SPJTRI's *Jonnycake Journal*), Hazard took aim at a reader who sent him an untraditional recipe for jonnycakes made with eggs, molasses, and baking soda. He accused the reader of, among other things, "being a descendant of . . . the very same wretch who discovered the art of making sausages of cat's meat and seasoning them with red pepper made of brick dust, and black of ground up shoe laces."

Today the defenders of jonnycakes use gentler language, but they are no less committed to the cause. They argue that jonnycakes are a food unique to Rhode Island. (And as you might have guessed, some people attempt to prick this balloon by pointing out that baked cakes made of corn are found in lots of places. Ever hear of hush puppies or cornbread?) They also spend a lot of time investigating the history of jonnycakes and planning and attending events in celebration of the jonnycake.

One who is particularly active in this area is Helene Tessler, the president of the SPJTRI. She admits that at times she wonders why there's so much fuss over jonnycakes, and why she puts herself in the middle of the fray. Then, Tessler says, she remembers: "It's because they taste so damn good."

Making jonnycakes is a little harder than making regular pancakes—it takes some practice. But we can honestly say that it's worth the effort. Be sure to use a cast iron skillet, and keep it well greased.

Retired miller John Hart and his grandson, Grayton Waite—both raised on Rhode Island jonnycakes.

Gray's is not the most glamorous place you've ever been to. The shelves sag, the floor creaks, and it's kind of dark inside. But this actually makes the store more interesting. It hasn't been sanitized like a lot of other old general stores.

There are a few edible offerings here worthy of note. At the top of the list: cornmeal for making Rhode Island jonnycakes, and other milled whole grains from neighboring Gray's Grist Mill (see page 181). As the name suggests, the store and the mill used to be owned by the same family.

Gray's Store is also a good place to visit if you're nostalgic and have a sweet tooth. They still make frappes (or "cabinets") at the old soda fountain, and they have a great selection of penny candy—everything from Mary Janes and Red Hots to Tootsie Rolls and Bingos. Some of the items still cost only a penny.

There is only one other food sold at Gray's that's worth mentioning, and it's probably their most famous product. But it is a hoax, as Grayton Waite freely admits. "Adamsville Cheddar" has a reputation for being especially tasty cheese, and at Gray's Store they always have a wheel of the aged cheddar on hand. Waite says he sells an awful lot of it. The cheese, however, is not made in Adamsville; it's not even made in Rhode Island. It's only aged in Adamsville for a few weeks. Many people know this, but they go out of their way to buy it anyway. People are funny sometimes. But in this case, at least, they are helping to maintain a historic landmark.

Jamestown

OUR DAILY BREAD
22 West Street, Jamestown, 02835; phone 401-423-BAKE. Hours: Tuesday–Friday 7 A.M. to 6 P.M., Saturday 8 A.M. to 5 P.M., Sunday 8 A.M. to 1 P.M.; closed Monday. Rhode Island checks accepted.

■ The emphasis is on whole grains at this family-run bakery. The bakers here produce a limited selection of cookies, pies, and pastry, but we suggest you stick to the beautiful and unusual breads. There's Farmhouse Potato Bread, made with mashed potatoes and raw wheat germ; subtly spiced Coriander Bread; rich and cheesy Cheddar Bread; whole grain Anadama Bread; Millet Bread; Lemon-Sesame Bread; and Wheat Germ Herb Loaf—over a dozen varieties in all. The Sourdough Rye Bread is a gorgeous golden brown loaf with a crunchy whole grain texture. It's a bread with substance, but not overly heavy like so many other whole grain breads.

Little Compton

THE COUNTRY STAND
West Main Road, Little Compton, 02837; phone 401-635-9511. Hours: mid-May through mid-October, seven days a week 10 A.M. to 5:30 P.M. Personal checks accepted.

■ Skip Paul is an artist who spends his winters painting and his summers growing vegetables and herbs. From mid-May through mid-October he runs one of Little Compton's most popular summer businesses, The Country Stand—a produce market/bakery/deli/fish store/charcuterie/flower shop.

Let's start with the produce. Paul describes himself as a "biological farmer," meaning he sprays only "when the pests create more damage than we can deal with." He says his ultimate goal is to run a totally organic farm. Paul grows all sorts of vegetables, including sweet corn, tomatoes, zucchini, and more unusual vegetables like radicchio, Italian broccoli, coriander, purple string beans, and Oxford carrots—a strange carrot shaped like a little round ball. He also sells locally grown berries, apples, and white peaches—an exceptionally juicy type of peach.

The Country Stand is also a fish store called The Net Result. Gill-netter Bill MacIntosh brings in a wide variety of local fish and shellfish daily. And 4 and 20 Blackbirds Catering supplies the breads, pies, tarts, cakes, soups, salads, pâtés, and frozen entrées sold at the stand. They also offer local and imported cheeses, deli meats, and gourmet food items. Skip Paul's wife is a floral designer and provides all the flower arrangements.

DELUCIA'S BERRY FARM
96 Willow Avenue, Little Compton, 02837; phone 401-635-2698. Hours: June 1 through October, seven days a week 8 A.M. to 5 P.M., or by

■ "I suppose it's the microclimate around here that makes this area so great for growing berries," said Norman DeLucia when asked why his berries are so good. "We don't get hit with extreme fluctuations in temperature and we rarely have an unexpected frost. That's a real blessing for a berry farmer.

"But the real trick," DeLucia went on, "is that we love berries and we pick them every day exactly the way we would want to eat them—when they're ripe and most

appointment. Cash only. Pick-your-own available; call ahead.

SAKONNET VINEYARDS

Route 77 (P.O. Box 572), Little Compton, 02837; phone 401-635-4356. Hours: from the weekend after Easter through the weekend before Christmas, seven days a week 10 A.M. to 5 P.M. Free tours and tastings held on Wednesdays and Saturdays, or by appointment, from Memorial Day through October. MasterCard, Visa, and personal checks accepted. Mail order available in parts of New England.

Sakonnet wines are also sold in liquor stores throughout Rhode Island and Massachusetts.

Sakonnet Vineyards displays its wines for tasting.

flavorful. Take strawberries, for example. Most wholesalers pick them when they're not quite ripe. They may redden up in transit but they never really ripen and develop that wonderful sweet flavor." DeLucia has a reputation for growing some of the most flavorful, plump, and juicy berries around. He supplies prominent Rhode Island restaurants as well as many local farm stands.

The season begins in early June with strawberries and then moves on to raspberries (both a summer and a fall crop), blueberries, and blackberries. DeLucia also grows gooseberries, a lesser-known berry that looks like a tiny watermelon with a green stripe. When gooseberries are picked green they are extremely tart and make excellent jam. However, DeLucia likes to let them get really ripe. "When they redden and sweeten up they make one of the best pies you've ever tasted," he explained.

You can visit the DeLucia farm throughout the season, and when there's a larger than usual crop, they allow visitors to pick their own berries. Call ahead for information about picking conditions.

■ We were standing at a counter with a small group, tasting the wines at Sakonnet Vineyards. The Vidal Blanc, explained the young woman conducting the tasting, is very similar in style to a French Blanc de Blanc. We sipped and swirled and shared our impressions. A subtle hint of green apples. "No, it's berries," someone insisted. Next came the America's Cup White, a pale yellow wine made from a blend of Seyval and Vidal grapes, aged in oak. "I taste hints of lemon and oak," said the man to our left. "No, it's bananas," we exclaimed enthusiastically. We went on to sample the Spinnaker White and Compass Rose. And then a refreshing semi-sweet blush wine called Eye of the Storm, named for Hurricane Gloria, which

Al Forno's Cannoli Cream

This is a lighter version of the cream filling used in Italian cannoli pastries. Created by Johanne Killeen, chef and owner of Al Forno restaurant in Providence, it is delicious poured over fresh strawberries, raspberries, peaches, or nectarines for a light summer dessert. (This recipe requires a food processor.)

2 pounds ricotta cheese, preferably freshly made
5 tablespoons sugar
1 cup orange marmalade

3 tablespoons Cointreau or other orange-flavored liqueur
1 teaspoon vanilla extract
3 tablespoons broken-up semi-sweet chocolate

In a food processor fitted with the steel blade, blend the ricotta until smooth. Add the sugar and blend for a second or two. Add the marmalade, Cointreau, and vanilla and blend another few seconds. Add the chocolate pieces and blend 1 second. Do not overprocess the mixture; the idea is to pulse for just a second or two after each addition. Serve spooned over fresh fruit. Makes about 4 cups.

---

swirled over Rhode Island in 1985. This, we all agreed, was a unique, highly appealing wine. Before we even got to the reds we had all become friends. We were also just a bit high.

We have tasted many New England wines, and our comments have ranged from "God help us" to "not bad." It wasn't until our visit to Sakonnet, a 45-acre vineyard located in the seaside town of Little Compton, that we could honestly say, "That's good wine."

Jim and Lolly Mitchell started Sakonnet Vineyards in the mid 1970s, hoping to produce "world class wines." They recently sold the vineyard to Earl and Susan Samson, but before leaving Sakonnet we had a chance to talk with Jim about their successful venture into winemaking. Mitchell explained that the area of Rhode Island where they chose to locate the vineyard has a microclimate that's ideal for growing grapes. It's close to the ocean, which helps moderate the temperature, and the growing season is similar to that of France's Burgundy region, one of the most famous wine-producing areas in the world. "Our climate is European," said Jim Mitchell, "so our style is European with American overtones."

If you think, as we used to, that the words "wine" and "New England" are incompatible, then we suggest you too visit Sakonnet Vineyards. It's one of the region's most beautiful vineyards, with row upon row of symmetrical grapevines growing within sight of the blue Sakon-

WALKER'S ROADSIDE STAND

261 West Main Road, Little Compton, 02837; phone 401-635-4719 or 635-4722. Hours: Mid-June through August, seven days a week 8 A.M. to 7 P.M. September and October, seven days a week 8 A.M. to 6 P.M. November, Friday, Saturday, and Sunday 8 A.M. to 6 P.M.; closed Monday–Thursday. Cash only.

net River. Not only are their wines very good, but the tours and tastings they conduct are informative and a lot of fun.

▪ We know several people who spend their summers in the Little Compton area, and all of them buy their fruit, vegetables, and herbs from Coll Walker. No one can really put their finger on why Walker's produce is so exceptional, so we decided to ask the farmer.

"I have no idea," Coll Walker stated flatly. "We farm about 50 acres of land and we're close to the sea, so we have a fairly long season. But other than that I don't know. The vegetables just do their thing."

Walker is one of the first farmers in the Little Compton area to have ripe tomatoes each spring. He starts them in a greenhouse, and by early June, when everyone else's tomato vines have only tiny hard green balls, Walker is selling perfectly ripe juicy tomatoes. As the season progresses there's lettuce (several varieties including red leaf, green ice, and tender buttercrunch), basil and other fresh-cut herbs, red and yellow sweet peppers, and sweet corn that has the reputation of being the best around. Toward fall there's broccoli and cauliflower, squash and pumpkin.

And then there's the fruit. ("Walker grows the most beautiful berries I've ever seen," swears a friend of ours.) There are plenty of plump raspberries and strawberries, and each fall Walker puts together beautiful displays of apples from his orchard—McIntosh, Paula Red, Empire, Red Delicious, and Winesap. He also presses his own cider.

Attached to the roadside stand is a bakery called The Bakery, where you'll find fresh-baked bread, cookies, pies, and cakes.

North Kingston

WICKFORD SHELLFISH

67 Esmond Avenue, North Kingston, 02852; phone 401-885-1100. Hours: Monday–Saturday 8 A.M. to 6 P.M., Sunday 9 A.M. to 6 P.M. Visa and MasterCard accepted.

▪ Driving along Wickford's Main Street, one really gets a feeling of the Rhode Island of the early nineteenth century. It's a tidy street with rows of beautifully restored houses on both sides—no fast food restaurants or modern architecture in sight. Directly off Main Street, overlooking Wickford Harbor, is Wickford Shellfish, where you'll find a good selection of very fresh fish from local waters. The day we visited, there were four types of clams (quahogs, littlenecks, cherrystones, and steamers), fresh conch, live lobsters, scallops, flounder filets, and squid. There's also a small selection of pickled herring and some excellent smoked fish. They will mail lobsters and preassembled clambakes.

4 and 20 Blackbirds Seafood Pasta Primavera

This recipe comes from Boo Hubbard, chef and owner of 4 and 20 Blackbird Caterers in Little Compton.

1 pound medium to large shrimp, peeled and deveined
1/2 head broccoli, cut into small florets
About 2 tablespoons olive oil
1 pound sea scallops
3 scallions, chopped
1 small yellow pepper, coarsely chopped
6 ounces mushrooms, sliced
2 small cloves garlic, minced
2 cups heavy cream
1 1/3 cups clam juice, fresh or bottled
2/3 cup dry white wine
Salt and freshly ground black pepper to taste
1 pound spinach and/or egg fettuccine
Chopped parsley for garnish

Fill a large pot with salted water and bring to a boil. Add the shrimp and boil 1 to 2 minutes, or until just opaque. Remove with a slotted spoon and set aside in a large bowl.

Add the broccoli to the boiling water and blanch until crisp and tender, about 2 minutes. Drain, and place in a bowl of cold water to cool. Drain, and add to the bowl with the shrimp.

In a large skillet heat the olive oil over moderate heat. Sauté the scallops until just opaque, about 2 minutes. Remove with a slotted spoon and add to the large bowl. Sauté the scallions 1 minute. Remove them with a slotted spoon and transfer to the large bowl. Sauté the peppers and mushrooms until barely tender, 3 to 4 minutes, adding additional olive oil if necessary. Again, remove with a slotted spoon and add to the bowl.

Add the garlic to the skillet and cook 30 seconds. Add the cream, clam juice, and wine, and bring to a boil. Continue boiling, uncovered, until reduced to 3 cups and slightly thickened. Season with salt and pepper to taste.

Meanwhile, bring a fresh pot of salted water to a boil. Add the fettuccine and cook until just tender. Drain, and place the pasta in a shallow serving dish. Add the seafood/vegetable mixture to the cream sauce and stir to warm it. Pour the sauce over the hot pasta and sprinkle with parsley. Serves 4 to 6.

Providence

A. & J. WHOLESALE
39 Hemlock Street, Providence, 02908 (in the Governor Dyer Market); phone 401-831-7420. Hours: Monday–Friday 5 A.M. to 2 P.M., Saturday 5 A.M. to 12 N., Sunday 8 A.M. to 10 A.M. Cash only.

■ If it's grown in Rhode Island or southeastern Massachusetts, chances are they sell it at A. & J. Wholesale. And while the name suggests that this fruit and vegetable market is open only to wholesale customers like restaurants and food stores, in truth everyone is welcome.

Gerry Ragosta, the slightly rotund proprietor, reels off a list of local produce he carries in season: "We've got local eggplants, local peppers, local green onions, local dandelion greens—"

His young assistant jumps in. "What about local squash, Gerry?"

Linguine with Clam Sauce

This is a simple clam sauce that requires the freshest ingredients. It takes only 10 minutes to cook, once all the ingredients have been cleaned, peeled, and chopped. The clams stay in the shell, so you don't have to shuck them. Be sure to have your water boiling, and add the pasta as soon as you start the sauce. This recipe makes enough sauce for 1 pound of linguine.

24 littleneck clams
3 tablespoons olive oil
2 tablespoons minced garlic
1/2 cup dry white wine
1/3 cup finely chopped flat-leaf parsley

Scrub the clams well under cold running water to remove any dirt or sea debris. Set aside.

In a medium saucepan, heat the olive oil over moderate heat. Add the garlic and sauté until it turns a light golden brown, about 2 minutes. (Do not let the garlic burn.) Add the clams and stir them around to coat the shells with the oil and garlic. Add the wine and half the parsley, and let simmer for a few seconds. Reduce the heat slightly, cover the pot, and let simmer 5 to 6 minutes or until the clams open completely. Pour the sauce over the hot linguine and top with the remaining parsley. Serves 2 to 4.

Ragosta continues: "We've got local potatoes, local melons, local strawberries, local horseradish—"

"Tell them about the squash, Gerry," urges the assistant. "We've got lots of different kinds of squash."

"That's not so important," Ragosta returns. "We've got local grapes, local apples, local peaches, local pears. Let's see, did I leave anything out?"

"What about squash," says the assistant, obviously seeing an opportunity.

"Oh yeah, we sell several different kinds of squash."

Prices at A. & J. Wholesale are reasonable. Retail customers will pay a bit more than wholesale, but it's still cheaper than shopping at most supermarkets or small farm stands. And even though their specialty is wholesale marketing, you don't have to buy a case of lettuce or a crate of strawberries. Most items are available in quantities that the average household can use.

ANTONELLI POULTRY COMPANY

62 DePasquale Avenue, Providence, 02903; phone 401-421-8739 or 621-9377. Hours: Tuesday–Saturday

■ It's a little like the United Nations at the Antonelli Poultry Company. The customers who come here for fresh-killed chickens, ducks, and rabbits hail from around the world. There are Cambodians, Nigerians, Liberians, Laotians, Portuguese, and Dominicans. Most of them are first-generation immigrants, says company owner Chris Morris. They come to his store because it's one of the few places in Providence where you can buy poultry and rabbits the way they do in the old country: by pointing to a live animal and having it slaughtered and cleaned on the spot. That way you know it's fresh.

The squawking of hens blends with conversations in three or four languages as customers wait in line for their purchases. All the dirty work goes on in the back room, behind thick plastic curtains. Some customers go back to watch, while others browse in the front of the shop, where there is a world of unusual ethnic foods to choose from, things like frozen *jute* leaves, dried okra, palm oil, and smoked shrimp—most of them used in African cooking.

Live chickens, rabbits, and ducks are always in stock here. Other types of live poultry are available with a day's advance notice, including pheasant, geese, quail, and squab. This store also sells quail eggs, double-yolk chicken and duck eggs, and some Latin American grocery items.

8 A.M. to 5 P.M., Friday 8 A.M. to 7 P.M.; closed Sunday and Monday. Cash only.

FARIA'S SWEET BREAD BAKERY

395 Wickenden Street, Providence, 02903; phone 401-331-0492. Hours: Monday–Saturday 24 hours a day, Sunday until 12 N. Cash only.

■ As the name indicates, this tiny Portuguese bakery specializes in sweet bread—a large round loaf capped with a golden-brown crown of a crust. This bread is distinctly sweet, with a soft, fluffy inside; it's the perfect accompaniment to hearty Portuguese-style soups or a sweet cup of coffee. At Faria's they bake bread round the clock, so your chances of getting a warm straight-from-the-oven loaf are quite good. On Sundays the bakers also make a fried dough called *malassada*.

THE GOLDEN SHEAF REAL FOODS MARKET

388 Wickenden Street, Providence, 02903; phone 401-751-9234. Hours: Monday–Friday 9 A.M. to 8 P.M., Saturday 9 A.M. to 6:30 P.M., Sunday 12 N. to 5 P.M. MasterCard, Visa, and personal checks accepted. Workshops, lectures, and classes offered.

■ The Golden Sheaf is a particularly good natural foods store. It's well stocked with organically grown produce and fruit, all sorts of Oriental ingredients and condiments, locally produced dairy products, cheeses from around the world, and whole grain breads and pastries. There's also a small cafe here, where you can sit and enjoy fresh-squeezed vegetable and fruit juices, homemade soups, meatless salads, and sandwiches. Right next to the cafe is a library of books on natural foods cookery, herbs, and health care.

The people who run Golden Sheaf are extremely knowledgeable about their products, whether it's finding a source for fresh goat's milk or using herbs for medicinal purposes.

JOE'S QUALITY MARKET/L'EPICUREO GOURMET FOODS

236-238 Atwells Avenue, Providence, 02903; phone

■ Whether you're a carnivore or a vegetarian, you're bound to be pleased with the selection of foods at this Italian market. One side of the store (Joe's Quality Market) is a butcher shop featuring top-quality veal, beef, chicken, and fresh Italian sausages. On the other side, L'Epicureo Gourmet Foods specializes in pasta sauces, soups, and ready-to-eat main courses.

401-521-3333 or 521-4526. Hours: Tuesday–Thursday and Saturday 8:30 A.M. to 6 P.M., Friday 8:30 A.M. to 7 P.M.; closed Sunday and Monday. Rhode Island personal checks accepted.

NEW ENGLAND TRUFFLE COMPANY
29 Okie Street, Providence, 02908; phone 401-831-0890. MasterCard, Visa, and personal checks accepted. Mail order only.

New England Truffles candies and sauces are sold in gourmet food stores throughout the Northeast.

A shop window on Federal Hill in Providence.

Most of these prepared foods are sold frozen, but on the day we visited they had just cooked up a few different pasta sauces, and we were able to buy them fresh. Chances are you can do the same.

The two sauces we tried were both meatless. One was a rich marinara sauce with big slices of mushrooms, peppers, and zucchini. It was superb served over ravioli from the nearby Venda Ravioli company (see page 196). The other was a cream sauce that contained chunks of green and yellow squash. It had a rich flavor, but the squash helped keep it light.

There are over a dozen other sauces that we didn't sample, including one made with four cheeses, a squid sauce, a pesto sauce, and a marinara sauce with bacon and onions. If the ones we did eat are any indication, you won't go wrong with any of these.

■ New England Truffles are flamboyant candies; they have personality and intrigue. The same can be said about the duo that runs the New England Truffle Company. Company president John Elkhay is best described with a phrase coined many years ago by *Mad* magazine: a "hip young upstart." In addition to the truffle business, Elkhay owns a trendy Providence restaurant, and he holds a Guinness record for omelet making (315 omelets in 30 minutes).

Candy maker Holly Drinkuth-Bradford is a bit quieter than Elkhay, but she has her own story to tell. Before starting the company, Drinkuth-Bradford "spied" on rival Champlain Chocolates in Burlington, Vermont. "I posed as a student from the Johnson and Wales College [pastry arts program]," she confided. In fact Drinkuth-Bradford did attend the school, but her mission to Vermont was not an innocent educational experience: "Neither of us knew much about chocolate making at the time. I got the people at Champlain Chocolates to show me everything. I feel kind of bad about it now." Maybe, but this sounds like the beginning of Trufflegate.

By hook or by crook, Elkhay and Drinkuth-Bradford have learned a lot about truffle making in the few years they've been in business. They produce confections that have genuine New England and American flavors. Their superb American Chèvre truffle is a creamy mixture of Massachusetts goat cheese and white chocolate, dipped in a dark chocolate shell. The Peach Melba truffle is made with New England peach wine. Gold Rush is a heady combination of white chocolate, golden raisins, and rum. And Mexican Chocolate combines ultra-rich dark chocolate with a hint of coffee flavoring, rolled in cinnamon cocoa.

The New England Truffle Company also makes very rich sweet sauces—Peach Melba, Champagne Cassis, Chocolate-Chocolate, and Caramel Crunch. They are de-

PALMIERI'S BAKERY

147 Ridge Street, Providence, 02909; phone 401-TE1-9145. Hours: Tuesday–Saturday 7 A.M. to 5 P.M., Sunday 7 A.M. to 12:30 P.M.; closed Monday. Personal checks accepted.

PROVIDENCE CHEESE & TAVOLA CALDA

407 Atwells Avenue, Providence, 02909; phone 401-421-5653. Hours: Monday–Saturday 8:30 A.M. to 6:30 P.M.; closed Sunday. Personal checks accepted. Catering available.

licious spooned over ice cream or poured over fresh fruit and berries.

■ "We've stayed in business by keeping it simple," responded Anthony Palmieri when we asked about the reasons for his bakery's success. Palmieri is the third generation of his family to run the business. It was started by his grandfather just after the turn of the century, and according to Palmieri not much has changed in the intervening years. He bakes only a few items in the bakery's large brick ovens, basically the same items that the Palmieri family has specialized in for the past eighty-six years.

There is crispy Italian bread—served in some of Providence's best restaurants—along with rolls, pepper biscuits, wine biscuits, and "homemade-style" pizza. The pepper biscuits are crunchy breadsticks spiced with flakes of pepper. The wine biscuits are slightly sweet breadsticks, twisted into the shape of a donut. We highly recommend all of these products, with the possible exception of the pizza.

■ To get the freshest, most authentic Italian foods in Rhode Island you must climb Providence's Federal Hill. Along Atwells Avenue, the main street of this old Italian neighborhood, you'll find dozens of bakeries, delicatessens, butcher shops, and restaurants. Providence Cheese and Tavola Calda is one of the most innovative shops in the neighborhood. Founded by the late Frank Basso, the store is a source of fresh pasta, homemade cheese, breads, and other Italian specialties. All of these foods are made with natural or organic ingredients.

Providence Cheese is *not* a health food store. Basso, born in 1912 just a few blocks from where the store is located, began his business with the idea that "eating, just plain eating, is a source of good health. It makes for a happy frame of mind." However, you must be selective about what you eat. So all the pasta, breads, and cakes at Providence Cheese are made exclusively with whole wheat flour. The pure white mozzarella, ricotta, farm cheese, and *latticini* are made from fresh cow's and goat's milk. No refined sugar is ever used, and salt is used sparingly.

That Providence Cheese is unique is apparent even before you enter the store. Colorful hand-painted signs embellished with primitive designs advertise the store's specialties. A pushcart decorated with American and Italian flags sits outside the front door, in summer laden with fresh vegetables, fruit, and strands of garlic and peppers.

Frank Basso's daughter, Ginny Wheatley, runs the store. She has been in charge since her father died in the fall of 1987. We visited Providence Cheese about six months before Frank Basso's death and had an opportunity to learn about his unique philosophy of food.

"Twenty years ago a popular expression was 'beatnik,'" Basso began. At this point we were not exactly sure what he was talking about. But after a few minutes it became clear that when he started Providence Cheese, Basso was the beatnik, selling natural foods before people knew what the term meant.

Today the same spirit of rebellion is evidenced by Providence Cheese. Because he believed that sugar "is an empty calorie," Basso and his daughter developed cakes

Providence Cheese and Tavola Calda—a wealth of organic foods.

and cookies sweetened entirely with minced fruit. We sampled a chocolate cake made with cocoa, whole wheat flour, and dried fruit. It was a little heavy, and not nearly as sweet as we're accustomed to. But after a few bites we had to admit that it really tasted good.

The fresh pasta, on the other hand, was an instant hit. There's a variety of colors, shapes, and flavors, all with a perfect texture and a wonderfully fresh flavor. We served the red wine linguine with Providence Cheese's pesto sauce, an exceptionally light pesto made with lots of olive oil and fresh, organically grown basil.

At Providence Cheese, the emphasis is on freshness. "When I decided that we were going to be natural," said

Basso, "I had to eliminate two things: the freezer and the can opener." As a result some items are available only in certain seasons. During the rest of the year Ginny Wheatley uses her imagination to create dishes for the store's *tavola calda* (selection of warm dishes).

When we visited, it was spring, and Ginny had made a spinach *focaccia,* a whole wheat pie baked with fresh spinach, mushrooms, onions, and ricotta cheese. It provided several satisfying meals for us as we traveled through Rhode Island looking for other places to write about. Two days after visiting Providence Cheese, we finished off the last crumbs and realized that we had done more than just consume delicious, healthy food. We had gotten a taste of the culinary rhythms that Frank Basso worked so hard to create.

SCIALO BROTHERS BAKERY

257 Atwells Avenue, Providence, 02903; phone 401-421-0986. Hours: Monday–Saturday 8 A.M. to 7 P.M., Sunday 8 A.M. to 6 P.M. Personal checks accepted.

■ Walking into Scialo Brothers Bakery is little like going back in time. There are the wonderful old art deco fixtures and the porthole windows set into the walls, displaying colorful mixtures of hard candy. The countertop decoration is a display of huge flowers made from sheets of dyed tissue paper. The shelves are spare, but what is displayed looks incredible—fresh-baked angel food cakes, rum pound cakes, flaky Italian pastries, and their own candies.

We first visited Scialo's because a friend told us they make the best nougat candy in the world. We asked the woman behind the counter about it and she said, "Yeah, yeah, it's good. Taste it." She cut off two chunks and handed them to us. We bit into that sweet, sugary mass of honey and whole almonds and had to agree. It was excellent.

"You should try the pepper sticks," the woman urged, handing us each a long breadstick. This was starting to get fun. Although our mouths were full of candy sweetness, the anise and pepper flavor of the breadstick came shining through.

Scialo Brothers also specializes in *sfogliatelle,* a crisp, flaky Italian pastry filled with pastry cream. You can order wedding cakes, and around Easter they bake *pastiere,* a special holiday rice cake made with fresh ricotta cheese.

TONY'S COLONIAL FOOD STORE

311 Atwells Avenue, Providence, 02903; phone 401-621-8675. Hours: Monday–Thursday 8:30 A.M. to 6 P.M., Friday 8 A.M. to 8 P.M., Saturday

■ "Taste it, taste it. There's no way you're not gonna love it." We were debating whether to buy some of Tony's hot pickled peppers stuffed with prosciutto and cheese. The stuffed green and red cherry peppers marinating in olive oil beckoned us. "I just made them today. Here, try one," he said, reaching over the shiny stainless steel counter to offer us a sample. We each delicately plucked a pepper from the long metal spoon where they rested and popped

The crew at Tony's Colonial Food Store.

8 A.M. to 6 P.M., Sunday 8:30 A.M. to 1 P.M. Cash only.

one into our mouth. Our teeth bit through the crunchy pepper, went on to the salty ham, and finally landed in the soft cheese. Our tongues tasted the flavors of all three ingredients, married with a thin coating of olive oil. Our noses filled with the mild hotness of the pepper. We were in love, just as the man said we would be.

It would be misleading to say that everything at Tony's evokes this kind of amorous response. But there are a number of items here that will get your juices flowing—sausages marinated in olive oil, dried Abbruzzese sausage, and fresh mozzarella and ricotta cheese to name a few.

Tony's is an exceptionally well stocked Italian deli and supermarket. There is literally a wall of imported Italian pasta, along with Italian cheeses, oils and vinegars, pickled and marinated vegetables—most at reasonable prices. There are even a few genuine bargains.

VENDA RAVIOLI
219 Atwells Avenue, Providence, 02903; phone 401-421-9105. Hours: Monday 9 A.M. to 12 N., Tuesday–Saturday 8:30 A.M. to 5 P.M., Sunday 8:30 A.M. to 12 N. Cash only.

■ This is top-quality fresh pasta. The ravioli are tender, and both the cheese and meat fillings are moist and well seasoned. Venda makes pasta in lots of different shapes and sizes. There's manicotti stuffed with ricotta and romano cheese, egg noodles, *pasta verde* (egg noodles with spinach), and tender potato gnocchi.

We made a terrific meal of Venda ravioli with sauce from L'Epicurio Gourmet Foods, located just a few doors down on Atwells Avenue (see page 191).

SAKONNET POINT PIER
Southern terminus of Route 77, Sakonnet Point, 02837.

Sakonnet Point

■ If you're a stickler for fresh fish, we suggest you visit the Sakonnet Point Pier at around 9:30 in the morning, just about any day of the week. That's when the fishing boats that work out of this harbor return to port with the day's catch. You can buy whole flounder, scup, mackerel, squid, bluefish, and other kinds of fish right off the boats.

Sakonnet Point is located where the Sakonnet River meets the Atlantic Ocean. It's a pretty place to have a picnic, walk on the beach, and breathe the salt air.

Tiverton

HELGER'S TURKEY RANCH
2554 Main Road, Tiverton, 02878; phone 401-624-4087. Hours: Monday–Saturday 9 A.M. to 5 P.M.; closed Sunday. Personal checks accepted.

■ Fresh turkeys are available here almost all year round. May and June are the only months when Helger's has only frozen birds on hand. The turkeys are broad-breasted, with lots of white meat. They cost quite a bit more than the frozen birds sold at the supermarket, but local residents say they are worth the price. Fresh turkeys must be ordered a week in advance.

MANCHESTER SEAFOODS
2139 Main Road (Route 77), Tiverton, 02878; phone 401-624-8000. Hours: seven days a week 8 A.M. to 5 P.M. Cash only.

■ When Johanne Killeen, owner and chef of Al Forno restaurant in Providence, told us that the only clams she ever uses are from Manchester Seafoods in Tiverton, we were puzzled. "You mean to tell us that there's not a single fish store in Providence or nearby that sells fresh clams?" we asked. "Not like these clams," she answered.

So we drove south to Tiverton and found a large abandoned-looking warehouse located on the Sakonnet River, with a faded sign advertising "Manchester's." Around the back of the building, next to a dock where fishing boats tie up, was a small shop with wire buckets filled with different kinds of clams. There were oversized quahogs, perfectly shaped cherrystones, petite littlenecks, and

Sakonnet Point.

PROVENDER
3883 Main Road, Tiverton Four Corners, Tiverton, 02878; phone 401-624-8096. Hours: Wednesday–Monday 9 A.M. to 6 P.M.; closed Tuesday. MasterCard, Visa, American Express, and personal checks accepted. Mail order and catering available. Gift baskets available; call or write for brochure.

Provender, in Tiverton—gourmet shopping.

meaty-looking steamers. There were also lobster tanks and a bushel basket of conch in their spiral shells.

We bought a dozen littlenecks and a dozen cherrystones and devoured the whole batch that evening. The littlenecks were consumed on the half shell, with just a squirt of lemon juice and some horseradish. They were exceptionally sweet and fresh tasting. The cherrystones went under the broiler with just a bit of chopped garlic and a dash of hot pepper sauce. They too were remarkably flavorful and tender. It is a rare treat to find clams that taste this fresh, alive, and full of the essence of the sea.

■ This is one of the most attractive gourmet food stores in all of New England—an old country store with a big front porch, tall ceilings, pale wood floors, and lots of gorgeous food. Now, it's true that looks can be deceptive. But in this case almost everything tastes just as good as it looks.

We peered behind the deli counter at the array of smoked meats, sausages, smoked fish, salads, olives, pâtés, and pickles. A large chalkboard advertised the daily soup and sandwich specials. We tried a strange soup called California Red (a purée of beets flavored with cloves) and a Dr. Bombay sandwich (a generous portion of curried chicken salad on homemade curry bread). The sandwich was spectacular. The soup was good, but took some getting used to.

Dessert and baked goods presented a whole other set of temptations. There were over ten varieties of freshly baked croissants, with flavors ranging from almond to Italian vegetable. Each day there are half a dozen different varieties of freshly baked bread, along with many

Grilled Swordfish with Herbs

You can use just about any combination of herbs with this recipe, as long as they are fresh. Tuna, mako shark, and halibut steaks work well also. Serve with charcoal-grilled leeks or scallions, fresh tomato and basil salad, and corn on the cob.

1 swordfish steak (2 pounds)
Juice of 1 large lemon
3 tablespoons olive oil
4 tablespoons chopped scallions
4 tablespoons chopped fresh herbs (basil, thyme, sage, and lemon balm)

Place the swordfish in a large bowl or pan. Add the remaining ingredients, making sure to coat the fish thoroughly. Marinate for about 2 hours, or cover and place in the refrigerator overnight.

Light a charcoal grill or preheat the broiler. Grill the swordfish about 4 to 6 minutes on each side, depending on thickness, basting with the herbal marinade. Serves 4.

---

kinds of pastries and oversized cookies. We tried a brownie—a chewy, gooey, nutty treat coated with rich chocolate icing—and decided that we wouldn't mind having lunch here every day. But price is another consideration. None of this wonderful food is cheap. For a brownie this good, however, we'd mortgage the house.

The rest of the shop is devoted to olive oils, vinegars, mustards, spices and herbs, teas and coffees, and imported cookies, biscuits, and chocolates, and regional foods.

Behind the shop is Provender Gardens, a small garden supply store that specializes in English garden tools, fresh herb and flower plants, seeds, planters, and freshly cut flowers. The garden that separates the two stores is open to the public for picnics and browsing.

Usquepaugh

■ *Usquepaugh.* The word kind of rolls off your tongue. You're not sure if it's the name of an Indian tribe or a kind of clam (it's neither). When you pull into the village of Usquepaugh (pronounced us-kuh-pawg) in Rhode Island's South County you find a collection of fine colonial houses perched on a hillside, and at the bottom of the hill, next to a millpond, the Kenyon Corn Meal Company. This is where they grind corn for the famous Rhode Island jonnycakes—those delicious flapjacks made from stone-ground cornmeal (see page 183 for more on jonnycakes).

If you pop your head in through the open door of the

KENYON CORN MEAL COMPANY

Usquepaugh, 02892; phone 401-783-4054. Mail order available. MasterCard, Visa, and personal checks accepted. Gift shop hours: Monday–Friday 10 A.M. to 5 P.M., Saturday and Sunday 12 N. to 5 P.M.

Thin Jonnycakes

These cakes can be served with melted butter and maple syrup. If you want to get fancy you can use them like crepes—top them with whipped cream and fruit preserves, crème fraîche, smoked salmon and dill sprigs, or a simple lemon-herb butter.

1 cup jonnycake meal or other cornmeal
1/2 teaspoon salt (optional)
1 teaspoon sugar (optional)
1 cup milk
1/2 cup water

Combine the dry ingredients in a bowl. Add the milk and water, and mix thoroughly.

Grease a large skillet with butter, margarine, or bacon fat, and place over moderate heat. Pour a few tablespoons of batter into the skillet to form a cake 2 to 3 inches wide. Fry until the edges of the jonnycakes are brown, then flip.

Keep the batter thin, adding more milk as necessary. Makes 10 to 12 jonnycakes.

Thick Jonnycakes

Serve with lots of butter and maple syrup. Rhode Islanders also serve thick jonnycakes with stews, instead of dumplings.

1 cup jonnycake meal or other cornmeal
1/2 teaspoon salt
1 teaspoon molasses (optional)
1 cup boiling water
1/8 cup milk

Combine the dry ingredients and molasses in a bowl. Pour in the boiling water, and stir until the dough is stiff. Let stand for 5 minutes. Thin the batter with the milk. Drop the cakes onto a skillet greased with butter or margarine. Cook slowly for 10 to 15 minutes on each side. Makes 6 jonnycakes.

(weekends only during winter and early spring).

Kenyon products are sold in supermarkets, health food stores, and specialty food stores throughout New England and New York.

mill you can hear the rumble of the heavy granite stones grinding the grain. The top stone, called the runner stone, and the bottom stone, called the bed stone, are set so close that you can just fit a sheet of paper between them. But they are perfectly balanced so they never touch when the runner stone spins on its axle. As a result the cornmeal that comes out is very fine, with just a bit of grittiness to give the jonnycakes texture.

This mill has been in operation since 1886, but according to Paul Drumm, Jr., who runs the Kenyon Corn Meal Company with his son Paul Drumm III, there have been mills at this site on the bank of the Queen's River since 1711. In years gone by there were lots of gristmills in

Rhode Island, not to mention other parts of the country. Today the Drumms are among a handful of millers who continue to practice stone grinding.

Kenyon's is probably Rhode Island's best known gristmill, and notoriety has helped them promote jonnycakes as well as the virtues of stone-ground grains. Even so, Kenyon's has its detractors who point out that Kenyon's cornmeal is not authentic because it's not made from Rhode Island white flint corn. The Drumms acknowledge that they use white dent corn imported from out of state, but they argue that the cornmeal they grind makes excellent jonnycakes. And in any event the debate over what kind of corn is best seems to add more intrigue to their product. After all, it's only dried corn that's been pulverized between two big rocks. You have to do something to keep the customers interested.

The Kenyon Corn Meal Company grinds other grains besides corn and sells them both separately and in mixes. There is whole wheat flour, graham flour, rye meal, scotch oat flour, corn muffin mix, Buckwheat Pancake Mix, Corn Meal Pancake Mix, Clam Cake and Fritter Mix, and lots more. None of these grains and mixes contain preservatives, so they must be treated as fresh products. This means either refrigerate them or keep them in a cool place.

FOX SEAFOODS
P.O. Box 464, Wakefield, 02880; phone 401-783-4646.
Available in fish markets throughout the northeastern U.S.

Wakefield

■ Fox Seafood smoked bluefish is exceptionally moist and flavorful. We have had it a number of times and have never been disappointed. This company also smokes several other kinds of fish and shellfish, including mackerel, cod, tuna, marlin, mussels, scallops, salmon, and trout.

WICKFORD GOURMET FOODS
21 West Main Street, Wickford, 02852; phone 401-295-8190. Hours: Monday–Saturday 9:30 A.M. to 6:30 P.M., Friday 9:30 A.M. to 7 P.M., Sunday 9:30 A.M. to 5 P.M. MasterCard, Visa, American Express and personal checks accepted. Mail order and catering available.

Wickford

■ There is something very welcoming about this gourmet food store. Enter from the parking lot in the rear, and you'll see a little cafe where you can sit and have a cup of hot soup, some fresh-baked bread, or one of their luscious pastries. When you're finished with lunch you can browse around this house, which is literally chock-full of goodies. There are condiments from around the world, jams and jellies, teas and coffees, herbs, chocolates, cheeses, pâtés, cookware, linens, kitchen equipment, and more.

Wickford Gourmet Foods offers cooking classes and wine tastings every few weeks.

Wyoming

MEADOWBROOK HERB GARDEN
Route 138, Wyoming, 02898; phone 401-539-7603. Hours: Monday–Saturday 9:30 A.M. to 5 P.M. Sunday 1 P.M. to 4 P.M. MasterCard, Visa, and personal checks accepted. Mail order available.

■ It was mid-April and it had been raining on and off for several weeks. We wandered into the Meadowbrook Herb Garden greenhouse, took a deep breath, and knew there was hope. The air there was rich with sweetness and the smell of the earth; it held the promise of spring. In one corner of the greenhouse there were twenty-five types of scented geraniums. We inhaled the essence of apple, apricot, and almond and then moved over to the lime, lemon, nutmeg, and old-fashioned rose geraniums. Next there was cinnamon-flavored basil, pineapple sage, lavender-scented thyme, flowering rosemary, and sweet chamomile with its tiny, delicate yellow and white flowers.

We walked inside the shop and looked at the vast array of dried herbs, herbal teas, herbal vinegars, and potpourris, all made from herbs and flowers grown at Meadowbrook. A young woman named Zelka explained a bit about Meadowbrook's philosophy: "All our herbs are grown biodynamically. That means everything is planted without fertilizers or pesticides. Instead we use a compost made up of herbal compounds." She paused and looked toward the sky. "And we always plant according to the phases of the moon," said Zelka with a mystical tone in her voice. We began to understand how unique this herb nursery is.

Make a point of visiting the gardens in the summer when the herbs are in bloom and everything is carefully labeled and identified. In addition to edible herbal products, the shop is filled with goodies—beautifully crafted toys from Germany, books on herbal cookery and organic gardening, and herbal cosmetics imported from Europe.

Rhode Island Farmers' Markets

Providence—Governor Dyer Farmers' Market, between Promenade and Valley streets, seven days a week from April through October, Monday through Saturday from November through March, 5 A.M. to 5 P.M. For further information, call Everett Petronio (401-273-8800).

South Kingston Farmers' Market, Government Center parking lot, Route 1, Saturdays from May through October, 10 A.M. until sold out. For further information, call Kevin Hartung (401-783-7671) or Gail Ambrose (401-789-3334).

South Providence—Northern Rhode Island Farmers' Market, Saint Martin de Porres Center, Cranston Street, Saturdays from July through October, 9 A.M. until sold out. For further information, call Stanley Luchka (401-647-3659).

Vermont

VERMONT

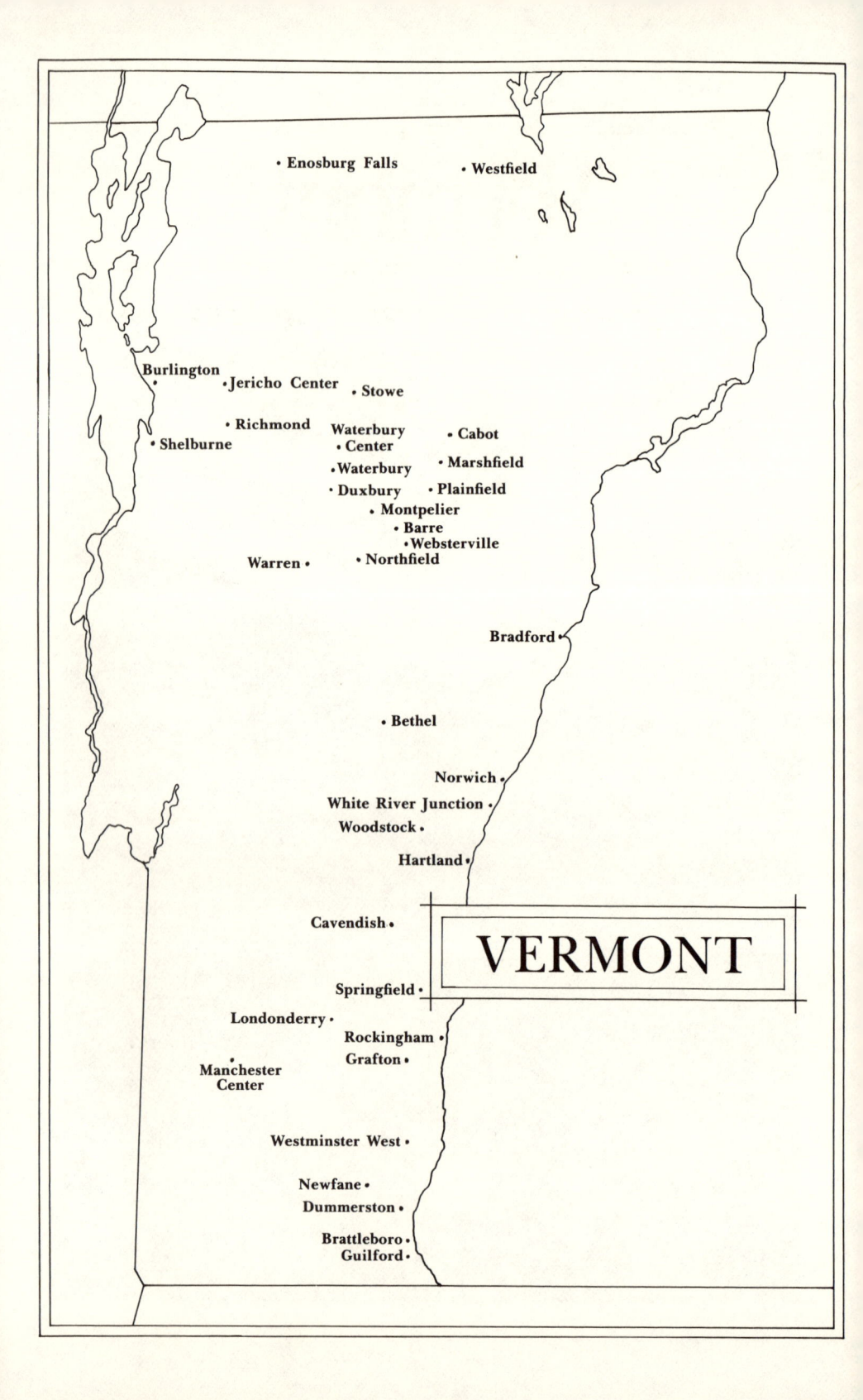

Barre

CHERRY HILL COOPERATIVE CANNERY

MR 1, Barre–Montpelier Road, Barre, 05641; phone 802-479-2558. Hours: Monday–Friday 9 A.M. to 5 P.M. Personal checks accepted. Mail order and tours available.

Cherry Hill products are sold throughout the northeastern United States.

■ The Cherry Hill Cooperative Cannery was founded in 1976 as a nonprofit co-op designed to help low-income Vermonters with their home canning. Members of the co-op brought their raw fruits and vegetables to the cannery, where they were taught to make home preserves using modern factory-type equipment.

Over the years the cannery has expanded. While still serving individual co-op members, Cherry Hill is now a profit-making company that produces some of the most delicious preserves and pickles we've tasted anywhere. We get almost as much satisfaction from eating their products as we do from opening a jar of our own homemade preserves.

Cherry Hill makes several different types of applesauce flavored with fresh berries. The Strawberry Applesauce is a thick, sweet, pink-colored condiment. The smell of fresh strawberries comes shining through as soon as you pop the lid off the pretty jar it's packed in. The same goes for the Raspberry Applesauce and the Cranberry Applesauce. All three are good served with roasted meats (instead of chutney), or spread on waffles or pancakes.

Pickled Fiddleheads are another excellent, and unusual, condiment from Cherry Hill. These wild Vermont fiddleheads, packed in a vinegar brine, are very crunchy and a bit peppery. The Maple Bread and Butter Pickles are made from sliced organically grown cucumbers sweetened with maple syrup instead of sugar. The Maple Beet Pickles also contain maple syrup and have a pleasant vinegary bite.

Cherry Hill offers several maple and honey products, including maple syrup, maple sugar granules, maple cream, Vermont honey, creamed honey, honey mustard, and honeycomb. Also good is their apple butter, and they offer three excellent varieties of berry preserves.

The Cherry Hill Cooperative Cannery is committed to supporting Vermont farmers. All of the raw produce they use is locally grown, and a good deal of it comes from organic farms. Maple syrup is the only sweetener used in their condiments. And none of the products contain preservatives.

In our view Cherry Hill is one of the finest food producers in New England.

COTTAGE STREET PASTA

4½ Cottage Street, Barre, 05641; phone 802-476-4024. Hours: irregular, call ahead.

■ Across the street from the tiny Cottage Street Pasta factory stands a statue honoring the Italians who came to Barre in the early twentieth century to work in the region's granite quarries. Those immigrants would have found favor with this pasta. It's sold fresh, and is tender and especially flavorful. Cottage Street Pasta comes in several different varieties including linguine, vermicelli,

Personal checks accepted.

Also sold at gourmet food stores, health food stores, and grocery stores in central Vermont.

RATHDOWNEY HERBS AND HERB CRAFTS
3 River Street, Bethel, 05032; phone 802-234-9928, or toll-free 800-543-8885. Hours: seven days a week, 9 A.M. to 5 P.M.; closed Sunday in March and April. MasterCard, Visa, and personal checks accepted. Mail order available.

and fettuccine (regular, spinach, and tomato flavor), meat ravioli (made with a blend of beef, pork, and chicken), and an outstanding cheese ravioli filled with cottage cheese, spinach, mozzarella, Asiago and Parmesan cheeses, garlic, and spices.

The company also makes two sauces; Bolognese, a red sauce with meat, and Marinara, a meatless red sauce.

Bethel

■ In a rambling house sandwiched between the railroad tracks and the White River, Louise Downey Butler has created an herb store that is a treat for all the senses. Bunches of herbs hanging from ceiling rafters, woven baskets on the floor overflowing with dried herbs, and shelves packed with glass canisters of herbs, spices, and herb blends give the place a cluttered but charming atmosphere. And as you walk from room to room the combination of herbs and spices creates powerful and compelling scents that are reminiscent of flower gardens and far-away open-air food bazaars.

We particularly enjoyed smelling (and tasting) many of the culinary herb and spice blends. Inhale the scent of a blend like Herb Sesame Chicken or New England Seafood Seasoning and you realize how much your memory

A herbal extravaganza—Rathdowney Herbs.

Also in Bridgewater, at The Marketplace, and in Hanover, New Hampshire, at Allen Street Herbal.

Rathdowney products are also sold in country stores and specialty food shops throughout New England.

DAD'S VERMONT MADE PEANUT BRITTLE

Box 634, Main Street, Bradford, 05033; phone 802-222-9325. Personal checks accepted. Mail order available.

Available at many specialty gift shops, candy stores, and country stores in New England and on the West Coast.

BRATTLEBORO FOOD COOP

49 Flat Street, Brattleboro, 05301; phone 802-257-0236. Hours: Monday–Friday 10 A.M. to 8 P.M., Saturday 10 A.M. to 6 P.M.; closed Sunday. Personal checks accepted.

of a good meal depends on the herbs that were used in the recipe.

Rathdowney is a complete herb store. Besides culinary herbs they sell their own herbal teas, local honey, decorative herbs and dried flowers, herb sachets, and supplies for making herb wreaths and herb displays. There is also an extensive selection of herb books, medicinal herbs, and such things as herbal insect spray, herbal flea collars for pets, herbal bath mixtures, and herbs for keeping moths out of your clothes.

Bradford

■ Remember peanut brittle? That sweet mass of peanuts and caramel sugar mixed together into a brick-like bar? Well it's been a long time since we've tasted the real thing, but when we met Noel Gaiser ("Dad") and tasted his Vermont Made Peanut Brittle we were flooded with fond childhood memories. This is actually much better than any peanut brittle we had when we were young. According to Mr. Gaiser, "We only use the best peanuts, sugar, Royal brand bourbon vanilla, and fresh Vermont butter. The secret ingredient is rich, dark Vermont maple syrup. And we never add salt or preservatives."

Gaiser, a former industrial engineer, began making peanut brittle at Christmastime for his kids and a few regular customers. "Everyone who tasted it loved the stuff," reports Gaiser. Before he knew it he was spending all his time making peanut brittle, and eventually it became a full-time occupation. Today Gaiser and his family make the candy in their house, built in 1869 and once the home of Governor Roswell Farnham. Try it crumbled over vanilla ice cream or devour it straight from the glass jar. Either way, you're in for a treat.

Brattleboro

■ The Brattleboro Food Coop is a little hard to find—it's in an old warehouse behind an auto supply store. But it's worth searching for, particularly if you want organic foods. There are organic fruits and nuts, vegetables, grains, cereals, dairy products, and more. Everything that is not organic is clearly marked.

They also sell lots of items in bulk at significant savings: things like cooking oil, miso, tahini, several different kinds of peanut butter, cashew butter, molasses, and syrups. This co-op also stocks a good selection of imported and domestic beer.

Homemade Maple Granola

Serve this granola with a pitcher of milk or a bowl of plain yogurt, lots of fresh fruit and berries, and a sprinkling of shredded coconut. The granola will keep for several weeks in an airtight jar.

6 1/2 cups rolled oats
3 cups mixed nuts and seeds (any combination of cashews, almonds, pecans, walnuts, filberts, pumpkin seeds, sunflower seeds)

1/2 cup honey
1/3 cup maple syrup
3/4 cup vegetable oil
1 1/2 cups raisins

Preheat the oven to 400°. Thoroughly mix all the ingredients, except the raisins, in a large roasting pan. Bake for 20 to 25 minutes, stirring the mixture every 5 minutes or so to prevent burning. (Beware: Granola can burn quickly. If the phone rings during the last 5 minutes of baking, don't answer it.) The granola is done when it's a light golden brown throughout.

Remove from the oven and let cool. If you like your granola loose, immediately mix it up with a spoon; if you prefer a chunkier, brick-like cereal, let it sit a few minutes longer and then break it up into clusters. Stir in the raisins and store in airtight jars. Makes about 10 cups.

HAMELMAN'S BAKERY

12 Elliot Street, Brattleboro, 05301; phone 802-254-6676. Hours: Monday–Saturday 6 A.M. to 6 P.M.; closed Sundays. Personal checks accepted.

■ When we hear people complain that there aren't any good European-style bakeries in New England, we get annoyed. Then we tell them about Hamelman's.

We discovered Hamelman's by accident. It was a freezing cold November morning and we needed a quick cup of coffee and a bite to eat before hitting the road. But as soon as we entered this warm bakery/cafe we knew we were on to something special. Loaves of bread coming out of the oven looked as though they were from a *"J'aime Paris"* ad. We saw patrons having their morning coffee at small marble tables, reading the local paper, listening to *Morning Pro Musica* on public radio. And then there were the display cases gradually being filled with the day's selections—fresh fruit danish on a croissant dough, napoleons oozing with *crème pâtissière*, remarkable-looking cheesecakes, Viennese tortes, thick sesame-studded breadsticks, and delicate little cookies sitting on mismatched Wedgwood plates. This was clearly not just another "let's-make-everything-with-whole-wheat" Vermont bakery.

Jeffrey Hamelman learned to bake in Ireland and Germany. After he returned to the U.S., he spent five years working in a European-style bakery in Northampton, Massachusetts, before he and his wife, Norma, opened their own bakery in Brattleboro. Bread—sourdough bread in particular—is his most popular item and the thing he likes best to bake. Hamelman's recipe comes from the Northampton bakery. "The bread they made was incredible," he recalls. "They worked with a sourdough starter that was over a hundred years old." Hamelman's sourdough is baked in a German convection oven; it has a firm brick-red crust, a soft, chewy inside, and a pleasing sour taste.

After devouring a little bit of everything we asked Jeffrey Hamelman why he settled in Brattleboro—his bakery could easily be a success in any major urban center. "It's nice being in a small town," he explained. "Here we are selling to our neighbors. It's not like being in the city where you can sell junk and get away with it. I feel we have an obligation to the community." The citizens of Brattleboro are fortunate to have the Hamelmans in their midst.

HIGH MEADOWS FARM MARKET

Putney Road, Brattleboro, 05301; phone 802-257-1450. Hours: Monday–Saturday 9 A.M. to 9 P.M., Sunday 9 A.M. to 7 P.M.; MasterCard, Visa, American Express, and personal checks accepted. Mail order available.

■ A visit to this roadside market may change forever your notions about the kind of place that sells organic fruits and vegetables. High Meadows Farm Market is a big, modern, suburban-style store, located on a strip of shopping centers and gas stations just north of downtown Brattleboro. But the fresh produce they sell has little in common with the plastic and neon that clutters the surrounding landscape.

Locally grown giant yellow peppers, handsome heads of deep green lettuce, gorgeous, juicy red tomatoes, sweet corn, and braids of organically grown garlic are part of the sumptuous selection offered here. Owner Howard Prussack grows many of the vegetables himself at his farm up the road in Westminster West. He is particularly proud of his Gilfeather turnips, a large, sweet root vegetable from a locally developed seed that is delicious boiled and puréed.

But there is more to this store than fresh vegetables. High Meadows Farm Market also stocks a big selection of natural foods including cereals, grains, and local dairy products. And in the spring they carry bedding plants, herb plants, and tomato plants.

STRAW AND HAY MARKETPLACE

71 Main Street, Brattleboro, 05301; phone 802-257-1277. Hours: Monday–Saturday 9 A.M. to 5:30 P.M.; closed Sunday. MasterCard, Visa, American Express, and personal checks accepted. Catering and mail order available.

■ Superb meats and poultry, imported cold cuts, pâtés, a big selection of cheeses, and imported chocolates are among the offerings here. This is the most upscale of Brattleboro's many specialty food stores.

The deli section is exciting. There is smoked Norwegian salmon, German-style wursts and bolognas, prepared salads, and breads from nearby Hamelman's Bakery (see page 208). Straw and Hay Marketplace will put together picnic baskets and boxed lunches.

They also make their own pasta, sauces, and salad dressings. Vermont-made products include several different types of cheese, candies, and maple syrup. During the Christmas and Thanksgiving holidays they carry locally raised turkeys and geese.

Burlington

CHAMPLAIN CHOCOLATE COMPANY

431 Pine Street, Burlington, 05401; phone 802-864-1808. Hours: Monday–Saturday 9:30 A.M. to 5:30 P.M.; closed Sunday. MasterCard, Visa, American Express, and personal checks accepted.

Also sold in candy stores and specialty food stores throughout New England.

■ Made with Belgian chocolate, rich Vermont cream and butter, and natural flavorings, these chocolates are among the classiest candies made in New England. American Truffles is the name they've given to a line of "dense, elegant nuggets" filled with sixteen various flavors including Grand Marnier, Amaretto Praline, and one of our favorites, Cappuccino. These oversized truffles are exquisitely decorated with thin ribbons of colored chocolate that remind us of party streamers.

Chocolates of Vermont, another variety, are chocolate disks flavored with mint, maple toffee, Vermont honey caramel, or almonds and raisins. Produced in molds, they are decorated with scenes of mountains, maple leaves, and so on.

For chocolate lovers, a trip to the Champlain Chocolate Company factory store in Burlington is definitely worthwhile. There are plenty of free samples, and you can watch chocolates being made from a glassed-in area perched above the factory floor. Slightly damaged chocolates are sold at reduced prices, and even the undamaged goods are a bit less expensive than in most stores.

CHEESE OUTLET

400 Pine Street, Burlington, 05401; phone 802-863-3968 or toll-free 800-447-1205. Hours: Monday–Thursday 9 A.M. to 5:30 P.M., Friday 9 A.M. to 6:30 P.M., Saturday 9:30 A.M. to 5 P.M.; closed Sunday. MasterCard, Visa, and personal checks accepted. Mail order and tours available.

■ It's only fair that Vermont, which long ago exceeded its quota of quaint shops selling cheddar, would have at least one cheese emporium built of cinder blocks and offering "outlet" prices. Cheese Outlet is the place to come if you love the food they sell in gourmet groceries but hate to pay gourmet prices. Here, a whole wheel of Brie sells for a little more than you would pay for two thirds of a wheel elsewhere.

Cheese Outlet sells cheeses from around the world, including Vermont cream cheese and goat cheese, Italian mascarpone, French camembert, Norwegian Jarlsberg, and of course several different kinds of cheddar. One of the best is their Truck Driver Cheddar, which has been aged for just under three years. It's so sharp and smelly that the salesman at Cheese Outlet told us the maker asks to remain anonymous for fear of ruining his reputation.

There is also a constantly changing selection of non-cheese foods (crackers, pickled herring, imported mustard, Vermont-made pasta, coffee beans) along with domestic and imported wines and sparkling cider. Many items are sold in large restaurant-size containers (for example, a 9-pound bucket of sweet Honeycup Mustard), so leave plenty of room in the trunk of your car and arrange with friends to share the food.

LA PATISSERIE

198 Main Street, Burlington, 05401; phone

■ An apple tart, sparkling in the display case, was the first thing that caught our fancy at La Pâtisserie. We were not disappointed. Made with Vermont apples, pastry cream,

802-658-3074. Hours: Monday and Saturday 8 A.M. to 5 P.M., Tuesday–Thursday 7:30 A.M. to 5:30 P.M., Friday 7:30 A.M. to 6 P.M.; closed Sunday. Personal checks accepted.

a delicate, buttery crust, and topped with a thin fruit glaze, this tart had the taste and texture we expect of fine French pastry. The chocolate éclair and napoleon were also well made, with just the right amount of sweetness. And the *pain de campagne* had a wonderfully crispy crust and a chewy white center.

La Pâtisserie also bakes croissants, several traditional varieties of French bread, butter cookies, and birthday cakes, and serves sandwiches, coffee, and tea at a few tables in the front.

Like the baked goods, the atmosphere is very French, right down to the brusque service that reminded us of the treatment we've gotten at some shops in Paris.

VERMONT PASTA COMPANY

156 Church Street, Burlington, 05401; phone 802-658-2575. Hours: Monday–Thursday 10:30 A.M. to 9:30 P.M., Friday 10:30 A.M. to 10 P.M., Saturday 11 A.M. to 10 P.M., Sunday 4 P.M. to 9:30 P.M. MasterCard, Visa, and personal checks accepted. Catering available.

■ There is something very soothing about a plate of warm pasta topped with sauce. Even before you put it to your lips, the whiffs of steam rising from the plate begin to calm your nerves while at the same time awakening your senses of taste and smell.

We can't prove that the spaghetti, linguine, and cheese-filled ravioli from Vermont Pasta Company are more soothing than other pastas, but that certainly seems to be the case. This pasta is fresh tasting, slightly chewy, and above all satisfying. Of all the Vermont-made pastas we've tasted, it's the best.

Vermont Pasta Company makes pasta in a whole variety of shapes and flavors. Some examples: scallion linguine and tomato fettuccine. They also prepare excellent pasta sauces. Among those we've tried are a pungent marinara sauce and both red and white clam sauces, made with generous amounts of garlic and whole baby clams.

In addition to selling pasta and sauces, breads, and pastries to take out, Vermont Pasta Company runs a large, informal restaurant. The menu is extensive, the atmosphere is congenial if not intimate, the prices are very reasonable, the portions are ample, and the food is well prepared.

Cabot

CABOT CREAMERY

Cabot Center (P.O. Box 128, Cabot), 05647; (the creamery is located in Cabot Center, between Montpelier and St. Johnsbury off Route 2); phone 802-563-2231. Hours: Monday–Saturday 8 A.M. to 4:30 P.M.; closed Sunday. MasterCard, Visa, and personal checks

■ The Cabot Creamery began in 1919 when a group of ninety-four dairy farmers banded together to form a cooperative. Members were paid for whatever milk they brought in, and at the end of the year they divided up the profits. Today there are five hundred dairy farmers from northeastern Vermont involved in the Cabot Co-op and, despite years of growth and expansion, the creamery is still run on the same basic principles.

Cabot is best known for its cheddar cheese, and for good reason. There are very few cheddars that can match this one in terms of quality and consistency. Cabot cheddar is available mild, sharp, and extra sharp. We are par-

accepted. Plant tours and mail order available.

Cabot dairy products are also sold at food stores throughout the region.

JOSEPH CERNIGLIA WINERY

Route 103, Cavendish, 05153; phone 802-266-7578, or toll-free 800-654-6382. Hours: seven days a week 10 A.M. to 5 P.M. MasterCard, Visa, and personal checks accepted. Tours and tastings available; call or write for information.

Joseph Cerniglia wines are also sold at gourmet food stores, supermarkets, tial to the extra sharp, aged for over fourteen months, with its snappy flavor. Cabot also produces butter, sour cream, yogurt, and Monterey Jack cheese.

You can visit the creamery and take a guided tour of the cheesemaking facilities. There's also a ten-minute video on the history of the Cabot Co-op. A word of advice: The best time to see the cheesemakers in action is before noon.

Cavendish

■ At the Joseph Cerniglia Winery they make varietal apple wines—wines made from a single variety of apple, rather than blended wines made from a mixture of several different types of fruit. There are nine apple wines in all, made from McIntosh, Golden Delicious, Red Delicious, Northern Spy, Empire, and so on. And while this may not sound particularly revolutionary, winemaker Joseph Cerniglia claims that "the difference between varietal apple wine and blended apple wine is like the difference between a really fine Cabernet Sauvignon or Riesling and table wine."

We wouldn't go that far, but from what we've tasted there is a difference. Cerniglia's McIntosh Dry Apple Wine is impressive—only slightly sweet with a full, tart apple flavor. We tried it with assorted cheeses and served it with a roast loin of pork. We also used it to deglaze the pan juices from sautéed lamb chops and it produced a wonderful apple-scented sauce (see recipe below).

New England Lamb Chops with Garlic, Rosemary, and Apple Wine

2 tablespoons olive oil
8 cloves garlic, peeled
4 sprigs fresh rosemary
4 loin lamb chops

About 1/3 cup apple wine or apple cider
Salt to taste
Freshly ground black pepper to taste

Heat the olive oil in a large skillet, and add the garlic and rosemary. Sauté over moderate heat until the garlic turns golden brown. Remove the garlic and rosemary and set them aside.

In the skillet over high heat, sauté the chops for 2 minutes on each side. Remove them and set aside. Add the apple wine to the hot skillet, and simmer for a few seconds. Add the reserved garlic, rosemary, and chops, and sprinkle with salt and pepper. Cook an additional 2 minutes on each side, adding additional wine if the skillet becomes dry. Transfer the chops to a serving platter, top with the pan juices, and serve immediately. Serves 2.

and liquor stores in Vermont and New Hampshire.

DWIGHT MILLER ORCHARDS
East Miller Road, Dummerston, 05346 (mailing address: RD 2, P.O. Box 835, Putney, 05346); phone 802-254-9158. Hours: seven days a week 8 A.M. to 5 P.M. Personal checks accepted. Mail order available.

Dwight Miller apple cider and maple syrup are also sold at farm stands and food stores in the Brattleboro area.

Products from Dwight Miller Orchards.

The winery also produces Old-Fashioned Hard Cider made from a blend of apples. Cerniglia calls it "light, sherry style" cider. According to the label: "Early settlers are said to have started the day with a tankard of the fragrant apple nectar." This stuff is a bit strong to swallow at breakfast, but it's pretty good with lunch or dinner.

You can visit this 40-acre apple orchard and watch the winemaking process. There's a small shop offering wine, apple jelly, wine jellies, cheese, and apple-related products.

Dummerston

■ There is a lot of history at Dwight Miller Orchards. The Miller family has been farming this piece of land for eight generations, and they claim to have the oldest apple tree in Vermont growing on their property. After tasting their apple cider it's obvious that they have learned a few things over the years. This cider is light, very refreshing, and a little bit on the sweet side. Bruce Newton, who is in charge of cider making, says people don't like a really tart cider, so he adds sweeter varieties like Golden Delicious when they are available. The best cider, according to Bruce, is available between October and April.

Dwight Miller Orchards grows about fifty kinds of apples (including a number of old-fashioned varieties), about twenty of which are available at any one time. If you don't know which to choose, they have a big chart on the wall that describes each kind of apple, its best use, and when it's in season. The apples are displayed in big wooden crates, and you can buy just one or two of each kind if you want to sample a lot of different varieties. Some of the more unusual varieties include Tolman

Sweet, Pound Sweet, Snow, 20-Ounce, and Blue Pearmain—a sweet, hard apple with a bluish blush on the skin, which tastes kind of like a pear. Dwight Miller Orchards also grows pears, plums, nectarines, apricots, peaches, strawberries, raspberries, blueberries, and blackberries. The apples, peaches, and berries are available for "pick your own."

The Millers also have a big maple-sugaring operation, which starts in the beginning of March and runs to the middle of April. At other times of the year their sugarhouse is used to boil down cider to make an excellent cider jelly. The sugarhouse is open to the public. They also have a flock of 200 sheep which look very pretty grazing on the farm's hilly fields. The sheep can be bought for freezer lamb.

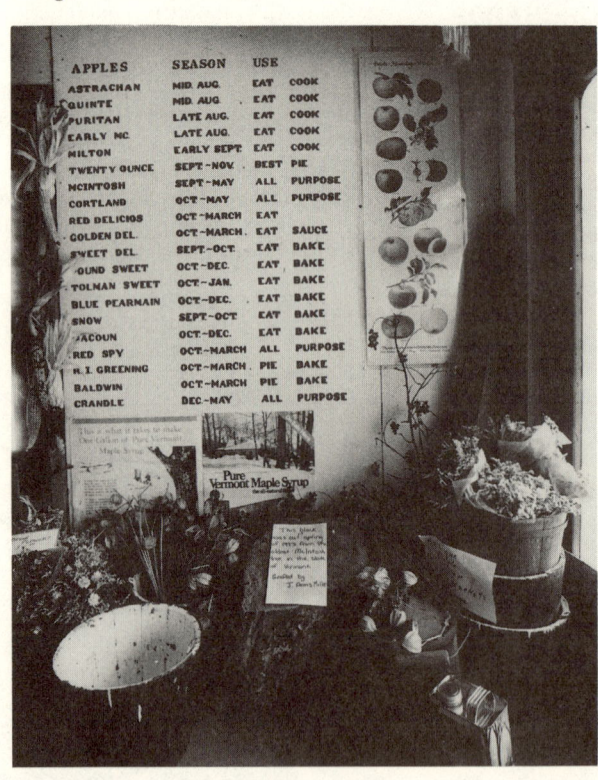

Having trouble choosing? Some help from Dwight Miller Orchards.

THE OLD MCDONALD FARM

Crossett Hill, Duxbury, 05676 (mailing address: RD 2, Box 1335, Waterbury, 05676); phone

Duxbury

■ The pigs at the Old McDonald Farm have a pretty good life. They're raised outdoors and are fed farm-grown corn mixed with soybeans and minerals. No cramped little pens, hormones, and low-level antibiotics for these hogs. As farmer Bert Senning explains it: "I make every effort to produce as lean and desirable a carcass as possible in a *natural* way."

802-244-8480. Hours: call ahead. Personal checks accepted.

VT'S CLEARVIEW FARMS

RD 1, Box 5070 NE, Enosburg Falls, 05450; phone: 802-933-2537. MasterCard, Visa, and personal checks accepted. Mail order available.

Also available at country stores and gourmet food shops throughout New England.

GRAFTON VILLAGE APPLE COMPANY

Route 121 (mailing address: Route 3, Box 236D, Grafton, 05146); phone 802-843-2406 or toll-free 800-843-4822. Hours: Monday–Friday 9 A.M. to 4 P.M.; open later and on weekends during fall foliage season. MasterCard, Visa, and personal checks accepted. Mail order available.

Each spring Senning writes his customers a pig newsletter, giving a pig progress report and current prices. In the fall, when the pigs are "ready," they are brought to a slaughterhouse in nearby South Barre. Old McDonald Farm will sell you a whole or half pig; they'll cure it, smoke it, and custom-butcher it to your specifications. These are what are called "long, bacon-type pigs," which are extremely lean and flavorful.

Pigs and raspberries may sound like an odd combination, but the Old McDonald Farm also has a reputation for its pick-your-own berries. (Be sure to call ahead for an update on picking conditions.)

Enosburg Falls

■ One of the golden rules of tasting condiments is to stay away from brands that have cute names. You know the ones: Tutti Frutti Jammy Jelly or Mother's Maple Marvel Mustard. A lot of cooks spend far more time coming up with the adorable names than worrying about what goes inside the jar.

So there we were with an assortment of relishes, jams, jellies, and sauces from Vermont's Clearview Farms. They looked good enough and the list of ingredients was impressive: nothing but fresh fruits and vegetables, maple syrup, honey, sugar, nuts, vinegar, and spices. But then there were those names: Braisin Raisin, Appreci-Date, Behind the Bush, and Baring Fruits. Cute—very cute. But something told us to plow ahead and taste these condiments despite their names, and we're glad we did.

We started with Original Sin—a thick, chunky combination of apples, raisins, walnuts, onions, green peppers, and spices. We tasted it on a cold roast beef sandwich and its fresh fruity taste made a rather ordinary sandwich come alive.

Actually, all the Clearview Farms products we tried were good—fresh tasting, not too sweet, with just the right amounts of spices and flavorings. Other favorites were Cranberry Orange Jam (excellent with baked ham), Appreci-Date (a chutney-like mélange of apricots, dates, brown sugar, and spices), and Blackberry Apple Jam (made without sugar). Perhaps there's a lesson in all this. Maybe we'll even try Tutti Frutti Jammy Jelly next week.

Grafton

■ Deliciously sweet apple cider, apples, fresh vegetables, cheddar cheese, maple syrup, Grafton Goodjam, and other Vermont foods. This store is located on a beautiful country road about 1½ miles west of the center of Grafton.

GRAFTON VILLAGE CHEESE COMPANY

Townshend Road, Grafton, 05146; phone 802-843-2221. Hours: Monday–Friday 9 A.M. to 4 P.M.; closed Saturday and Sunday. Personal checks accepted. Mail order available.

GRAFTON VILLAGE STORE

Main Street, Grafton, 05146; phone 802-843-2348. Hours: Monday–Saturday 8:30 A.M. to 6 P.M.; Sunday 9 A.M. to 6 P.M. Personal checks accepted. Mail order available.

GUILFORD CHEESE COMPANY

Lee Road (RD 2, Box 420), Guilford, 05301; phone 802-254-9182. Hours: call ahead. Mail order available; also available through the Shelburne Farms catalogue (see page 231). Tours available.

Also sold in many cheese shops and specialty food stores throughout the country.

- Cheddar cheese and sage-flavored cheddar with a smooth consistency and a nice sharp bite. You can watch the cheese being made here, sample the different kinds they make, and picnic, hike, and cross-country ski on the surrounding grounds.

- Grafton has the look of a museum, but it is a real town, with real people. A restored village of old homes, white-steepled churches, country inns, and winding country roads, it also happens to produce some of the finest traditional Vermont products available anywhere. And the Grafton Village Store is probably the best place to experience the full panorama of the village's culinary output.

Grafton Goodjam is a rich fruit preserve sweetened with maple syrup. It comes in strawberry, blueberry, raspberry, and wild blackberry. The berries in the jam are still whole, and the addition of maple syrup seems to heighten the natural fruit flavor. It's excellent on pancakes or used as a glaze for baked ham.

Cider from the Grafton Village Apple Company is also available, along with cheeses from the Grafton Village Cheese Company.

Another item to look for at the Grafton Village Store is their own fresh pork sausage. It's a very lean breakfast sausage with a subtle sage flavor.

The Grafton Village Store is a good place to put together a picnic lunch before heading off for a walk or cross-country ski trip on the trails surrounding the village.

Guilford

- The Dixon family, owners of the Guilford Cheese Company, have been making cheese for less than a decade, but after tasting their French-style Brie and camembert you would swear that they had been at it for generations. These cheeses, made with pasteurized milk from the Dixon's own herd of Jersey cows, come very close to the exquisite flavor and texture of cheeses made in France from unpasteurized milk. The camembert, which is sold under the name Mont-bert, has a tangy flavor, a pure white rind, and a creamy center. It has none of the unpleasant ammonia flavor you often find in camembert—both imported and domestic varieties. The Mont-brie is a bit milder than the camembert, but it has the same outstanding qualities—a creamy texture and a rich, mellow flavor that improves as the cheese ripens.

Ann and John Dixon began making cheese almost by accident. They started dairying at their Vermont farm in 1981 with the idea of selling their rich Jersey milk as a premium product. It was bottled the old-fashioned way—unhomogenized, with a thick layer of cream floating on

The important first step in making Guilford's cheeses.

Leading the Jerseys back to pasture.

top. But the idea didn't work. The Dixons soon discovered that, as Ann put it, "milk is a commodity. You have to add something to it to give it greater value." Three years later they began making cheese. Their first product, Verde-mont, a fresh cow's-milk cheese (available plain or flavored with herbs and garlic), was the beginning of a great success story for the Dixons. The Guilford Cheese Company is now one of New England's leading farmstead cheesemakers.

A farmstead cheese is one that's made on the farm, solely with milk from the farm's own herd. At one time this was a common practice, but until recently it had almost disappeared. Now the Dixons are helping to revive farmstead cheesemaking. Their two sons, Peter and Sam, are intimately involved in the operation, making this a true family farm.

But the Dixons have also gone outside the family in an effort to perfect their cheeses. French cheesemakers have visited their farm, offering guidance as well as secrets that have been part of French cheesemaking for years. As a result the cheeses made by the Guilford Cheese Company are unique both in their flavor and in the level of satisfaction they offer.

Hartland

TALBOTS' HERB AND PERENNIAL FARM
(RR 1, Box 197)
Hartland-Quechee Road,
Hartland, 05048; phone
802-436-2085. Hours:
Tuesday–Sunday 9 A.M. to
5 P.M. or by appointment;
closed Monday. Personal
checks accepted.

■ This farm, operated by David and Patty Talbot, is a great resource for anyone who wants to start growing herbs or to expand an existing herb garden. The Talbots offer a wide choice of culinary herbs, all of them raised organically.

The herbs here are potted as well as field dug, meaning that you can browse through the Talbots' garden, select the plants you want, and have them dug up to take home for replanting. There is a lot to choose from; a dozen varieties of thyme and mint, and over a dozen members of the onion family, from chives to Egyptian onions—a majestic perennial that propagates itself by growing pungent little onions at the end of its long green stalks.

The Talbots know a lot about herbs, both growing them and cooking with them, and they are happy to share their knowledge with visitors. They will wander with you along the narrow paths of their garden, offering hints on herb culture and breaking off a leaf here and there for you to taste and smell. They also conduct occasional workshops on cooking with herbs.

Jericho Center

VERMONT COUNTRY MAPLE
P.O. Box 53, Jericho
Center, 05465; phone
802-864-7519. Personal
checks accepted. Mail
order only.
   Maple Sprinkles are
available at gourmet and
health food shops
throughout New England.

■ When Lyman Jenkins was working for the U.S. Forest Service several years ago, one of his projects was to research maple syrup and find better uses for the dark, less expensive grades. "I stumbled upon a process that essentially removes the water content from cane sugar. I got excited and decided to try this idea with maple syrup. After all, syrup is two thirds natural sugar and one third water." Of course, admits Jenkins, there's nothing new about removing the water from maple syrup. "People have been doing it for hundreds of years and calling it maple sugar," he says. "But most maple sugar producers only take out *part* of the water. Our process removes *all* that water. We take Grade C dark syrup and vacuum-dry it."

Jenkins's Maple Sprinkles are different from old-fashioned maple sugar. Open the canister and the sweet scent of maple syrup fills the room. It looks like brown sugar, but the taste is undeniably maple. Sprinkle the light brown granules on hot or cold cereal, toast, ice cream, yogurt, fresh fruit salad, or in your morning tea. Because they contain no water, Maple Sprinkles are great to bring on a camping trip or to send to friends who live far away. (According to Jenkins, Maple Sprinkles are a big hit in Japan.) And, if you want, you can simply mix the sprinkles with boiling water and you're back to step one—maple syrup.

Tomato-Garlic Soup with Rouille

This is a simple, very fresh tasting soup that can be made in the spring with canned plum tomatoes or in the summer with fresh ones. The sharp bite of the rouille gives the soup a full, garlicky flavor. (Rouille is a classic French sauce traditionally served with fish soups. It can also be used in other soups, in stews, as a topping on grilled meats or fish, or mixed with sour cream to make a dip.)

1 large sweet red pepper
1 two-inch-thick slice French bread
9 cloves garlic, peeled
3 1/2 tablespoons olive oil
2 pounds very ripe plum tomatoes, or 1 can (16 ounces) plum tomatoes
2 tablespoons unsalted butter
1 large onion, thinly sliced
1 bulb "spring" or "new" garlic or 1 shallot, thinly sliced
1 rib celery, thinly sliced
2 1/2 tablespoons chopped fresh basil, or 1 1/2 tablespoons dried
4 cups light chicken stock, preferably homemade
Minced fresh basil or parsley (optional)

Make the rouille: Place the red pepper directly on a gas burner and grill until completely charred on each side. (If you don't have gas, place the pepper on a piece of tin foil and set under a hot broiler for about 4 minutes on each side, until completely charred.) Place the pepper in a paper bag or piece of foil for 1 minute, then peel off the skin and remove the seeds. Slice into small pieces.

Soak the bread in water and then squeeze out all the moisture.

Place 3 cloves of the garlic and the red pepper in a blender or food processor and finely chop. Add the drained bread and 2 1/2 tablespoons of the olive oil, 1/2 tablespoon at a time. Purée until smooth and thick. Cover and refrigerate until needed. (If you make the rouille more than an hour ahead of time, place 1 tablespoon of olive oil over the top of the rouille and refrigerate.)

Prepare the soup: Bring a large pot of water to a boil. Drop in the fresh tomatoes for about 10 seconds, then remove them and place them in a bowl of cold water. Peel and cut the tomatoes into quarters. Set aside.

In a large soup pot, melt the butter and remaining 1 tablespoon olive oil over moderate heat. Add the onions, new garlic, remaining 6 cloves garlic, celery, and basil, and sauté about 8 minutes, or until soft. Add the tomatoes and stock, cover, and let simmer for 15 minutes. Remove, and purée in batches in a blender or food processor. Reheat and taste for seasoning. Serve in soup bowls with a dollop of rouille and a sprinkling of fresh basil or parsley. Serves 6.

Londonderry

THE COOK'S GARDEN

Junction of Routes 100 and 11 (P.O. Box 65), Londonderry, 05148; phone 802-824-3400.

■ So you think you're on top of things because you've developed a taste for radicchio and arugula? Well, get hip. There's a whole new world out there just waiting to be tasted—Val d'Orge, Rougette du Midi, Radian, Rigoletto, Kinemontpas, and Tetue de Nimes. No, these are not undiscovered operas. These are just some of the

220   THE GREAT NEW ENGLAND FOOD GUIDE

Hours: May through Columbus Day weekend, seven days a week 10 A.M. to 5 P.M. MasterCard, Visa, and personal checks accepted. Mail-order seed catalogue available.

more than forty types of lettuce available at The Cook's Garden in downtown Londonderry.

We first learned about The Cook's Garden when a friend served us a gorgeous arugula salad a few summers ago. When we asked her where she found such beautiful lettuce, she proudly told us she had grown it. We hadn't known that this pungent variety of Italian lettuce would take to a New England garden. Then she started to rave about this wonderful gardening catalogue, a place in Vermont that offered seeds for all sorts of exotic vegetables, herbs, and flowers. So we immediately sent away for a catalogue and the following summer we served our friends spectacular salads made of black-seeded Simpson mixed with Prado, Voluma, and Lollo Rossa.

Shephard and Ellen Ogden, owners of The Cook's Garden, have been gardening organically since the late 1970s. They got the idea for the business when Shephard's grandfather, Sam Ogden, a renowned gardener and gardening writer, passed away. The couple decided to take over his garden, and they supplemented the usual crops of corn, tomatoes, and squash with unusual varieties of lettuce and vegetables. They bought seeds for French *cornichons* (those small cucumber pickles traditionally served with pâté), Italian white eggplant, Italian peppers, golden baby beets, red Italian onions, thin French beans called *haricots verts,* and French shelling beans called Flageolets Chevrier. Before long they were selling seeds, produce, and plants to their neighbors and the business began to boom.

The Cook's Garden catalogue includes fourteen types of chicory, plus baby vegetables, edible flowers, sprouting broccoli, and ornamental vegetables. Just about every vegetable listed in the catalogue is available fresh at The Cook's Garden produce stand each summer. You'll also find a good variety of herb and flower plants in season.

MOTHER MYRICK'S CONFECTIONERY AND ICE CREAM PARLOUR
Route 7A, P.O. Box 1142, Manchester Center, 05255; phone 802-362-1560. Summer hours: Monday–Thursday 8:30 A.M. to 11 P.M., Saturday and Sunday 8:30 A.M. to 12 M. Winter

Manchester Center

■ It hits you all at once when you walk in the door. There's the rich smell of fudge slowly cooking in deep copper kettles; a dazzling array of handmade chocolates laid out in gleaming metal, glass, and wooden cases; and a fantastic display of brightly colored ornaments and lights, giving the whole place a happy glow. Mother Myrick's is a candy lover's fantasyland—a place you will not want to leave even if you think you are too old for such childlike seductions.

Look across the room at the two giant polished brass kaleidoscopes filled with jelly beans. Turn the crank and the wheels slowly spin until you come to the flavor you want. Open the shoot and the jelly beans spill out until

hours: seven days a week, 10 A.M. to 5:30 P.M., until 10 P.M. on Saturday and holidays. MasterCard, Visa, American Express, and personal checks accepted. Mail order available.

you've had your fill. Turn around, and a few steps away you can peer over etched glass panels at the candy makers at work. There are vats of bubbling chocolate and trays of freshly made candies set out to cool. Perhaps you'll see dried apricots being dipped in dark chocolate, or chocolate truffles being made with Frangelico, Grand Marnier, or rum flavoring. And maybe you'll have a chance to see them making Mother Myrick's Buttercrunch, an incomparable combination of crunchy toffee surrounded by milk chocolate and freshly roasted chopped almonds and cashews.

By this time you've probably developed an uncontrollable urge to eat something sweet. No problem, just step into the ice cream parlor, where they serve ice cream sundaes topped with Mother Myrick's thick and creamy hot fudge sauce. There are also flaky croissants, fresh danish pastry, and an assortment of extraordinary cakes including a chocolatey Grand Marnier Torte and their award-winning Vermont Harvest Cheesecake. It's made entirely from Vermont products; cream cheese, maple sugar granules, and a topping of native apple marmalade and raspberries.

According to owners Ron Mancini and Jacki Baker, the business was named after a woman who lived near Manchester in the eighteenth century. "Mother Myrick was a midwife and healer," Ron told us. "There is a mountain named after her. I figured she must have had such power for them to name a mountain in her honor that, what the hell, I might tap into some of that power by using her name as well."

Mother Myrick's, in Manchester Center: a fantasyland of confections.

RAINBOW SWEETS AND CAFE

Route 2 (P.O. Box 121), Marshfield, 05658; phone 802-426-3531. Hours: Monday, Wednesday, and Thursday 9 A.M. to 6 P.M., Friday and Saturday 9 A.M. to 9 P.M., Sunday 9 A.M. to 3 P.M.; closed Tuesday and March and April. MasterCard, Visa, and personal checks accepted. Catering and mail-order catalogue available.

Marshfield

■ Rainbow Sweets and Cafe is a culinary gem set in the mountains of central Vermont. But according to Bill Tecosky, the energetic co-owner of this cafe and bakery, these kinds of riches have not always been available. "When I came to this area in the mid '60s, you couldn't get anything good to eat," recalls Tecosky. "That's why I opened this place."

Tecosky and his partner and wife, Patricia Halloran, have brought a delicious and eclectic array of food to the town of Marshfield. Their business is both a bakery featuring European-style breads and cakes and an informal restaurant where you can choose from specialties including *empanadas*, stuffed brioches, and flaky *spanikopita*. It is one of the most civilized small-town bistros we have visited, combining the funkyness of Vermont's back-to-the-land movement with big-city amenities. Order a glass of wine and you get real Italian Chianti, not some undrinkable liquid out of a big plastic jug from California. Eavesdrop on the conversation at the next table and it's just as likely to be about current literary trends as it is to be about the price of chain saws.

Rainbow Sweets also does a big mail-order business, shipping cakes and pastries to consumers around the country. One popular mail-order item is the Engadiner Nusstorte. It's a chewy sweet cake that reminded us a little of baklava. The recipe is based on a Swiss formula using walnuts, caramel flavored with kirsch, and butter rum pastry. Other cakes available by mail include Linzertorte and English Fruitcake made with dates, raisins, filberts, and cognac.

A visit to Rainbow Sweets, however, is necessary if you are to become acquainted with their full baking repertoire. They make a wonderful black cherry cheesecake as well as dense, sweet date bars, baklava, and a rich Sicilian-style cake they call Mafia Torte—a three-layer white cake with whipped cream, ricotta cheese, and chunks of chocolate between the layers, iced with chocolate frosting.

LA BRIOCHE BAKERY AND CAFE

26 Elm Street, Jailhouse Common, Montpelier, 05602; phone 802-229-0443. Hours: Monday–Friday 7:30 A.M. to 3:45 P.M., Saturday 7:30 A.M. to 1 P.M.; closed Sunday. MasterCard, Visa, American Express, and personal checks accepted.

Montpelier

■ Students at the New England Culinary Institute, working under the watchful eye of their instructors, bake all the croissants, brioches, cakes, cookies, and breads sold at La Brioche. The bakery's style is European, and the quality is excellent. The croissants we sampled were exceptionally buttery and flaky, and the cookies were the kind you expect from a fine French *pâtisserie*.

There are a few tables where you can enjoy pastry and a cup of tea or *café au lait*. The bakery also serves lunches from the adjacent Tubbs restaurant, which is also part of the New England Culinary Institute.

HORN OF THE MOON CAFE

8 Langdon Street, Montpelier, 05602; phone 802-223-2895. Hours: Monday 7 A.M. to 3 P.M., Tuesday–Saturday 7 A.M. to 9 P.M., Sunday 10 A.M. to 2 P.M. Personal checks accepted. Catering available.

STATE STREET MARKET

20 State Street, Montpelier, 05602; phone 802-229-9353. Hours: Monday–Friday 9:30 A.M. to 6:30 P.M., Saturday and Sunday 9:30 A.M. to 6 P.M. MasterCard and Visa accepted.

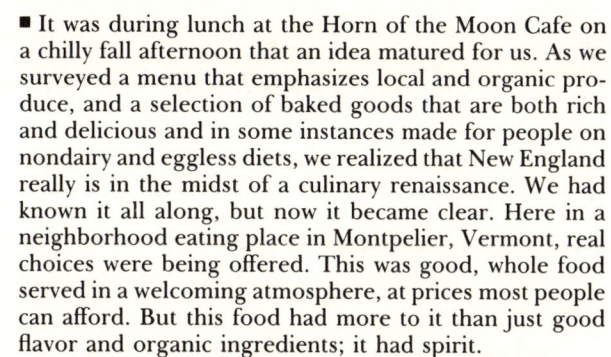

DUTTON BERRY FARM

Mailing address: RFD 1, Box 118, Newfane 05345; phone 802-365-4168. Call for hours of pick-your-own berries (see details at right). Farm stand hours: seven days a week 9 A.M. to 6 P.M. May 1 to November 1 (see details at right).

■ It was during lunch at the Horn of the Moon Cafe on a chilly fall afternoon that an idea matured for us. As we surveyed a menu that emphasizes local and organic produce, and a selection of baked goods that are both rich and delicious and in some instances made for people on nondairy and eggless diets, we realized that New England really is in the midst of a culinary renaissance. We had known it all along, but now it became clear. Here in a neighborhood eating place in Montpelier, Vermont, real choices were being offered. This was good, whole food served in a welcoming atmosphere, at prices most people can afford. But this food had more to it than just good flavor and organic ingredients; it had spirit.

In addition to serving vegetarian, Mexican, Indian, and Greek dishes, along with salads and soups, Horn of the Moon has a full line of bakery items. Among the ones we've tried are the fruit bars and apple strudel, both excellent. They also bake pies, several varieties of whole grain bread, muffins, coffee cake, cookies, and much more.

■ If you crossed a food co-op with a gourmet food store, you would probably come up with the State Street Market. This store carries many of the organic and locally made foods that are found in co-ops and health food shops, but unlike those stores the State Street Market is a slick, '80s-style supermarket. You could do all of your shopping here, but you probably wouldn't because the prices are high.

Among the market's outstanding offerings: a big selection of breads from bakeries around Vermont, organically raised beef, locally grown organic vegetables, Vermont cheese and yogurt, fresh seafood, Oriental ingredients, and a great collection of beers from boutique breweries in New England and other parts of the country. They also sell beer-making equipment.

In the back of the market there's a small, attractive cafe where they serve salads, soups, sandwiches, muffins, and sweets.

Newfane

■ Gorgeous plump raspberries and strawberries are what attract people to the Dutton farm. You can pick-your-own in season (call ahead to check conditions) or stop by the Dutton farm stand. This is one of the nicest farm stands in the area. When we visited in late October it was the only one that still had perfectly ripe tomatoes, and they were among the best we had had all season. We also found a large selection of sweet peppers, chilies, lettuce, pears, apples, pumpkins, gourds, and squash. At the end of the season the fruit and vegetables are sold by the bushel at extremely good prices; they're ideal for "putting up" your own jellies, jams, and relishes.

Spicy Shrimp Sauce

This recipe makes enough sauce for about a pound of grilled medium-size shrimp.

¾ cup New England Chunky Ketchup*
2 large cloves garlic, minced
About ½ teaspoon Tabasco or other hot pepper sauce
1 tablespoon safflower oil
2 tablespoons water

In a small serving bowl, mix the ketchup, garlic, and Tabasco. Add the oil and water and stir until thoroughly incorporated. Pour into a small saucepan and place over a very low heat. Taste for seasoning; if you want a very spicy sauce, add an additional ½ teaspoon of Tabasco. Serve hot.

*If you can't find Blanchard & Blanchard's thick, chunky ketchup you can substitute ¾ cup regular ketchup mixed with 1 teaspoon tomato paste and ¼ cup finely chopped green and red peppers.

For pick-your-own berries, go to the farm on Grassy Brook Road, Brookline (1 mile from Newfane flea market and Route 30). Their farm stands are on Route 30, Newfane, and also on Route 7A, Manchester Center (¼ mile north of The Jelly Mill).

Northfield

DEETER'S BAKERY
Main Street (Route 12), Northfield, 05663; phone 802-485-3002. Hours: Monday–Friday 8 A.M. to 5 P.M.; Closed Saturday and Sunday. Cash only.
Also sold at local gourmet food stores and food co-ops.

■ Central Vermont is dense with good bakeries. By the time we got to Deeter's, we figured we had tasted all the area had to offer. Wrong again. This Swiss bakery makes extraordinary breads, including Whole Wheat, Four-Grain, and Swiss Loaf—a combination of sourdough starter and wheat and rye flours. This hand-shaped loaf has a primitive, organic appearance, like a large stone taken from the beach. But the crust is light and flaky and the loaf has a chewy, slightly sour middle. Daily specials include homemade pretzels, pizza, and exquisite Swiss pastries.

ELLIE'S FARM MARKET
Route 12, Northfield, 05663; phone 802-485-7968. Hours: seven days a week 8:30 A.M. to 7:30 P.M. MasterCard, Visa, and personal checks accepted.

■ Ellie's is a good farm stand to visit any time of year, but at Halloween it's really special. The pumpkin patch here is particularly prolific. What do you do with all those pumpkins? "Well," explained one of the farm hands, "we figured we could just sell them and clutter up the farm, or have a festival. A real Halloween-time pumpkin festival."

In anticipation of Halloween Eve some five hundred pumpkins are carved with a variety of designs: smiling faces, ghoulish faces, stupid faces, silly faces.... A candle is placed inside each one and around sunset on both Halloween Eve and Halloween, all the pumpkins are lit. People come from all around to see the magical sight. There's hot cider and apples and lots of uncarved pumpkins for sale.

Ellie's is a great place to stop for apples. Huge wooden bins line the outside of the farm stand, filled with close to a dozen varieties. Inside you'll find fresh fruits and vegetables, a wheel of sharp cheddar cheese, fresh eggs, locally pressed cider, maple syrup, and farm-grown popcorn.

Norwich

FRASERS GENERAL STORE (DAN & WHIT'S)
157 Main Street, Norwich, 05055; phone 802-649-1602. Hours: seven days a week, 7 A.M. to 9 P.M. Personal checks accepted.

■ Dan & Whit's, as everyone calls Frasers, is really not much different from dozens of other country stores scattered across Vermont. It has a disorganized, slightly run-down look. The aisles are piled high with dog food and hunting clothes. The wooden floors creak with age. But this place has something extra: character.

The first hint comes from the illuminated clock mounted outside the store, which proclaims "Time for Budd's Beverages." Inside there's always activity. Local residents stop in to pick up a newspaper and a quart of milk, get some gas for the car (or the pickup truck), and in the meantime swap local gossip or a joke. If you arrive at Dan & Whit's and forget what you came for, there's a phone in the back where you can make a free two-minute call home.

Early Sunday mornings, when it seems as if everyone in the Upper Valley is awake and shopping at Dan & Whit's, the line at the butcher counter is long. Thick-slab bacon is what most people want. There are local eggs for your morning omelet, fresh-baked bread, cookies and sweet rolls, and a selection of Sunday papers. You can even pick up some thick Vermont cream and yogurt.

KILLDEER FARM STAND
Bullock Road, Norwich, 05055; phone 802-649-2852. Farm stand on Route 5 in Norwich. Hours: mid-May through October, Monday–Saturday 10 A.M. to 5:30 P.M. Personal checks accepted.

■ Overlooking the Connecticut River, the Killdeer Farm offers one of the most beautiful displays of seasonal fruits, berries, and vegetables around. You can visit the farm or stop by the farm stand on Route 5. Particularly good is the tender young zucchini they sell in the early summer.

Plainfield

HILL FARM OF VERMONT
RD 1, Box 740, Plainfield, 05667; phone

■ "Smaller is better" is an idea that frequently comes up when we speak with the farmers, chefs, and merchants who are part of New England's culinary renaissance. No place demonstrates this concept better than Hill Farm of Vermont. Farmers Peter Young and Nancy Everhart milk

802-426-3234. Tours of the farm can be arranged by writing ahead of time.

Hill Farm Cream Topped Milk and Crunchy and Fresh Sauerkraut are sold at food stores in central Vermont. The sauerkraut is available in other parts of the country under the Organic Farms brand name.

less than half a dozen Brown Swiss and Jersey cows. Working with their small herd, and following the principles of organic agriculture, Young and Everhart produce milk that is richer, creamier, and more delicious than most we have tasted.

This milk is unhomogenized, and it comes with a thick layer of cream on top. It's pasteurized using an old-fashioned method—still permitted by the U.S.D.A.—which Young says preserves flavor that is lost when more modern pasteurizing techniques are employed. According to Young, his philosophy is to process the milk as little as possible but at the same time make it safe for the consumer "beyond the shadow of a doubt." This milk costs a bit more than milk you buy at the supermarket, but it's definitely worth it.

Also excellent is Hill Farm of Vermont sauerkraut. Like the milk, it's an organic product. It has a great crunchy texture and a nice snappy taste. This sauerkraut is sold fresh and must be refrigerated.

Zucchini-Walnut-Ginger Muffins

These muffins are light and fluffy, with the fresh flavor of zucchini and a subtle hint of ginger. They can be made ahead of time and refrigerated, or can be frozen for several months. For breakfast or a nice afternoon snack, serve them with a crock of sweet butter, a large bowl of fresh fruit, and a pot of hot lemon tea.

1 1/2 cups unbleached flour
1/3 cup sugar
2 teaspoons double-acting baking powder
1 1/2 teaspoons ground ginger
1 teaspoon ground cinnamon
1/4 teaspoon salt
2 small eggs

3/4 cup milk
2 tablespoons unsalted butter, melted
1/4 teaspoon vanilla extract
Grated peel of 1 lemon
1 packed cup grated fresh zucchini
1/3 cup chopped walnuts

Preheat the oven to 400°F. Generously grease a 12-cup muffin tin. In a large bowl, sift the flour, sugar, baking powder, ginger, cinnamon, and salt, and set aside.

In a small mixing bowl, lightly whisk the eggs. Then whisk in 1/2 cup of the milk, the melted butter, vanilla, and lemon peel.

Gently mix the zucchini and walnuts into the flour mixture. Add the egg and milk mixture, and using a spatula, gently stir until the flour is moistened. (If the batter seems too dry, add an additional 1/4 cup milk.) Spoon the batter into the muffin tin, filling each cup about two-thirds full. Bake about 20 minutes, or until the muffins are puffed and golden. Turn the pan upside down over a cooling rack, remove the muffins, and serve hot or cool. Makes 12 muffins.

UPLAND BAKERS

Hollister Hill Road, Plainfield, 05667; phone 802-454-7119. Hours: irregular, call ahead. Cash only. Workshops on breadmaking and bread oven building are held from time to time. Tours must be arranged in advance.

Also sold at health food and gourmet food stores in central Vermont.

■ So much love and hard work goes into Upland Bakers bread that you can taste it. And there are other virtues too—creativity, a sense of community, idealism. This bread is more than a mixture of flour, water, salt, and sourdough starter. It is the expression of an idea, put forth more eloquently than words ever could.

Upland Bakers is the creation of Jules and Helen Rabin. They are the company's sole employees; they grind the organic flour that goes into the bread, shape the loaves by hand, and tend the fire in a massive brick and fieldstone oven that they built themselves.

The Rabins are idealists, and virtually every aspect of their bakery reflects this. They began baking bread in the late 1970s in an attempt to kindle a communal spirit in their town. Their oven—an imposing 8-foot-high, 5-foot-wide structure—is modeled after an eighteenth-century community oven they saw in southern France. The Rabins originally intended to replicate the ancient custom of village residents bringing their dough to a central oven a few times a week to be baked. "It didn't work," says Jules, an anthropologist who has studied European communal ovens. "European peasants can walk to the village oven. Here, people who want to use our oven have to drive several miles up a mountain, over bumpy Vermont roads. It's not the same thing."

Today neighbors occasionally do visit the Rabins' hilltop bakehouse to put a pot of beans in the still-warm oven after all the bread has been baked. But the Rabins do all the bread baking themselves. And what incredible bread it is. The sourdough flavor is tangy and delicious. The crust is thick and chewy. "A brick oven makes that heavy crust," says Jules. "It may be because the oven is very, very dry. The bricks absorb all the moisture."

The Rabins bake only three days a week. But they are long, exhausting days. At around 5 in the morning the fire is lit. The oven has only one chamber, so the pine

*Upland Bakers'
sourdough bread.*

Jules Rabin of Upland Bakers in Plainfield, next to his stone oven.

slabs the Rabins use for fuel are set ablaze in the same place where the bread will be baked later on. About eight hours later all that remains is a pile of glowing coals and ash. The oven, which is shaped like a giant beehive, is then swept out and the loaves of bread are placed inside. The heat that has been trapped in the oven's mass of stone and brick is what bakes the loaves to their deep brown color. There is enough heat to bake for about six hours, and the Rabins take advantage of every minute. Their workday generally ends at around 10 in the evening.

The Rabins bake several different varieties of bread. There is traditional French bread, also rye bread with caraway seeds, whole wheat, light wheat made with half whole wheat and half white flour, and *pain de campagne* made with whole wheat and white pastry flour. All the breads are made with sourdough starter. None contain any baker's yeast.

These breads can be found only in central Vermont. The Rabins believe that bread should be baked and consumed locally. "Our bread stays close to home," says Jules. "We and our neighbors know each other a little better through the bread. Our bread has become part of our bond with our community."

Richmond

HARRINGTON'S
Main Street, Richmond, 05477; phone 802-434-4444. Hours: Monday–Friday 8 A.M. to 5 P.M.; closed Saturday and Sunday. MasterCard, Visa, American Express, Diners Club, and personal checks accepted. Mail order available.

Also in Shelburne, on Route 7; Stowe, on Route 100; Manchester Center, in the center of town; and in Greenwich, Connecticut, at 278 Greenwich Ave.; and Wellesley, Massachusetts, at 277 Linden Street. Most of these stores are open on weekends as well.

■ When we were kids our parents often took us skiing in Stowe, and the trip was never complete without a visit to Harrington's. The big attraction was the free samples: plates of smoked ham, cheddar cheese, and sausage, all displayed under glass covers that, when lifted, would emit wonderful, rich, smokey aromas that made our mouths water.

We still visit Harrington's when we come to Vermont, and wonder (as we did when we were young) if the women behind the counter ever notice how many little chunks of ham we are popping into our mouths.

Harrington's sells a complete line of smoked products including ham, turkey, turkey breast, pheasant, bacon, Canadian bacon, pork sausage, salmon, and beef. Other products available through their catalogue include several kinds of cheese, beef, lamb, cakes, and candies.

If you visit their store you'll find a very good selection of Vermont-made products that are not offered in the catalogue. Things like preserves, jellies, and mustards. They also sell some wine, along with imported cheeses and cookbooks.

At the Richmond store (their headquarters), you can tour Harrington's smokehouse.

Pea Soup with Smoked Ham and Sherry

When you think you can't get another scrap of meat off your holiday ham, it's time to use the bone in this hearty, smokey-flavored soup.

1 large ham bone, meat scraped off and reserved
2 ribs celery, chopped
2 carrots, chopped
2 medium onions, peeled and quartered
2 cloves garlic, peeled and chopped (optional)
2 sprigs fresh parsley, chopped
2 bay leaves
3 peppercorns
3/4 pound dried green peas
1 large carrot, thinly sliced
About 1/3 cup dry sherry
Salt to taste

Place the ham bone, celery, chopped carrots, onions, garlic, parsley, bay leaves, and peppercorns in a large soup pot and cover with cold water. Bring to a boil over high heat. Cover, and reduce the heat to a gentle simmer. Cook 1 1/2 hours, or longer, until the broth has a good ham flavor. Strain the broth, reserving the ham bone.

Bring the broth to a boil and add the peas and sliced carrot. (If you like, put the ham bone back in the soup at this point.) Let the soup simmer for 1 to 1 1/2 hours, or until the peas are tender. Add any reserved pieces of ham, and taste for seasoning. Add salt if needed. Stir in the sherry.

Serve the soup boiling hot. Serves 4 to 6.

Rockingham

VERMONT COMMON CRACKERS

The Vermont Country Store, Route 103, Rockingham, 05101; phone 802-463-3855. Hours: Monday–Saturday 9 A.M. to 5 P.M., Sunday 10 A.M. to 5 P.M. MasterCard and Visa accepted. Tours of the cracker factory can be arranged ahead of time. Mail order available (Vermont Country Store, Mail Order Office, P.O. Box 3000, Manchester Center, 05255-3000; phone 802-362-4647).

Also sold at gourmet food shops, country stores, and health food stores throughout New England.

■ New Englanders love tradition, and that includes traditional foods—things like cheddar cheese, maple syrup, boiled lobster, and country smoked ham. But we've never been able to figure out why Vermont Common Crackers, a hard white cracker that looks like a stale biscuit, has been popular for so many years. To solve this riddle we called The Vermont Country Store in Rockingham, where the crackers are made, and spoke to Cracker Manager Bob Mills.

According to Mr. Mills, who has been making the crackers for close to twenty years, the story goes something like this: "The cracker was first made in 1825 by Mr. Timothy Cross. Back then they were known as 'Cross Crackers.' The Cross family made the crackers well into the 1900s, when the business was sold to the Edson family. They continued the tradition right up until 1981. Then the family put the business up on the auction block and Vrest Orton, owner of The Vermont Country Store, bought the cracker-making equipment and the original recipe. Mr. Orton was the one who changed the name to Vermont Common Crackers."

Today visitors can look into the cracker room located at the back of The Vermont Country Store and watch the crackers being manufactured the same way they were made in the 1800s. "The machinery dates back to 1825," said Mr. Mills. "Originally it was run by horsepower. The horse would run the machine one day, and then the next day he'd pull a cart into town to sell the crackers. That's kind of nice, isn't it? Today, of course, we run it with electricity."

What exactly is a Vermont Common Cracker? It's a mixture of wheat flour, potato flour, shortening, water, baking soda, and salt. (There are now salt-free and cheddar cheese versions of the cracker.) According to Bob Mills, they're a "bland, almost tasteless cracker.

"It sounds crazy to call them bland, but that's the real truth," he continued. "People love 'em anyway. They're best used as a base to bring forth the taste of something else. If you've made something and you're real proud of it and you don't want anything else to interfere with this flavor, well then, that's when you serve Vermont Common Crackers.

"The most popular way of eating the crackers," said Mr. Mills, "is to put your finger along the seam and press it in half. Butter each half lightly and toast until golden brown. They're darn good that way." Other people, Mr. Mills reported, like to soak them in milk and eat it all up with a wedge of sharp Vermont cheddar.

Before we hung up, we asked Mr. Mills once again: Why have these crackers endured over the years? "You know, I really couldn't tell you. It must have to do with

Shelburne

SHELBURNE FARMS
Bay Road, Shelburne, 05482; phone 802-985-8686. Hours: cheese shop open seven days a week 9 A.M. to 5 P.M. Guided tours and walking trails in operation from June through mid-October. Call for information about programs and special events. MasterCard, Visa, American Express, and personal checks accepted. Mail-order catalogue available.

▪ There is a coach barn at Shelburne Farms, a commanding red brick structure situated at the edge of Lake Champlain on this 1000-acre estate. Around the turn of the century, when the estate was in its prime, the building housed dozens of horses, carriages, and sleighs that were used by the founders of Shelburne Farms, Dr. William Seward Webb and his wife, Lila Vanderbilt Webb, and their guests. The coach barn is an unusual building: a large rectangle built around a central courtyard, each of its four sides rendered in a different architectural style. From a distance, the barn almost looks like a little village, with its gray slate rooftops slanting in every direction.

The coach barn is a metaphor for all of Shelburne Farms. This is a fanciful environment with a real purpose. The estate, which has been run by a private nonprofit corporation since 1972, is a place to see how the other half lived at the turn of the century. It's also an educational institute devoted to conservation and a working farm that produces top-quality foods.

Shelburne Farms is probably best known in culinary circles for its cheddar cheese, made with milk from their own Brown Swiss cows. During guided tours of the farm you can watch the herd being milked and see the cheddaring process. This involves stacking large blocks of

Silos, farmhouse, and dairy barns—the soul of Vermont life.

Pure mountain water flows through the heart of Vermont.

WOOD'S CIDER MILL
RFD 2, Box 477, Springfield, 05156; phone 802-263-5547. Personal checks accepted. Mail order available.

The Woods' products are also available in gourmet and health food shops and country stores around New England.

fresh cheese curd under carefully controlled temperatures to help the formation of lactic acids. These acids in turn help the cheese to age properly. Shelburne Farms is one of the few places that we know of where the public is invited to see this operation on a regular basis.

But cheese, and the chance to see it being made, is only one reason why it's worth making a special trip to Shelburne Farms. There is the Webbs' sixty-room mansion on a bluff overlooking the lake, which has recently been converted to an inn and restaurant specializing in regional foods. The grounds, too, are impressive. The sweeping vistas and forest groves were designed by Frederick Law Olmsted, who also designed New York's Central Park and the string of Boston parks known as The Emerald Necklace.

When the Webbs bought up thirty small farms in the late 1800s to create Shelburne Farms, they intended the enterprise to be an agricultural model. The most modern machinery was used, and new farming and conservation techniques were constantly being tried out. Today the farm is at the forefront of organic agriculture. Among the food producers who have taken up residence here are David Miskell, who raises organically grown vegetables, and the O Bread Bakery, manufacturers of dense European-style breads made with organic wheat.

All of the products made on the farm are available at Shelburne Farms' cheese shop. They also sell organically raised beef, organic apples from a nearby orchard, and a wide selection of foods from around Vermont.

Springfield

■ When you grind apples and squeeze out the juice, you get cider. When you boil that cider down, it eventually transforms itself into a thick concentrate called boiled cider. And if you boil that syrupy substance down even further, you will get a natural apple cider jelly—a rich, dark-colored jelly full of the flavor of fresh apples. Boiled cider and cider jelly are traditional New England favorites. We've tasted literally dozens of brands over the years, but found none to be quite as sweet and tart and tangy as those made by Willis and Tina Wood.

The Woods own a small family farm in southern Vermont where they grind their own apples, press their own cider, and then cook it all up to make boiled cider and jelly. "My family has been boiling cider since 1882," says Willis Wood. Tradition has real meaning in the Wood family.

Tina and Willis Wood cook down 7 gallons of cider to make each gallon of Boiled Cider. What results is a sweet, thick syrup that is delicious added to applesauce, mincemeat, pies, and gravies.

The Woods' Cider Jelly is a 9 to 1 concentration—that

Custom-Pressed Apple Cider

Years ago most cider mills custom-pressed apples for their customers. You would pick a variety of apples from your own trees, deliver them to the mill, and pick up your fresh-pressed cider the next day. You could drink the cider fresh or set it "down cellar" to age into hard cider. Today there are only a handful of cider mills left that still offer this service.

The advantage to having a mill press cider for you is that you can custom-design your own blend—a few apples for sweetness, another variety to add tartness, and still others for a fruity finish. If you don't grow your own apples, simply visit your favorite orchard and pick your own, or buy three, four, even five varieties at your favorite farm stand.

Most of the mills listed below will press your apples in season, on just a few days notice. It's best to call ahead to make an appointment and find out exactly when they do custom pressing.

Cider Hill, Windsor; phone 802-674-5293

Kramer's Cider Mill, Route 12, Northfield; phone 802-485-7969

Ogden's Cider and Grist Mill, Hartland; phone 802-436-2481

Turnpike Road Orchards (formerly Brigham's Orchard), Norwich; phone 802-649-3999

Wood's Cider Mill, Springfield; phone 802-263-5547

---

means it's even thicker, sweeter, and more appley. We like to spread this jelly on toast, hot biscuits, or pancakes. It adds great flavor to roast turkey sandwiches, and makes wonderful gravy when added to the pan juices from roast chicken or pork.

The Woods also tap their maple trees for syrup and sell four grades, ranging from Fancy to Grade C. Some of the syrup gets mixed with boiled cider to create something called Cider Syrup. This maple/apple combination is delicious drizzled over ice cream, pound cake, or pancakes. Also try mixing a few tablespoons into a basic vinaigrette for a sweet apple dressing; serve it with duck or chicken salad mixed with almond slivers and tiny wedges of tart apple.

Stowe

FOOD FOR THOUGHT
Route 100, Lower Village (P.O. Box 82), Stowe, 05672; phone 802-253-4733. Hours: Monday–Thursday and Saturday 9 A.M. to 6 P.M., Friday 9 A.M. to 7 P.M., Sunday 10 A.M. to

■ Racks filled with freshly baked breads, sticky buns, and muffins, bottles of Champagne in the cooler, and a display of lush organically grown vegetables all tell you that this is no ordinary health food store. The baked goods are the real stars here—braided challah, a slightly sweet poppy seed loaf, and dense sourdough bread to name a few. (Many of the breads are dairy-free.)

There is also a big assortment of local and regional foods—Vermont cheese, yogurt, and condiments, dried

6 P.M. MasterCard, Visa, and personal checks accepted.

PURCELLS' COUNTRY FOODS

Green Mountain Inn, Main Street (Box 220), Stowe, 05672; phone 802-253-7494. Hours: seven days a week 10 A.M. to 5 P.M. MasterCard, Visa, American Express, and personal checks accepted. Mail order available.

edible seaweed from Maine, fresh seasonal fruits and vegetables from area farms. Other offerings include a small but good selection of beer and wine, and some Chinese and Japanese ingredients.

■ It may seem strange to use the word "prolific" to describe people who make condiments, but in the case of Don and Debbie Purcell the term fits. Working in a small kitchen at the Green Mountain Inn in Stowe, they turn out an astounding array of mustards, fruit butters, and preserves. What's even more impressive is that most of these condiments are very good. There are a few clunkers, but that's to be expected when you are dealing with something in the neighborhood of twenty-two different recipes.

One of the real winners is Good Stuff Mustard Sauce. It's hot and sweet at the same time. In addition to going well with ham and sausages, this mustard makes a nice dipping sauce for egg rolls and Chinese-style spare ribs.

The Purcells' fruit preserves come in a dozen different flavors. The Wild Blueberry L'orange won rave reviews from nearly all of our friends who tasted it. It's thick and gooey with whole blueberries and bits of orange rind. This condiment would make an unusual glaze for ham. The Spiced Apple Butter is thick and flavorful, but it's a bit too spicy for people who expect apple butter to be more bland.

Another type of condiment made by the Purcells is fruit butter fortified with alcohol. Brandied Apple and Peach Bourbon are two examples.

If you visit the Purcells' store you may get a chance to see the condiments being made. The kitchen is out in the open, and when things are cooking the whole store fills with the smell of simmering fruit and spices.

THE WARREN STORE

Main Street (Box 259), Warren, 05674; phone 802-496-3864. Hours: Monday–Saturday 8 A.M. to 7 P.M., Sunday 8 A.M. to 6 P.M. MasterCard and Visa accepted for non-food items only. Personal checks accepted. Catering and mail order available.

Warren

■ If Bloomingdale's were a country store it would look like The Warren Store. While this idea may be a turn-off for some people, we hasten to add that The Warren Store is not snobbish. What the two do have in common is an incredible array of beautiful food, clothing, crafts, and antiques from around the world.

According to Carol Lippincott, who has owned The Warren Store since the early 1960s, Warren used to be a thriving community with seven operating sawmills. More than half a century ago the building now occupied by the store was a stage coach inn that rented rooms to traveling salesmen and others passing through town. Later the structure was converted to a general store, and today The Warren Store caters mainly to vacationers and skiers who frequent the nearby Glen Ellen and Sugarbush ski areas.

The Warren Store: a classic country store.

There is an ambience of warmth and plenty here. A large display of wine, along with jars of locally made preserves and beautiful bottles of locally produced vinegar, are the first things to catch your eye. From the back of the store comes the smell of cookies and cakes baking: The Honest Loaf Baking Company has its bakery and store here. There are long French *baguettes* with a wonderfully crisp golden crust, croissants, tarts, cookies, muffins, and scones. In the cooler you'll find their superb bread loaf–shaped Vermont Butter Cakes—similar to pound cake, only more moist and flavorful. They come in a variety of flavors including Lemon, Chocolate Chocolate Chip, Chocolate Rum, and Chocolate Sherry. Vermont Butter Cakes are perfect for picnic lunches, afternoon teas, or a light dessert. They can be ordered by mail.

Next to the bakery is the deli counter. We put a picnic lunch together one afternoon and had a hard time choosing between several pâtés, salads, and sandwiches they make on the premises. We finally settled on The Warren Store Pâté, a creamy chicken liver pâté studded with walnut chunks, flavored with black pepper and cognac, and wrapped in grape leaves.

In the warmer months you can have your breakfast or lunch at the store's outdoor cafe, which overlooks a brook and waterfail.

GREEN MOUNTAIN COFFEE ROASTERS

33 Coffee Lane, Waterbury, 05676; phone 802-244-5621, or toll-free 800-223-6768. MasterCard, Visa, and personal checks accepted. Mail order only.

Retail shops at Mad River Green, Waitsfield; the Champlain Mill, Winooski; Tinguini's, Shelburne Road, South Burlington; and 15 Temple Street, Portland, Maine.

VERMONT EPICUREAN

DeMeritt Place (P.O. Box 327), Waterbury, 05676; phone 802-244-8430. MasterCard, Visa, and personal checks accepted. Mail order only.

Sold in food stores and gift shops throughout New England.

COLD HOLLOW CIDER MILL

Route 100, Waterbury Center, 05677; phone

Waterbury

■ Selecting a coffee or tea at Green Mountain Coffee Roasters can be mind boggling because there are so many to choose from, all with tantalizing, pungent aromas. Hawaiian Kona, Colombian Supremo, Sumatran Mandheling Decaf, and Yemen Mocha Mattari are among close to four dozen coffees they carry (many with unpronounceable names). All the coffees are roasted on the premises, and many may be purchased "green" if you prefer to roast them yourself.

The choice of teas is more limited, but equally alluring. In addition to old standards like English Breakfast and Earl Grey, they blend their own herbal teas from herbs and flowers grown in Vermont. Green Mountain Magic Tea combines the flavor of mint with the sweetness of licorice. Vermont Fruit and Flowers is a tart brew made from lemon grass, rose hips and flower essences. There's also a good selection of decaffeinated teas and teas flavored with fruit essences including black currant, raspberry, and wild cherry.

Green Mountain Coffee Roasters also sells coffee makers, coffee grinders, and other paraphernalia for making the perfect cup. All their stores have attractive cafes where you can enjoy pastry along with your favorite brew.

■ Vermont Epicurean Tangy Maple Mustard is about as good as mustard can be. As the name suggests it's tangy, with just a bit of sweetness from maple syrup, and it's grainy, which gives it a delightfully crunchy texture. We eat it on anything that goes with mustard, and some things that don't. It's that good.

Vermont Epicurean produces some other outstanding condiments, all made without preservatives. The Cucumber Jelly is so cool and refreshing that it reminded us of the sensation of jumping into the ocean on a hot summer day. It's made from finely grated cucumber in a light, not-too-sweet jelly. We tasted it on crackers with cream cheese, added it to an omelette, served it with cold poached salmon, and spread it on a roast turkey sandwich. Also excellent are the Pepper Jelly and a sweet and soothing Lemon Honey Jelly that can be spread on your breakfast toast or added to a cup of hot tea.

Waterbury Center

■ If we hadn't already tasted Cold Hollow Cider, we would have driven right by this long red barn on the road between Waterbury and Stowe. It's the kind of place we usually try to avoid, a tourist trap to be exact. But the cider is superb, as are the cider jelly and cider syrup.

802-244-8771, or toll-free in Vermont 800-U-C-CIDER or elsewhere 800-3-APPLES. Hours: seven days a week 8 A.M. to 7 P.M. MasterCard, Visa, American Express, and personal checks accepted. Mail order available.

Cider and Cran-Cider are also sold in supermarkets, health food stores, and gourmet stores throughout New England.

Owners Eric and Francine Chittenden blend McIntosh apples with several other varieties including Empires, Macouns, Cortlands, and Delicious to make a cider that is rich and spicy. At an apple-cider tasting we conducted with a group of friends, Cold Hollow Cider was the clear favorite. Another point in its favor: it's made with alar-free apples.

Cold Hollow's Apple Cider Jelly and Cider Syrup are made from fresh cider that has been boiled down, so they have the same delicious flavor as the cider itself, only stronger. The Chittendens stress that no sugar or pectin is used in either of these products.

Most cider makers agree that the secret to good cider is blending different kinds of apples—some tart, some sweet. As a result many cider mills shut down in the winter when the only apples available are McIntosh that have been kept in cold storage. But the Chittendens have found a way around this dilemma by creating Cran-Cider. The tartness of cranberry juice offsets the sweetness of the McIntosh. The result is a rich, tangy drink with an inviting deep red color.

If you visit Cold Hollow Cider Mill during apple sea-

Apple aficionado Eric Chittenden of Cold Hollow Cider.

son, you'll have a chance to watch cider being made in their big mechanical press. They also operate a large gift shop and a bakery that produces apple pies, cakes, and terrific donuts. The hot donuts are best when accompanied by a glass of cold cider or Cold Hollow's Hot Spiced Cider (which is available in a concentrated form through their mail-order catalogue).

Other items sold here include maple syrup, smoked meats, herbs and spices, honey, candy, pancake mixes, kitchen equipment, and cookbooks.

Websterville

VERMONT BUTTER AND CHEESE COMPANY
Pitman Road (P.O. Box 95), Websterville, 05678; phone 802-479-9371. Hours: Monday–Friday 8 A.M. to 4 P.M.; closed Saturday and Sunday. MasterCard, Visa, and personal checks accepted.
  Also available at many Vermont and Massachusetts gourmet food stores and cheese shops.

■ The Vermont Butter and Cheese Company makes a variety of superb cheeses and fresh cream products. Their *chèvre* is the fresh, creamy, spreadable type and comes in a variety of shapes and flavors: plain, coated in coarsely ground black pepper, or smothered with herbs. The *crème fraîche* tastes as good as anything you'd find in France; we first tried it on top of fresh raspberries and fell in love. It's also delicious as a topping for baked or mashed potatoes, a thick, hearty soup, or pancakes. The *fromage blanc* tastes incredibly rich, but surprisingly, it's not nearly as caloric as cream cheese. It can be used to make cheesecake or eaten on its own. Try it with a generous drizzle of Vermont maple syrup and watch out.

Freshly made butter is also available. This isn't your everyday American butter, but a low-moisture, unsalted, cultured butter similar to the kind you find in the French countryside. They will also be making various herb butters. Other future products include Petit Suisse, a luscious combination of *fromage blanc, crème fraîche,* and fresh native fruit (it's eaten as a dessert, much like yogurt), and *tortas,* fresh cheeses layered with fresh basil, smoked salmon, and a variety of other fillings.

Visitors can visit the Vermont Butter and Cheese Company and watch the cheesemaking process. Each day a different product is made.

Westfield

BUTTERWORKS FARM
Westfield, 05874; phone: 802-744-6855.
  These products are available in food coops, health food stores, and supermarkets throughout Vermont. Also available in

■ On the whole, yogurt made by small New England dairies like Butterworks Farm is vastly superior to the Dannons and Columbos of the world. There's none of that dry, chalky flavor you find in many supermarket yogurts. But all New England yogurts are not created equal. As far as we're concerned, the very best is the ultra-creamy yogurt made by Jack and Anne Lazor at Butterworks Farm in north central Vermont, about 10 miles south of the Canadian border.

Eating Butterworks Farm yogurt is a sensual experience. Open the lid and there's a thick layer of heavy

Hanover, New Hampshire, and in natural foods supermarkets in Boston.

cream floating on top. Mix it up and notice the smooth, silky texture. If you're lucky enough to be eating their Maple Yogurt (there's also plain Low Fat Jersey Milk Yogurt and Whole Jersey Milk Yogurt), you'll taste rich, sweet syrup woven throughout. This is what yogurt should taste like.

Butterworks Farm yogurt is made from the milk of Jersey cows. As the Lazors explain, "We run an organic operation. Our cows receive their nourishment from grain and hay grown ecologically on our farm. Barley, oats, and wheat are grown in rotation with alfalfa, timothy, and clover." It's obviously a diet that works well.

Butterworks Farm also produces Heavy Cream—a thick, yellowish cream that resembles the exquisite stuff you find in England or the French countryside. And they make Farmer's Cheese a few times a year. Unfortunately these products are too perishable for mail order.

Westminster West

LOAFERS' GLORY

Bemis Hill Road (RFD 3, Box 895), Westminster West, 05346; phone: 802-869-2120. Hours: call ahead. Write or call for mail-order information.

Products are also available in many Vermont, Boston, and Rhode Island gourmet and health food stores.

■ "When I was pregnant with my daughter," says Gaelen Ewald, "I wanted to maintain a whole grain diet. That was in '69 and there wasn't much whole grain food around. So a friend taught me to bake whole grain bread and I fell in love with baking."

Today Ewald bakes over a dozen varieties of bread, as well as biscuits, rolls, shortbread, granola, and cakes. Almost all of her products contain organic whole wheat flour (some of which is grown by a local farmer). But don't get the wrong idea about this stuff. Loafers' Glory baked goods may be loaded with natural ingredients, but they have none of that bland "health food" taste. They are delicious.

The Black Russian Rye Bread is a hearty hand-shaped black loaf, rich with molasses and honey. The Onion-Herb Bread is flecked with bits of fresh herbs and onion and is excellent toasted and served with soups and stews. And Sunday supper will never be the same without Ewald's light and cheesy Vermont Cheddar Dinner Rolls.

Gaelen's Maple Shortbread is a revelation. We expected a dry whole-grain rendition of this popular Scottish confection, but were happily proven wrong. This shortbread is perfectly buttery, with a subtle degree of maple sweetness. It looks as good as it tastes—a golden brown, round cake with a bas relief design.

Ewald bakes in a small, cozy building that her husband built for her, with a large picture window looking out into the woods. Ewald's teenage kids and their friends work along with her. Her philosophy is simple: "If you're going to eat something rich, delicious, and decadent," she says, "it should at least give your body something good in return. Foods need to be above zero in terms of what they do for our bodies. A candy bar is a zero." By

CATAMOUNT BREWING COMPANY

58 South Main Street (P.O. Box 457), White River Junction, 05001; phone 802-296-2248. Hours: Wednesday–Saturday 1 P.M. to 5 P.M.; closed Sunday–Tuesday. Personal checks accepted. Tours of the brewery available.

Catamount beer is sold in Vermont and parts of New Hampshire.

F. H. GILLINGHAM & SONS

16 Elm Street, Woodstock, 05091; phone 802-457-2100. Hours: Monday–Saturday 8:30 A.M. to 5:30 P.M.; closed Sunday. MasterCard, Visa, American Express, and personal checks accepted. Mail order available.

Ewald's own standards, and ours, Loafers' Glory baked goods definitely score.

White River Junction

■ "Be patient," we told ourselves. We were in a package store in Montpelier, and the clerk told us that she was sold out of Catamount beer. It was the fourth store we had gone to that day in search of beer from Vermont's one and only brewery. We had waited a long time to try this beer. It had finally come on the market after months of delays and beer lovers we had spoken to had raved about it, but now Catamount beer was proving as elusive as the wily mountain lion it was named for.

Several more weeks went by. We were still thirsting for Catamount beer. Finally a friend went to the brewery and secured a case for us (which represented an astounding one tenth of one percent of the brewery's average weekly output of one thousand cases). We poured ourselves a mug of Catamount Amber, inhaled its hoppy aroma, and took a sip, expecting our tastebuds to be thrilled. Instead, we had to say to ourselves, "Be patient." This beer, with its dark amber color, was pretty strong stuff. We had to drink several bottles over the course of a few days before we really began to enjoy its rich, tangy flavor.

Catamount beer (both Catamount Amber and the lighter-colored Catamount Gold) is not for those who customarily down a six-pack or two in an evening. This is a thinking person's beer, beer that wants to be studied and savored, beer that challenges your intellect as well as your taste buds. If that's the kind of challenge that appeals to you, then you'll probably enjoy this beer. But remember, at first you have to be patient.

Woodstock

■ This is it, the big daddy of New England general stores, the ultimate exercise in putting everything you'll ever need under one roof. Yes, it's true that Gillingham's, which first opened its doors in 1886, has been gentrified and yuppified in recent years. But where else will you find a kitchenware section that features eighteen different kinds of strainers and at least six types of ice cream makers? At Gillingham's you can buy the seeds to sow a garden, the tools to cultivate it, the pots in which to cook your garden's bounty, the plates to serve it on, and wine to drink with your meal.

If you're not into raising your own food, there's plenty of it to buy here: smoked meats from William's Smokehouse and Harrington's, a big selection of New England honeys, pasta from Putney Pasta, locally grown produce (in the summer and early fall), Vermont cheeses, condiments, and more.

A historic rendering of F. H. Gillingham's, one of Vermont's oldest country stores.

For a cook, however, the real pleasure in visiting this store is the chance to browse through the extensive collection of kitchen gadgets and cookware. From the tiniest saucepan to an 80-quart stockpot, they have it all. There are food processors, waffle irons, knives, woks, apple corers, and a lot of gizmos you never even knew existed.

Prices here are a bit high, but that's to be expected when you're dealing with the Cadillac of general stores.

SUGARBUSH FARM
RFD 1, Box 568,
Woodstock, 05091-9985;
phone 802-457-1757.
Hours: Monday–Friday
7:30 A.M. to 4 P.M.,
weekends and holidays
10:30 A.M. to 4:00 P.M.
(Call ahead for directions and road conditions, especially between January and mid-May.)
MasterCard, Visa, American Express, and Diners Club accepted. Mail order available.

■ The town of Woodstock is pretty touristy. So, according to Betsy Ayers Luce, one of the owners of Sugarbush Farm, people drive up the long, steep dirt road to her farm "when they are looking for someone real to talk to."

You will encounter these "real" people in what passes for the farm store. It is, in fact, a small factory room in the back of the farmhouse, where workers wrap blocks of cheese and seal them with colored wax. Sitting amid vats of hot wax and stacks of cardboard boxes, you'll get a chance to sample the cheeses and enjoy a bit of conversation. A trip to Sugarbush Farm is also worth it for a chance to see the countryside around the farm and the spectacular mountainside views.

No cheese is made at Sugarbush Farm. The cheddar comes from cheesemakers around New England, and is then aged at the farm for up to two years. Betsy Ayers Luce claims that this allows the farm to choose only the best cheddar, and to offer cheese that is of consistently good quality. It *is* good cheese, sharp with a somewhat grainy texture. They also package a sage cheddar, smoked cheese, Green Mountain Jack (similar to Monterey Jack), and Green Mountain Bleu, a creamy and mild blue cheese.

Cheese is the main product sold at Sugarbush Farm, but they also produce delicious maple syrup. Hundreds of trees are tapped behind the old farmhouse early each spring, and the sap is boiled down over a wood fire in the farm's new sugarhouse. They make light, medium, and dark amber syrup.

Vermont Farmers' Markets

Call or write the Vermont Department of Agriculture for further information on locations and hours: 116 State Street, Montpelier, 05602; phone 802-828-2500 or toll-free within Vermont 800-622-4247.

Bennington Farmers' Market, Methodist Church, Main Street, Fridays from mid-May to October and Wednesdays from July 1 to October, 12:45 P.M. to 5 P.M.

Brandon Farmers' Market, call for information on location and times.

Brattleboro Farmers' Market, two locations: Mink Farm on Route 9W, Saturdays from mid-May through early October, 9 A.M. to 4 P.M.; and Town Common, Wednesdays from mid-June through September, 10 A.M. to 2 P.M.

Burlington Farmers' Market, Burlington City Hall Park, College Street, Saturdays from mid-June through October and Wednesdays from mid-July through October, 9 A.M. to 2 P.M.

Charlotte Farmers' Market, call for location and times.

Chelsea Farmers' Market, on the common in Chelsea Village, Wednesdays from mid-May through September, 3:30 P.M. to dusk.

Enosburg Farmers' Market, Lincoln Park, Main Street, early June through early October. Call for days and times.

Fair Haven Farmers' Market, in the park in the center of town, Fridays from late June through early August, 9 A.M. to 2 P.M.

Manchester Farmers' Market, downtown Manchester Center, Fridays from mid-June through mid-October, 1 P.M. to 5 P.M.

Middlebury Farmers' Market, College Street School, on Route 125 (College Street) in Middlebury Village, Wednesdays and Saturdays from June through October, 9 A.M. to 12 N.

Montpelier Farmers' Market (Capital City Farmers' Market), County Courthouse parking lot, Elm Street just off State Street, Saturdays from early May to late October, 9 A.M. to 1 P.M.

Morrisville Farmers' Market, on the green in downtown Morrisville, junction of Routes 2 and 15A, Saturdays from mid-June through mid-October, 9 A.M. to 12:30 P.M.

Newport Farmers' Market, Newport City Garage, Causeway Access Road to I-91, Saturdays from late June through early October, 9 A.M. to 1 P.M., and Wednesdays from early July through early October, 1 P.M. to 5 P.M.

Randolph Farmers' Market, center of town, Saturdays from late June to mid-October, 9 A.M. to 12 N.

Rutland Farmers' Market, Unitarian Church, West Street, Saturdays from May through October, 8 A.M. to 2 P.M., and Wednesdays from July through September, 9 A.M. to 3 P.M.

St. Albans Farmers' Market (Northwest Farmers' Market), Taylor Park, Main Street (Route 7), Saturdays from mid-June through mid-October, 10 A.M. to 2 P.M.

St. Johnsbury Farmers' Market, call for location. Saturdays from July through September and Wednesdays in July and August, 9 A.M. to 12 N.

Windsor-Norwich Farmers' Market, State Street Common, one block west of Main Street, Saturdays from mid-June to mid-October, 10 A.M. to 1 P.M.

Recipes and Featured Essays

Specific recipes are listed in *italics*.

Al Forno's Cannoli Cream, 187
Appetizers (recipes), 55, 142, 157, 170

Baked Asparagus with Garlic-Lemon Butter and Parmesan, 82
Baked Beans, 174
Baked beans, 173
  recipe, 174
Baked Bluefish with Onions, Tomatoes, Basil, and New Potatoes, 134
Baked Buttercup Squash, 52
Baked Green Bean Bundles Wrapped in Prosciutto, 157
Beans-in-the-Hole, 173
Bill Bell's New England Boiled Dinner, 53
Boston's Haymarket—The Original New England Market, 97
Breads (recipes), 6, 164, 226

Chile Dilly Beans, 122
Chowder. *See* Soups.
Clams on the Half Shell, Martha's Vineyard Style, 118
Classic New England Clam Chowder, 40
Cold Spinach Soup with Nutmeg and Cream, 27
Common Ground Country Fair, 72
Crabmeat Salad with Almonds, 176
Cranberry World, 132
Cranberry-Orange-Ginger Sauce, 103
Cream of Fiddlehead and Asparagus Soup, 61
Custom-Pressed Apple Cider, 233

Desserts (recipes), 78, 80
  sauces (recipes), 103, 187
Drinks (recipes), 8, 26

Entrées (recipes)
  glazes for, 152
  meat, 53, 126, 212
  salad, 176
  sauces for, 103, 224
  seafood, 55, 134, 141, 189, 190, 199
  vegetable, 38, 142

Fairs and festivals, 10, 62, 68, 70, 72, 97. *See also* Farmers' markets
Farmers' markets
  Connecticut, 31
  Maine, 83
  Massachusetts, 146
  New Hampshire, 178
  Rhode Island, 202
  Vermont, 242
Festivals. *See* Fairs and festivals.
Fiddlehead ferns, 46
  recipes, 51, 61
Fiddleheads, Fiddleheads, 46
4 and 20 Blackbirds Seafood Pasta Primavera, 189

Garlic, Leek, and Onion Tart, 38
Getting a Taste of the Portuguese Community, 10
Glazes (recipes), 152
Golden Cheese Tart, 142
Granola (recipe), 208
Great Rhode Island Jonnycake Debate, The, 183
Grilled Shiitake Mushrooms Oriental-Style, 124
Grilled Swordfish with Herbs, 199

Herb Baguette, 164
Homarus Americanus—Cooking the Sweet Maine Lobster, 42
Homemade Maple Granola, 208

James Haller's Smoked Mussel Cream Chowder, 75
Jonnycakes, 183
  recipes, 200
Judie's Lemon Rice Ricotta Bread, 6

Lemon Verbena Iced Tea, 8
Linguine with Clam Sauce, 190
Lobster, 42, 55

Maine Festival, The, 68
Maine Maple Sunday, 62

Maple Sugaring—A Wife's Lament, 67
Maple syrup, 49, 62, 67, 208

New England Afternoon Tea, A, 26
New England Lamb Chops with Garlic, Rosemary, and Apple Wine, 212

Orzo Salad with Greek Olives, Tomatoes and Feta Cheese, 167

Pancakes (recipe), 49
Pea Soup with Smoked Ham and Sherry, 229
Picnicking at Tanglewood, 115
Portuguese Sausage Stew, 126
Potatoes Edwin, 71

Red Cabbage Salad with Blue Cheese and Bacon, 113

Salads (recipes), 113, 167, 176
Sauces (recipes), 103, 187, 190, 224
Sautéed Fiddlehead Ferns, 51
Seafood, 42, 118
 fish (recipes), 134, 141, 199
 shellfish (recipes), 40, 55, 75, 176, 189, 190, 224
Shiitake Mushrooms in Cognac-Cream Sauce, 125

Soups (recipes), 27, 40, 61, 75, 219, 229
Spicy Shrimp Sauce, 224
Spirited Rabbit Liver Pâté, 170
Squire Tarbox Inn Chèvre Pound Cake, 80
Steamed Lettuce with Chinese Oyster Sauce, 94
Stir-Fried Chinese String Beans with Chinese Sausage, 93
Sylvia's Apple Spice Buckle, 78

Terrine of Fresh Corn with Lobster, 55
Thin Jonnycakes, 200
Thick Jonnycakes, 200
Three Glazes for New England Smoked Ham, 152
Tips on Cooking Pheasant, 136
Tomato-Garlic Soup with Rouille, 219
Trout in Orange Herb Sauce, 141

Vegetables, 46, 71, 173
 recipes, 51, 52, 55, 82, 93, 94, 122, 124, 125, 157, 174

Washburn-Norlands Living Center, 70
Whole Wheat Almond Pancakes with Maple-Nut Syrup, 49

Zucchini-Walnut-Ginger Muffins, 226

Index

Apples
Connecticut
  Bethel/Blue Jay Orchards, 3
  Derby/McConney's Farm Cider Mill, 12
  Guilford/Bishop's Orchards, 17
  Northford/Bishop's Northford Farm Market, 17
  Sharon/Ellsworth Hill Farm, 27
Maine
  Alfred/Gile Orchards, 35
  Eliot/King Tut's Cider Mill, 50
Massachusetts
  Acushnet/Flying Cloud Orchard, 87; Peters Family Orchard and Cider Mill, 87
  Bolton/Bolton Orchards 89
  Colrain/Pine Hill Orchards, 105
  Ipswich/Goodale Orchards—The Russell Family Store and Cider Mill, 113
  Littleton/Chase Farms, 116
  North Grafton/Creeper Hill Orchard, 126
  Phillipston/Red Apple Farm, 129
  Richmond/Bartlett's Orchard, 131
  Sterling/Faneuil Cider Company, 138
  Westhampton/Outlook Farm, 142
New Hampshire
  Contoocook/Gould Hill Orchards, 154
  Greenland/Ye Olde Allen Farm, 160
  Hampton Falls/Applecrest Farm, 161
Vermont
  Dummerston/Dwight Miller Orchards, 213
  Grafton/Grafton Village Apple Company, 215
  Springfield/Wood's Cider Mill, 232
  Waterbury Center/Cold Hollow Cider Mill, 236

Bakeries
Connecticut
  Branford/Judie's European Baked Goods, 5, 6
  Bridgeport/Chaves Bakery, 6
  Danbury/International Bakery, 11
  Greenwich/Versailles Restaurant, 17
  Hartford/Hartford West Indian Bakery, 19; Top Taste Jamaican Bakery, 20
  New Haven/Atticus Bookstore/Cafe, 20; Bob Cardinale's Marjolaine Pastries and Confections, 21
  Westport/Atticus Bookstore/Cafe, 20
Maine
  Bangor/Bagel Shop, The, 35
  Bath/Kristina's Bakery and Restaurant, 37
  Portland/Port Bakehouse, 66
  South Portland/Port Bakehouse, 66
  Thomaston/Sylvia's Cakes and Breads, 77, 78
Massachusetts
  Belmont/Eastern Lamejun Bakers, 88
  Boston/Hing Shing Pastry, 94; I & A Bakery, 95; Modern Pastry Shop, 95; A. Parziale and Sons Bakery, 91
  Brookline/Kupel's Bake and Bagel, 98
  Cambridge/Rosie's Bakery, 103
  Chestnut Hill/Rosie's Bakery, 103
  Falmouth/Peach Tree Circle Farm, 108
  Ipswich/Goodale Orchards—The Russell Family Store and Cider Mill, 113
  Lenox/Suchèle Bakers, 114
  Martha's Vineyard/Scottish Bakehouse, The, 118
  Methuen/Middle East Bakery, 120
  New Bedford/Pastelaria Colmeia, 122
  Northampton/Bakery—Konditorei Normand, 127
  Phillipston/Baldwin Hill Bakery, 129
  Pittsfield/George's Bread, 130
  Shelburne Falls/Marty's Riverside Restaurant and Bakery, 135
  Sherborn/St. Julien Macaroons, 135
  Southwick/Putnam Farm, The, 137
  Stockbridge/Nejaime's of the Berkshires, 139
  Watertown/Massis Bakery, 89; Sevan Bakery, 89
  Williamstown/Caretaker Farm, 143
  Woods Hole/Pie in the Sky, 145
New Hampshire
  Concord/La Boulangerie Cafe and Bakery, 154
  Keene/Drake's Duck, 164
  North Conway/Great Northeastern Pastry Works, The, 167
  North Hampton/Little Marvel Farm, 168
  Portsmouth/Cafe Brioche, 171; Ceres Bakery, 172
Rhode Island
  Jamestown/Our Daily Bread, 185
  Little Compton/Country Stand, The, 185; Walker's Roadside Stand, 188
  Providence/Faria's Sweet Bread Bakery, 191; Palmieri's Bakery, 193; Scialo Brothers Bakery, 195
Vermont
  Brattleboro/Hamelman's Bakery, 208
  Burlington/La Pâtisserie, 210
  Manchester Center/Mother Myrick's Confectionery and Ice Cream Parlour, 220
  Marshfield/Rainbow Sweets and Cafe, 222
  Montpelier/Brioche Bakery and Cafe, La, 222; Horn of the Moon Cafe, 223
  Northfield/Deeter's Bakery, 224
  Plainfield/Upland Bakers, 227
  Rockingham/Vermont Common Crackers, 230
  Shelburne/Shelburne Farms, 231
  Stowe/Food for Thought, 233

INDEX

Warren/Warren Store, The, 234
Westminster West/Loafers' Glory, 239
Beer and wine
Connecticut
  Coventry/Nutmeg Vineyard, 9
Maine
  Camden/Wine Emporium, The, 43
  Portland/Geary's Pale Ale, 64; Portland Lager, 66
Massachusetts
  Bolton/Nashoba Valley Winery, 90
  Colrain/West County Cider, 106
  Martha's Vineyard/Chicama Vineyards, 116
  Westport/Village Store, The,/Root and Vine, 143
Rhode Island
  Little Compton/Sakonnet Vineyards, 186
Vermont
  Cavendish/Joseph Cerniglia Winery, 212
  White River Junction/Catamount Brewing Company, 240
Breads. *See* Bakeries.
Breweries. *See* Beer and wine.
Butchers. *See* Meat and poultry.

Cakes. *See* Bakeries.
Candy and snack foods
Connecticut
  Ansonia/Vonetes Palace of Sweets, 12
  Bethel/Hauser Chocolatier, 3
  Bolton/Munson's Chocolates, 4
  Branford/D and P Old Fashioned Candy, 4
  Danbury/Chocolate Lace, 10
  Derby/Vonetes Palace of Sweets, 12
  Enfield/Crand's Candy Castle, 12
  New Haven/Thomas Sweet, 23
Maine
  Bangor/Bangor Taffy, 35
  Corinna/Cock Pheasant Farm Popcorn, 45
  Damariscotta/John Hannon Chocolatier, 54
  Gardiner/John Hannon Chocolatier, 54
  Lewiston/Seavey's Needhams, 56
  Ogunquit/Harbor Candy Shop, 62
  Portland/John Hannon Chocolatier, 54
  Waldoboro/Claudette Boggs's Peanut Butter Balls, 78
  York Beach/Goldenrod, The, 82
Massachusetts
  Amherst/Sweeties Fine Chocolate and Confections, 88
  Boston/Dairy Fresh Candies, 93
  Concord/Priscilla Candy Shop, 109
  Gardner/Priscilla Candy Shop, 109
  Hyannis/Cape Cod Potato Chips, 112
  Methuen/Royal Feast Potato Chips, 120
  Northampton/Sweeties Fine Chocolate and Confections, 88
New Hampshire
  Exeter/Chocolatier, The, 159
Rhode Island
  Providence/New England Truffle Company, 192
Vermont
  Bradford/Dad's Vermont Made Peanut Brittle, 207
  Burlington/Champlain Chocolate Company, 210; Sweeties Fine Chocolate and Confections, 88
  Manchester Center/Mother Myrick's Confectionery and Ice Cream Parlour, 220
Cheese. *See* Dairy products.
Cider. *See* Apples.
Coffee and tea
Connecticut
  New Haven/Willoughby's Coffee and Tea, 23
Maine
  Portland/Green Mountain Coffee Roasters, 236
Massachusetts
  Boston/Coffee Connection, The, 100; Polcari's Coffee, 96
  Cambridge/Coffee Connection, The, 100
  Great Barrington/Berkshire Coffee Roasting Company, The, 109
  Lexington/Coffee Connection, The, 100
  Newton Center/Coffee Connection, The, 100
  Northampton/Coffee Gallery, 128
Vermont
  South Burlington/Green Mountain Coffee Roasters, 236
  Waitsfield/Green Mountain Coffee Roasters, 236
  Waterbury/Green Mountain Coffee Roasters, 236
  Winooski/Green Mountain Coffee Roasters, 236
Condiments
Maine
  Bowdoinham/Hattie's Kitchen, 39
  Deer Isle/Nervous Nellie's Jams and Jellies, 45
  Eliot/Back Fields Farm, 50
  Hope/Gingham Shop, The, 56
  Medomak/Hockomock Hollow, 58
  New Sharon/Firths' Fruit Farm, 59
  North Waldoboro/Morse's Sauerkraut, 61
  Rangeley/First Farm, 73
Massachusetts
  Charlemont/Charlemont Apiaries, 104
  Sterling/Faneuil Cider Company, 138
New Hampshire
  Alstead/Bascom's Sugar House, 151
  Lyme/Fox More Than a Mustard, 165
  North Hampton/Little Marvel Farm, 168
Vermont
  Barre/Cherry Hill Cooperative Cannery, 205
  Dummerston/Dwight Miller Orchards, 213
  Enosburg Falls/VT's Clearview Farms, 215
  Jericho Center/Vermont Country Maple, 218
  Plainfield/Hill Farm of Vermont, 225
  Springfield/Wood's Cider Mill, 232
  Stowe/Purcells' Country Foods, 234
  Waterbury/Vermont Epicurean, 236
  Woodstock/Sugarbush Farm, 241
Country stores. *See* Specialty stores.

Dairy products
Connecticut
  Falls Village/Connecticut Farmhouse Cheese Company, 13
  Woodbury/Old World Dairy Pure Farm Yoghurt, 30
Maine
  Dover-Foxcroft/Peacefield Farm, 47
  New Sharon/York Hill Farm Cheese, 60
  Old Orchard Beach/Kate's Butter, 63
  Rockland/State of Maine Cheese Company, 74
  Wiscasset/Chevalier Farms, 79, 80
Massachusetts
  Boston/Purity Cheese Company, 96
  Greenfield/New England Country Dairy, 111
  Hubbardston/Westfield Farm, 111
  Lee/High Lawn Farm, 114
  Martha's Vineyard/Nip-N-Tuck Farm, 117
  Monterey/Monterey Chèvre, 121
  Wenham/Craigston Cheese Company, 140
  Winchendon/Smith's Country Cheese, 144

248   INDEX

New Hampshire
  Keene/Drake's Duck, 164
  Salem/Anoosh Yogurt Spread, 176
  Wilton/Stonyfield Farm Yogurt, 177
Rhode Island
  Providence/Providence Cheese & Tavola Calda, 193
Vermont
  Burlington/Cheese Outlet, 210
  Cabot/Cabot Creamery, 211
  Grafton/Grafton Village Cheese Company, 216
  Guilford/Guilford Cheese Company, 216
  Plainfield/Hill Farm of Vermont, 225
  Shelburne/Shelburne Farms, 231
  Websterville/Vermont Butter and Cheese Company, 238
  Westfield/Butterworks Farm, 238
  Woodstock/Sugarbush Farm, 241

Ethnic foods. *See* Bakeries; Specialty food stores.

Farm stands. *See* Fruits and vegetables.
Farmers' markets. *See* Recipes and Featured Essays index.
Fish and shellfish
Connecticut
  Greenwich/Bon Ton Fish Market, 14; Lobster Bin, The, 15
  Newtown/Newtown Fruit and Flounder, 24
  South Norwalk/So No Seafood Mart, 28
  Westbrook/Shoreline Lobster, 29
Maine
  Bath/Gilmore's Seafood Market, 37; Plant's Seafood, 38
  Camden/Caspian Caviars, 41
  Lincolnville/Ducktrap Fish Farm, 57
  Portland/Harbor Fish Markets, 65
  Rockland/Skansen Food Packers, 73
  Saint George/Kohn's Smokehouse, 74
  South Bristol/John's Bay Seafood, 75
  Tenants Harbor/Great Eastern Mussel Farms, The, 77
  Waterboro/Horton's Downeast Foods, 79
  York/Finestkind Fish Market, 81
Massachusetts
  Allston/Cao Palace, 87
  Belmont/Greer's Sea Foods, 89
  Boston/Chung Wah Hong Company, 92; Giuffre Fish Market, 94
  Cambridge/Chapin's Fish and Meat Market, 100; New Deal Fish Market, 102
  Dennis/Aquagems, 107
  Falmouth/Harbor View Fish Market, 108
  Martha's Vineyard/Poole's Fish, 118
  Pittsfield/Guido's Fresh Marketplace, 130
  Sandwich/Joe's Lobster and Fish Mart, 133
  Sunderland/Red-Wing Meadow Farm, 139
New Hampshire
  Hampton Beach/Sanders Lobster Company, 175
  Portsmouth/Sanders Lobster Company, 175
Rhode Island
  Little Compton/Country Stand, The, 185
  North Kingston/Wickford Shellfish, 188
  Sakonnet Point/Sakonnet Point Pier, 196
  Tiverton/Manchester Seafoods, 197
  Wakefield/Fox Seafoods, 201
Fruits and vegetables
Connecticut
  Andover/Hurst Farm and Greenhouses, 3
  Bethel/Blue Jay Orchards, 3
  Greenwich/Greenwich Produce, 14
  Guilford/Bishop's Orchards, 17
  New Haven/Chico's Farm Fresh Fruit and Produce, 21
  Newtown/Newtown Fruit and Flounder, 24

  Northford/Bishop's Northford Farm Market, 17
  Sharon/Ellsworth Hill Farm, 27
Maine
  Bar Mills/Snell Family Farm, 36
  Bath/Swango Farm, 81
  Bowdoinham/Hattie's Kitchen, 39
  Camden/Caspian Caviars, 41
  Cape Rosier/Funny Farm, The, 44
  East Lebanon/Sirois Family Farm, The, 47
  Eliot/Back Fields Farm, 50
  Franklin/Maine Coast Sea Vegetables, 51
  Freeport/Good Earth Farm and Market, 52
  Gorham/Patten's Farm, 54
  Kennebunkport/Patten's Farm, 54
  North Waldoboro/Morse's Sauerkraut, 61
  Presque Isle/New Penny Farm, 70
  Rangeley/First Farm, 73
  Steuben/Maine Seaweed Company, 76
  Woolwich/Swango Farm, 81
Massachusetts
  Acushnet/Peters Family Orchard and Cider Mill, 87
  Bolton/Bolton Orchards, 89
  Boston/Cheng-Kwong Seafood Market, 92
  Cambridge/Le Jardin, 101; Savenor's Market and Supply Company, 104
  East Falmouth/New Alchemy Institute, 107
  Falmouth/Peach Tree Circle Farm, 108
  Great Barrington/Taft Farms, 110
  Ipswich/Goodale Orchards—The Russell Family Store and Cider Mill, 113
  Lexington/Wilson Farms, 115
  Littleton/Gary's Farm Stand, 116
  Martha's Vineyard/Nip-N-Tuck Farm, 117; Solviva, 119
  Monterey/Tall Pine Farm, 121
  Nantucket/Bartlett's Ocean View Farm, 121
  North Adams/Delftree Corporation, 123
  Pittsfield/Guido's Fresh Marketplace, 130
  Sandwich/Crow Farm, 132; Quail Hollow, 133
  Seekonk/Four Town Farm, 134
  Southwick/Putnam Farm, The, 137
  Watertown/Kay's Fruit, 140
  Westfield/Fowler Farms, 141
  Westhampton/Outlook Farm, 142
  Williamstown/Caretaker Farm, 143
New Hampshire
  Center Conway/Earle Family Farm, 153
  Dover/Tuttle's Red Barn, 156
  Durham/Emery Farm, 158
  East Kingston/Maplevale Farm, 159
  Greenland/Ye Olde Allen Farm, 160
  Hampton Falls/Applecrest Farm, 161
  Litchfield/Wilson Farm of New Hampshire, 165
Rhode Island
  Little Compton/Country Stand, The, 185; DeLucia's Berry Farm, 185; Walker's Roadside Stand, 188
  Providence/A. & J. Wholesale, 189
Vermont
  Brattleboro/High Meadows Farm Market, 209
  Brookline/Dutton Berry Farm, 223
  Duxbury/Old McDonald Farm, The, 214
  Londonderry/Cook's Garden, The, 219
  Manchester Center/Dutton Berry Farm, 223
  Newfane/Dutton Berry Farm, 223
  Northfield/Ellie's Farm Market, 224
  Norwich/Killdeer Farm Stand, 225
  Shelburne/Shelburne Farms, 231
  See also Apples.

Gourmet foods. *See* Specialty food stores.
Grist mills. *See* Specialty food stores.

INDEX

Health foods. *See* Specialty food stores.
Herbs
Connecticut
  Branford/Bittersweet Herb Farm, 4
  Coventry/Caprilands Herb Farm, 7
Maine
  Bar Harbor/Northern Lights Garlic and Herbs, 36
  Cape Elizabeth/Ram Island Herb Farm, 44
  Eliot/Back Fields Farm, 50
  New Gloucester/United Society of Shakers, The, 59
  Rangeley/First Farm, 73
  Waldoboro/Fox Fern Herb Farm, 79
  York/Wild Iris Herb Farm, 81
Massachusetts
  Lenox/Naomi's Herbs, 114
  Lexington/Wilson Farms, 115
  Martha's Vineyard/Solviva, 119
  Nantucket/Bartlett's Ocean View Farm, 121
  South Lee/Naomi's Herbs, 114
  Williamstown/Caretaker Farm, 143
New Hampshire
  Canterbury/Canterbury Herbs, 152
  Hopkinton/Fragrance Shop, The, 163
Rhode Island
  Wyoming/Meadowbrook Herb Garden, 202
Vermont
  Bethel/Rathdowney Herbs and Herb Crafts, 206
  Hartland/Talbots' Herb and Perennial Farm, 218
Honey. *See* Condiments.

Jam. *See* Condiments.

Maple products. *See* Condiments.
Meat and poultry
Connecticut
  Fairfield/Drotos Brothers, 13
  Goshen/Nodine's Smokehouse, 14
  Greenwich/Harrington's, 229; Manero's Meat Market, 15; Sausage Emporium, 16
  Guilford/Gozzi's Turkey Farm, 17; Prime Cut, 18
  Hartford/Adolf's Meat and Sausage Kitchen, 18
  Norwalk/Norwalk Pork Store, 25
Maine
  Brooks/Smith's Log Smokehouse, 39
  East Lebanon/Sirois Family Farm, The, 47
  Freeport/Wolfe's Neck Farm, 53
  North Nobleboro/Rivendell Farm, 60
  Saint George/Kohn's Smokehouse, 74
Massachusetts
  Boston/Angelo Deluca Meat Market, 90; Sulmona Meat Market, 98
  Cambridge/Chapin's Fish and Meat Market, 100; Le Jardin, 101; Mayflower Poultry Company, 102; Savenor's Market and Supply Company, 104
  Dalton/Burgner Farm, 106
  Lenox/Burgner Farm, 106
  Newton Center/John Dewar and Company, 123
  North Dartmouth/Gaspar's Sausage Company, 125
  North Otis/Otis Poultry Farm, 127
  Norwell/Smokehouse, Inc., 128
  Pittsfield/Guido's Fresh Marketplace, 130
  South Hadley/Lukasik Game Farm, 136
  Southampton/Pine Hill Farm, 137
  Sunderland/Red-Wing Meadow Farm, 139
  Wellesley/Harrington's, 229; Smokehouse, Inc., 128
  Westhampton/Outlook Farm, 142
New Hampshire
  Barrington/Calef's Country Store, 151
  Concord/Blake's Turkey Farm, 154
  Dover/Brookford Farm, 155
  East Kingston/Maplevale Farm, 159
  Greenland/Hodgdon's Turkey Farm, 160
  Nottingham/Val's Rabbitry, 168
  Portsmouth/Bavarian Pantry, The, 170
  Wendell/Glen Echo Farms, 177
Rhode Island
  Providence/Antonelli Poultry Company, 190; Joe's Quality Market/L'Epicureo Gourmet Foods, 191
  Tiverton/Helger's Turkey Ranch, 197
Vermont
  Duxbury/Old McDonald Farm, The, 214
  Manchester Center/Harrington's, 229
  Richmond/Harrington's, 229
  Shelburne/Harrington's, 229
  Stowe/Harrington's, 229
Milk. *See* Dairy products.
Mustards. *See* Condiments.

Orchards. *See* Apples.

Pasta. *See* Specialty food stores.
Pastries. *See* Bakeries.
Pick-your-own. *See* Fruits and vegetables.
Poultry. *See* Meat and poultry.
Produce. *See* Fruits and vegetables.

Restaurants
Connecticut
  Coventry/Caprilands Herb Farm, 7
  Derby/Vonetes Palace of Sweets, 12
  Greenwich/Manero's Meat Market, 15; Pasta Vera, 15; Truffles, 16; Versailles Restaurant, 17
  New Haven/Atticus Bookstore/Cafe, 20; Bob Cardinale's Marjolaine Pastries and Confections, 21; Thomas Sweet, 23; Willoughby's Coffee and Tea, 23
  South Norwalk/So No Seafood Mart, 28
  Westport/Atticus Bookstore/Cafe, 20
Maine
  Bangor/Bagel Shop, The, 35
  Bath/Center Street Grainery, 37; Kristina's Bakery and Restaurant, 37
  Portland/Battambang Restaurant, 63; Foodworks, 64; Portland Wine and Cheese Company, 69
  York/Finestkind Fish Market, 81
  York Beach/Goldenrod, The, 82
Massachusetts
  Allston/Cao Palace, 87
  Amherst/Black Sheep Deli & Bakery, The, 88
  Boston/Genji, 97; Roka's Market, 97
  Colrain/Pine Hill Orchards, 105
  Falmouth/Peach Tree Circle Farm, 108
  Great Barrington/Berkshire Coffee Roasting Company, The, 109
  New Bedford/Pastelaria Colmeia, 122
  Shelburne Falls/Marty's Riverside Restaurant and Bakery, 135; McCusker's Market & Deli, 135
  Westhampton/Outlook Farm, 142
  Williamstown/Slippery Banana, The, 144
  Woods Hole/Pie in the Sky, 145
New Hampshire
  Alstead/Bascom's Sugar House, 151
  Concord/La Boulangerie Cafe and Bakery, 154
  North Conway/Great Northeastern Pastry Works, The, 167
  Portsmouth/Cafe Brioche, 171; Ceres Bakery, 172; Emilio's Foods, 173
Rhode Island
  Providence/Golden Sheaf Real Foods Market, The, 191

Index

Tiverton/Provender, 198
Wickford/Wickford Gourmet Foods, 201
Vermont
  Brattleboro/Hamelman's Bakery, 208
  Burlington/La Pâtisserie, 210; Vermont Pasta Company, 211
  Manchester Center/Mother Myrick's Confectionery and Ice Cream Parlour, 220
  Marshfield/Rainbow Sweets and Cafe, 222
  Montpelier/Horn of the Moon Cafe, 223; La Brioche Bakery and Cafe, 222; State Street Market, 223
  Northfield/Deeter's Bakery, 224
  Shelburne/Shelburne Farms, 231
  Warren/Warren Store, The, 234
  Waterbury/Green Mountain Coffee Roasters, 236

Seaweed. *See* Fruits and vegetables.
Shellfish. *See* Fish and shellfish.
Smokehouses. *See* Fish and shellfish; Meat and poultry.
Snack foods. *See* Candy and snack foods.
Specialty food stores
Connecticut
  Clark's Falls/Clark's Falls Grist Mill, 7
  Danbury/Bali Oriental Foods, 9; Fernandes Food Store, 11; Lisboa Food Market, 11
  Darien/Good Food Store, The, 11
  Fairfield/Hay Day, 29
  Farmington/Ann Howard Cookery, 13
  Greenwich/Harrington's, 229; Pasta Vera, 15; Truffles, 16
  Hartford/DiFiore's Pasta Shop, 18; Ravioli Kitchen, 20
  New Haven/Chico's Farm Fresh Fruit and Produce, 21; China Trading Company, 22; DeRose's, Inc., 22; Edge of the Woods, 23
  New Milford/Silo, The, 24
  Newtown/Newtown Fruit and Flounder, 24
  Norwalk/Stew Leonard's, 25
  Riverside/Hay Day, 29
  West Hartford/Ann Howard Cookery, 13; Nanshe's, 28
  Westport/Hay Day, 29
Maine
  Bath/Center Street Grainery, 37
  Camden/Wine Emporium, The, 43
  Damariscotta/Margo's Market, 45
  East Union/Morgan's Mills, 48
  Freeport/L. L. Bean, 52
  Orono/Store, The, 63
  Portland/Battambang Asian Market, 63; Foodworks, 64; Good Day Market Co-op, 65; Model Food Imports, 66; Portland Wine and Cheese Company, 69; Whip and Spoon, The, 69
  Rockport/Market Basket, The, 74
  South Portland/Whip and Spoon, The, 69
  Wiscasset/Treats, 80
Massachusetts
  Allston/House of Spices, 87
  Amherst/Black Sheep Deli & Bakery, The, 88
  Belmont/Eastern Lamejun Bakers, 88
  Boston/Cheng-Kwong Seafood Market, 92; Chung Wah Hong Company, 92; Erewhon Natural Food Grocery, 101; I & A Bakery, 95; L'Espaliers Great Food Store, 95; J. Pace and Son, 96; Roka's Market, 97; Trio's Ravioli Company, 98
  Brookline/Bread & Circus Wholefood Supermarkets, 99; Erewhon Natural Food Grocery, 101
  Cambridge/Bread & Circus Wholefood Supermarkets, 98; Chapin's Fish and Meat Market, 100; Erewhon Natural Food Grocery, 101
  Great Barrington/Locke, Stocke & Barrel, 110
  Greenfield/Foster's Supermarket, 110
  Hadley/Bread & Circus Wholefood Supermarkets, 99
  Lenox/Crosby's Gourmet Shop, 115; Loeb's Foodtown, 115; Nejaime's Stockbridge Wine Cellar and Cheese Shop, 115
  Newton Four Corners/Bread & Circus Wholefood Supermarkets, 99
  Northampton/Coffee Gallery, 128
  Pittsfield/Guido's Fresh Marketplace, 130; Mazzeo Importing Market, 131
  Sandwich/Dexter Grist Mill, 133
  Shelburne Falls/McCusker's Market & Deli, 135
  Wellesley/Harrington's, 229
  Wellesley Hills/Bread & Circus Wholefood Supermarkets, 99
  Westport/Village Store, The,/Root and Vine, 143
  Williamstown/Slippery Banana, The, 144; Wild Oats Food Coop, 144
New Hampshire
  Barrington/Calef's Country Store, 151
  Concord/Anthron's, 153
  Dover/Tuttle's Red Barn, 156
  Exeter/Cook's Choice, The, 160
  Hanover/Hanover Consumer Cooperative Society, 162
  Manchester/Angela's Pasta and Cheese Shop, 166; Bakolas Market, 166
  Portsmouth/Angelina's, 169; Bavarian Pantry, The, 170; Emilio's Foods, 173
Rhode Island
  Adamsville/Gray's Grist Mill, 181; Gray's Store, 182
  Providence/Golden Sheaf Real Foods Market, The, 191; Joe's Quality Market/L'Epicureo Gourmet Foods, 191; Providence Cheese & Tavola Calda, 193; Tony's Colonial Food Store, 195; Venda Ravioli, 196
  Tiverton/Provender, 198
  Usquepaugh/Kenyon Corn Meal Company, 199
  Wickford/Wickford Gourmet Foods, 201
Vermont
  Barre/Cottage Street Pasta, 205
  Brattleboro/Brattleboro Food Coop, 207; Straw and Hay Marketplace, 209
  Burlington/Cheese Outlet, 210; Vermont Pasta Company, 211
  Grafton/Grafton Village Store, 216
  Manchester Center/Harrington's, 229
  Montpelier/State Street Market, 223
  Norwich/Frasers General Store (Dan & Whit's), 225
  Richmond/Harrington's, 229
  Shelburne/Harrington's, 229
  Stowe/Food for Thought, 233; Harrington's, 229
  Warren/Warren Store, The, 234
  Waterbury Center/Cold Hollow Cider Mill, 236
  Woodstock/F. H. Gillingham & Sons, 240
Syrup. *See* Condiments.

Tea. *See* Coffee and tea.

Vinegar. *See* Condiments.
Vineyards. *See* Beer and wine.

Wine. *See* Beer and wine.

Yogurt. *See* Dairy products.